CS Ackley

UTRECHTSE KUNSTHISTORISCHE STUDIËN IV

THE BAROQUE TOWN HALL OF AMSTERDAM

THE TOWN HALL SEEN FROM THE DAM

Painting by Jacob Berckheyde 1672 · Rijksmuseum, Amsterdam

KATHARINE FREMANTLE

ART HISTORY INSTITUTE, UNIVERSITY OF UTRECHT

THE BAROQUE
TOWN HALL
OF AMSTERDAM

1959

HAENTJENS DEKKER & GUMBERT

UTRECHT

ACKNOWLEDGEMENTS

This book is based on research which was largely carried out in Holland, and, with the exception of Chapters V and VI, which were added later, it was presented as a Ph. D. thesis at London University in 1956. Hence my debt of gratitude is a double one, owed in two countries, and it has been increased by the dependence on other people's help which is inevitable when one first undertakes research in a foreign country. Unfailingly this was met with great generosity. I am indebted to a great number of people, for help of many kinds, and since not all of them can be named here I should like to thank them together, most warmly, for the contributions that they have made to this work, as well as thanking those mentioned below for the special help that they have given.

In the first place I am very greatly indebted to Her Majesty the Queen of the Netherlands, who has given her gracious consent to the publication of photographs taken in the Royal Palace, Amsterdam, and in the Huis ten Bosch.

In addition I should like to express my gratitude to Jonkheer Ir. P. F. O. R. Sickinghe, who with great kindness arranged for me to make detailed studies in the Royal Palace, and both there and in the Royal Archives has given every assistance.

The study owes its existence, jointly, to Professor Johannes Wilde and Professor J. G. van Gelder. Professor Wilde has inspired it, and its scope and completion in this form result from his unfailing and patient guidance. Professor van Gelder provided the setting, which has been an ideal one, in which it could be carried out, and the constant encouragement which was essential to it. He also introduced me to much of the documentation of Dutch seventeenth-century culture, in literature and visual records, which is referred to, and has made it possible for this work to appear in the series Utrechtse Kunsthistorische Studiën. Past and present members of the staff of the Courtauld Institute of Art of London University have given indispensable help during the course of my study and have provided the incentive for many of my explorations. I have specially valued the detailed criticisms and suggestions made there by Mr. Kerry Downes and Mr. Michael Kitson, who have done much to push an unwieldy text in the direction of clarity and informativeness. My colleagues and others at the Institutes of Art History and Archaeology of the University of Utrecht have also given invaluable assistance. They have provided much wise and practical guidance in my search for information, have made suggestions for which I am most grateful, and have saved me from countless pitfalls in the making of translations. Among them I should like to thank in particular Professor M. D. Ozinga, Professor J. H. Jongkees, Professor W. S. Heckscher – who has made valuable suggestions concerning the Town Hall's iconographic scheme – Dr. J. Bruyn, Mr. J. A. Emmens, Dr. C. Isings, and Miss E. Verwey.

Among those who have helped me at the Rijksmuseum and Rijksprentenkabinet, Amsterdam, special thanks are due to Mr. J. Leeuwenberg for his assistance in the study of models for the sculpture of the Royal Palace and for information about them, and to Mr. Th. H. Lunsingh Scheurleer, to whom I owe the idea which formed the starting-point for this study. At the Amsterdam City Archives Dr. S. Hart brought works to my notice which have provided important information, and without the patient help which he and many others have given me there my attempts to read and find my way in the city records would certainly have foundered. Jonkheer W. J. H. B. Sandberg kindly allowed me to photograph and study in detail the models which are in the Amsterdam Historical Museum, The Waag. Mr. A. Perfors has given much-valued help and information during my studies at the Royal Palace.

Among those who have helped me in other places I should like to thank in particular Mr. F. Baudouin and Dr. E. Haverkamp Begemann for their kindness in discussing suggestions made here concerning Rubens and his influence, Dr. L. D. Ettlinger and Professor E. H. Gombrich for suggestions concerning parts of the Town Hall's symbolism, and Professor J. M. C. Toynbee, who in a short but most illuminating discussion during my stay at the British School at Rome contributed generously to my exploration of the emulation of antique sculpture in seventeenth-century Holland. I am also indebted to members of the staff of the National Library of Scotland and of Register House, Edinburgh, who with great perseverance helped me in the search for information about stone exported to Amsterdam from Scotland. Finally, and with deep gratitude, I should like to mention Mr. and Mrs. H. E. Covens-Wijsman and their family, whose generous invitation given many years ago to an English schoolgirl who was quite unknown to them led to my first acquaintance with Holland and ultimately to the making of the present study.

For financial help I am indebted to the Ministry of Education, Arts and Sciences of the Netherlands who most generously provided scholarship for two and a half years' study in Holland, and also to the Central Research Fund of London University for grants covering the expenses of visits to Belgium and Italy and for material needed for research. The publication of this book, with its many illustrations, has been made possible by the kind help of the Board of Curators of the State University of Utrecht.

I am most grateful to the museums and other owners of works illustrated who have given permission for the publication of reproductions. Acknowledgements for photographs reproduced will be found at the end of the List of Illustrations.

The book owes its form to Mr. H. L. Gumbert's complete understanding of the intention of this book and to the precise and scholarly care with which he has shaped it accordingly. Miss Elsa Scheerer has given me guidance on many points concerning the preparation of the manuscript, and Mrs. M. Singelenberg-Van der Meer expert help with its revision, with proof-reading, and with the index. For the careful preparation of many of the photographs I am indebted to Miss Ursula Pariser and other members of the Photographic Department of the Courtauld Institute of Art and to Mr. H. A. van Dijk of that of the Art History Institute, Utrecht. In conclusion I should like to thank N.V. Drukkerij Trio, The Hague, and Cliché-fabriek Utrecht N.V., Rommerts en Van Santen, for the very special care that they have given to the preparation and printing of this volume.

KATHARINE FREMANTLE

Utrecht, 1959

CONTENTS

Holland's nature and geographical position (5) – Origins of Dutch trade (6) – Amsterdam's origins (7) – Increase in trade and prosperity (9) – The nature of the city (10) – Its extensions and public buildings (12) – Growth of the city government (15) – The power of the burgomasters (16) – Foundation of the administrative departments (18) – Allotment of rooms in the seventeenth-century Town Hall according to precedence (19) – The mediaeval Town Hall (19) – Its state in the seventeenth century (20) – Need for replacement (23) – Organization of this undertaking (24) – Relationship of Amsterdam with the States of Holland (26) – With the States General (26) – Rivalry with the Stadholder (27) – Role of Amsterdam in peace negotiations with Spain (27) – The Stadholder's aspirations (27) – The Peace of Munster concluded (28).

Significance of the Peace of Munster (30) – The new Town Hall a memorial to it (31) – Early records of the design (34) – Its nature (34) – The decoration planned for the tower (36) – That of the eastern pediment and façades (38) – General description of the interior (39) – Planning of the central hall and galleries (41) – Their decoration designed to form a miniature universe (42) – Amsterdam's history represented within this (48) – The building's classical form appropriate (51) – Possible emulation of Rome's first Senate House (51) – Unity and complexity of the Town Hall's symbolism (55).

Amphion and Argus as symbols of good government (57) – Function of the Town Hall in civic life (59) – Poetry and painting held to be equivalent (61) – Architecture and sculpture used with these in symbolism of Town Hall (62) – Didactic function of poetic imagery (63) – Defence of such imagery against objections (64) – Its use in the Town Hall to inspire civic virtues (65) – The burgomasters' chamber and its decoration (66) – Their council-room (69) – Further decoration in the central hall and galleries (71) – Office of Trustees of the City Orphans (74) – The office for matrimonial affairs (74) – The magistrates' court (74) – The gallery for public announcements (78) – The *vierschaar* (78) – The chamber of justice (86).

LIST OF ILLUSTRATIONS

'Right' and 'Left' in this list refer to the spectator's viewpoint. Where publications from which illustrations have been taken are mentioned in the Bibliography they are referred to here by shortened titles.

153. Rubens. Triumphal Entry decorations, 1635: Arch of the Infante Ferdinand. Engraving by Van Thulden. Gevartius, *Pompa*, Pl. p. 108 A.

154. Rubens. Triumphal Entry decorations: The Infante Ferdinand at the Battle of Nordlingen. Engraving by Van Thulden. Gevartius, *Pompa,* Pl. p. 99 B.

155. Van Campen. Prince Frederik Hendrik Crossing the Three Rivers. Painting in the Oranjezaal, Huis ten Bosch, The Hague. *(Bildarchiv Foto-Marburg.)*

156. Rubens. Triumphal Entry decorations: Doors of the Temple of Janus. Engraving by Van Thulden. Gevartius, *Pompa*, Pl. p. 117 B.

157. Van Couwenberch. Painted doors. Oranjezaal, Huis ten Bosch, The Hague. *(Bildarchiv Foto-Marburg.)*

158. J. Duquesnoy the Younger. Tomb of Bishop Triest. 1642–54. Detail. St. Bavo, Ghent. *(Copyright A. C. L. , Brussels.)*

159. Faydherbe. Tomb of Archbishop Cruesen. 1660. Detail. Cathedral, Malines. *(Copyright A. C. L., Brussels.)*

160. Quellien. Ara Coeli Madonna. Ste Gudule, Brussels.

161. F. Duquesnoy. St. Andrew. Designed 1627. St. Peter's, Rome. *(Photo Alinari.)*

162. Faydherbe. St. Simon. Ste Gudule, Brussels.

163. J. Duquesnoy the Younger. St. Thomas. Ste Gudule, Brussels.

164. Quellien. Plantin printer's mark. 1639. Plantin-Moretus Museum, Antwerp. *(Copyright A. C. L., Brussels.)*

165. Rubens. Plantin printer's mark. Drawing. c. 1627–8. Plantin-Moretus Museum, Antwerp. *(Copyright A. C. L., Brussels.)*

166. Quellien. Model for door-top for Amsterdam Town Hall. Rijksmuseum, Amsterdam.

167. F. Duquesnoy. Tomb of Ferdinand van den Eynde. Commissioned 1633. Detail. S. Maria dell' Anima, Rome.

168. Quellien. Justice. Model for front pediment of Amsterdam Town Hall. Rijksmuseum, Amsterdam.

169. F. Duquesnoy. St. Susanna. 1629–33. S. Maria di Loreto, Rome. *(Photo Alinari.)*

170. Quellien. Sleeping child. 1641. Walters Art Gallery, Baltimore.

171. F. Duquesnoy. Tomb of Ferdinand van den Eynde. Detail. S. Maria dell' Anima, Rome.

172. Quellien. Holy Family. 1644. St. Paul's, Antwerp.

173. Quellien. Holy Family. Detail. St. Paul's, Antwerp.

174. Rubens and others. High Altar. c. 1621. St. Charles Borromeo, Antwerp.

175. A. Quellien the Younger and others. High Altar. 1686–9. S. Jacques, Antwerp.

176. Van Campen and Quellien. Organ case. c. 1650–5. New Church, Amsterdam.

177. Van Logteren and others. Organ case. 1735–8. Detail. St. Bavo, Haarlem.

178. Van Campen and Quellien. Organ case. Detail. New Church, Amsterdam.

179. Van Campen and Quellien. Organ case. Detail. New Church, Amsterdam.

180. Former Town Hall, Amsterdam. Front pediment.

The author is greatly indebted to the following, who have provided photographs used for illustrations and have kindly consented to their reproduction. (Illustrations not mentioned in this list have been made direct from the original engravings or are from photographs taken by the author.)

AMSTERDAM
    Gemeentelijke Archiefdienst: Nos. 6–10 and 190.
    Intendance Koninklijk Paleis: Nos. 193–4, 199–200, and 203–4.
    Rijksmuseum: Frontispiece, Nos. 4, 5, 95, 100, 120, 153, 166, 168, 185–7, 189, 192, and 195–8.
    Stedelijk Museum: No. 2.
    Stichting Centraal Projectie- en Lichtbeelden Instituut: Nos. 40, 52, 62, 89, 98, 99, 109, and 181.

    Scheltema en Holkema's Boekhandel en Uitgeversmaatschappij N.V.: No. 103.

ANTWERP
    Stadsarchief: No. 146.

BALTIMORE
    Walters Art Gallery: No. 170.

BRUSSELS
    Institut Royal du Patrimonie Artistique (A.C.L.): Nos. 140, 158–9 and 164–5.

FLORENCE
    Alinari: Nos. 161 and 183.

GRONINGEN
    Groninger Museum voor Stad en Ommelanden: No. 201.

HAARLEM
    Stichting Haarlem's Bloei: No. 177.

THE HAGUE
    Algemeen Rijksarchief: No. 117.
    Dienst voor Schone Kunsten der Gemeente 's-Gravenhage: No. 116.
    Gemeente-Archief: No. 121.
    Rijksbureau voor Kunsthistorische Documentatie: No. 73.
    Rijksdienst voor de Monumentenzorg: Nos. 11–13, 83, 110, and 113–15.

    A. Dingjan: No. 191.

LONDON
    Courtauld Institute of Art: Nos. 122, 127, 129, and 132.
    Alec Tiranti Ltd: No. 124.

MADRID
    Biblioteca Nacional: Nos. 182 and 184.

MARBURG
    Bildarchiv Foto Marburg: Nos. 152, 155, and 157.

MUNICH
    Staatliche Grafische Sammlung: No. 39.

ROME
    Anderson: Nos. 137, 169, and 202.

STOCKHOLM
    Riksarkivet: No. 123.

UTRECHT
    Bibliotheek der Rijksuniversiteit: Nos. 3 and 101.
    Kunsthistorisch Instituut der Rijksuniversiteit: Nos. 33, 71, 75, 76, 80a, b, and c, 147, and 180.

INTRODUCTION

Perhaps the main historical interest of the seventeenth-century Town Hall of Amsterdam, the great building in the centre of the city which is now the Royal Palace, lies in its significance as a record of the life and culture which produced it: those of Holland at the greatest moment of her history, and of Amsterdam itself. In this book the building is examined as such a record. At present, however, no very detailed study of the subject can be made; it appears that such an approach to the study of a complex work of architecture, with its decoration, is a comparatively new one, and because of this few of the points in the landscape of cultural history on which bearings might be taken have been singled out, and the country that must be passed through in making the approach is very largely unexplored. It has therefore seemed best to seek out points of reference in this surrounding landscape, and to plot the Town Hall's position in relation to them, rather than to attempt to make an exhaustive examination of the building itself. For until its position in the history of Dutch and of European culture has been defined the significance of the building cannot be fully understood.

Although it was built to provide accommodation for the numerous departments of the city government the Town Hall was designed as a statement, made in visual terms but comparable to a vast oration, concerning the city's history and status, its civic life, and the ideals of its government. It was to testify to the city's glory and to its civic virtues, and in doing so was to confirm and encourage them. This statement was expressed – more completely than its makers can have realized – by means of the relation of the building to its surroundings and of its arrangement and use, and in terms of its symbolic decoration, of its architectural and sculptural forms, and of the baroque design of its decorative scheme, in which the citizens who visited the building or did business or worked there were themselves included. It was also expressed in the paintings carried out as part of the whole design, whose formal composition probably did not form part of the original scheme and here, except in one instance, is not examined. These means of expression together form a language, as perhaps it may be called, which now has to be interpreted because the meanings and connotations of many of its words have changed and others have been forgotten. Since here an attempt is made to construe some of the most important passages of the Town Hall's oratory and to understand their historical connections, other works of art which convey their meaning in a similar way, and comparable statements made in other terms (most often those of literature) must be referred to, for these may provide a key to the Town Hall's meaning. At the same time means of expression that are used in the building – the style of its architecture, the baroque design of its decoration, and the style of its sculpture – will be considered historically, since the lines of their development, meeting in the Town Hall, may be used to determine its position in cultural history.

Although some parts of the scheme were not carried out and others were altered in the later stages of building and decoration the principal parts of the Town Hall were largely carried out according to the designs of its architect, Jacob van Campen. It has been extremely well preserved, and although damaging alterations were made at the beginning of the last century when it became King Louis Napoleon's palace it has now been restored to much of its original splendour. Even its setting in Amsterdam has not entirely altered. The streets round it and the square on which it stands have in general kept their former outlines, and although most of the buildings that flank them are higher than their seventeenth-century predecessors the Palace still is dominant. The waterways that were once so important to its meaning, however, have been filled in, and the masts which could be seen across the square from its windows have long since vanished.

Both the development of the Town Hall's design and Van Campen's intentions for those parts which were not executed are very well documented. A wooden model for the building has been preserved and also many models for its sculpture, engravings which show preliminary versions of the architectural design and of the design of the sculpture on the pediments, and drawings for parts of the decoration. After the scheme was modified engravings were published which show the architect's original intentions, and there is written evidence which adds further to our knowledge. This evidence includes papers concerning much of the sculpture written in Quellien's own hand. All these sources of information have been drawn on in making the present study, and some of them are discussed in detail here for the first time.

The sources which have provided information about the Town Hall's meaning and its relationship to its setting are more various. They include works of antique, Italian renaissance, and Dutch seventeenth-century literature, seventeenth-century accounts of Amsterdam, of its history and its government, and of its Town Hall itself, drawings and engravings, records made by travellers, public shows performed, decorations designed, and medals struck to mark special occasions, works of architecture, sculpture, and painting both in Holland and elsewhere, and a number of seventeenth-century documents. Since the many sources used are uneven in value, and since in some cases they have to be seen in their context before they can be interpreted correctly, explanatory notes have been provided in many cases in the List of Sources and in the Bibliography. Where passages are quoted double quotation marks are used for those given in the original language and single marks for translations. English translations are those of the present author unless it is stated otherwise. Where passages have been transcribed from manuscripts the rules for the publication of historical records laid down by the Historisch Genootschap (*Regels voor het uitgeven van historische bescheiden*, revised by D. Th. Enklaar and A. J. van de

Ven, Utrecht, 1948) have been followed, though with the utmost conservatism in making changes in orthography and punctuation. Square brackets, however, have not been used in accordance with these rules, but here retain their usual function of marking editorial interpolations.

Modern literature that has been referred to is mentioned in the Bibliography and footnotes, but no attempt has been made to give a list of all the literary sources and later writings on the Palace. Such a list would cover many pages. The present author is very deeply indebted to those who have written on the Palace earlier, and in doing so have made this study possible. Her apology for adding to the list consists in the new approach to a major work of architecture that is suggested here, in the reconsideration of primary sources concerning it, and in the re-examination of developments in the arts in Holland and abroad by which the building's design was affected. In this process of revaluation it has been possible to piece together evidence concerning parts of the Town Hall's decoration about which very little was known, to see the decorative scheme, together with the architecture, as a single, very complex, symbolic design, and to attempt to define the nature of its symbolism. The origins to certain of the Town Hall's features in antique and renaissance art and literature on art, and in works designed by Rubens, have also become evident, and new information has been brought forward about the two major artists concerned with the building in the early stages, Jacob van Campen and the sculptor Artus Quellien. In addition it has proved possible to reassess the nature of certain of Rubens' decorative designs and of others derived from them, and also of the classical architecture developed in Holland in the 1630s, and, in examining their presence in works of the visual arts, new light has perhaps been thrown on the seventeenth-century Baroque of northern Europe and on Dutch seventeenth-century classicism.

The renaissance, in a worthy sense of the name, came slowly to the northern countries, and in Holland the Classical and the early Baroque arrived at very nearly the same time. Their union there was very fruitful, and the Palace at Amsterdam is perhaps one of the greatest works which resulted from it. This study therefore, if it succeeds in its purpose, will not only give back to that splendid building some part of its original meaning, but will also add to what is known of the nature of seventeenth-century Dutch culture, by indicating the process by which some of its elements reached Holland or arose there, and in doing so by adding to what is known of the relation of Dutch seventeenth-century culture to that of Europe as a whole.

At the beginning of his description of Amsterdam, one of the works most often consulted in writing this survey, Olfert Dapper, in 1663, referred to a passage written by Seneca. He echoed rather than borrowed Seneca's words, in a way in which classical themes were very often employed in Holland in the seventeenth-century. Today, at least in literary matters, it is the custom to quote exactly, even where the thought is expressed in laboured terms. So, in an unembellished translation, it seems appropriate to end with Dapper's statement. For he expressed feelings, and hopes for his work, which in introducing this book the present writer shares:

> As Seneca rightly said . . . that *those who came before us have done much, but yet have not done all; and that there still is and always will be much to find; and no-one, even if it were a hundred thousand years from this day, would ever be deprived of the opportunity to add something more* – so it is to be hoped that the remainder which is lacking here, and perhaps indeed will make up the greatest part (of the study), will be added in time by other and more exact inquirers, and that so by degrees this work – if it receives that honour – will be brought to perfection.

On the 29th of July 1655, a Thursday, two sermons were preached in the morning, one in the Old, the other in the New Church. In the New Church the minister Melchior Johannes preached a very neat and edifying sermon, taking as his text Psalm [30], the first and second verse, in which – having been pursued by his son Absalom, in which pursuit the said Absalom was killed – the royal prophet David has come back to Jerusalem and the Temple has been rededicated.

After the sermon the members of the city government came out of the church and into the Prinsenhof, where the Town Hall had been since the burning of the old building, and thus in the following order went to the new Town Hall:

The mounted guard (that is, those who guard the Town Hall) all with new halberds . . .

The city messengers, or rod-carrying messengers, all bareheaded

My lord the sheriff, going alone, at whose side the rod of justice was carried

The burgomasters in office

The magistrates in office

The ex-burgomasters

The treasurers

The trustees of the city orphans

The council, without any distinction as to whether they were ex-magistrates or not

The secretaries

The clerks . . .

Having come to the Town Hall in the aforesaid order, and standing in a circle in the burgomasters' large apartment, Burgomaster de Graeff, being president, gave a short address, and after that they went into their ordinary chamber and the magistrates into a room (next to their ordinary chamber, which was not yet ready) prepared for this provisionally; and the treasurers and the trustees of the city orphans went into theirs, and the council disbanded.

The burgomasters having come into their chamber and being seated, representatives from the officially recognized churches, including the French, English, German, and other churches, attended by elders, arrived and congratulated their noble worships.

And a small barrel of Rhenish wine was sent to the house of each of the ministers, that is, all the ministers who are in church service.

In the afternoon the gentlemen, sitting at table in the burgomasters' apartment in the order in which they had gone in the morning, were feasted with all dignity.

The citizens marching up, to wit six companies of the yellow regiment, with very fine and efficient discipline, the same standing in battle order, the captains and lieutenants or their representatives were requested to come into the Town Hall and were brought into the chamber of justice, being served with some twisted-stemmed glasses and flute-glasses of wine, and after three salvo of discharges had been fired with muskets the militia withdrew about seven o'clock in the evening, and the members of the city government did the like at about half past eight in the evening.

And everything went on with merry cheerfulness at the feast.[1]

It has seemed appropriate to begin with this description, and to give it in full, to set the key for this whole study. For it appears that the historian's first task is to make his readers sense past events as though they were taking part in them, so that in trying to understand them they may re-live them in their minds. The quiet realism of the native tradition of Dutch painting has put the history of everyday life in Holland as it were into storage for us, so that the rich interplay of its textures, lights, and colours emerges unimpaired. Hans Bontemantel, in his account of the inauguration of the seventeenth-century

---

[1] Bontemantel, MS. *Resolutien*, I, ii, pp. 175–7 (for Dutch text see p. 192 below). This is his earliest account of the inauguration (others in MS. *Civ. en mil. reg.*, I, pp. 240–3 and III, pp. 458–61; publ. Kroon, *Stadhuis*, pp. 54–57 and Kernkamp, *De regeeringe*, II, pp. 59–62 respectively). The accounts differ little, but that published by Kernkamp shows that the sermons began at 7.30 a.m., thus the celebrations lasted more than twelve hours.

In de *Statenvertaling* (translation ordered by States General, 1637) the psalm referred to (Vulgate 29) begins:
    1. Een Psalm, een liedt der inwyinge van Davids huys.
    2. Ik sal u verhoogen, HEERE, want ghy hebt my opgetrocken, ende mijne vyanden over my niet verblijt.
Though the number was not filled in this text, here from an early folio edition (Leiden, n.d., before 1640), is identified by the notes in such editions, which give the occasion as David's return though they state that his house was purified and do not mention the Temple. Recent translations – e.g. Pontifical Biblical Institute, 1945 – mention a feast of the dedication of the Temple in the heading (v. 1 above) and the minister may have referred to the Hebrew text. The 1945 translation, Latin from the Hebrew, gives "quoniam liberasti me" and the reference to liberation was appropriate, as will be seen. In English (1611) the passage reads:
    [Heading] A Psalm and Song at the dedication of the house of David.
    1. I will extol thee, O Lord; for thou hast lifted me up, and hast not made my foes to rejoice over me.

Town Hall of Amsterdam, the palace in the centre of the city which is our subject, has preserved a single event in very much the same way, so that we are privileged to witness the solemn procession that crossed the city's central square on a summer day three hundred years ago, and may sense the simplicity and humanity of the occasion as well as its dignity, becoming acquainted as we do so with the pattern of the civic life which was represented there.

Descriptions, however, are limited, and if we are to attempt to understand the significance of the new building, in which this pattern is reflected, we must add to our knowledge by considering records of other kinds. For since the senses become dulled to the most familiar conditions of life, the soil in which history grows, these are seldom spoken of unless by strangers, and information about them is most often recorded unconsciously, in the forms of material objects and by other means, while ideas, which shape history, are conveyed most directly in the form of symbols from mind to mind.

On the medal that was struck to commemorate the inauguration,[1] where the scene on the city square is depicted as though in a photograph (illus. 1a), certain figures appear which Hans Bontemantel was not able to describe. Mercury flies above the assembled crowd, his caduceus and the ample hat of liberty[2] grasped firmly in his hands; an antique column and a sculptured bust lie on the cobble-stones; and Amphion sits in the foreground, playing his lyre.[3] These figures represent trade, bringing with it liberty, past history as it is re-embodied in present times, and civic life, which together have nourished and shaped the history of Amsterdam and brought her Town Hall into being. So we shall be concerned with them. They are depicted for us in the seventeenth-century Town Hall itself, as they are in this picture, in the solid forms of architecture and sculpture and in terms of symbolism which, like the music of Amphion, had the power of encouraging good citizenship.

---

[1] By G. Pool, Amsterdam, 1655. *Cat. gedenkpenningen*, I, nos. 840 and 842; Van Loon, *Historiepenningen*, II, pp. 399–401. The reverse of no. 842 is described on p. 169 below.

[2] See Ripa, *Iconologia*, 1624, p. 397, description of Liberty: "Se le dà il capello ... perciòche quando volevano i Romani dare libertà ad un servo dopò d'havergli raso i capelli gli facevano portare il cappello, e si faceva questa ceremonia nel tempio di una Dea [Feronia] creduta prottetrice di quelli, ch'acquistavano la libertà, e la dimandavano". The words OMNIBVS IDEM, 'The same for all', appear on the brim of the hat on the medal.

[3] For this figure's significance see pp. 58–59 below.

CHAPTER I

MERCURY ARRIVES

Soo ley hy eer een groene Kra[n]s van eiken
　　Een kruik gewyde wyn,
　　Voor 't pronkbeelt van Jupyn,
Die 't hooft des Dondergods niet kon bereiken:
Als ik, die niet in top weet op te halen
　　Hoe 't needrig Amsterdam
　　Tot zulk een hooghte quam,
Doe nu met my haar hoogheit nederdalen.
Ik kan haar lof ten vollen niet verklaren,
　　Maar kip daar uit alleen
　　Haar deughden in 't gemeen,
Als uit een oeugst een luttel korenaren:
Zy is zoo hoog ten eertroon opgeklommen,
　　Datz' in haar wal bevat
　　Zoo kostelyk een schat,
Het tegenwicht van 's werelts Koningdommen.

Wat zalze nu, op het aanhoudend' smeken
　　Der Vrede, zacht van zin,
　　Al voordeel en gewin
Opsteken, met haar swaarden op te steken.
Zy liet den Kryg in al dat bloedt versmoren,
　　Die nu niet prikt noch steekt,
　　Doordien hem magt ontbreekt.
En mint de Roos en Leli noch die doren?
O Perel aan de Lantkroon, noit volprezen,
　　O Hollants wonderding!
　　Was Nederlant een ring
Gy zout, ô Stadt, de diamantsteen wezen.
O Vaders, wien, op 's hemels welbehagen,
　　De Stadt is toebetrouwt:
　　De stoffe maakt my stout,
Om dit geschenk u dankbaar op te dragen.

ANSLO, Dedication to Burgomasters, 1648 [1]

Almost the whole of Holland [2] is delta country, and much of it has been won and kept from marsh and sea by the hard work and constant watchfulness of its inhabitants. They have fenced out the sea, controlled the rivers, and drained inland waters, so that it might almost be said that they have made the land itself. Even the houses, over large parts of the country, have to be built on piles driven laboriously into the soft ground so that their weight may rest on the comparatively solid sand below. In a sense, therefore, economic life there starts at a disadvantage, which is triumphantly overcome, and it is not surprising that everyday life, with all that goes to make it up, is treasured and cherished in such a country.

---

[1] From 'Het gekroonde Amsterdam', quoted from *Olyf-krans*, 1750, pp. 165–6. "Roos en Leli" denote France and England, "Holland" the Province of Holland, and "Nederland" the Dutch Republic. 'As, of old, he who could not reach the head of the God of Thunder laid a green oaken Wreath, a pitcher of hallowed wine, before the great statue of Jupiter; so I, who am not able to display how the lowly Amsterdam came to such a height, make her highness descend to me. I cannot declare her praise to the full, but choose out of it only her virtues in general, as out of a harvest a little ear of corn. She has climbed so high to the throne of honour that she contains within her wall such a costly treasure, the counter-weight to the world's Kingdoms. How shall she now, at the continued beseeching of gentle-natured Peace, put in her purse all advantage and profit by sheathing her swords. She let War stifle in all that blood, who now neither pricks nor pierces because he is powerless. And do the Rose and Lily still love that thorn? O Pearl in the crown formed by this land, never fully praised, O Holland's wondrous thing, were the Netherlands a ring you, O city, would be the diamond stone. O Fathers, to whom the city is entrusted by the goodwill of heaven, the subject makes me bold to dedicate this present to you gratefully.'

[2] 'Holland' is used in this book in the English sense to denote the whole country except in Dutch quotations, where it signifies the Province of Holland only. The Provinces of Holland are mentioned in the text as such. The present-day provinces of North and South Holland together formed the single province of Holland and West Friesland in the seventeenth century.

The position of Holland, at the mouths of the river Rhine and the Maas, opposite England, and providing a traffic route through sheltered waters between the region of the Baltic and north Germany and that of Flanders and France, nevertheless brought her advantages, and her rivers and the harbours that they form became highways for the transport of goods by water and the starting-points for overseas trade.[1] Tacitus shows that the inhabitants of the country were competent seamen in Roman times,[2] and in the seventh and eighth centuries their trade was widespread. At that time there were Frisian settlers in cities along the Rhine, in England, in north Germany, and in Sweden, where the long trade route through Russia to the Levant began. Frisian territory stretched from the northern coast as far south as Dorestad, now the village Wijk-bij-Duurstede, a fortified trading settlement at the point where the Rhine divides into branches leading west and north. During the centuries that followed Friesland gradually declined, but inland centres of trade grew up on the branches of the Rhine, one of which, the river IJsel, formed an alternative route leading northward. Toll was extracted from foreign merchants as they passed through these centres and the inhabitants formed staples for the organization and protection of their commerce, so that gradually, with this new security, civic life in the northern Netherlands began, based from the first on her waterways and her overseas trade. The merchants of Tiel, on a western branch of the Rhine, traded with England and the upper Rhineland. Utrecht, which was first important as the centre of the bishopric which covered the greater part of the northern Netherlands, under the protection of the Church became a merchant centre and a place of transhipment on the northern branch of the Rhine which linked the Rhineland and the route to England with the Baltic Sea. So great was the trade of this city that round about the year 1200 and perhaps even earlier a new canal was made there which had spacious wharves and cellars for the storage of goods to either side of it. Up till about the middle of the thirteenth century, when the cog, a seafaring vessel built for the carrying of merchandise, was introduced, goods were transported over land on the northern route, by Schleswig and Ripen or by Hamburg and

[1] The writer is indebted to J. Huizinga's account of Dutch 17th-century culture and its origins, *Nederland's beschaving in de zeventiende eeuw*, Haarlem, 1941, and to the following: P. Geyl, *Geschiedenis van de Nederlandse stam*, revised ed., Amsterdam [etc.], 1948–; J. F. Niermeyer, *De wording van onze volkshuishouding* (Servire's Encyclopaedie), The Hague, 1946; Jan Romein and others, *De lage landen bij de zee*, Utrecht, 1934. For accounts in English see P. Geyl, *The Netherlands Divided (1609–1648)*, London 1936, and G. J. Renier, *The Dutch Nation, an Historical Study*, London, 1944.
[2] *Historia*, IV, xv and xvi.

6

Lübeck, between the North Sea and the Baltic, but from this time the sea route round Denmark and through the Sont was used. Heavier goods could then be transported, and traffic on the inland waterways of the northern Netherlands increased in consequence. The towns on the IJsel route, the most direct route between the Rhineland and the north, came into prominence, while Utrecht, where the support of the Church had weakened, declined. At the same time settlements on the sheltered waters of what is now the IJsel Lake, then a large inlet of the open sea, and on the islands of Zeeland, became ports used for overseas trade. Among these ports was Amsterdam, which may well have originated as a fishing village. In the seventeenth century its citizens were justifiably proud of its growth from such humble beginnings into an important centre of world trade.[1]

The earliest record in which Amsterdam is named dates only from 1275, and is a document in which the "homines manentes apud Amstelredamme" were granted freedom from toll in the whole of the province of Holland, which indicates that at that time there were already traders among these people.[2] Their settlement was beside the dam on the river Amstel, which runs northwards into the wide mouth of the river IJ near the point where it opens into the IJsel Lake, and it is probable that this dam had been made by the year 1204, since it appears that by this year the surrounding country had been dyked. The dam was not placed across the mouth of the river, but a short distance upstream, and there were dykes along the river banks between the dam and the sea, so that a sheltered harbour was formed. Goods carried along the river must have been transhipped at the dam, and it was natural that a market-place should come into being beside it and should eventually take its name. This was evidently the origin of the Dam at Amsterdam, the market-place in the centre of the city on which the mediaeval Town Hall and its seventeenth-century successor stood.

While the traffic through Utrecht declined in the thirteenth century a winding inland waterway was formed, which led through what are now the provinces of Holland and linked the IJ with the western estuaries of the Rhine mouth and with the ports of Zeeland. Transhipment was not necessary along the course of this new route, and although at first it was used for local traffic it

---

[1] See for example the passage by Vondel quoted on p. 30 below.
[2] For the growth of Amsterdam the following in particular have been consulted: chapters by W. F. H. Oldewelt and A. E. d'Ailly in *Zeven eeuwen*, I. pp. 1–40, pp. 37–63 respectively; H. Brugmans, *Opkomst en bloei van Amsterdam*, Amsterdam, 1911. For maps documenting the city's growth see d'Ailly, *Catalogus van Amsterdamsche plattegronden*, Amsterdam, 1934. Early descriptions are listed by Wouter Nijhoff, *Bibliographie van Noord-Nederlandsche plaatsbeschrijvingen tot het einde der 18e eeuw*, revised ed., The Hague, 1953.

developed into a thoroughfare used for overseas trade. The inhabitants of both Holland and Zeeland began to sell their local agricultural products, goods made from these in the towns, and preserved fish, along the Rhine, in England, and later in north German markets, while towards the end of the thirteenth century the merchants of Hamburg began to use Amsterdam instead of Utrecht as their main port for goods sold in the northern Netherlands and in particular for the import of large quantities of German beer, finding a new market in the towns of north and south Holland, which because of the development of their trade and industry were increasing in prosperity. By the middle of the fourteenth century Amsterdam was the principal port in the northern Netherlands not only for goods from the Baltic destined for these provinces, but also for those which were sent further afield, to Zeeland, Flanders, and Brabant, its inhabitants and those of the surrounding country at first mainly acting as carriers for German merchants but later trading on their own account. In the fifteenth century, helped by their allegiance to the House of Burgundy, they came to compete successfully with the merchants of the Hanseatic League, whose principal market in the Netherlands was at Bruges, while the German merchants themselves, prefering the shelter of the inland waterway to the risks of the open sea, and attracted by the flourishing market at Amsterdam, contributed to the city's prosperity.

These changes were decisive in Dutch history, for they account for the rise of the western towns, where the main centres of Dutch trade are concentrated even today, and for the importance of the western provinces in the days of the Republic; they laid the foundations for Amsterdam's further development, and they determined her character, which from the start was that of a merchant city, dependent for its position and its wealth on the activities of its citizens rather than on the protection of ecclesiastical or of secular authorities. It has been shown by Professor Huizinga that the expansion of Holland's trade was largely due to her very lack of central organization, and that physical conditions in the northern Netherlands favour not the landowner and the man on horseback, but the man who owns a boat.[1] In Amsterdam the man with a boat triumphed, and it is not surprising that the cog found its way into the city's mediaeval coat of arms (see illus. 188).[2]

---

[1] Op. cit., pp. 30–36 and 23 respectively.
[2] The cog appeared on the city's seal from 1300 (the earliest known) until after 1484, when the present coat of arms of the city, three diagonal white crosses on a vertical black band on a red shield surmounted by an imperial crown, was granted by Maximilian of Austria; see W. H. F. Oldewelt, 'De stadszegels van Amsterdam', *Jaarboek Amstelodamum*, XXXIII, 1936, pp. 17–30.

Once the foundations were laid Amsterdam's trade expanded rapidly, favoured by external circumstances. In the middle ages Dutch trade had been helped by the war between England and France, which for many years hindered the economic development of these countries, and in the sixteenth century the shift of the centres of European trade from the Mediterranean to the North Sea coast, which in part resulted from the discovery of America, brought further advantages. About the year 1500, largely because of this shift, and with the silting up of the harbours of Bruges, Antwerp became the world's most important trading centre, and there for the first time in renaissance Europe a city exchange open to the merchants of all countries was set up in 1531. When Antwerp's trade came to an end with the closing of the Scheldt by the United Provinces in 1585 Amsterdam was in a position to succeed her, and took her place. By then Dutch merchants had a footing in all the North Sea ports, they had been trading not only with the Baltic but also with France and the Iberian Peninsula from late mediaeval times, and Amsterdam was already the most important centre for the corn trade. By the end of the sixteenth century the United Provinces were also trading with Italy and the Levant, and were sending expeditions to the Cape Verde Islands, Africa, and the East Indies. For such expeditions a large amount of capital was necessary and merchants, who during the fifteenth and sixteenth centuries with the development of insurance had begun to own ships rather than divide their goods among ships owned by others, now combined to finance expeditions and to share the proceeds. The holding of shares by those who were not merchants also began. In 1602 the Dutch East India Company was formed by the groups of merchants who were concerned with trade on the route round the Cape, and in this company all citizens of the United Provinces could hold shares. In 1621 the Dutch West India Company was founded on the same model. The power of these companies became very great, and as early as 1607 it was declared that trade done on the Cape route was the principal contributor to Amsterdam's finances.[1] In the early seventeenth century the city council of Amsterdam itself set up a bank and a pawnbroker's office, both of which proved to be very profitable although they were set up in the first place to encourage trade and to help the poorer citizens. They also founded a city exchange. The revolt against Spain did not hold back the country's progress, nor did it prevent the Dutch from trading with the enemy, who hardly set foot in the Province of Holland and West

[1] Statement made by the city council of Amsterdam; cited by P. J. Bouman in Romein, op. cit., p. 313.

9

Friesland after 1575; rather it was Dutch trade, and very largely that of Amsterdam, that made the long war for freedom possible.

It has been shown in a recent study[1] that the population of Amsterdam increased from about 31,000, in 1587 to 1590, to about 139,000 in 1631 to 1640; that is to say it increased by almost four and a half times. These figures give some idea of the growth of the city which was linked with its increasing prosperity. During roughly the same period Amsterdam trebled its area, and in the course of a single century, from 1575 to 1675, its size increased by about six times. The Dam and the harbour at the river mouth, however, kept their old importance, and even present-day maps of the city show how its roads and canals encircle or converge on them, while early maps provide further information about its nature and its growth.

The earliest known map of Amsterdam (illus. 2),[2] which dates from 1536, is very fortunately a painted one, so that the modern observer may see the city of that time stretched out before him, as though from an aeroplane. It is a walled city which glows with the colours of brick and tile and it is set in a flat landscape of low-lying meadows which stretch as far as the eye can see, divided only by rivers and water-channels, and of the vivid green which is proper to such country. Like the meadows the city itself is surrounded by a girdle of water,[3] and on the northern side, which significantly is placed in the foreground, it is bordered by the blue waters of the river IJ, in which a great number of ships come and go or lie at anchor, their pennants flying gaily in the wind; by this time the city has large harbours lying outside the mouth of the Amstel, defended by a palisade. The harbour within the river mouth is crowded with smaller vessels, which are tied up beside the wharves and warehouses along its banks to unload or take on cargo, and this inner harbour, the Damrak, or 'Dam reach', of the Amstel, stretches to the very centre of the city, crossed by two wooden bridges under which boats may pass. At its end is the Dam itself, on which the stalls of the fish market, and a number of houses, appear, and next to the Dam is the market-place which shares its name. Beyond the Dam the river provides a wide thoroughfare through the southern part of the city and leads, through a gap in the city walls, which is defended by a fort, to the open

[1] P. Schraa, 'Onderzoekingen naar de bevolkingsomvang van Amsterdam tussen 1550 en 1650', *Jaarboek Amstelodamum*, XLVI, 1954, pp. 1–33. The figures quoted are from p. 27.
[2] Painted map by Cornelis Anthonisz. dated 1536, Amsterdamsch Historisch Museum, The Waag, Amsterdam (d'Ailly, *Catalogus* cit., no. 27). See also his woodcut map of 1544 (d'Ailly no. 30), in which the proportions of the larger buildings shown are less exaggerated.
[3] The canal named the Singel, or 'girdle', in present-day Amsterdam originally formed part of this defensive strip of water.

country beyond. There are few roads within the city, and those that there are are by modern standards very narrow ones. The more important of them evidently came into being along the top of the dyke which runs through it, on which the ground was firm, and so the line of this dyke can be seen on the map quite clearly and is recorded in the street names: the Zeedijk, the Nieuwendijk, and the Haarlemmerdijk.[1] The road along the remaining section of the dyke is called the Warmoesstraat; a vegetable market was evidently held there.[2] Still narrower continuations of the Warmoesstraat and the Nieuwendijk, which flank the Damrak, lead upstream along the river, a small road furnished with stone bridges runs across the city, and another encircles it within the walls as part of its system of defence. In addition there are only passages and alleys between the closely-packed houses, quays beside the waterways, and a few open spaces of very limited extent. It is clear that transport by land was at a disadvantage in sixteenth-century Amsterdam and that water traffic was all-important. In the seventeenth century wheeled traffic was not allowed within the city, goods being transported by road where it was necessary by horse-drawn sleigh or by hand barrow,[3] yet prosperity continued. The blue of the city's waterways, meanwhile, is almost as prominent as the colour of the houses in the painted map, and they form highways through all its quarters which link them with the Rokin, the reach of the Amstel above the Dam. Along them goods could be carried direct to the houses, where they were hauled up by pulley into attics or rolled into cellars from the quays or from the boats themselves, to be guarded by their merchant owners, who lived on the intervening floors,[4] and to be shipped again in due course as easily.

The houses themselves seem to jostle for places beside the water and on the streets, their ridged roofs placed at right-angles to them so that as many as possible are accommodated, and so that there is the end of a strong roof-beam at the top of each façade to which if it is required a beam with a pulley capable of bearing heavy weights may be attached. All these houses, and indeed all the buildings of the city, rest on piles driven into the marshy ground, and when

[1] The 'sea dyke', the 'new dyke', and the 'Haarlem dyke'. The first was the part of the dyke facing the sea at the mouth of the IJ, the second that on the 'new', or western, side of the Amstel, and the third that on the road towards Haarlem. The terms Old and New Side distinguished the parts of the city to either side of the Amstel.

[2] *Warmoes* is equivalent to the English 'pot herbs'.

[3] Vividly described by the brothers De Bovio; Brom, 'Reisbeschrijving', *Bijdragen*, 1915, p. 106: "Le carozze sono prohibite; non si vedono per la città altri cocchi che certuni tirati da un solo cavallo, non havendo ruote, e scorrono per la città come le slitte". For travellers' accounts of Amsterdam see J. N. Jacobsen Jensen, *Reizigers te Amsterdam*, Amsterdam, 1919, and Supplement, 1936.

[4] See A. A. Kok, *Amsterdamsche woonhuizen* (Heemschut Serie), Amsterdam, 1946.

Cornelis Anthonisz. made his map many of the yards behind the houses near the harbour were stacked high with tall tree-trunks brought from overseas, not only for use in the extensive shipyards which he depicted on the banks of the river IJ, but also to form foundations in the city itself. Yet in spite of this limitation, which in part must account for the modest scale of the houses, two great stone churches dominate the city, a tall tower draws the attention of the observer to the group of buildings on the western side of the Dam which together form the Town Hall, and the walls are defended by solid gatehouses and by many turrets.

Amsterdam's earliest defensive walls dated from the beginning of the fourteenth century, when the settlement on the river Amstel was first granted the rights of a city. They were of earth, and their position is recorded in the names of three of the city's waterways, the Oudezijds Voorburgwal, the Oudezijds Achterburgwal, and the Nieuwezijds Voorburgwal;[1] the Spui, or 'Sluice', lay outside the walls on the city's western side. The brick walls shown in the painted map were begun in 1481, and it can be seen that by that time the city had already expanded considerably. After the map was made it grew still more rapidly. It was realized before the war with Spain began that the walls no longer provided adequate protection, and after Amsterdam had joined the rebellion in 1578, when the matter had become urgent, the making of new defences was embarked upon. Land was added to the city on all but the north-eastern and the harbour sides, and a strong wall with bastions, protected by a wide moat, was constructed round it. On the north-eastern side an area used for ship-building, an all-important industry in Amsterdam, was taken up by the defences, and a further extension was made soon afterwards, presumably because of the difficulties that this caused. The level of the fields along the IJ on the eastern side of the city was raised so that they could be used for building and for industry, a new island was added by filling up an area near the river bank, and the defensive wall was carried round these new additions. With this extension of the waterside Amsterdam became roughly semicircular in form, and the outer harbours as well as the river mouth became important in the shaping of the city. These two extensions were made before the end of the century, and the area of the city was doubled by them. A map published in 1609[2] shows that by then the greater part of the land that was added had been taken into use.

---

[1] "Voor" and "achter burgwal" denote 'in front of' and 'beyond the city wall', and again the Old and New sides of the city are referred to.
[2] d'Ailly, *Catalogus* cit., no. 88.

12

The city's spectacular growth continued in the seventeenth century. By 1609 a large number of houses had been built outside the walls, and these, with the artificially raised land on which they were built, were a danger to the city. Because of this danger it was decided in that year that new enlargements and defences should be made, plans were approved by the city council in 1610, and work was begun soon afterwards. Three wide canals with quays to either side of them were to be constructed round Amsterdam, reaching to the IJ at either end, with strips of land between them wide enough for the building of houses along the quays, which would provide dignified accommodation for the wealthiest inhabitants and would have gardens behind them. On the western side of the city beyond these new canals a less spacious quarter was to be made, designed for industry and to accommodate less wealthy citizens; further islands were to be added to the city along the banks of the IJ, and there was to be a new system of defences. This extensive project, which trebled the area of the city, was accomplished in the course of about fifty years, with very little modification. By the middle of the century the western part of the extension and its accompanying defences had been completed, and thousands of new houses had been built (illus. 3).

These successive extensions, undertaken primarily in the interests of defence and trade, and in addition providing for an increasing population and symbolizing the new status of its leading inhabitants, in themselves testify to the wealth of Amsterdam and the power of its government. Much property was purchased by compulsion and many houses on the edge of the city were destroyed before the final extension and its defences were completed, and in making these alone many miles of canals were dug, walled, and bridged by hand labour; quays, founded on piles, were shaped and paved, land was raised for building, islands were made, old works of fortification were levelled or filled in, and the new walls, with in all twenty-six bastions and six gates, four of them with handsome gatehouses,[1] were laboriously constructed. Yet while the extensions were being made, and before the middle of the century, other improvements were carried out by the city government, many of them made necessary by Amsterdam's rapid growth. These too show its wealth, and they also give some impression of the wide range of the responsibilities of the government. Churches were built in the newly-added districts, the city orphanage was enlarged, a house was built for the aged, and houses of correction were founded. In 1637 a

---

[1] All these gates, now destroyed, are illustrated by Wagenaar, *Amsterdam*, I, pls. facing p. 50.

theatre was built, whose profits were to contribute to the support of the dependents of the city. It was designed by Jacob van Campen, later to become the architect of the new Town Hall, in emulation of the theatres of the antique world.[1] Two arsenals and a gun-foundry were set up, while four of the turrets which had formed part of the city's earlier defences were turned into towers for the adornment of the city; the carillon and clock from the tower of the old Town Hall were placed in one of these after the spire had become unsafe and had been taken down,[2] so that the time still passed to the accompaniment of music. Many facilities were also provided for the city's ever-expanding trade. As early as 1565 a weigh-house, nearly square in form and ornamented with a classical balustrade, had been built on the Dam. Later new market-places were made in districts added to the city, and two of them were furnished with market halls. Warehouses, a corn-exchange, a house for measuring corn, a cloth hall, and an excise house were also built by the city government, as well as the Exchange, whose foundation has already been referred to. The Exchange was finished and taken into use in 1608, and part of the Rokin near the Dam was roofed over to make room for it. Its designer, the city stonemason and architect Hendrik de Keyser, was sent over to see the Royal Exchange in London,[3] itself Flemish in design and largely modelled on that of Antwerp[4], before building it. He followed the pattern of the London Exchange very closely, so that the building came to be designed in an internationally accepted style. It was built 'for the general use of merchants of whatever nation and language, and for the ornament of the city',[5] and was generous in scale, dwarfing the fair-sized Gothic houses that stood beside it. In both style and scale it symbolized the new status of the city as a leading centre of world trade, and it evidently pleased the engravers and painters who recorded its appearance

---

[1] Records concerning this building's authorship are confused because the *bouwheer*, i.e. the person commissioning or supervising the work, was Jacob van Campen's relation, the city councillor Nikolaas van Campen. Wagenaar describes him as being 'not inexperienced' in architecture and refers to him as the *bouwmeester*, i.e. architect, of the building as well as the *bouwheer* (op. cit., II, pp. 398 and 400). Yet Jacob van Campen clearly was the architect. Houbraken, *Schouburg*, III, p. 381, mentions the theatre as being by him and its style supports the attribution. The theatre has been destroyed but is known from engravings.
[2] *Beschryvinge van 't Stadhuis*, 1782, p. 7, and Wagenaar, op. cit., II, p. 4.
[3] Neurdenburg, *De Keyser*, p. 8.
[4] Robert Hedicke, *Cornelis Floris und die Florisdekoration*, Berlin, 1913, p. 192 and pl. XL, 1 and 2; John Summerson, *Architecture in Britain 1530–1830* (Pelican History of Art), London [etc.], 1953, pp. 113-14.
[5] Quoted from the legend on a contemporary print, illus. Neurdenburg, op. cit., pl. XVIII: S. P. Q. AMST. IN PUBLICUM NEGOTIANTIUM CUIUSCUNQ. NATIONIS AC LINGVÆ USUM URBISQ. ADEO SUÆ ORNAMĒTV̄ ANNO MDCVIII A SOLO EXTRUI CURAVIT. The illustration of the Antwerp Exchange in Lodovico Guicciardini, *Descrittione . . . di tutti i Paesi Bassi* [etc.] (ed. Antwerp 1588, p. 6) bears a comparable inscription.

to show strange figures from foreign countries doing business in its spacious courtyard, among the soberly-dressed merchants of Amsterdam. The gentlemen of the city government, who were responsible for these many improvements, meanwhile continued to meet in the mediaeval Town Hall. It came to be too small for them, for with the growth of the city their activities increased, more departments were set up, and more officials were appointed.

Amsterdam was first governed by a sheriff, the representative of the overlord, and by magistrates, whose duty was to represent the citizens although they too were appointed by the overlord or on his behalf.[1] These officials together were responsible for justice and for the other administrative functions of government, though in a charter which dates from 1300 it was laid down or confirmed that the magistrates of a higher court should be consulted in difficult legal cases, and 'counsellors' of the sheriff and magistrates are mentioned in the same document. The function of these counsellors was at first purely advisory but during the fourteenth and fifteenth centuries the sheriff and magistrates delegated some of their duties to them, and only supervised the way in which they were carried out. The counsellors were put in charge of the city's dependents and entrusted with its finance, they were empowered to levy taxes, and in 1411 they were made responsible for the swearing-in of new *poorters*, burghers whose fixed home was in the city and who enjoyed certain privileges. After this time the counsellors came to be known as the 'burgomasters' of the city. The sheriff and magistrates specialized more and more in the making of statutes and in the administration of justice, and delegated their other functions to the burgomasters, who came to hold a leading position in the city government and were no longer subject to their supervision.

In documents dating from the early fifteenth century another advisory body is mentioned, the *vroedschap*, which here is referred to as the city council, though its powers were more limited than those of the city councils of modern times. At first this body consisted of twenty-four leading citizens chosen by the community to give advice to the officials of the government, but in 1477 the number of its members was raised to thirty-six, and it was laid down that they should be appointed for life and that new members should be co-opted. After this arrangement was made representatives of the citizens or of their leading organizations continued to be consulted in certain cases by the city government, but the practice fell into disuse soon after the Republic of the United

[1] For particulars concerning the city government G. W. Kernkamp, in *Amsterdam in de zeventiende eeuw*, I, ii. pp. 1–143, and Wagenaar, *Amsterdam*, III, pp. 269–502, have been referred to.

Provinces was formed, when the leading councils of the government came to be concerned more with political issues than with civic affairs, and by the seventeenth century ordinary citizens were in no way represented in the deliberations that went on in the Town Hall. In the first half of the century this does not seem to have caused much resentment, and perhaps this was in part because until about 1650 the members of the city government generally were or had been in trade or industry themselves, and many of them continued to do business like other citizens in the modest houses in which they lived, so that there were no very obvious grounds for jealousy. It was only in the second half of the century that a generation arose whose members could live entirely on invested money and could build themselves houses of some splendour beside the canals of Amsterdam and in the country outside the city.

The rise of the burgomasters to a position of importance was made possible by the way in which they were elected. They were never chosen by the city council as they were in the other towns of Holland, but three of them were elected annually by the ex-burgomasters and ex-magistrates of the city, and these three then chose one of the retiring burgomasters to hold office with them. It became an accepted custom that only ex-burgomasters and ex-magistrates should be elected, so that the same people served as burgomasters again and again and the magistrates, hoping to receive promotion in future elections, took care to vote according to the burgomasters' wishes. By the seventeenth century the magistrates themselves were also chosen by the burgomasters, for although fourteen candidates were nominated each year by the city council and seven of these were then appointed by the overlord, the nominations came to be made on the burgomasters' advice, and from 1565 for more than a century the candidates whom they recommended to the Stadholder were always appointed, while the seven new magistrates, not independently but together with the four burgomasters, elected two of the retiring magistrates to act as their president and vice-president. Even the sheriff was chosen by the burgomasters, who for many years during the fifteenth and sixteenth centuries rented the right of appointment from the overlord. In 1564 it was purchased by a final payment, and from then onwards it was laid down that the sheriff should fulfil his functions according to the burgomasters' 'counsel and advice'.

By these means the burgomasters, whose predecessors were appointed as the advisors of the sheriff and magistrates, acquired supreme power in the management of the city's affairs; they not only came to perform the administrative duties that had at first been delegated to them, but made themselves

16

responsible as well for one of the oldest and most important functions of the city government, the administration of justice itself. They were under an obligation to consult the city council in all decisions of importance, but it seems that they often did so summarily, without providing information on which an independent judgement could be based and often when it was too late for consultation to be of use, while the councillors themselves were not entitled to bring subjects forward for discussion. It was stipulated in particular that financial matters were to be laid before the city council, and a balance-sheet was presented to them each year. Yet it is doubtful whether even the treasurers understood the whole of the working of the city's finances. No modern historian has as yet been able to fathom them although the account-books survive, and it seems that secrets concerning very large sums of money died with the burgomasters themselves. The system of election, moreover, brought the virtual power of the city government into the hands of a few leading families, and though there were rules to prevent close relations sitting together on the various councils and limits of age were set, their oligarchy remained supreme. The members of these families decided on Amsterdam's policy in external affairs. The nature of the city's justice was determined not only by tradition but also by their interpretation of it. They appointed, or approved the appointment, of the admirals, the clergy, the grave-diggers, the midwives, the market cleaners, the professors, the schoolmasters, the stonemasons, the city smith, and the other employees of public institutions and of the city.[1] Their business sense led to the setting up of the city bank and the pawnbroker's office, it was they who decided that the organ was to be played during the singing of psalms in the Amsterdam churches, or that the city orphans were to be taught a trade 'suitable to their capacities' and were not to be sent to the Latin School. Their ideas and tastes were impressed on every aspect of the civic life of Amsterdam. They as well as tradition determined the nature of the city's public celebrations, and they determined the appearance of Amsterdam as the city renewed itself. They too, when the time was ripe for its building, were ultimately responsible for the design of the new Town Hall. Yet it was by Amsterdam and the nature of the life that went on in it that the leading families, and the personalities of each of their members, were first formed and were shaped continually. In this sense, though in this sense only, the government was made by, and represented, the city itself.

[1] These and the following instances are drawn from MS. *Res. Burg. en Oud-Burg.*, 1625–1700.

It has already been stated that certain functions of government were delegated to the predecessors of the burgomasters in early times. The burgomasters in their turn, as their work increased with the growth of the city and as new needs had to be met, delegated the less important of their functions to subordinate colleges. These colleges remained under their supervision, and those of them which dealt with legal matters could refer difficult cases to the sheriff's court. All were elected annually, the financial colleges by the burgomasters and magistrates jointly, and all were composed of members of the government and had burgomasters or ex-magistrates for their presidents. The duties to be delegated earliest were those mainly concerned with finance. In the fifteenth century colleges of Treasurers, of Trustees of the city's Orphans, and two Collectors of Excise[1] were appointed, and a subordinate college of treasurers, the Treasurers Extraordinary, was set up to reduce the duties of the treasurers themselves. The delegation of judicial matters, which in early times were entirely in the hands of the sheriff and magistrates, began only after the 'alteration', Amsterdam's change in 1578 from the support of Spain in the war of rebellion, to the rebel side. In that year Comissioners for Matrimonial Affairs were appointed to register marriages, since with the official change to Protestantism that accompanied the 'alteration' this responsibility no longer rested with the Church, and to deal with legal cases concerned with marriage. In 1598 two more subordinate benches were set up, the Chamber of Insurance and the College of Peacemakers, which in 1611 was replaced by the college of Commissioners for Petty Affairs. In the Chamber of Insurance legal cases concerning insurance were heard, while the Commissioners for Petty Affairs relieved the magistrates' court of minor cases in which only goods or sums of money of small value were involved; in the years up to 1650 the limit of value was gradually raised from forty to six hundred gulden, or about sixty English pounds of the value of that time, so that this court very quickly became one of importance. In the first half of the seventeenth century four further colleges were also formed. When the city bank and the pawnbroker's office were founded in 1609 and 1614 colleges of commissioners were appointed to control them, in 1641 a Chamber of Marine Affairs was set up to deal with legal cases concerning seafaring except those in which insurance was involved, and in 1644 a Bankruptcy Office was set up to regulate the affairs of bankrupts, either

---

[1] The Collectors of Excise did not at first form a college of the city government, and so did not have the right of precedence accorded to the Treasurers and the Trustees of the Orphans as members of senior colleges. For this reason they did not walk in procession with these officials at the opening of the Town Hall.

feigned or genuine, to make inventories of their possessions, and to enquire into their creditors' claims.

The new Town Hall (Frontispiece) was designed expressly for the use of these many departments and to meet their needs, and the places of the senior colleges in it were allotted according to their rights of precedence (see illus. 15).[1] Thus a high court of justice, or *vierschaar*, was placed in the centre of the eastern façade, which faces the Dam. On the first floor the burgomasters had their chamber to the south of the *vierschaar*, and there was a room devoted to justice to the north of it, while beyond these again on the eastern side of the building were, to the south, the council-room of the burgomasters and, to the north, that of the city council. The magistrates' court was placed at the centre of the western side of the Town Hall, and the city's Secretary, whose office dated from the fourteenth century, was accommodated with his staff in a large room at the centre of the southern side. At the southern corner of the building on the side of the Dam the Treasurers had their offices, and at the northern corner were those of the Trustees of the Orphans. At the southern corner of the western façade was the office of the Treasurers Extraordinary, and at the northern corner was the Accounts office. The Collectors of Excise had been accommodated in a separate building and did not move into the new Town Hall, the Commissioners of the City Bank were given rooms on the ground floor which had cellars for the storage of gold under them,[2] and the other younger colleges were housed with less regard for seniority in smaller quarters on the western and northern sides of the building on the first floor and in further rooms upstairs.

There can have been no such systematic accommodation of the government departments in the old Town Hall (illus. 4), since it was founded for the use of a mediaeval city government, and in later times was enlarged mainly by the addition of buildings designed for other purposes which happened to adjoin it. Very few facts are known about its early history, but it is known that by about 1395 a town hall existed,[3] that in 1418 a separate court of justice was added to an earlier Town Hall which already stood on the western side of the Dam, and that after the great fires which ravaged the city in 1421 and 1452 both these

---

[1] The allocation of the rooms is given by Vennekool, *Afbeelding*, pls. A. and B, and in early descriptions. It was thought out at a very early stage; although there are slight variations in it in the plans of 1648 and 1650 these show the magistrates' court, the main councils, and the two most senior colleges as they were finally arranged.

[2] The position of these cellars is noted on the prints of 1648 and they are mentioned in descriptions of the building.

[3] W. F. H. Oldewelt, in *Zeven eeuwen*, I, p. 30; C. G. 't Hooft, 'Op zoek naar de oudheid van het middeleeuwsche Stadhuis', *Jaarboek Amstelodamum*, XXXIII, 1936, pp. 1-2; Wagenaar, *Amsterdam*, II, p. 4.

buildings were either rebuilt or very much restored. On grounds of style it is now considered that both the court of justice as it was in the seventeenth century, and also the tower that by then stood beside it, may have dated from soon after the second fire,[1] and the earliest known illustration of the group of buildings, that which appears in the painted map of 1536, shows that by this date both the tower and the court of justice already had the general form that is known from seventeenth century records. Towards the end of the fifteenth century buildings which were previously occupied by a hospice were added to the Town Hall, and it was enlarged still further in 1557 by the annexation of houses built on neighbouring sites, which were to provide further accommodation for the city government itself, as well as extra prisons. Prisons, therefore, as well as the court of justice, must have existed in the complex of buildings earlier, and it is known that by the middle of the sixteenth century the burgomasters met in a room under the tower.

The Town Hall as it was about 1640 took up the greater part of the western side of the Dam, then very much smaller than it is at present (illus. 6).[2] It had streets to either side of it (to the south the Gasthuissteeg, on which the former hospice stood, and to the north the Vogelsteeg) and it reached westwards about half-way from the Dam to the Nieuwezijds Voorburgwal. A three-storey house, built mainly of brick but with its lowest part of stone, stood on the north-eastern part of this site. It was irregular in plan, with a sharp angle at the street corner, and it had a broad gable-end facing the Dam. In the lowest part of this house the city bank was accommodated, and above it was a large room

[1] E. H. ter Kuile, in *Duizend jaar bouwen*, I, p. 356. C. G. 't Hooft, op. cit., pp. 1–16, concludes that the earliest parts of the Town Hall were of the thirteenth century and that the court of justice was of the period of transition from Romanesque to Gothic architecture.

[2] For the building and its use in the seventeenth century see: [1] Johannes Isacius Pontanus, *Rerum et urbis Amstelodamensium historia* [etc.], Amsterdam, 1611, pp. 110–11. [2] Plan showing the former Town Hall and its immediate surroundings, 1639, copied from one by Danckerts, the city surveyor, Splitgerber Coll., Amsterdam, no. 260. [3] 'Plan of the [ground floor of the] Old Town Hall, copied from the original, which is kept in the treasury there' the copy being by the same hand as [2] above, Splitgerber Coll., no. 261. (It is likely that [2] and [3] were made following a resolution of the city council of Jan. 1639; Boeken, 'Over de voorgeschiedenis', *Jaarboek Amstelodamum*, 1919, pp. 5 and 27.) [4] Pieter Saenredam (a) painting of the former Town Hall of Amsterdam, loaned by the city to the Rijksmuseum, Amsterdam, signed and dated 1657 and based on a drawing (of 1641) from the building itself; (b) drawing (Gemeente-Archief, Amsterdam): see P. T. A. Swillens, *Pieter Janszoon Saenredam*, Amsterdam, 1935, cat. nos. 204 and 155 respectively. [5] Wagenaar, *Amsterdam*, II, pp. 4–5. Pontanus' account was the main source of information for later writers. Wagenaar, however, provides a wide range of further information. Yet his account of the rooms is misleading. He based it on Pontanus but apparently took his "insuper", used in listing a number of rooms, in its literal sense, and so describes three rooms mentioned after the word as being on an upper floor. The mention of a fourth room, the court of justice, completes Pontanus' list and it is clear that he used the word figuratively; moreover Wagenaar describes the city bank as being on the first floor whereas no. [3] above shows that it was on the ground floor.

which had been used for many years for the marking of cloth with the city's seal,[1] from which proclamations were read out to the public assembled on the Dam below. On the south-eastern part of the site was the court of justice, or *vierschaar*, a building consisting of an open arcaded space with a single storey over it. This type of open court of justice was to be found as part of many mediaeval town halls in the Netherlands and Germany.[2] That of Amsterdam was built of stone and was nearly square in form, and it had a high-pitched roof which sloped on all four sides from a short central ridge. It was arcaded on the eastern and southern sides, and had one of its longer sides on the Dam. Under the arcade there was a space open to the public, and behind this, with a separate entrance in the back wall, which linked it with other parts of the Town Hall, was a space separated from the public by railings. This was to some extent a stronghold, for about twenty arquebuses were kept there to defend it. Above the railings stood wooden statues of the Counts of Holland,[3] apparently facing outwards, and behind them the sheriff sat, accompanied by the magistrates, to administer justice on the overlord's behalf, watched by the crowd outside. Public punishments were carried out in the *vierschaar*, where a post for scourging, surmounted by a figure of Justice, was set up.[4] These punishments were never carried out in the corresponding *vierschaar* of the new Town Hall, which was reserved exclusively for the pronouncement of the death sentence, but after it was in use they were still administered in public, on a scaffold set up in front of the Town Hall.[5] Between the three-storey house and the *vierschaar*, and joining them, stood the tower, which was square and was built of brick. For many years it bore a tall spire, which dominated the triple façade on the Dam. It was surmounted by a weather-vane in the form of a three-masted ship,[6] the successor of the cog as the bringer of fortune to the city, and it had bells in it which played at the hours and half hours to keep the city's time. In 1615, after an earlier attempt to save it, the spire had to be taken

[1] Wagenaar, op. cit., I, p. 397 and II, 42. From 1626 this work was done elsewhere.
[2] Lederle, *Gerechtigkeitsdarstellungen*, p. 5.
[3] Their feet are visible in Saenredam's painting. See further Bontemantel, *De regeeringe*, I, p. 50, note, and A. Quellien, MS. Papers, no. 20. The figures were set up on the Treasury book-cases in the new Town Hall. Now on loan to the Rijksmuseum, Amsterdam; *Cat. beeldhouwwerken*, nos. 189–92.
[4] A gilded statue of Justice which in earlier times was set up on the post was kept in the Treasury of the new Town Hall; *Beschryvinge van 't Stadhuis*, 1782, p. 87. In Vennekool, *Afbeelding*, p. 9, a bronze statue of Justice above the door in the Chamber of Justice is mentioned. Quellien was paid 50 gulden for making, or perhaps repairing, 'a wooden statue representing Justice'; A. Quellien, MS. Papers, no. 16 (account receipted 27 Oct. 1656).
[5] Bontemantel, *De regeeringe*, I, pp. 50–51.
[6] Clearly shown in the engraving of the Town Hall by Claes Jansz. Visscher, published in Pontanus, op. cit., and in the drawing for it, Gemeente Archief, Amsterdam.

down and the bells set up elsewhere, as has already been stated. Afterwards only a single bell remained, and in later years it could be seen hanging from a beam set up above the desolate roof of the tower. This bell, the City Bell, was essential to the Town Hall, since it was rung to summon the public to hear proclamations and to witness the administration of justice.[1] Below it, in a ground floor room within the tower, the burgomasters continued to direct the city government.

The *vierschaar* projected on to the Dam, and behind it, lying on the Gast-huissteeg, was the former hospice, whose principal room was a large hall of irregular shape whose use is not recorded. It had a separate entrance with an inscription over it commemorating the rising of the Anabaptists, who captured the Town Hall in 1535, and their final overthrow. One of the smaller rooms inside the building, that used for the Chamber of Petty Affairs, had a series of paintings of this event, which was of great importance in the city's history, round its walls, and was known as the 'painted room' in consequence.[2] Beyond this nothing is known of the decoration of the interior of the old Town Hall except that it contained a fragment of a painting of the Nativity by Pieter Aertsz., which later was to be seen in the new Town Hall.[3] To the west of the hall was the magistrates' court, which was also used for meetings of the city council,[4] and beyond this was the torture chamber. It had been laid down in the first instance as an exception to the usual practice, that a criminal could be punished by the city authorities for a crime to which he had confessed without

[1] Its importance is evident from the statement that 'A bell was hung at once out of the highest window' of the inn where the burgomasters and councillors found temporary accommodation when the Town Hall was destroyed by fire in 1652 (Bontemantel, op. cit. II, p. 60, n. 2) and also from its occurring to Bonte-mantel to record the fact.

[2] Wagenaar, *Amsterdam*, I, p. 246, where he states that the paintings were in a room used by the Com-missioners for Petty Affairs known as the "geschilderd kamertje" or 'painted room', the term implying that the room was small. According to Dapper, *Beschryving*, p. 333, the paintings were in the magistrates' chamber, also used as the council chamber, which was $29\frac{1}{2}$ by c. 26 feet by $22\frac{1}{2}$ feet high. Possibly, though not demonstrably, the Commissioners also used this room. The decoration would be suitable to a room used as a court since the series culminated in a scene showing Anabaptists being executed. Engravings based on the paintings were published in Lambertus Hortensius, *Van den Oproer der Wederdooperen*, Enkhuizen, 1614, pp. 2–24, and drawings connected with them survive (see G. J. Hoogewerff, *De Noord-Nederlandsche schilder-kunst*, The Hague, 1936–47, III, pp. 507–10).

[3] Van Dyk, *Schilderyen op het Stadhuis*, p. 136. The fragment, attributed by Van Dyk to Rubens, is in the Rijksmuseum, Amsterdam, on loan from the city. It is thought to be part of a painting by Pieter Aertsz. made for the New Church, Amsterdam and damaged during the Reformation; *Catalogus der schilderijen . . . tentoongesteld in het Rijksmuseum te Amsterdam*, Amsterdam, 1934, no. 6, and Van Mander, *Schilder-boeck*, fol. 244 r.

[4] See Bontmantel, MS. *Resolutien*, II, i, pp. 625–7; id. MS. *Civ. en mil. reg.*, I, pp. 486–7; and id. *De regeeringe*, I, p. 243 and II, p. 8. In all these works diagrams of the arrangement of the room as magistrates' court and as council room are given.

the case being referred to a higher court, and the extraction of confessions by torture had become usual in consequence. To the north of this room, and separated from it by an open court, were the gaoler's quarters and presumably also the prisons, some of which at least were under ground. Between the gaoler's quarters, which were on the Vogelsteeg, and the city bank, was accommodation for the caretaker, and a room between the bank and the great hall was occupied by the city Secretary. It seems that the Chamber of Insurance was in an upstairs room in the northern part of the Town Hall. Beyond this the use of the rooms is not recorded, and the arrangement of those on the upper floors remains unknown. It is known, however, that as well as the departments already mentioned the Treasurers, the Trustees of the Orphans, the Treasurers Extraordinary, the Accounts Office and the Bankruptcy Office were all packed into the old Town Hall.[1]

There is no doubt that the building was seriously overcrowded,[2] and it had also become extremely inconvenient as the number of departments increased. There was a shortage of storage space. There were not enough fireplaces and one was either frozen or singed. The rooms were unhealthy and verminous, and both they and the people in them were 'overcrowded and mixed together and entangled with each other', to quote the words of a contemporary who must have seen it in that state.[3] Those who worked there were disturbed by the wrangling of the lawsuits which, with the increase of Amsterdam's population, had become so numerous. In the minute of a resolution passed by the city council in 1655 concerning the completion of the new Town Hall it was recorded 'that in view of our flourishing commerce it is necessary daily to found new colleges and, because of the manifold business coming to hand, to provide the old with more space or chambers',[4] and it is evident that the need had first arisen much earlier. Nevertheless it was not because it was over-crowded that the city council decided to replace the old Town Hall, but because it was derelict.

---

[1] Deducible from Bontemantel's account, *De regeeringe*, II, p. 60, n. 2, of the temporary quarters found in 1652 for the departments which had occupied the Town Hall. All the city departments except the Excise Office, the Pawnbroker's Office, the Commissioners for Matrimonial Affairs and the Chamber of Marine Affairs are mentioned. These are known to have been housed elsewhere, though the two last later moved to the new Town Hall.

[2] See Dapper, *Beschryving*, p. 330, where the overcrowding is given as the reason for replacing the building, and Vondel, *Inwydinge*, lines 1233-70, where the terrible condition of the prisons is also described.

[3] Vondel, op. cit., lines 1240-1: "Verdrongen en gemengt, En onderling verwert".

[4] MS. *Res. Vroedsch.*, 10 Feb. 1655: "Dat men, ten opsichte van de gesegende commercie, dagelijx genoodsaeckt wordt nieuwe Collegien te institueren, ende de oude, van weghen de meenigvuldige voorvallende zaeken, met meerder ruijmte off camers te voorsien".

'Young crutches' supported the old building,[1] and drawings of it, as well as a painting by Pieter Saenredam which faithfully records its appearance,[2] show that the stonework of the *vierschaar* was rotting and crumbling away. This part of the Town Hall, however, according to the account given by Dapper, was 'still pretty firm and strong' compared with the rest.[3] In 1639 the burgomasters proposed to the city council that 'since the Town Hall is pretty ruinous in many places, so that it is feared that at some time or other some accident will happen because of it' the possibility of having a new town hall built should be considered, and a commission, consisting of the burgomasters and treasurers of the time together with the ex-burgomaster Pieter Hasselaer, was set up to enquire into the matter.[4] In the following year their report was considered. The building had been found to be 'entirely ruinous' and in constant danger of collapsing, and that being so it was decided to build a new town hall. The commission was authorised to purchase sufficient property at the city authorities' valuation to provide an ample site with streets twenty-five to thirty feet wide to either side of it, and to have plans made, which were to be laid before the city council.[5] In the years that followed many plans were made, and the proposals for the new Town Hall were altered repeatedly,[6] while the old continued to stand. Eventually it was burnt down by accident, but this only happened after the new building was rising behind it.[7] A committee was set up to take charge of the making of plans and the arrangements for the new Town Hall, and 'after mature deliberation' a plan by Jacob van Campen was chosen.[8] At first this was carried out under his supervision and with the assistance of Daniel Stalpaert, who was appointed city architect from August 1648.[9] Later Van

[1] Vondel, *Werken*, V, p. 542, in the poem 'Op het verbranden van 't Stadhuis van Amsterdam', 1652.
[2] See p. 20 n. 2 [4] above, and illus. 4. Drawings such as those by Willem Schellinks, Splitgerber Coll., Amsterdam, nos. 198, 262, and 264, reveal further details about the condition of the *vierschaar*.
[3] Dapper, op. cit., p. 330: "Noch vry vast en hecht".
[4] MS. *Res. Vroedsch.*, 28 Jan. 1639. "Alzoo het Stadthuijs vrij wat bouvalligh is tot veele plaetsen, zulx datter t'eenen oft t'anderen tyde eenigh ongeluck uyt gevreest worden te zullen ontstaen . . .".
[5] MS. cit., 28 Jan. 1640.
[6] Early proposals and designs for the building are discussed by Boeken, 'Over de voorgeschiedenis', *Jaarboek Amstelodamum*, 1919, pp. 1–30, which has been consulted here, and quoted (see List of Sources s.v. MS. *Res. Vroedsch.*).
[7] An engraving of the former Town Hall after the fire and the new behind it, by R. Roghman, shows that the walls of the southern end had been built to the first cornice by July 1652 when the fire took place. This is certain, since demolition started immediately; Dapper, *Beschryving*, p. 333. Vondel, *Inwydinge*, lines 297–308, states that the flames reached the scaffolding of the new building and that Daniel Stalpaert was active in saving it.
[8] The setting up of this second committee is not mentioned in the city council's minutes. Vondel, op. cit., line 162, and later writers name its members: Cornelis de Graeff, Anthony Oetgens van Waveren, Joan Huydecoper, and Jan Cornelisz. Geelvinck. The quoted phrase is from Dapper, op. cit., p. 331.
[9] For Stalpaert see A. W. Weissman, 'Daniel Stalpaert', *Oud-Holland*, XXIX, 1911, pp. 65–85.

Campen withdrew from the work for reasons which are not fully explained,[1] and after he left Stalpaert must have been in charge of it.[2] Meanwhile in 1647, because of the unprecedented amount of building in stone being undertaken by the city, Willem de Keyser was appointed to the office of city stonemason, although for a time this position had been vacant,[3] and in the same year a city smith was appointed for the first time.[4] In 1650 an under master stonemason was appointed to assist in looking after the stonemasons' works in general, and in particular to supervise work being done for the Town Hall,[5] and in 1653 an Englishman recorded that he saw "a Cloister, where hundreds of men are dayly employd in hewing and working of Stone for ye new Stadt-house" when he visited Amsterdam.[6] A further mason's yard was set up for the making of the building's sculpture, and was directed by Artus Quellien, who came from Antwerp to carry out this part of the work. It is clear that great powers of organization and management and also the weight of the authority of the city government were brought to bear on the making of the new building, and if there were complaints about the enormous expenditure involved, or about the compulsory purchase and the destruction of much valuable property in the centre of the city, no attention was paid to them.[7]

[1] The city authorities paid for living expenses incurred by Van Campen in Amsterdam between 17 Apr. and 1 Dec. 1654 (record cited by Kroon, *Stadhuis*, p. 51) and no evidence of his presence there later is known. He apparently withdrew because of a quarrel caused by envy, discussed by A. W. Weissman, 'Jacob van Campen in 1654', *Feest-bundel Dr. Abraham Bredius* (publ. Oud-Holland), Amsterdam, 1915, pp. 283–91; see also Asselijn, 'Uytvaart' [etc], in *Hollantsche Parnas*, pp. 419–20. It is likely that the quarrel was connected with the 'envy' which broke up the artists' brotherhood in Amsterdam between the St. Luke's days of 1654 and 1655, in which year their feast was evidently in abeyance (Houbraken, *Schouburgh*, III, pp. 329–33).
[2] He evidently directed its execution earlier since the under master stonemason appointed in 1650 was to be responsible to him (and to the city treasurers) for work done for the building; MS. *Res. Thes. Ord.*, 16 Aug. 1650. The records do not mention any other architect being called in after Van Campen withdrew. Jan Vos, at an unknown date, implied that Stalpaert was author of the building; 'Op d'afbeelding van den E. Daniel Stalpaardt &c.', *Gedichten*, II, p. 174, but Anslo, 'Het gekroonde Amsterdam', in *Olyfkrans*, 1750, p. 173, gives unquestionable evidence from before the quarrel that the design was Van Campen's.
[3] MS. *Res. Burg. en Oud-Burg.*, 27 Sept. and 3 Dec. 1647; Weissman, 'Jacob van Campen', *Oud-Holland*, 1902, p. 155.
[4] MS. cit., 27 Nov. and 5 Dec. 1647. The earlier resolution states that he was to be appointed because of the new Town Hall and New Church tower.
[5] MS. cit., 16 Aug. 1650.
[6] Bargrave, MS. *A Relation*, fol. 91 r.
[7] The tone of parts of Vondel's *Inwydinge* suggests that one of his purposes in writing was to satisfy his readers that the erection of such a building was justified, and he states, lines 337–8, that the rising Town Hall 'met with reproach and affront, and kept the same course'. In a passage clearly based on Vondel's lines, Vennekool, *Afbeelding*, p. 4, this statement is elaborated: "Jaa men ontsagh 't niet, overdaadigh en verquistend' kostelijk te noemen, gestadigh murmurerende op 't getal der Burger-huysen, die tot 'et Stadt-huys af ghebrooken waren [yet the work was continued without alteration]" ('Indeed people did not forbear from calling it excessively and extravagantly costly, continually grumbling about the number of citizens' houses which were broken down for the Town Hall').

A description has already been given of some of the main activities of the city government within Amsterdam itself, but the part that it played in external affairs and its relations with the Stadholder must also be outlined.[1] The city was represented in the provincial government, the States of Holland and West Friesland, by its Pensionary, an official chosen by the burgomasters though the pensionaries of other cities were chosen by their city councils. The Pensionary of Amsterdam was briefed by the burgomasters and reported to them, though in theory he was responsible to the city council. The burgomasters of Amsterdam were thus exceptionally well represented in the provincial government. Their position was further strengthened by the city's great wealth, for though the college of nobles and the cities of the province had votes of equal weight in the provincial council, and though theoretically the passing of all important measures had to be unanimous, the minority opinions of the smaller cities were in fact often ignored; otherwise negotiations would have come to a standstill. If, however, a measure was opposed by so wealthy a city as Amsterdam there was no use in passing it, for if she witheld her support the provincial government would be powerless. Hence in practice the cities represented in the States of Holland and West Friesland were by no means equal in their authority, and Amsterdam, by far the richest city in the province, and thus her burgomasters, could dominate the provincial government.

The situation was very much the same in the States General, where the delegates of the seven sovereign provinces which together formed the Republic of the United Netherlands met and negotiated with each other like the ambassadors of allied states over matters in which they were commonly concerned.[2] Each province had a single vote, and it was laid down that decisions in matters of war and peace and in certain financial matters must be unanimous. Yet, as in the provincial government, members frequently had to see measures passed against their wishes. As there the city of Amsterdam so here the province of Holland was in a strong position, for she supplied the States General with about fifty-seven per cent of the money contributed by the provinces for common expenses. The next largest quotas, those of Friesland and Zeeland, were each not more than about eleven per cent of the total. Holland's voice, in practice, was therefore a strong one, and ultimately, though quite unofficially, the burgomasters of Amsterdam were of influence in the States General.

[1] See Robert Fruin, *Geschiedenis der staatsinstellingen in Nederland tot den val der republiek*, ed. Colenbrander, The Hague, 1901, as well as the works on Holland and on Amsterdam already referred to.
[2] See concise descriptions of the States General by Geyl, *Geschiedenis*, I, pp. 439 and 442.

As early as 1579 it was complained that in the States General the deputies seemed more concerned to make decisions that were to the advantage of their own provinces than to consider the general welfare,[1] and throughout its history the republic was handicapped in framing its foreign policy and in warfare by the independence of its members and by their conflicting interests. Their dissentions made it possible for Prince Frederik Hendrik, after he became Stadholder in 1625,[2] steadily to increase his influence in the States General, over which he presided, and to pursue a policy of his own with a good chance of success. Only the Province of Holland, able to bargain over the supply of money and herself dominated by the merchant aristocracy of Amsterdam, whose interests were not served by the Stadholder's policy, could rival him.

The rivalry between Amsterdam and the Stadholder was perhaps most evident in controversies concerning the conclusion of peace with Spain, in which Amsterdam ultimately triumphed.[3] In the early 1630s the division of opinion in the United Provinces on this issue became evident for the first time. Friesland and Groningen, for religious reasons, and Zeeland because she could profit from trade in Spanish waters while it lasted, were in favour of continuing the war. A party representing the opinion of the merchants of Amsterdam was in favour of ending it, because if the Southern Netherlands were conquered the Scheldt could no longer be kept closed and their trade would be threatened by the rivalry of Antwerp; the Scheldt might well be kept closed under the terms of a peace treaty. This party was led by Adriaen Pauw, Pensionary of the States of Holland and West Friesland and a former Pensionary of Amsterdam, and by Andries Bicker, a leading member and spokesman of Amsterdam's city government. For a time Pauw took the lead in conducting peace negotiations, and these had the Stadholder's approval, but later a special French ambassador arrived in The Hague and the Stadholder was persuaded to support him. In 1635 a treaty was signed by which it was agreed that neither the United Provinces nor France should make peace with Spain separately. Pauw was forced at the last moment into assisting in the conclusion of this treaty, but he was nevertheless replaced by one of the Stadholders' supporters when his term of office as Pensionary ended.

The French ambassador himself considered that the Prince's change to the

---

[1] Complaint by Prince Willem I, see Fruin, op. cit., p. 179.

[2] The Stadholder of the Province of Holland so predominated that he is referred to by custom as 'the Stadholder' without qualification.

[3] See Geyl, op. cit., I, pp. 404–53, and G. W. Kernkamp, in *Amsterdam in de zeventiende eeuw*, I, ii, pp. 161–72.

support of France was due to his dynastic interests, and it is clear that his position was gradually altering. He must have seen the possibility of governing the country at the head of an obedient States General, and he seems to have worked to that end. He had many adherents in the States General itself, he gained control of the Council of State, which dealt with military and other matters, and in 1630 a Secret Council composed of his adherents took over the day-to-day management of foreign affairs; the members of this council were in theory delegates of the provinces but they were sworn to secrecy even from those they represented. At the same time the Stadholder's personal status altered. After his conquest of Bois le Duc in 1629 the provinces of which Prince Frederik Hendrik was Stadholder one after another, though not all of them willingly, granted the succession of his office to his son. In 1637 he acquired the title of Highness, which gave him new rights of precedence. In 1640 he became the Stadholder of all the provinces but one. In 1641 the young prince, later the Stadholder Prince Willem II, was married to Mary Stuart, the eldest daughter of Charles I of England, an alliance which brought Prince Frederik Hendrik further prestige. At that moment it must have seemed that the leadership of the House of Orange in the Republic was established, and that further conquests in the Spanish Netherlands, in particular the taking of Antwerp, would add to its almost royal glory. Yet the attempts made by the Stadholder to march on Antwerp were unsuccessful; he appears to have acted indecisively, and throughout his campaigning he was short of money.

The treaty with France was renewed in 1644, in spite of opposition, which was led by Bicker, in the States General, but by this time the Hapsburgs and their enemies were already holding a conference at Munster. In 1646, after two years had been spent in drawing up their instructions, delegates from the United Provinces arrived there, with Pauw as one of their principal spokesmen. In the same year Spain initiated secret negotiations with France, which were in fact a blind intended to break her alliance with the Republic, over an exchange of Catalonia for the Spanish Netherlands, and the Stadholder, who was promised Antwerp in exchange for Maastricht, was made a party to these negotiations. When his treachery was discovered he was unable to pursue his policy further, and on 30th January 1648 a treaty was signed by the United Provinces and Spain in which France did not participate. Its ratification was delayed until 15th May of the same year because of the opposition of Utrecht and Zeeland, and even then Zeeland witheld her signature, but when the peace was proclaimed on 8th June 1648 she too had realized that further resistance was useless, and those who had championed the cause of peace and of trade without the competition of Antwerp were satisfied.

In the ratification the city of Amsterdam and the Province of Holland triumphed, for it was their representatives that had brought the peace about. Amsterdam had shown that she was indeed the principal city of the United Provinces, that she could rival the Stadholder, and that she was of consequence internationally in politics as well as in trade. It was natural that the old Town Hall of such a city should be replaced by one worthy of her status and of the virtues of her government, which might declare her greatness within the city and to the admiring world.

CHAPTER II

LIBERTY

ZANG

Athene en Rome dragen bey
Een zonderlinge lieverey
Van kunsten, elck in zijn gewest.
De Bouwkunst voeght Athene best,
En andre wetenschappen meer;
Het strijtbre Rome voeght een speer
En schilt, gelijck een krijghsheldin,
Op datze 't aertrijck overwinn',
En met den Burgemeestersrock
Dan alles wat zy overtrock
Met vliegende Arenden, haer Goôn,
Berechte, en onder haer geboôn
Doe zwichten d'overheerde liên,
Die 't aertsgebiet naer d'oogen zien.
Dus zijnze, beide in lof zoo rijck,
Elckandre in zegen ongelijck,
Het zy by noodlot, of geval;
Want een bezit het zelden al.

TEGENZANG

Maer AMSTERDAM, zoo zwaer met gout
Gekroont, en uit Godts schoot bedouwt
Met zegen, voert haer oorloghsvlagh
Tot in den ondergaenden dagh,
Van 't blozende Oosten, en beklimt,
Van daer de steile Noortbeer grimt,
De Zuidas met haer stoute kiel.
Zy mint den Vrydom als haer ziel,
En na dien dierbevochten schat
Zoo kroontze 't mercktvelt van de stadt,
Den Visschersdam, met een gebouw
Waer voor d'Athener strijcken zou,
En stom staen met zijn' open mont;
Hoe wel hy zich den bouw verstont:
Hy zou gerief en majesteit
En tijtverdurende eeuwigheit
Verknocht zien in een Hooftgesticht,
De glori van mijn bouwgedicht.

VONDEL, On the new Town Hall, 1648[1]

The Peace of Munster set the seal on Holland's prosperity and guaranteed the liberty, as an independent nation, of her inhabitants. It was defined in its opening clause as an Eternal Peace, and it was known as such. It signified the relinquishment of all Spanish claims in Holland and on Dutch territory abroad. The Scheldt could be kept closed, the two countries were to trade with one another 'with every guarantee of security',[2] and the rights of each, on trade-routes and in colonial territory, were to be defined and thereafter respected.

It was pointed out when the treaty was ratified that only a few old people

---

[1] From the 'Bouwzang' (Building Song), *Werken*, V. pp. 370–1, on the laying of the foundation-stone. The term given as 'consul's toga' could also be translated 'burgomaster's gown'. In the final lines the three principles of architecture laid down by Vitruvius and his followers – convenience, durability, and beauty – are evidently referred to. *Hoofdgesticht* may be regarded as a careful Dutch translation of the word Capitol. 'Athens and Rome each wear an especial livery of arts, each in his region. Architecture, and other sciences as well, suit Athene best; a spear and shield suit the valiant Rome, like a heroine of war, so that she may conquer the earth, and then, in the consul's toga, govern all that she marches over with flying eagles, her gods, and cause the conquered people, who stand in awe of the rulers of the earth, to yield. So, whether by destiny or chance, these cities, both so rich in praise, each have different blessings; for it is seldom that one possesses all. But Amsterdam, crowned so heavily with gold, and weighed down with blessing from the lap of God, with her strong keel carries her flag of war to the sunset from the blushing east, and climbs from where the high North Bear scowls, to the South Pole. She loves freedom as her own soul, and because of this dearly fought-for treasure she crowns the market-place of the city, the Fisherman's Dam, with a building before which the Athenian would lower his flag and stand silent and gaping, although he understood architecture. He would see convenience and majesty and everlasting eternity knit together in a Capital Edifice which is the glory of my building-song'.

[2] The text appears in Dutch in *Olyf-krans*, 1649, pp. 1–50. Quotation from p. 7: "In alle verseeckertheyt".

could remember the days before the war with Spain began.[1] During their lifetime, in spite of internal stresses, the United Provinces had banded themselves together and, as a small nation pitted against a larger one with military experience and longstanding power, had shaken free of Spanish domination. Moreover the war had become a war of religion, in which freedom of belief and for Protestant worship had been secured. The sense of relief at the end of this long and apparently interminable struggle was of necessity overwhelming, and it must have seemed that a golden age had at last begun. In the speech made to the States of Holland and West Friesland in honour of the peace there are words which herald this new era as though with the blast of a trumpet 'Holland is beginning, as of old, to grow, to blossom, and the golden age in which our forefathers lived, and which we have longed for so many years, is setting in'.[2]

The peace was celebrated in Amsterdam on the day of the proclamation with every kind of rejoicing:

> The white flag of peace flew with its pennant above the weathercock on the tower ... Plays and splendid pageants were produced. Bells rang with joy; canon thundered. All were welcome: poets and orators praised the peace; joy rose with shouting and applause to the undying glory of Amsterdam. One displayed his wit and learning; another spared no expense or extravagance to take part in the general rejoicing. At the news of the Peace the citizens came out everywhere in their best clothes, looked happily at each other, and fell on each other's necks.[3]

On 28th October of the year of this great rejoicing four children, the sons and nephews of the burgomasters in office, laid the foundation-stone of the new Town Hall of Amsterdam.[4]

Although plans had been made for it much earlier the building was regarded as a symbol of the peace. Indeed in Reinier Anslo's verses addressed 'To Peace, on the foundation of the Town Hall' it was stated that the building was founded

---

[1] 'Trompet of lofrede', *Olyf-krans*, 1750, p. XXXVII.

[2] Op. cit. p. XLVII. "Nederlandt begint, gelyk van oudts, te groeien, te bloeien, en de goude tyt gaat in, daar onze Voorvaders in leefden, en wy zoo lang naar verlangden".

[3] Op. cit. p. XLV. "De witte vredevlag en wimpel waaiden boven den weerhaan van den toren ... Men stelde spelen en heerelyke vertooningen toe. De klokken luiden van vreught, de kortouwen donderden. Het was open hof: dichters en redenaars loofden den pays: de blyschap daagde op met juichen en handtgeklap tot onsterffelyke eere van Amsterdam. D'een toonddde zyn vernuft en geleertheit: d'ander spaarde geen kosten, noch overdaat, om de gemeene blyschap by te wonen. Op de mare des vredes quamen de burgers met hun beste kleederen uitgestreken, en toonden onderling een bly gelaat, en vielen elkandere om den hals".

[4] For an eyewitness account of the ceremony see P. van Eeghen, '300 jaar Stadhuis-Paleis', *Maandblad Amstelodamum*, XLII, 1955, p. 85.

in honour of the Peace, or in the honour of Peace herself who, it was implied, had entered the city's walls and was expected to stay there.[1] The demolition of the houses which stood on parts of the site had in fact been begun in 1643 and pile-driving ten days before the signing of the treaty.[2] A map dated 28th April 1648 which is in the city archives shows the site of the new building (illus. 9).[3] It is marked 'The ground of the new Town Hall that is to be built: the breadth and length of the work going up'.[4] In this map the measurements of the site are 280 by 225 feet, measurements which differ by ten feet only, in one direction, from those of the final work, whose orientation is the same. Yet a road thirty feet wide is shown running across this site, dividing it into two rectangles of unequal size.[5] The measurements of the two parts are only given separately. Since the part of the site to the south side of the road, that on which the inscription is written, measures 165 by 225 feet, and so almost corresponds with the measurements – 160 by about 250 feet – which were decided on by the council on 3rd December 1646,[6] it is possible that the plan was made in connection with the transition from what was then proposed or from an intermediate project to the final design. If this is so the new plans were decided on by the burgomasters, and preparations for their execution were made, before the matter was brought before the council. Only on 18th July 1648, thus after the Peace of Munster had been ratified, was a larger plan officially accepted.[7] It was of 280 by about 200 feet, the size of the building as it stands today if the central salients, which add 35 feet to the depth, are not considered. The introduction at this point of a new and grander project, which involved the destruction of further houses on the Dam, was due not only to the express wish to give 'a work of such expense its full scope, status, and dignity,[8] but also to the hope of settled prosperity that the peace had brought in train. Only this could make the accomplishment of such a project possible, as the alarms of the years that followed were to emphasize, for in 1653, when

[1] 'Aan de Vreede, op de grondtbouw van 't Stadthuis', in *Olyf-krans*, 1750, pp. 181–2. The verses form part of Anslo's 'Het gekroonde Amsterdam' [etc.] and appeared in the first edition of *Olyf-krans*, whose introduction is dated 30th January 1649.
[2] MS. *Res Vroedsch.*, 28 Jan. 1643. Dapper, *Beschryving*, pp. 330–1.
[3] Gemeente-Archief, Amsterdam, Topografische Atlas, Stadsgedeelten no. 92.
[4] "T 'Erff vandt nieuw te maaken Stadt Huijs de wijdtte en lanckte van 't op gaend werck". Work 'already going up' or 'about to go up' may be referred to.
[5] The road does not correspond with any previously crossing the site.
[6] MS. *Res. Vroedsch.*, 3 Dec. 1646.
[7] MS. cit., 18 July 1648, where the particulars that follow are given.
[8] MS. and loc. cit. The plan would have to be enlarged "indien men een werck van zooveel costen zijn volcomen beslagh, standt en ansien wilde geven".

the country was at war with England, it was decided that the scheme should be modified for the sake of economy, and after the signing of the Peace of Westminster the city council withdrew the decision.[1] Dapper records that the plan was changed as a result of the announcement of the peace, the depth of the building, that is, 230 feet, remaining the same but the breadth being increased to the present measurement, though many piles had been driven in positions where, after the change, they became unnecessary.[2] It may be added that by September 1650, and probably earlier, it had been decided that the figure of Peace should crown the front pediment of the building, although her great bronze statue was not hauled into position until more than ten years later.[3]

There was the best possible precedent for making such a building a monument of peace. In the speech already quoted which was made to the States of Holland and West Friesland in 1648, reference was made to the Roman Caesar Augustus, who, having established peace throughout the Roman Empire, 'Brought the lands to fertility, the arts to their former splendour, and ornamented the city of Rome with excellent statutes and laws and magnificent buildings'.[4] Vitruvius, in dedicating his treatise on architecture to Augustus, had written: 'Furthermore, with respect to the future, you have such regard to public and private buildings, that they will correspond to the grandeur of our history, and will be a memorial to future ages'.[5] It is likely that the example of Augustus was in the minds of the members of the city government of Amsterdam who were responsible for the building, and that they intended not only to provide for present needs, but also that the new Town Hall should become a monument of just this kind, and that the final plans were prepared accordingly.

---

[1] MS. cit., 27 June 1653 and 10 Feb. 1655.

[2] Dapper, *Beschryving*, p. 336. See also Vondel, *Inwydinge*, lines 601–4. If in fact the burgomasters anticipated the council's decision piles might have been driven according to the original plans at least from January to April 1648.

[3] The figure appears in this position in the prints of 1650, whose privilege dates from 1st September of that year. A figure of Peace apparently similar in design to that on the building appears on the model for it, probably of 1648 or soon after, and its composition suggests that it was for a central position. Yet the figures are detachable and have been restored, and the model's date is not proveable, so that neither Peace's position on the model nor the early date are certain. When Dapper's description was published (1663) the bronze figure was not in place; it was there when Cosimo III de' Medici visited Amsterdam in 1669 (*Beschryving*, p. 339; Hoogewerff, *De twee reizen*, p. 316).

[4] 'Trompet of Lofrede', *Olyf-krans*, 1750. p. XXIX: "... de landen tot vruchtbaarheit, de kunsten tot hunnen ouden luister broght, en de stadt Rome met uitnemende keuren en wetten en heerelyke gebouwen vercierde".

[5] *De Architectura*, I, Preface, para. 3. "Reliquo quoque tempore et publicorum et privatorum aedificiorum, pro amplitudine rerum gestarum ut posteris memoriae traderentur, curam habiturum." Quoted, with translation, from Granger.

Two prints which are in the city archives of Amsterdam show the ground and first floor plans of the building in an early form (illus. 10).[1] Only the outlines of these plans are printed, they have been coloured by hand, and here and there they have been altered in the colouring. The outside measurements are those decided on in 1648 and the general design is the same as that finally executed although some details of the interior planning are different. The measurements were filled in by hand, as well as the names of the rooms, whose 'general distribution' was indicated when the decision was taken,[2] and in one case what represents a single room in the plan has the names of two rooms written on it, those of the Chamber of Insurance and the Bankruptcy Office. This proposed space was afterwards divided to accommodate the two rooms,[3] but the division is not indicated on the plan. The inconsistency is significant, for the plans cannot have been made before the meeting at which the project was enlarged, except in preparation for it, while if they had been made afterwards the division between the rooms would have been drawn in. Moreover since the city council had thirty-six members a duplicated plan must have been necessary for their deliberations. It can only be concluded that these prints represent the project which according to the minutes of the meeting the burgomasters 'had had drawn', which was discussed by the council in 1648, and that a copy of it, on which the arrangement of the rooms which had been decided on was indicated, was put away with the city records, where it remains to this day.[4] The wooden model (illus. 5), in the Waag Museum, Amsterdam, appears to correspond with these earliest prints, and since it is likely to date from before the prints of 1650 in all probability it provides the earliest record of the building's elevation.[5] The prints of 1650 (illus. 11–13)[6] show a further stage in the development of the whole design and record some parts of the project which were never executed. Finally a set of prints which was made by Jacob Vennekool, Van Campen's draughtsman, and first published in 1661,[7] shows the architect's matured intentions for the building.

The Town Hall was to be of a size hitherto unknown in Amsterdam, built on a scale comparable with that of the Renaissance palaces of Rome, which

[1] See List of Sources, s.v. Prints of 1648.
[2] MS. *Res. Vroedsch.*, 18 July 1648, from which further details about the meeting are also taken.
[3] The prints of 1650 show the division.
[4] Noach has connected the prints with the meeting of 1648; 'Een vergeten ontwerp', *Jaarboek Amstelodamum* 1936, p. 153.
[5] Photographs by the Rijksmuseum, Amsterdam, negs. 1036–7, show parts of the model's interior.
[6] See List of Sources s.v. Prints of 1650.
[7] See Bibliography s.v. Vennekool.

themselves reflect the scale of those of antiquity, and vying with the civic buildings of the merchant cities Venice and Antwerp. It was to tower above the Gothic buildings of the city centre (illus. 23–24) and even above the Exchange, and both the resolutions of the city council and one of the early projects for the Town Hall show to what extent town planning, rather than the mere replacement of one building, was involved in the preparations (illus. 8).[1] In connection with another project it was proposed that one side of the Nieuwezijds Voorburgwal, to which the Town Hall extended towards the west, should be widened.[2] Wide streets were allowed for to each side of the new building, its orientation was discussed, and by the clearances on the north side of the site the New Church was brought on to the Dam, so that it came to form part of the same complex (illus. 7). The New Church was also to be furnished with an extremely tall tower designed by Van Campen, but although this was proudly included in illustrations of the Dam as it was to appear in the future it was never completed.[3] Such was to be the grandeur of the new city centre that Vondel, in his poem on the dedication of the Town Hall, described the Dam and the buildings on it, the New Church, the Weigh-house, the Fish Market, the Exchange and the Town Hall itself as:

> An undeniable token of majesty and power, illustrious to see, for now the Dam does not yield in fame before St. Mark's Square or even the Field of Mars, which was so widely famed among the ancients, who saw Rome in its power and at the height of its splendour, at the time when Augustus, Caesar's successor, rode up the sacred Capitol in his Triumph when there was complete peace.[4]

[1] MS. *Res. Vroedsch.*, 28 Jan. 1640, 5 Mar. and 10 Dec. 1642, 8 Apr. 1647 and 18 July 1648. The project is known only from the plan illustrated here, dated 1643, which is in the Topografische Atlas of the Gemeente-Archief, Amsterdam. Not mentioned by Boeken. Van Luttervelt, *Raadhuis*, p. 22, mentions it briefly. It shows a building of about 185 by 205 feet including salients, whose main façade, on one of the shorter sides, is on the Dam. To the north and south buildings are indicated which run parallel to its sides, forming streets about 35 feet wide that flank the Town Hall. A line is drawn down the centre of the northern street to indicate that it provides a vista which culminates in the Weigh-house. Another shows that the centre of the Town Hall is aligned on to the Fish Market, and a third that the building to the north ends opposite the north-west corner of the Kalverstraat, the street at the south-west corner of the Dam. What was to remain of the Gasthuissteeg was to be screened by an arch or doorway and the New Church was to be approached through an arch or arcade with three openings. The plan, which is a copy, bears a careful tracing of the signature of Cornelis Danckerts de Rij in its usual form: "C. de Rij". This identification, for which thanks are due to Mr. P. Wuisman, cannot be questioned. Since Danckertsz. was city surveyor in 1643 the plan probably was official and of a project which was seriously considered.
[2] Ms. *Res. Vroedsch.*, 8 Apr. 1647.
[3] Two models for the tower, one with classical and the other with Gothic architectural motifs, are in the Rijksmuseum, Amsterdam. The foundations of the tower were finished before work began on those of the Town Hall (MS. *Res. Vroedsch.*, 8 Apr. 1647). The lowest storey was built and in part survives. The tower is shown in a painting by Jacob van der Ulft, Musée Condé, Chantilly (F.-A. Gruyer, *Musée Condée, notice des peintures*. Paris, 1899, no. 137, signed and dated 1659), in engravings after this painting, and in other works. These records show, and the remains suggest, that the more Gothic design was decided on.
[4] Vondel, *Inwydinge*, lines 470–6:

The Town Hall was sober in form, and was planned with a classical balance and symmetry, in every particular, outside and inside and on every floor, which was often remarked on, so new was the idea in mid-seventeenth-century Amsterdam.[1] It was ornamented with two orders of giant pilasters of the gayest kind[2] and was hung about with richly carved festoons which, with the pictorial reliefs in the pediments and the figures that stood above them, are essential to the building's form as well as its significance. They appear as part of the wooden model and in the prints of 1650 and are part of the whole design. It would be hard to imagine a greater contrast between this design and that of the previous Town Hall, and the difference was symbolic of the momentous changes that had taken place in Amsterdam in the course of her short history, and of the changes in life and thought that lay behind them. Yet the continuity of her history had remained unbroken, and the functions of her government were essentially the same. These functions were expressed in the new Town Hall as they were in the old, only, since thought had changed, they were conceived differently, and so were expressed in different terms. The language of the new building was rhetorical, and was based on the language of antiquity with scholarly exactness in so far as this was understood and could be adapted to new purposes.

The bell-tower of the old Town Hall was replaced by a cupola (illus. 17), with an open drum below it housing a carillon, and with a lantern at the top to contain the City Bell. It was intended as a Tower of the Winds, for the prints of 1650 show eight figures that were to have stood above the half-columns of the drum, and Vennekool's prints show in addition the swivelling figure of a mermaid or Triton at the summit of the cupola (illus. 16).[3] The figures of the

> . . . geen onkenbaer teiken
> Van majesteit, en maght, die nu doorluchtigh blijckt,
> Naerdien de Dam in naem Sint Markus plaets niet wijckt,
> Noch zelf het velt van Mars, zoo wyt befaemt by d'ouden,
> Die Rome, in zijne kracht en middaghglans, aenschouden,
> Toen, Cezars erfgenaem, August, in vollen vre,
> Het heiligh Kapitool in zijn triomfe opre.

[1] The passage describing this symmetry in Dapper, *Beschryving*, p. 335, suggests that its writer found the subject bewildering.

[2] The orders, each with the height of one floor with a mezzanine above it, are Composite and Corinthian. No precedent for the arrangement of the orders is apparent, but that in the reconstruction of Solomon's Temple in [Jerónimo de] Prado and [Juan Bautista] Vilalpando, *In Ezechielem explanationes et apparatus urbis, ac templi Hierosolymitani*, Rome, 1596–1604, has some features in common with it. Van Luttervelt, *Raadhuis*, pp. 13–16, 18, and 23–24, draws attention to this and to evidence of Van Campen's interest in the work, suggesting it was one of his sources. Yet except in the giant pilasters there are few resemblances. In Ch. IV below further possible sources for the Town Hall's architecture are mentioned.

[3] Vennekool, *Afbeelding*, pls. D, F., G and I.

winds were mentioned as such by Everard Meyster in his description of the design,[1] so that the figures planned for the tower cannot have been intended only as a formal decoration. A weather-vane representing the cog was put on the summit of the building itself and the figures were never made. Vitruvius describes the Tower of the Winds built by Andronicus of Cyrrha at Athens, an octagonal tower on which representations of the winds were carved 'opposite their several currents', which was surmounted by the figure of a Triton with a rod in his hand which indicated the direction of the wind that was blowing as he turned.[2] The design of this tower seems to have been adapted in the plans for the new building, and this is not surprising when one remembers the importance of the winds to the trade and so to the prosperity of seventeenth-century Amsterdam. It is possible that they were also intended to carry her fame with them in their eight directions, for the mermaid or Triton of the Town Hall design is equipped with wings, and has not a rod, but a double trumpet such as was used in ancient Rome, although this has the serious dis-advantage of pointing in two directions at once.[3]

One noticed the cupola first, whether one approached the city by sea or land, and it may be seen as an introduction to the building's rhetoric. The figures surrounding it were to have been enormous, like those of the virtues which stand on the pediments below. Peace, the heaviest of the virtues, weighs over 8,000 pounds.[4] In every part of the building size and weight have their effect upon one, and this must have been intended. It has stone and marble floors and much stone vaulting, as well as very massive walls, though it is built only on a forest of wooden piles, which still bear it without shifting. The greater part of the stone, all of which had to be imported, was brought from Westphalia and the marble from Italy,[5] much of it in blocks which were

[1] Meyster, *Land-spel*, I, p. 27. Meyster mentions the weather-vane as having the form of a mermaid.
[2] *De Architectura*, I, vi, 4. Quoted from Granger.
[3] The figure is perhaps comparable, as a marine version of Fame, with the winged tritons which blow conches on the tomb of Admiral Tromp (d. 1653), Old Church, Delft, which was designed by Van Campen. See further p. 140 n. 5 below.
[4] A MS. sheet without title giving the weights of the figures in an 18th-century hand, Gemeente-Archief, Amsterdam, Library, section H, gives her weight as 8150 pounds.
[5] Vondel (*Inwydinge*, line 560) and other writers refer to stone from Bentheim. A copy of one contract for purchasing stone from merchants at Bremen and minutes concerning other purchases survive in MS. *Res. Thes. Ord.*, 1594–1657, folios 152 r. and 154 r. (referred to and quoted by Kroon, *Stadhuis*, pp. 119–21). Kroon states (p. 118) that 'all the white marble' for the building was shipped from Leghorn, citing accounts in the city archives. The claim made by Alexander Boswell writing to his son James in 1763 that "the Stadthouse [of Amsterdam], which is a noble edifice, was all built with stones furnished by your great-grandfather the Earl of Kinkardine" (quoted by Frederik A. Pottle, *Boswell in Holland, 1763–1764*, Melbourne [etc.], 1952, p. 51) is at least exaggerated. Yet Vondel (line 561) refers to 'the western marble cliff' and commenting on this J. van Lennep (*De werken van Vondel*, Amsterdam, 1855–69, VI, p. 676, note) states

of a very exceptional size for stone imported into Holland. The trees for the piles were brought from Norway.[1] It is certainly not surprising that the Town Hall of Amsterdam was often called the eighth wonder of the world.[2]

Below the bronze figures on the front pediment, but high above the Dam, where boats were brought in to be unloaded and markets were held, sea gods and water creatures gather to do homage to the symbolic figure of Amsterdam, Venus rises from the sea at the city's feet, and a crowd of mermaids races to crown her with wreaths of laurel (illus. 18–20, 180, 205a).[3] The jostling host, carved in the relief of the tympanum, seems to be present, not merely represented, and in light and shadow or against a watery sky it seems alive and moving. It must have been closely related to the noisy scene below, supplementing the evidence of all that the spectator saw around him as he walked across the Dam, and recording Amsterdam's present glory for him and for posterity in what were in principle the terms of antique art. The festoons (illus. 22) which form part of the architectural scheme of the walls provide the spectator with further information, for some are made of fruit and flowers, others of shells, sea-creatures, or ships' instruments; others again contain wreaths of oak leaves, the ram's head that symbolises Jupiter's authority, or the lion's wolf's and dog's heads which are appropriate to wise deliberations.[4] There was no element of chance in the design of these ornaments, for models made for them by Artus Quellien were sent down to the workshops of the city mason,[5] where the designs were carved in stone, each from a single block. In some of the capitals for the corners of the building sphinxes, the symbols of

that 'The marble for the Town Hall was to a large extent brought from Scotland', citing 'old documents' seen in Edinburgh; these cannot now be traced. Also it was said at Tulliallan in 1794 that "the principal houses of AMSTERDAM, and the Stadt-House of Holland" were built of stone from a local quarry; John Sinclair (compiler), *The [First] Statistical Account of Scotland*, Edinburgh, XI, 1794, pp. 552–3. Scottish stone, however, has not been recognized in the building; see *Economic Geology of the Stirling and Clackmannan Coalfield* (Geological Survey, Scotland), Edinburgh, 1932, p. 199.

[1] Vos, 'Inwijding', *Gedichten* [1], p. 337.

[2] Asselijn, in 1654, referred to the building as the first of the seven wonders (see p. 51 below), and Meyster, *Land-spel*, II, p. 3, as one of them. Constantijn Huygens, 'Geluk aan de EE. Heeren regeerders van Amsterdam' [etc.], 1655 (quoted in Vennekool, *Afbeelding*, p. 10), called it the eighth wonder of the world in his opening line. The term was used by Vos, op. cit. [1], pp. 341 and 345, and by later writers. Its use descended to absurdity in a verse in which C. Gravesteyn tells his Cloris that he has seen the Town Hall, the eighth wonder of the world, but asks permission to apply the term to her; 'Aen Cloris, Amsterdam en het nieuw Raadthuis gezien hebbende', in *Hollantsche Parnas*, I, p. 317.

[3] The design is faithfully given by H. Quellien, *Statuen*, pl. 1. A drawing for this engraving is in the Louvre; Frits Lugt, *Inventaire générale des dessins, école Flamande*, Paris, 1949, II, no. 1003.

[4] Ripa, *Iconologia*, 1624, pp. 121–4 (*Consiglio*). Meyster's explanation, *Land-spel*, I, pp. 23–24, shows that this meaning was intended. The symbol appears again in the frieze of the north chimney-piece of the meeting-room of the city council. The history of the symbol, and the derivation of this frieze from Ripa, are discussed by Erwin Panofsky, *Meaning in the Visual Arts*, New York, 1955, pp. 146–68.

[5] See p. 166 n. 3 below.

wisdom, were carved (illus. 21). Others are ornamented with an eagle supporting the imperial crown which, by grant of Maximillian of Austria, surmounts
the city's coat of arms.

Seven rounded arches take the place of the arcade of the old Town Hall and
the *vierschaar* lies behind them with equal entrances to the building on either
side of it,[1] and since Amsterdam was the chief city of a republic it was symbolic
that there should be no main door. The seven openings of the entrance arches
were taken to signify the seven provinces,[2] but the design was not necessarily
made with the seven provinces in mind. The *vierschaar* takes up the full height
of two storeys. It gets most of its light from the first floor through openings
out of the publication gallery, a narrow room above the central arches used for
the reading of proclamations and known as the *puy*, or 'well'.[3] This forms a light
well comparable with those traditional in seventeenth-century Amsterdam in
merchants' houses and presumably derived from them, though here the traditional *puy* took on a new guise. Under the arcade the public can look into the
vierschaar through window openings barred by bronze railings, which, like
those of the old Town Hall, were intended for defence; a row of holes designed
to take the muzzles of muskets forms part of their ornament.[4] To each side
of the *vierschaar* there were guard-rooms, where the watch was kept. The rest
of the ground floor (illus. 14) housed, on the south side, the city bank, an ammu-
nition store, and the caretaker's quarters. On the north side were prisons with
dungeons under them,[5] as well as a torture chamber and accommodation for
the gaoler.

A double stair leads up behind the inner wall of the *vierschaar* to the first
floor (illus. 15), here a *piano nobile* in the Italian sense, and directly into the
Burgerzaal, the 'citizens' hall'. The stairs were designed to be dark, whereas
the hall is of dazzlingly white marble and stone and very evenly lit.[6] It runs

---

[1] For the arrangement of the rooms see Vennekool, *Afbeelding*, pls. A, B, and C.

[2] The supposed symbolic meaning is not mentioned in the poems written in 1655 on the building, nor
in the introduction to Vennekool's prints, and seems to have been thought of later. Vitruvius' basilica at
Fano, whose use must have been comparable with that of the Amsterdam Town Hall, was divided into
seven bays on the forum side (Vitruvius, *De Architectura*, V. i. 6); the front façade of the Capitol Palace is
also so divided. Possibly the arrangement in these buildings was emulated. For the suggestion concerning
the basilica thanks are due to Mr. W. A. Keuzenkamp. For a further parallel with this building see p. 112 below.

[3] Its use is summed up by Dapper, *Beschryving*, p. 376.

[4] Dapper, op. cit., p. 349.

[5] The position of the dungeons is noted on the prints of 1648 and they are mentioned in descriptions made
later.

[6] The contrast is now lost, the stairs being lit by windows in the upper part of the inner wall of the *vierschaar*, but Vennekool, *Afbeelding*, pls. B and K, shows the wall as being continuous, and in a passage in
which the type has been disturbed, p. 6, it is stated that it has been broken through. The decision 'to make

39

right across the centre of the building and there are open courts to each side of it round which run galleries that open out of the Burgerzaal at either end. All the light for the hall and galleries was to come from the two courts, and it was proposed at first that these, like the outside walls of the building, should be ornamented with giant pilasters.[1] In the centre of each court was to have stood a fountain of allegorical significance, but these fountains were never made.[2] The principal council-rooms and departments of the city government were on the first floor, ranged round the galleries according to their order of seniority as has already been described. The burgomasters' chamber, beside the Dam as it was in the old building, was provided with a window (see illus. 84) through which the burgomasters could look down when the *vierschaar* was in use, to give their sanction to the sentencing of the prisoner.[3] It was arranged that from the chamber of justice the sentenced man could be led on to a scaffold set up against the building for his execution; the condemned prisoners had been led out on to the scaffold from an upper window of the old Town Hall. The larger rooms of this principal floor take up the height of the second storey, but the smaller rooms have a mezzanine floor above them which, with the rooms of the upper part of the Town Hall, housed some of the younger departments of the city government and other offices. The council chamber of the Civic Guard, known as the 'War Council chamber'[4], was the only room of

a light on the great stairs in the wall of the *vierschaar*' is recorded in MS. *Res. Thes. Ord.*, 9 Mar. 1660. Three lights were made – see an early 18th-century drawing of the Burgerzaal by one of the De Moucheron family, Koninklijk Oudheidkundig Genootschap, Amsterdam, Atlas Amsterdam, portfolio 17 – and these remain today. Miss L. Frerichs kindly brought this drawing to the writer's notice.

[1] Indicated in the prints of 1648 and 1650, and shown in the model of the building, Waag Museum, Amsterdam.

[2] There are models for these in the Rijksmuseum, Amsterdam; *Cat. beeldhouwwerken*, no. 277, 13. (The particulars of date and price in this entry, apparently from Kroon, *Stadhuis*, p. 114, are inaccurate, and there can be no doubt of the models' identity.) They are mentioned, with descriptions, one of them as a model for a fountain, in lists of works first in the Kunstkamer, later in the Academy, of the city; these works were transferred from the Academy to the Rijksmuseum. See unnumbered papers, H, Stadsmuseum [etc.], Gemeente-Archief, Amsterdam, Library. Two such models, paid for at 24 gulden each, are mentioned in A. Quellien's Papers, on sheets 4 and 6 (both of 1652, one repeating information from the other) and on sheet 11 (where the same particulars are summarized). The burgomasters decided in 1664 that the sculpture for the courts should not be made; MS. *Res. Thes. Ord.*, 26 Feb. 1664. Larger models were also prepared, for during his final settlement of accounts with the Treasurers in 1665 Quellien claimed 1000 gulden for models of sculptures ordered for the fountains. The claim was fulfilled only in part since 'it was not satisfactorily shown that they had been ordered'; MS. cit., 1 May, 1665. One model represents Cimon and Pero, with two further prisoners; it must have been for the fountain of the north court, this being reached from the prison precincts and bordering on them. The other, thus for the south court, has the form of a ship borne on the shoulders of four allegorical figures: Minerva, Hercules, Mercury, and one unidentified. In descriptions in the papers referred to, one of which is of 1769, it is stated that the ship is that of the city's coat of arms, and that "de Zeevaart", i.e. 'navigation' in its widest sense, is represented.

[3] For the procedure see p. 83 below.

[4] Bontemantel describes the council's functions; *De regeeringe*, I, pp. 191–214.

40

great size at second floor level. This was over the magistrates' court and had no further floor above it, but reached to the roof. There were upper galleries at the same level, and above the remaining rooms of this floor was a great armoury, in which the city's supply of military equipment was kept.[1]

This summary description can give little idea of the character of the building, of its practical planning and of the grandeur of its scheme. Each of the main departments had its own entrance from the galleries, either direct, or through a small vestibule. Each was self-contained, having a large room and smaller offices, and at certain points there were private stairs connecting the first floor rooms with those of the mezzanine above. At the ends of the galleries leading north and south from the Burgerzaal were the main staircases, whose rising flights were originally seen through pairs of arched openings, though these have now been fitted with doors. Where the upper galleries abutted on to the walls of the Burgerzaal, which takes up the full height of the first and second floors and has its barrel-vault under the roof, there were to have been further openings. From these and from openings in its end walls, on the west out of a narrower gallery and on the east from a room under the tower, it would have been possible to look down into the great hall and to watch the small figures of the citizens who passed to and fro across the marble floor below. The openings in the end walls of the Burgerzaal were certainly made, together with four extra ones, those in the western wall opening out of the council chamber of the Civic Guard instead of the gallery that was planned,[2] but they were not provided with the balustrades that should have ornamented them.[3] The omission of some of these openings and the filling in of others very seriously damages the design of the great hall, for, seen from below, the on-looker leaning over a balustrade or parapet to look down from his high

---

[1] Vondel, *Inwydinge*, lines 1037–62; Dapper, *Beschryving*, p. 348. When Dapper's account was published, 1663, the armoury was not ready for use, but in 1668 Duke Cosimo III de' Medici was shown arms for 12,000 persons there; Hoogewerff, *De twee reizen*, p. 84.

[2] The openings above the ends of the galleries were probably never made. They are not mentioned in the minute, MS. *Res. Thes. Ord.*, 20 Oct. 1665, recording the burgomasters' decision to put four of Quellien's full-scale models for the bronze pediment statues above the cornice in the Burgerzaal, though four of those put there stand where the openings would have been. Moreover the vaults of the galleries were made higher than was first intended, so that no upper galleries could be made above them from which to look down. The narrow gallery at the west end of the hall on the second floor, which would have linked the upper galleries north and south of it, was designed by Van Campen but eliminated in the building itself to make more room for the council chamber of the Civic Guard; see Bibliography s.v. Vennekool.

[3] The openings are shown in De Moucheron's drawing, see p. 39 n. 6, above, but without the balustrades which Vennekool shows, *Afbeelding*, pls. H, R, and S. He shows the openings at the sides of the hall without balustrades, but these have them in the model, Waag Museum, Amsterdam. The extra openings, shown by Vennekool only in pl. Q, which brought the number at each end from two to four, formed part of an early version of the design. They appear, though in differing forms, in both model and drawing.

position would have become part of the decoration of the room, as painted spectators do in the decorations of Veronese and his followers,[1] and, with spectators as their *staffage*, the openings would have added greatly to its scale and to its splendour. The Burgerzaal and galleries were evidently designed to reflect the newly-won status of the citizen who, as it seems, could wander about them at will.[2] His freedom was also suggested in their decoration, which was designed with him in mind. Indeed the architecture of the Town Hall and its decoration cannot with justice be considered separately, for they were very closely related to each other by their symbolism, purpose, and harmony of form.

As he walked across the Burgerzaal (illus. 25–37, 65–66, 68, 77–79) the citizen traversed the terrestrial hemispheres, correctly orientated, depicted in two great maps which were drawn in coloured mosaic lines and with brass divisions and lettering in the stones of the floor.[3] The discoveries made by Tasman on the coast of Australia during his voyage of 1642 to 1644 were shown on the map of the old world, and were proudly marked as 'New Holland'.[4] In the words of a contemporary writer 'you can . . . make your way across the whole world in a moment' in this room.[5] But more than the world was represented, for in the Burgerzaal and the galleries together the spectator was to have been placed in his setting in the universe. Between the maps of the terrestrial hemispheres

---

[1] For decoration of this kind in Holland see p. 136 below.

[2] Vennekool shows many figures standing about in his view of the Burgerzaal, and in that of one of the galleries a boy is shown patting a dog, a baby is being promenaded, and three figures appear to be strolling in the distance; op. cit., pls. R and W. The *Beschryvinge van 't Stadhuis*, 1782, p. 102, mentions a wooden fence round the carved panel below the figure of Diana in the south gallery, put there 'to prevent hands eager to damage' from further mischief. It is unlikely that deliberate damage would have been done by people on business there.

[3] The 'coloured inlaid small stones' are mentioned in Dapper's account, *Beschryving*, p. 354, and by other writers. The *Description de l'Hotel de Ville d'Amsterdam*, Amsterdam, 1714, p. 55, describes some of the 'stones' as being of coloured plaster; in the *Beschryvinge van 't Stadhuis*, 1782, p. 50, the 'stones' are stated to be of plaster and much damaged by wear. This later description may well apply to the original mosaic since in 1742 restorations were needed and these, also to be made with some such material, were not completed. The terrestrial globes were not replaced in the Burgerzaal until 1953. For their restoration and later history see V. F. H. E. van Schaick, 'Het inlegwerk in de vloer van de burgerzaal', *Jaarboek Amstelodamum*, XLVI, 1954, pp. 47–59. The date of these maps is unknown. A list of payments to the cartographer and publisher J. Bleau, receipted 28 Dec. 1652, mentions a payment of 160 gulden to Jan Wijbrantsz. Colck "voort maecken en schilderen, vergulden verschuren vande grooten sphera planeten ende den Quodiacq". ('for the making and painting [or colouring] gilding and rubbing down of the great sphere planets and the Zodiac'); MS. *Res. Thes. Ord.*, 1594–1657. fol. 149 v. The dates of some of these payments are recorded but do not indicate the date of that referred to here. The entry has been connected by Kroon, *Stadhuis*, p. 62, and others, with the decoration of the Burgerzaal floor, where one of the celestial hemispheres, showing signs of the zodiac, is depicted between the terrestrial maps; Van Schaick points out that the signature of Y. W. Kolck appears on this central hemisphere.

[4] R. Posthumus Meyjes, *De reizen van Abel Jansz Tasman en Franchoys Jacobsz Visscher 1642–1644* (Lin-schoten Vereeniging), The Hague, 1919, p. 261. The maps were later altered, presumably during restorations. Their original form is shown by Vennekool, op. cit., pl. O.

[5] Zoet, 'De Zaale van Oranje', *Werken*, p. 183.

is depicted the northern hemisphere of the sky, and painted above it in the central compartment of the ceiling, whose divisions were to have mirrored those of the floor below, the southern celestial hemisphere was to have been represented, in a sky in which, to the south, the Fall of Phaeton was taking place and where, to the north, Boreas was carrying away Orithyia.[1] There was to have been a painting of Aurora fleeing before Apollo in the lunette of the eastern wall of the hall, and one of Diana driving her chariot up into the heavens and Apollo disappearing, in the western lunette,[2] and each of these paintings was to have contained a band in which signs of the zodiac appeared, though it seems that no horoscope was to have been included in the building's decoration. These scenes would have been correctly placed at the four main points of the compass, so that the spectator would have stood below them as though in an ordered universe. In the introduction to the book of engravings by Vennekool the two lunette paintings are described as representing sunrise and sunset, and in an eighteenth-century edition of Vennekool's and Quellien's plates the painting of the fall of Phaeton is described as 'A neat lesson for the ambitious, who want to raise themselves too high, and for those who strive after positions which are beyond their powers'.[3] The symbol was used in this sense, and very pointedly, on a medal struck in Amsterdam on the death of Prince Willem II in 1650, soon after he had attempted to capture the city by laying siege to it[4] and a play on this meaning may well have been in mind when plans were made for the decoration of the Burgerzaal. In the remaining compartments of the ceiling the sky was to have been continued, with birds flying about in it; unfortunately the engravings that record the design do not make their species clear, but they may well have been intended as auguries.[5] Between the balustraded openings of the eastern wall, which were to have been flanked on the outer sides by panels decorated with trophies, there was to have been a painting of some story in which Neptune calms the waves, and in a corresponding position on the western wall one of Jupiter punishing the giants who

---

[1] Shown by Vennekool, op. cit., pls. P and R. Both Phaeton and Boreas are named in *Bouw schilder en beeldhouwkonst*, p. 7, description of pl. XXXVIII.

[2] Shown by Vennekool, op. cit., pls. H and R. The subjects are recognizable and are also mentioned, p. 7, as follows: "In 't Oosten vertoont sich Phoebus, der Sonnen opgangh, en ten Westen, der Sonnen ondergangh, uytbeeldende" ('In the east appears Phoebus, representing the sunrise, and, in the west, the sunset'). Quite possibly these representations were inspired by the carved figures of the Sun and Moon which had ornamented Jupiter's temple on the Roman Capitol. For these see p. 174 n. 1 below.

[3] *Bouw schilder en beeldhouwkonst*, p. 7, description of pl. XXXVIII: "Een fraije les voor de heerzuchtigen, die zich te hoog willen verheffen, en voor hun, die amten bejagen, welke hunne krachten te boven gaan".

[4] Medal by Sebastian Dadler; *Cat. gedenkpenningen*, I, no. 794; Van Loon, *Historiepenningen*, II, pp. 353–4.

[5] Thanks are due to Dr. L. D. Ettlinger for this suggestion.

rebelled against him.[1] It has already been stated that the sea paying tribute to Amsterdam is shown on the eastern pediment of the building and, as will be shown, the continents pay their tribute to her in the relief on the western tympanum. Here, and perhaps to correspond with these scenes on the outside of the Town Hall, the gods were to have been seen supporting law and order by sea and land at the eastern and western ends of the Burgerzaal. Unhappily no records are known of the intended meaning of the scheme of paintings as a whole, and no text has been found which corresponds to them, but it seems as though the scenes showing Phaeton, Boreas, Neptune and the Giants may well have represented the four elements, fire, air, water and earth. If this is so, whether by chance or intention, the rising moon of the western lunette would have appeared opposite the element of water, which she governs, and the element of earth would have been opposite the rising sun.[2]

On the spandrels of the great arches which lead from the hall to the galleries the four elements are quite clearly represented, carved as figures in marble, two to an arch. Since there are four arches each element appears twice, and in each case the symbolism corresponds very closely with the descriptions of the elements given by Cesare Ripa in his *Iconologia*, first published in Italy in 1593 and published in a Dutch translation in 1644. There can be no doubt that they were based on these descriptions, since Ripa's account itself is a compilation, and since in the representations above one pair of arches, that at the western end of the Burgerzaal, his first set of descriptions is followed while in those above the other pair his further descriptions are used together.[3] Above the representations of the elements, and to either side of the points at which openings should have linked the Burgerzaal with the upper galleries, hanging bunches of symbols connected with the elements are carved in relief. These,

[1] Shown by Vennekool, op. cit., pls. H and R. The *Gigantomachia* (Ovid, *Metamorphoses*, I, lines 151–62) is clearly identifiable. The second painting, in which Boreas carries Orithyia away above Neptune, may represent the incident described by Virgil, *Aeneid*, I, line 102, in which after Aeneas' ship has been hit by a gust of wind from the north Neptune notices the uproar and stills the waves: cf. Rubens' 'Quos Ego', 1634–5, formerly Gemäldegalerie, Dresden; Rudolf Oldenbourg, *P. P. Rubens* [etc.] (Klassiker der Kunst), 4th ed., Stuttgart and Berlin, n.d., p. 362. Alternatively the story of the flood as told by Ovid (I, lines 262–347) may be shown though Deucalion and Pyrrha do not appear. In this case the pendant paintings would show two connected stories. Boreas appears with Orithyia in the illustrations of the Winds in many editions of Natales Conti, *Mythologiae* (e.g. ed. Padua, 1637, p. 452) much as he does in the paintings including him planned for the Town Hall, and for a model for the North Wind this may have been referred to.
[2] The author is indebted to Dr. J. Bruyn and Mr. J. Emmens for this suggested interpretation.
[3] See H. Quellien, *Statuen*, II, pls. C and E, and Ripa, *Iconologia*, 1624, pp. 194–8 (*Elementi*). The use of Ripa's treatise in the Town Hall has been mentioned in general terms by A. Zijderveld, 'Cesare Ripa's Iconologia in ons land', *Oud-Holland*, LXIV, 1949, pp. 117–18, and an instance given by Panofsky (see p. 38 n. 4 above). For connections with Ripa in the sculpture of the west pediment see pp. 176–81 below.

however, if they are not the invention of the person who designed them, were taken from another source of information, for they do not correspond with Ripa's account. In the next chapter it will be shown that symbols of the seasons and of the times of day, as well as further signs of the zodiac, appear in the Burgerzaal above the eastern entrance, as part of the universe of space and time which was to surround the citizen; that the figure of Amsterdam, appearing as Peace and accompanied by Strength and Wisdom, takes a prominent place on the eastern wall, surrounded by representations symbolising good government and authority; and that Justice appears above the entrance in the western wall which leads to the magistrates' court.[1] It is evident that the principal functions of the government of the city were to be seen there as part of a universal harmony.

The symbolic scheme of the Burgerzaal is extended into the galleries (illus. 38–64, 67) to either side of the hall, where the seven planets and Cybele are depicted as standing figures, life size and in high relief, on the end walls, surrounded by their attributes. They were not placed in the conventional order, and it cannot be supposed that in the seventeenth century and in a building of this kind this was due to ignorance or to any lapse of memory. It seems that they were suited so far as possible to the departments whose entrances they guarded.[2] Since, as has been shown, the main departments of the city government took their place in the building in order of their seniority in a regular scheme, the planets, if they were to be related to them, had of necessity to abandon their own order of precedence, inviolable as it might seem, and to dispose themselves accordingly, to the greater glory of Amsterdam.[3] Mythological figures symbolic of the use of the various rooms were to be found in earlier town halls[4], and in the Town Hall of Amsterdam this invention was evidently elaborated, and both the symbolic figures on the end walls of the Burgerzaal and the planets in the galleries were designed, by virtue of their dual significance (their particular meaning and their meaning in relation to the general scheme) to link the actual departments of the city government with the universe that was represented three-dimensionally in the centre of the

---

[1] See pp. 71–72 and 75 below.
[2] H. Brugmans and A. W. Weissman, *Het Stadhuis van Amsterdam*, Amsterdam, 1914, p. 110, connect the planets with the various departments though with an interpertation rather different from that given here.
[3] Erwin Panofsky, *Early Netherlandish Painting*, Harvard, 1953, I, pp. 146–8, shows how in a painting by Jan van Eyck the laws of nature were broken in order that a particular meaning might be expressed. Although this does not provide a parallel the idea lying behind the symbolism is in some respects comparable with that referred to here.
[4] See Lederle, *Gerechtigkeitsdarstellungen*, p. 3.

building. The various rooms, even to the smallest detail of their symbolic decoration, and by implication also the people who occupied them, were thus given their place in this scheme, and were related each to its other elements.

Diana appears beside the door of the treasury, surrounded by a profusion of trophies of the chase among which preponderate fish and lobsters, pearls, shells, and coral, so that one may conclude that she is in this instance a sea huntress, as is suitable to Amsterdam. Mercury too appears near to the treasury, money-bag in hand, and it may be because he is a messenger that he is between the treasury and the Secretary's office, and not in Diana's place; he also guards the stair that leads down to the city bank. Cybele, who is 'the mother of the gods'[1] and is also the personification of mother earth, is appropriately placed beside the entrance to the office of the Trustees of the Orphans. Between the arches of the staircase near to her appears Saturn, who takes his place beside two offices in which legal cases involving money were dealt with, the Chamber of Insurance and the Bankruptcy Office; it may be presumed that this planet is connected with them because by long-lasting tradition he rules over Melancholy, who in turn is associated with money.[2] These planets are depicted on the eastern side of the building. On the western side Apollo appears beside the door leading to the office of the Treasurers Extraordinary, which, perhaps because it is an offshoot of the treasury, has no separate planet associated with it. He is also next to the door of the room occupied by the Commissioners for Petty Affairs, and since these were the successors of the College of Peacemakers[3] Apollo was appropriate to them as the maker of harmony. At the western end of the northern gallery Venus guards one of the staircases that lead up to the Chamber of Matrimonial Affairs and that of Marine Affairs, both of which fall under her jurisdiction.

The disposition of these six planets in relation to the offices of the city government may thus be accounted for quite naturally, although there is no written evidence which explains it.[4] Supposing, further, that these six planets had been

---

[1] Vennekool, *Afbeelding*, p. 7. Cybele, as the Earth, was mother of all that grows on the earth (Ripa, *Iconologia*, 1624, p. 195, *Elementi*) and so was suited to act as guardian to the city's dependents. The symbolic meaning was in keeping with that of the room itself, in whose decoration the theme of adoption was illustrated; see p. 74 below.

[2] The writer is grateful to Professor W. S. Heckscher for pointing this out. For the connection of Saturn with Melancholy and of Melancholy with money see Erwin Panofsky, *Albrecht Dürer*, Princeton, 1943, I, pp. 166 and 163–4 respectively. The stair guarded by Saturn was probably one of the routes by which members of the public could ascend to the 'tower', which housed the main timepiece of the city. Since Saturn is symbolic of time this may add to the appropriateness of his position.

[3] See p. 18 above.

[4] The interpretation of the iconography of the planets suggested here is hypothetical, but in putting it

given their places, there would remain no college of government housed within the building that was not in some way connected with one of the symbolic figures of either the Burgerzaal or the galleries, for the Accounts Office, like the office of the Treasurers Extraordinary, may be considered to be under the shadow of the treasury. Of the planets Jupiter and Mars would remain to be given places, and two places would remain unfilled, one guarding a staircase, and one near to the figure of Venus. In such a case the most suitable arrangement for the figures would be obvious. Jupiter, as the highest commander, should guard the staircase, which is one of those leading to the council chamber of the Civic Guard, and, like all the main staircases, also led to the immense supply of arms which was kept at the top of the building. It seems likely that he was placed beside the staircase for this reason, while Mars, giving pride of place to Jupiter, remained as a companion for Venus. Mars and Venus are accordingly to be seen looking fondly at each other across the north-western corner of the galleries.

The history of the building shows that the decoration of the galleries was considered to be of special importance, as its place in the iconographic scheme suggests. When the earliest prints of the plan of the Town Hall were made in 1648 the decoration of the galleries had not been decided on. The stairs were to be in their final positions at the ends of the galleries running north and south, but were not all to be alike in form, and were to be approached through single openings. By the time that the prints of 1650 were made the design for the staircases had been changed and, except for a difference in the thickness of the walls, they had been given their final form. The pairs of openings which lead to the stairs from the galleries are shown in these prints, and their position corresponds to that of the arched door openings in the walls at right-angles to them, which are at the ends of the remaining galleries, so that the views down all the galleries are in harmony. The short lengths of wall between the pairs of openings, both of arches and doors, provide fields suitable for sculptural decoration, and it is on these, above panels which were known as 'pedestals',

forward a tendency of thought prevalent in 17th-century Amsterdam has been borne in mind: that by which aspects of everyday life were discussed and illustrated in the terms of, and were seen as being related to, humanist knowledge. This tendency is evident in literature and pictorial symbolism. In the oration made by Caspar Barlaeus at the opening of the Athenaeum Illustre, the predecessor of the city's university, the connection between trade and humanism was discussed; *Mercator sapiens, sive oratio de conjugendis mercaturae et philosophiae studiis*, Amsterdam, 1632 ('The Wise Merchant, or Oration Concerning the Union of Mercantile and Philosophical Studies'). Thanks are due to Professor W. S. Heckscher for drawing attention to this work, which he discusses in his book *Rembrandt's "Anatomy of Dr. Nicolaas Tulp", an Iconographic Study*. New York, 1958, pp. 110–11 and n. 212.

that the reliefs of the planets are set up, so that they are centrally placed at the end of each gallery.[1] It seems likely that the final arrangement was planned with such decoration in mind, for the prints of 1650 also show details of the arrangement of the *vierschaar* that are very closely connected with its scheme of decoration.[2] Before 24th October 1651 models for the reliefs of Apollo and Diana and for fillings for the lunettes over the doors beside them had been completed, and at the same time what must have been the first of all the marble sculptures for the building were carved: the Apollo and two of the lunettes for which models had been made.[3] No further carvings were made for the galleries for at least a year, though the making of marble decorations for the *vierschaar* went forward, so that it is evident that at this time the work of building had not reached the point at which it was necessary to put the sculpture of the galleries into place. The three marble works must have been made in advance, as samples to show what the decoration would be like, which shows that this part of the scheme was given precedence. It may also be concluded that the Apollo was carved by Quellien himself, for the making of such a sample would not be left to a pupil. This work is the only piece of sculpture in the building which can be shown with complete certainty to be by Quellien's own hand, although he must have executed very many more of them.[4] By 1655, the year of the inauguration, the main features of the sculptural decoration of the *vierschaar*, galleries, and Burgerzaal, had been decided on and much of it made,[5] and paintings of the deeds of the ancient Batavians were to appear in the lunettes of the galleries, which fill the spaces above the planets and below the vault.[6]

[1] On the pedestals facing east and west the central panels bear carved reliefs. The panels of those facing north and south are plain and are flanked by garlands; chandeliers were to stand against them (see Vennekool, *Afbeelding*, pl. T).

[2] See p. 79 below.

[3] A. Quellien, MS. Papers, nos. 5 and 11. The first payment recorded on no. 6, which follows no. 5 chronologically, was made on 24th October 1651. It may thus be assumed that the work listed on no. 5 had been completed by that date. See also List of Sources s.v. A. Quellien.

[4] The writer is indebted to Mr. A. Perfors for pointing out that the monogram A. Q. is carved in the relief showing Mars, on the head of his battleaxe; there is no conclusive evidence as to whether it refers to the elder or the younger Artus Quellien.

[5] This statement is based on an analysis of the parts of the decoration referred to by Meyster, *Land-spel*, by Vondel, *Inwyding*, and in the 'Inwyding' of Vos, all written in 1655 or, in the case of the first, perhaps very slightly earlier (see Bibliography). None of the paintings designed for the Burgerzaal are clearly referred to in these works. A. Quellien's MS. Papers show that much of the sculpture had been made by this date.

[6] Mentioned by Vondel, op. cit., lines 1117–30. For an account of the paintings and their history see Van de Waal, *Geschied-uitbeelding*, I, pp. 235–8. The sources of 1655 do not mention the paintings of strong men of the Old Testament in the spaces above the great arches leading to the Burgerzaal, two of which are described by Van Dyk, *Schilderyen op het Stadhuis*, p. 78. Since the vaulting of the galleries was made higher than was first planned the fields for all these paintings were originally to have been of a different shape. The earlier design is shown consistently in Vennekool's *Afbeelding*.

The history of the city, being shaped in the rooms round the galleries and illustrated by the splendour of the Town Hall itself, was to be further embellished by representations showing the glory of her past history.

During the rebellion against Spain the story of the Batavians had been brought into prominence. Tacitus, in his *Germania*, had described the outstanding valour of this people, a tribe which occupied an island in the Rhine and a small part of the river bank,[1] and although the exact location of this island was uncertain, and was not in fact in the immediate neighbourhood of Amsterdam, it was believed there in the seventeenth century in all seriousness that the Batavians were the ancestors of the people of the province of Holland, and therefore of the citizens of Amsterdam themselves.[2] These ancestors had, it was thought, been the allies and friends of the Romans but had come to be oppressed by them and to suffer great injustices at their hands. Tacitus describes how they were incited to rebellion by one of their chieftains, named Julius Claudius Civilis, at a feast in a holy wood, and how they swore loyalty to him. Claudius Civilis led the tribe in a series of successful campaigns against the Romans, defeated them on the Rhine, and gained ground far into Germany, but they were finally cut off from their own territory and the Roman general Cerealis sent secret offers of peace to the Batavians. A meeting between the two leaders was arranged. Unfortunately in the middle of Tacitus' account of the negotiations his narrative breaks off, but it was believed that the Batavians entered into an honourable alliance with the Romans. They were no longer to be oppressed or taxed. All that they had to do was to provide help for the Romans when it was required. Moreover a 'very old stone' had been dug up on Dutch soil, which bore a Latin inscription: GENS BATAVORUM AMICI ET FRATRES ROM. IMP.[3] This in itself was enough to show their honourable position.

In view of the well-known greatness of ancient Rome the story was clearly an encouraging one, and, in particular during the Twelve Years' Truce of 1609 to 1621, striking parallels were drawn between the rebellion of the Batavians and the revolt of their descendants against the modern powerful oppressor Spain. The historian Pontanus included such a comparison in his description and history of Amsterdam, first published in the year 1611, in a

[1] *Germania*, xxix.
[2] Here Tacitus, *Historia*, IV, xii-xxxvii and liv-lxxix, and V, xiv-xxvi, and Dapper, *Beschryving*, pp. 2–8 and 365–9, have been referred to. Dapper mentions among authorities for the story the antique writers Dion, Julius Caesar, Pliny, Plutarch, Suetonius and Tacitus.
[3] Dapper, op. cit., p. 8, citing Hadrianus Junius: 'The Batavian people, friends and brothers of the Roman Empire'.

passage entitled: 'A digression in which the present revolt of the Dutch against the Spaniards, led by the Prince of Orange, is compared with that which took place in past times under Claudius Civilis, when these same Batavians or Dutchmen were vexed by the Roman yoke, which was not at all unlike this Spanish one'.[1] In the year that followed engravings by Tempesta based on illustrations of the Batavian Rebellion by Otto van Veen were in circulation, and Van Veen also made paintings of the rebellion, composing his works with an antiquarian's care.[2] Added to this, translations of Tacitus into Dutch, not all of them accurate, were published in 1612, 1614, 1616, and 1630, which suggests that there was a growing interest in the subject.[3] P. C. Hooft made a further translation which was scholarly and accurate. It was begun about 1630 but was not published until 1684.

In 1648 the parallel drawn between the rebellion of the Batavians against the Romans and that of the United Provinces against Spain became an exact one, and the likeness between the two events was pointed to triumphantly. The story of the Batavians was illustrated in the second of the three shows given by order of the burgomasters of Amsterdam during the celebration of the proclamation of the peace[4]. Scene by scene, and heralded by trumpets, the Batavian heroes and the events of their history appeared and were likened to the heroes and events of the rebellion against Spain. Moreover in the oration made to the States of Holland and West Friesland on the occasion of the proclamation the speaker, after hailing Augustus as the founder of peace and granting that he had been carried in triumph preceded by the trophies of war, turned to the Batavians, and addressed them rhetorically with these words:

> You, columns of Batavians, have put out the fire of war by word and deed and authority, and shall triumph with a better right (you who put on show the horrible Erinys, menacing Bellona and blood-besprinkled Tisiphone fettered and chained) and shall be called 'Protectors of the Human Race'; yes, what is more, your likenesses will be seen hanging in a row in galleries, displayed in market places, skilfully cast in bronze, cut in ivory, carved in marble, and put on show, so that even the houses, sharing in your praise, triumph in it and spur on the lords of future times to virtue.[5]

[1] Johannes Isacius Pontanus, *Rerum et urbis Amstelodamensium historia* [etc.], Amsterdam, 1611, p. 53. "Digressio in comparationem Defectionis hujus Hollandorum ab Hispanis, duce Auriaco; et ejus, quae facta est olim, auspicijs Claudii Civilis, cum ijdem Batavi sive Hollandi jugo Romanorum, Hispanico isti haud absimili, divexarentur."

[2] See Van de Waal, op. cit., I, pp. 210–15.

[3] H. Bruch, *P. C. Hooft, Boexken van Cornelis Tacitus . . . in het Nederlands vertaald* [etc.] (Kleine Dietse Keur), The Hague, n.d., pp. 5–6.

[4] Geeraardt Brandt de Jonge, 'Beschryving van de zes middelste vertooningen; die, door last der E.E. Heeren Burgermeesteren, t' Amsteldam vertoont zyn', in *Olyf-krans*, 1750, pp. 103–10. Dapper, *Beschryving*, pp. 249–51, describes all three shows and the way in which they were presented.

[5] 'Trompet of lofrede', in *Olyf-krans*, 1750, p. XXIX. "Gy, *Kolommen der Batavieren*, hebt met raad en daat

It was thus natural that representations of the Batavian Rebellion should be 'put on show' in a prominent position in the new Town Hall, the city's principal monument of the peace and at the same time a solid expression of her present greatness.[1] The events chosen for depiction were among those illustrated by Van Veen and engraved by Tempesta, and likenesses show that the works of these artists were referred to in making the designs. The incidents represented in the show given at the peace celebrations were not the same, but the two series, as was inevitable, ended with the same scene: 'The swearing of the peace with Cerealis, Vespasian's general, who accepted the brave Batavians once again as the allies and friends of the Roman people'.[2]

If borrowings from the ancient world were common throughout western Europe at the time here at least they must have seemed to be justified by history. The agreement between Claudius Civilis and Cerealis might be taken to be a symbol of the equal greatness of the Batavians and the Romans, and the glory of ancient Rome was taken to be the prototype of Amsterdam's present splendour. Perhaps this accounts for the gusto and exuberance with which antique forms and motifs were used in the Town Hall, both in its architecture and formal decoration, and in its decoration with ideas expressed symbolically. It was to be: 'Not the last but the first of the seven wonders so widely famed throughout the world'.[3] It was in fact to surpass the wonders of the ancient world.

The poet Asselijn, from one of whose works this quotation is taken, wrote that the inauguration of the new building, which would be 'censed by Peace', would be like that of the temples and the Town Hall of Rome, which were dedicated by Numa Pompilius when, in a time of peace, he went up into the Capitol.[4] Vondel made a similar comparison in his song on the laying of the foundation-stone of the new Town Hall,[5] and in his poem on its inauguration, after describing the fire which destroyed the old building, he commended the

en gezagh den brandt des oorloghs uitgebluscht, en zult met beter recht mogen triomfeeren, die de gruwelyke Erinnis, dreigende Bellone, en met bloedt besprenkelde Tisifone geboeit en geketent ten toon voert, en *Behoeders van het menschelyke geslacht* genoemt wort: ja, dat meer is, men zal uwe afbeeldingen in galeryen op een ry zien ophangen, op merkten pralen, kunstig van koper gegoten, van ivoor gesneden, in marmor uitgehouwen, en over al te pronk gestelt, zoo dat ook zelfs de huizen, deelachtigh van uwen lof, hier mede triomfeeren, en de nakomende Heeren tot deught zullen aanprikkelen."

[1] For a discussion of these paintings, and further references, see Van de Waal, op. cit., pp. 215–38.

[2] Brandt, op. cit., p. 110: "'t besweeren der Vreede met Cerealis de Veldt-Heer van Vespasiaan, die de dappre Batavieren weêr voor Bontgenooten en Vrienden van 't Roomsche Volk aan neemt".

[3] Asselijn, 'Broederschap der schilderkunst', in *Hollantsche Parnas*, p. 28: ". . . het laatste niet, maar d'eerste van de zeeven Der wonderen zo wyd de Werelt door berucht".

[4] Op. cit., p. 29.

[5] 'Bouwzang', *Werken*, V. pp. 368–9.

competence of the city council to choose and to keep to a good plan for the new. Then, as a parallel and by the context suggesting that it may to some extent have been regarded as a model, he described what he called "Latinus raethuis", 'the town hall of Latium', in a passage based on Virgil's description of the building in the *Aeneid*, of which Vondel had published his prose translation in 1646.[1] The parallel is not exact, but by the time Virgil's description of the building as a senate-house had been expanded and references to the sanctity of the place, to the dedication of kings which took place there, and to sacrificial feasts had been suppressed it was tolerably close, and the particulars of the building itself and of its decoration have some likeness to those of the Town Hall of Amsterdam. As it was described by Virgil[2] the Palace of Latium, 'stately and vast, towering with a hundred columns', stood in a prominent position in the city. It was decorated with statues of the Latin kings:

> . . . carved of old cedar – Italus and father Sabinus, planter of the Vine, guarding in his image the curved pruning-hook, and aged Saturn, and the likeness of two-faced Janus – all standing in the vestibule; and other kings from the beginning, and they who had suffered wounds of war, fighting for their fatherland. Many arms, moreover, hang on the sacred doors, captive chariots, curved axes, helmet-crests, and massive bars of gates; javelins and shields and beaks wrenched from ships.[3]

The full edition of Vondel's translation of the *Aeneid* into verse, which was published in 1660, was dedicated to Cornelis de Graeff, a patron of the arts in Amsterdam who, as a member of the committee set up in the early stages to consider plans for the Town Hall, and as a burgomaster in 1648, 1651, 1652 and 1655 and treasurer in the intervening years, must have been concerned with its scheme throughout its development.[4] In his dedication Vondel describes

[1] *Inwydinge*, lines 1289–1306. The source is pointed to by Kronenberg and by other commentators.
[2] *Aeneid*, VII, lines 170–86.
[3] Quoted, with translation, from H. Rushton Fairclough, *Virgil* (Loeb Classical Library), London [etc.], II, 1918, p. 15:
  . . . antiqua e cedro, Italusque paterque Sabinus
  vitisator, curvam servans sub imagine falcem,
  Saturnusque senex Ianique bifrontis imago,
  vestibulo adstabant aliique ab origine reges
  Martiaque ob patriam pugnando volnera passi.
  multaque praeterea sacris in postibus arma,
  captivi pendent currus curvaeque secures
  et cristae capitum et portarum ingentia claustra
  spiculaque clipeique ereptaque rostra carinis.
[4] Dapper, *Beschryving*, p. 331, writes of the committee responsible, which included De Graeff: "En hebben ook deze Bouwmeesters hun overvliegend verstant en schrandre herssenen, aen dit meester stuck, zoodanigh doen blijken, dat de lof en eere, die hen 'er van toekomt, noit der vergetel zal overgelevert worden" ('And

how Virgil's account of the rise of Rome from small beginnings reminds De Graeff, whom he addresses, of the rise of the fishing village of Amsterdam, the new city of the Batavians, built by them and shining out before the whole world.[1] From this, Vondel continues, you go on to remember the events of the rebellion of the Batavians of antiquity against Roman oppression, and, in remembering them, 'your vigilant mind is anxious to clothe the city's Capitol and arches with a series of victorious wars painted with art, illustrating them from the beginning, to the end where Rome recognizes our Batavians as allies'.[2] The train of thought is unexpected; it was Tacitus and not Virgil who wrote about the Batavians and might be supposed to inspire De Graeff with such ideas for the decoration of the new Town Hall. Yet when the contemporary view of history and of the circumstances in which Virgil wrote are considered with it, Vondel's reasoning seems probable enough, and the poet himself had described these circumstances in the life of Virgil with which he prefaced his prose translation of the Aeneid in 1646, beginning it with the words:

> When Octavius Augustus, Julius Caesar's successor and heir, had happily concluded the civil war . . . it was useful that his princely honour and authority as well as the dignity of the new kingdom and of its most excellent and oldest families, should be increased and confirmed by some magnificent and excellent work of Latin poetry . . . about the Latin predecessors and leaders who, with so great a praise and renown, spread the illustrious deeds of the ancient heroes, their forefathers and fellow-countrymen, over the wide world, and exalted them. . . . Then for [the making of] such a masterpiece a genius was required corresponding to the greatness and importance of the matter; and for this it was a remarkable piece of good fortune that . . . Publius Virgilius Maro flourished at that time.[3]

these men who were responsible for the building have shown their excellent understanding and ingenious brains to such an extent in this masterpiece that the praise and honour that is due to them will never be handed over to oblivion'). Vermeulen, *Handboek*, III, pp. 232–3, claims that the completion of the main floor of the Town Hall was largely due to De Graeff and to his financial support. De Graeff composed the inscription on the panel in the *vierschaar* commemorating the laying of the foundation-stone (Vondel, *Inwydinge*, lines 598–604). He was in close contact with Flinck (Houbraken, *Schouburgh*, II, p. 22), and his brother and successor in the city government, Andries, conveyed payments and a gift from the city to Jordaens (MS. *Res. Thes. Ord.*, 28 Apr. and 13 June 1662); both these artists worked for the Town Hall.

[1] 'Parnasloof', *Werken*, VI, pp. 88–89.

[2] Op. and loc. cit., lines 105–9. Quoted by Van de Waal, op. cit., I, pp. 219–20, who points out that the passage suggests De Graeff was prominent in working for the inclusion of the story of the Batavians in the Town Hall's decoration. "Schikt" might also be translated 'takes care'.

> Dan schikt uw wackre geest stadts Kapitool en boogen
> Te kleeden met een ry zeeghaftige oorelogen,
> Geschildert naer de kunst, van vore tot het endt,
> Daer Rome ons Bataviers voor bondtgenooten kent.

[3] Op. cit., VI, p. 45. "Toen Ocktaviaen August, Iulius Cezars nazaet en erfgenaem, den burgerlijcken oorloogh gelukkigh had beslecht, . . . was het dienstigh, dat 's Vorsten eere en gezagh, oock het aenzien van 't nieuwe Rijck en des zelfs voortreffelijckste en outste geslachten vermeert en bevestight werden, door

If Virgil was seen in this light in mid-seventeenth-century Amsterdam his work may well have been one of the sources of inspiration for the new Town Hall, the visible monument of the city's new status and dignity. It may not only have inspired the series of paintings depicting the deeds of the Batavians, 'they who had suffered wounds fighting for their fatherland', but may have provided ideas for other features of the building as well: for the splendour of its architecture, for the figures of the antique gods, in default of further distinguished ancestors, 'all standing in the vestibule', and for trophies, though here many of these are of a peaceful kind.[1] Vondel's borrowing is therefore of interest, and the connection with De Graeff is important. It suggests that he was instrumental in including the history of the Batavians in the decorative scheme[2] and provides one of the very few pieces of evidence as to the scheme's authorship that have so far come to light. This evidence points (though it does no more) in a likely direction, for De Graeff was brought up in humanist circles, his father was a friend of Lipsius and of the historian and translator of Tacitus P. C. Hooft, and he was himself Hooft's son-in-law.[3] It would not be surprising if Hooft had suggested or inspired the inclusion of the Batavian scenes in the decoration of the new Town Hall, or if the scheme as a whole was conceived in the intellectual circle which he had dominated.[4]

eenigh heerlijck en uitstekende werck van Latijnsche Poëzye, . . . der Latijnen voorgangers en aenleiders, die, met zoo groot eenen lof en naemhaftigheit, de doorluchtige daden der aeloude helden, hunne voorvaderen en lantslieden, over de wijde weerelt uitbreidden, en in top haelden; . . . Tot zulck een meesterstuck dan wert een vernuft ge-eischt naer mate van de grootheit en 't gewight der zaecke; en hier toe besloegh wonder wel, dat . . . ten dien tijde PUBLIUS VIRGILIUS MARO bloeide."

[1] Military trophies were to have been represented in the Burgerzaal (Vennekool, *Afbeelding*, pls. H and R); further designs representing trophies destined for the Town Hall are shown by H. Quellien, *Statuen*, II, pl. T. It is not clear whether the trophies planned for the council chamber of the Civic Guard were part of the original design (see Bibliography s.v. Vennekool). The panels within the arches between galleries and stairs bear carvings of objects connected with the planets near them, arranged in the form commonly used for trophies in Renaissance art.

[2] De Graeff's concern with the building and interest in the arts strongly support the suggestion. In the dedication of his *Batavische Broeders*, 1663, to Simon van Hoorn, *Werken*, IX, p. 901, Vondel described how on looking at Tempesta's prints of the Batavian story his "lust vast verlangde dat die historien, door last der Burgermeesteren treflijck geschildert, de galery van ons Kapitool, op eene ry, moghten bekleeden" ('[his] desire greatly longed that those histories, in a series, excellently painted by order of the Burgomasters, might clothe the gallery of our Capitol'), and his zeal to write the tragedy was aroused. Yet as Van de Waal points out, op. and loc. cit., this does not necessarily imply that the paintings were Vondel's idea in the first place. Van de Waal analyses the relationships between the paintings and Tempesta's engravings which Vondel's words suggest.

[3] He married Cornelia Hooft as his second wife in 1635. Hooft died in 1647, when plans, though not the final ones, had already been made for the new Town Hall.

[4] Constantijn Huygens was a member of this circle, the Muiderkring. In 1640 he had visited it with Van Campen; see Huygens, *Werken*, III, p. 134, note. At this time the decision to rebuild the Town Hall had not been taken.

Throughout the whole of its structure and decoration the Town Hall has a triumphant mood and a serious purpose, and it is as though a great oration concerning the nature of the city's life had been given visible form in it. The events of the time in which the Town Hall was built and their apparent relation to past history helped to create the statements made in it and to determine the language in which they were expressed, and history itself, as part of the cosmos of the life of Amsterdam, also found expression in it. The passages in which history takes pride of place may provide a key to the understanding of the rest, and so they have been given precedence in this discussion. But the symbolism of each passage can only be fully understood in relation to the whole and to the life that went on in and around the building, which gave it scale and completed the parallels that it drew. The Town Hall must be seen as a single statement of a most complex kind, extended in space to beyond the limits of the building, and cumulative in its effect.

The sculptures of the two gable-ends of the Town Hall are linked up by the garlands of shell and ships' instruments, of fruit and flowers, that hang round the building, and by the merchandise brought in from sea and land that was unloaded outside its doors. Together they form a single figure of the glory of Amsterdam. In one of the reliefs the sea does homage to her and in the other, in which the trade of Amsterdam is represented,[1] the land. She is surrounded by virtues, the figures that stand on the pediments' ends. On the western pediment Atlas supports the globe of the heavens above her and the world is at her feet. She appears in this complex representation very much as she did in the last of the shows given on the Dam during the peace celebrations of 1648, in a scene which was entitled 'The Mother of Peace':

> Bless'd Amsterdam, surrounded by water-multitudes, now wields Neptune's fork as empress of the freshwater and salt waves. Her head is bewigged with a crown of prows. Fame bestrides her throne and blows her trumpet of praise. Justice, the strength of cities, Freedom, the aged Discipline, Religion and Peace are arrayed at her right side. She has Trade, Plenty, Wealth, Unity and Faithfulness, whose nature is sincere, at her left hand. All her city wards are swarming with foreign traders. Black-coloured Africa gives her ivory, blood coral and gold. America gives her sugar-cane, and silver, and wood which the unexplored forest of the west may boast of. And Asia gives her silks, and pearls, and flowers, with censers and other treasures. Their princes stand amazed now that they see the rich city on the Amstel blazing so gloriously on her throne. Good fortune gives

---

[1]   See pp. 171–85 below. The subject is so named in Dapper's *Beschryving*, p. 339, and in other descriptions.

her her hand. Those who denounce disastrous War greet her from afar as the
Mother of Peace. So Rome boasted in the time of Augustus.[1]

With this splendid spectacle Amsterdam's official celebration of the 'Eternal
Peace' was brought to an end:

> ... But the joy and happiness of the citizens was reflected by heaven and earth
> that night, with thousands of tar-barrels, and fireworks, which were let off into
> the air not only on the towers but throughout the whole city. And Amsterdam,
> after quenching the fire of war, seemed to be on fire everywhere. With this
> great splendour and illustrious preparation the peace was celebrated after eighty
> years of war.[2]

[1] Vos, 'Beschryving der Vertooningen', *Gedichten* [1], pp. 585–6:
Gezeegendt Amsterdam, omheint van Waaterschaaren
Zwaait nu, als Kaizerin der zoet' en zoute baaren,
De gaffel van Neptuin: haar hooft is met een kroon
Van steevens geperruikt. de Faam beschrijt haar troon,
En steekt haar loftrompet. 't Gerecht, de kracht der Steede',
De Vryheidt, d'oude Tucht, de Godsdienst en de Vreede,
Bekleên haar rechte zy. de Neering, d'Overvloedt.
De Rijkdom, d'Eendracht, en de Trouw, oprecht van moedt,
Heeftz' aan haar slinkehandt. het krielt in al haar wijke'
Van vreemde handelaars. het zwart geverfd' Afrijke
Beschenkt haar met yvoor, met bloetkraal, en met goudt;
Amerike met riet, met zilver, en met hout,
Daar 't ongebaande bosch in 't westen op mach roemen;
En Azië met zijd, met paarlen en met bloemen,
Met wierooktellegen, en allerhande schat.
Haar Vorsten staan verbaast, nu zy de rijke stadt
Aan d'Aamstel, op haar troon zoo heerelijk zien blaaken.
't Geluk biedt haar de handt. die 't heillooz' Oorloogh wraaken
Begroeten haar van veer voor Moeder van de Rust.
Zoo bralden 't oude Room' in 't leeven van August.

[2] Dapper, *Beschryving*, p. 251, passage following a description of the shows on the Dam. "... maer de
vreught en blyschap der Burgeren, deed des nachts hemel en aerde weerlichten, door duizenden van teer-
tonnen, en vuur-werken, die niet alleen op de toorens, maer door de gansche stadt in de lucht geschooten
wierden. En Amsterdam, na 't blussen van den brandt des oorloghs, scheen geheel in vlam te staen. Door
zoo veel glans en doorluchtigen toestel, wiert hier de vrede, na tachtentigh Jaren oorloghs, geviert."

CHAPTER III

THE SONG OF AMPHION

Two of the three shows that were given on the Dam during the peace cele-brations of 1648 have been referred to, but the third, with which the proceedings opened, must be mentioned here.[1] It began with a scene in which the virtues of Prince Willem I were shown 'in the form of Amphion'[2] to the wondering public, and, lest there should be any doubt about the identity of these virtues, their personifications surrounded Amphion on the scene. The author of the show, Samuel Coster, listed seven of them, Justice, Wisdom, Prudence, Valour, Constancy, Strength, and Impartiality, and left it to the imagination of the reader to supply the rest. The scene bore the title "Moderata Durant"[3] and a verse written in Dutch by which the figure was explained:

> As Amphion, by his virtues and good-naturedness, and by being indulgent, brought the city of Thebes to the very greatest dignity, [so] Prince Willem, by good judgement, draws together people of every kind and every occupation here in this country.[4]

In the scenes that followed the virtues of Prince Maurits, Prince Frederik Hen-drik and Prince Willem II were represented in much the same way by the figures of Numa Pompilius, who established religion and preserved it by his just government, Fabius Maximus, who withstood the campaigns of Hannibal, and Augustus, under whom peace was established in Rome. The virtues of the States of Holland and West Friesland were then represented, in a scene entitled 'Whoever owns the cow, catch her by the horns',[5] which showed:

> Argus, with a hundred eyes, by which are meant the Lords of the States of Holland, who will never let themselves be played to sleep by a crafty Mercury . . . but, as careful watchmen, will look after the cow (that is, the fatherland which is dear to all of them).[6]

[1] Described by Samuel Coster in 'Korte verklaring der zes eerste vertooningen, gedaan binnen Amsterdam, op de Eeuwige Vreede, door last der E.E. Heeren Burgemeesteren' in *Olyf-krans*, 1750, pp. 111–14. Partic-ulars and quotations are from this source unless otherwise stated. The six scenes are illustrated in an engraving by Pieter Nolpe.

[2] Dapper, *Beschryving*, p. 249.

[3] Translated as "Maat hout staat"; '[What has] measure endures [or supports the state].'

[4]   Gelyk *Amphion* door zyn deughden en goed-aerdicheyt,
    En bot te vieren, bracht tot d'alderhoogste waerdicheyt
    De Stad van Thaebe, lokt *Prins Wellem* door verstand
    Het volk van alle slagh en neering hier in't Land.

[5] "Die de Koe zyn is, vatze by de Hoornen".

[6] "*Argus* met hondert oogen, daer mede bediedende de Heeren Staten van Holland, die haer, door het lieflyk pypen van eenen Loozen *Mercurius* . . . nimmermeer in 't slaep laten spelen, maer de Koe (dat is haer elk aengename Vaderland) als wakende sorg-dragers, wel sullen bewaren."

The verse explaining this scene read as follows:

> I notice, I see, I know, how craftily everyone has tried to get this milking cow into his possession. But no, I'm not asleep, I shall not get caught by Mercury's lovely piping as others have done.[1]

It was only necessary to show Mars being chained, Vulcan being forbidden to make arms, and soldiers receiving their dismissal to bring this series of scenes to a happy conclusion.

Amphion was represented, as we have seen, on the medal cast to commemorate the inauguration of the new Town Hall of Amsterdam which took place seven years later, and two great reliefs (illus. 65–66), one representing Amphion playing his lyre before the rising walls of Thebes and the other Mercury piping to a watchful and determined Argus, were placed in the Burgerzaal above the doors at its eastern end that led to the chamber of justice and the burgomasters' chamber. The relief representing Mercury and Argus is to the southern side and so was above the entrance to the burgomasters' chamber, and it is evident that the symbol of the eternally watchful Argus was applied to them; here the figure of Argus is based on the Farnese Hercules, to indicate his incomparable strength. Hubertus Quellien, the brother of Artus, in his book of engravings of the sculpture of the Town Hall, connects the relief with the room and describes it in these words: 'Mercury, who fain would play Argus to sleep, while Argus stands and watches, so that this cow shall not be taken away from him'.[2] Here the cow, in fact, no longer represents the United Provinces of the Netherlands, but symbolises the rich city of Amsterdam, watched over by its burgomasters. In a later description of the relief it is pointed out that it serves as a reminder to the burgomasters themselves.[3] The relief representing Amphion, 'who by harmony built the city of Thebes',[4] was described by Hubertus Quellien as being above the chamber of justice, and by a later writer as being applicable to it.[5] The figure was also applicable to the whole purpose of the building and to the Burgerzaal itself, for it told the story of the origins of citizenship:

---

[1]   Ik merk, ik zie, ik weet, hoe listich elk getracht
       Heeft, deeze Mellik-Koe te krygen in zyn macht.
       Maer neen ik slaepe niet, ik zal my niet vergrypen
       Als andre deeden door *Mercurius* Lieflyk pypen.
[2]   *Statuen*, II, Index, entry for pl. A. "Mercurius, die Argus geeren in 't slaep wilde speelen, maer Argus die staet en waeckt, op dat hem die Koe niet ontnomen en wort."
[3]   *Bouw schilder en beeldhouwkonst*, p. 8, description of pl. XLV.
[4]   *Statuen*, II, Index, entry for pl. B. ". . . die door 't goedt accoort de Stadt van Theben opbouwden."
[5]   *Bouw schilder en beeldhouwkonst*, p. 8, description of pl. XLIV.

Pausanias said ... that he and Orpheus were Egyptians and that they excelled in magic arts. They say that he was expert in music and that he was wont to lead wild animals and stones where he liked; for by the sweetness of his speech he civilized hard and savage people and won them over to building cities and to observing the cities' laws.[1]

This account of Amphion, which was given by Natales Conti in his *Mythologiae* of 1551, was taken over by Van Mander in his explanation of Ovid's *Metamorphoses*.[2] Van Mander added, it appears, further opinions of his own about unity and government, and omitted the end of Conti's story, which describes how Amphion was punished for usurping the powers of the gods. Van Mander's description was borrowed in Dapper's account of the Town Hall, with only minor alterations of wording, to explain the meaning of the relief,[3] and the theme was taken up again in eighteenth-century guide-books to the building. The explanation given in one of these, intended for the English visitor, may be quoted:

> This Amphion was a Man, who by his wit, eloquent speeches, and easy govern-ment gather'd the unruly people that liv'd of great distances from one another, in one body by good laws and manners, and made them to dwell together, he taught them to build houses and walls about the cities, and us'd them to live easy and quiet.[4]

The two reliefs provide an effective contrast between the eloquence that achieves noble results and eloquence that beguiles, though this contrast is not referred to by the authors who explain them.

The oratory of the Town Hall itself, like that of Amphion, seems to have been of a dynamic and a constructive kind, for the building was not only designed to express Amsterdam's newly-won glory and to serve, as we have seen, as a 'memorial to future ages'. Vondel likened it to a refuge where the watchful eye of the members of the city government [like the many eyes of Argus] guarded the citizens. He likened it to a house, enclosing, and by its government

---

[1] Conti, *Mythologiae*, p. 462. "Hunc [Amphion] & Orpheum fuisse Aegyptios & magorum scientia excelluisse ait Paus [anias] ... Aiunt hunc musicae fuisse peritum, & saxa ac feras, quo vellet, ducere solitum: quoniam per orationis suavitatem duros & agrestes homines mansue fecerit, & ad extruendas civitates, civitatumque legibus obtemperandum delinierit."

[2] *Wtleggingh*, fol. 52 r.

[3] *Beschryving*, p. 376. This account was based on Van Mander but not on Conti, since the writer took over not only Van Mander's addition but also a misreading by Van Mander of Conti's text. Where Conti gives "Fuisse Aegyptios ... ait Paus." Van Mander has "*Pausanias* schrijft, dat een Egypter hem eens seyde" ('Pausanias writes that an Egyptian once told him') and Van Mander's phrase is taken over word for word in Dapper's account.

[4] From an English edition of *Beschryvinge van 't Stadhuis; Description of the Cityhouse of Amsterdam*, Amsterdam, 1782, p. 54.

supporting, the many thousand houses of the city, and to a heart, nourishing the members of the community and keeping them alive:

Human weakness needs to be strengthened by reward and punishment. This demands authority and lawful order. Authority and order at once point to the distinction between the people and citizens, and the office of the Government. That office demands a place, a house chosen for it, for the service of the city. So the Town Hall is born here out of necessity, for the benefit of the republican State. So town halls serve everywhere as refuge and sanctuary for the people, who, free from all cares, peacefully carry on their trade, and go to sleep on those assurances [i.e. the town halls, which may be compared to] the Fathers' eye that watches over the children and takes heed before the storm comes near to the gates and walls. So the people suffer no trouble from shipwreck when the squalls of war blow up, which strike republics and throw them to the ground unless protection is given by heaven. Heaven maintains the Lords of the city government and, by means of such pillars as they, supports many thousands of houses as though they were enclosed in one Town Hall, the heart of the whole city and of the faithful fellow-citizens. These thank the heart for its living glow, while it nourishes all the members of the civic body and keeps them alive for many hundreds of years.[1]

The Town Hall was evidently intended, in being a symbol of Amsterdam's risen glory and a memorial to it, in providing fitting accommodation for the departments of the city government, and also by embellishing and illustrating the functions which Vondel mentioned in all their diversity and in detail, to

---

[1] Vondel, *Inwydinge*, lines 49–69. As M. E. Kronenberg notices there is a play between the words *vryborg*, 'sanctuary', and *borgen*, 'assurances'. In the phrase 'the Fathers' eye' City Fathers (burgomasters) are referred to.

De zwackheit van den mensch behoeft gestut te worden
Door loon, en straf, dit eischt gezagh, en wettige orden:
Gezagh en orden melt terstont het onderscheit
Van volck en burgerye en 't ampt der Overheit:
Het ampt vereischt een plaets, en huis, hier toe gekoren,
Ten dienst der stede; aldus wort hier 't Stehuis geboren,
Uit een nootwendigheit, tot heil van 's burgers Staet.
Stadthuizen dienen dan alom ten toeverlaet
En vryborgh van het volck, dat, vry van alle zorgen,
Gerust zijn' handel dryft, en heenslaept op die borgen,
Het oogh der Vaderen, dat voor de kindren waeckt,
En toeziet, eer de storm de poorte en wal genaeckt.
Dus lydt het volck geen' last van schipbreucke, in 't verheffen
Der oorloghsbuien, die de burgerstaeten treffen,
En storten in den grond, ten zy 't de hemel schutt',
Die Heeren hanthaeft, en door zulcke pylers stut
Veel duizent huizen, als in een Stehuis gesloten,
Het hart van al de stadt en trouwe stadtgenooten,
Die 't hart bedancken voor zyn' levendigen gloet;
Terwijl het al de leên der burgerye voedt,
In 't leven onderhoudt, veel honderden van jaeren.

nourish the civic life of Amsterdam and to encourage the virtues of good government and of citizenship.

Geerardt Brandt, Vondel's biographer and the author of one of the shows given on the Dam during the peace celebrations of 1648, describes how at the feast held on St. Luke's day 1653 in Amsterdam the arts of poetry and painting were symbolically united, and how the poet Vondel was crowned by a person representing Apollo as he sat in the place of honour at the painters' feast.[1] In recognition of this honour Vondel dedicated his translation of the poetry of Horace, published in 1654, 'to the painters, sculptors, draughtsmen and their well-wishers' who were present, and in his short foreword to the work,[2] which was addressed to them, he discussed the relationship of poetry and the visual arts, and stated: 'Everyone is saying now, from Plutarch, that painting is silent Poetry, Poetry speaking painting'.[3] The close relationship between poetry and painting, a theme which runs through Renaissance criticism,[4] had been brought to the fore in Holland during the first half of the seventeenth century, and it seems to have triumphed at this moment in Amsterdam. The publication in the early years of the century of Van Mander's explanation of the *Metamorphoses* of Ovid, stated on the title-page to be 'Very useful to painters, poets, and art lovers,[5] was in itself an acknowledgement of the equivalence of the two arts. Franciscus Junius, in his book on the painting of the ancients, which was published in Latin in 1637 and in Dutch in 1641, discussed the subject at length.[6] The publication in 1644 of the Dutch translation of the *Iconologia* of Cesare Ripa by Dirk Pietersz. Pers,[7] an acquaintance of Vondel and his first publisher, shows that a more extensive handbook on the use of poetic and pictorial imagery than that of Van Mander was by then in demand in Holland. The very large number of emblem books which were published there from the sixteenth century onwards shows that there was a general preoccupation with

---

[1] P. J. Leendertsz. Jun., *Het leven van Joost van den Vondel door Geerardt Brandt*, The Hague, 1932, pp. 44–45.

[2] Vondel, *Werken*, VII, pp. 261–2. Dated 27 Nov. 1653.

[3] "Van Plutarchus heeft elck nu in den mont dat schildery stomme Poëzy, de Poëzy spreeckende schildery is."

[4] For its history see Rensselaer W. Lee, 'Ut Pictura Poesis; the Humanistic Theory of Painting', *Art Bulletin*, XXII, 1940, pp. 197–269.

[5] The *Wtleggingh*, published with Van Mander's treatise on painting in 1604: "Seer dienstich den Schilders, Dichters, en Constbeminders".

[6] *De pictura veterum libri tres*, Amsterdam, 1637, and *De schilder-konst der Oude, begrepen in drie boecken*, Middelburgh, 1641. Chapter IV of Book I is devoted to the relationship between poetry and painting.

[7] See Bibliography s.v. Ripa. B. H. Molkenboer discusses the relationship between Pers and Vondel, 'Vondel's drukkers en uitgevers', *Vondel-Kroniek*, XII, 1941, pp. 34–62.

symbolism of this kind,[1] and the tendency to think in emblematic terms was a very strong one.[2] There was moreover a fashion which was very marked in Holland for writing verses in which the significance of paintings was described, for adding such verses to engravings, and for painting them on the frames of pictures so that, as in the emblem books and in the pageants given on occasions of public rejoicing, pictorial and poetic arts were used together to convey a single symbolic meaning.

Poetry was combined with painting in this way in the Town Hall of Amsterdam, where explanatory verses were painted under many of the pictures, and further, the visual arts of architecture, sculpture, and painting were combined there to convey its message. This was recognized at the time, for in the poem *Broederschap der Schilderkunst*, which was written by Thomas Asselijn on the occasion of the artists' feast held a year after that at which Vondel was crowned,[3] the god Mercury describes their gathering and how these artists bring glory to the goddess of painting in these words:

> These are the Phoenixes whose brave heroic pieces brag forth her praise, no age shall oppress her. Each one makes himself famous by his art. Architecture and Sculpture now [are] coupled to her brush; these seem to burn with love for one another.[4]

'In this way', Mercury adds, 'a state, a kingdom, can be immortalized'. It is clear from the context of the passage as well as from the circumstances in which the poem was composed that in writing these lines Asselijn must have had the Town Hall foremost in his mind,[5] and it may justifiably be assumed that they characterize it. The poet in all probability was in contact with the leading

---

[1] For Dutch emblem books see A. G. C. de Vries, *De Nederlandsche emblemata* [etc.], Amsterdam, 1899, and Mario Praz, *Studies in Seventeenth-century Imagery* (Studies of the Warburg Institute), London, 1939–47, Vol. II (Bibliography).

[2] See W. A. P. Smit, *Van Pascha tot Noah* [etc.], Zwolle, 1956–, I, Introduction. In this work the emblematic character of Vondel's dramas is pointed out and analysed.

[3] See Bibliography s.v. Asselijn.

[4] 'Broederschap der Schilderkunst', in *Hollantsche Parnas*, pp. 30–31:
Dit zyn de Fenixen, wiens dappre helden-stukken,
Uitbrallen haren lof, geen tyt zal haar verdrukken.
En ieder maakt zich hier door zyne konst ve[r]maardt.
De Bouw en Beeldkonst nu aan haar Pençeel gepaart;
Die schynen onderling van liefde hier te blaaken.

[5] The passage from which the lines come closes with another reference to sculpture, and to architecture, 'which shows the splendour of her glory while she thus rises daily to the heaven[s]' (p. 31). In its context the word 'thus' can only refer to the description earlier in the poem of the buildings of Amsterdam. Of those mentioned only the Town Hall, the last referred to, was being built when the poem was written, and Asselijn described it in almost the same words, as 'the Town Hall . . . whose façade rises daily' (p. 28). For the circumstances of the poem's composition see Bibliography s.v. Asselijn.

artists among those who decorated the building and he was an admirer of Van Campen, for he pleaded after the architect's death that honour should be done to his memory, calling him the support of Dutch architecture.[1] It is not likely that Asselijn recognized the use of the three arts as a single means of expression in the building by considering plans, models, or the half-finished work itself, nor that he stumbled on the principle by chance as a poetic fiction, and it seems much more probable that he heard it discussed in artistic circles in Amsterdam. If this is the case it is most likely that the complementary use of architecture, sculpture, and painting in the Town Hall to produce one complex statement was deliberately and consciously thought out during the planning of the building, as the changes made in the design in the years 1648 to 1650 seem to indicate,[2] and as the building itself suggests. It is perhaps worth noticing that no second statement to the effect of that made by Asselijn has as yet been found, and that only he, of all the writers whose works have bearing on the nature of the building as a whole, seems to have had close connections with this circle. Of such writers only Meyster, whose tendency was to miss general principles by his short-sighted contemplation of a wealth of detail, is likely to have been able to draw his information from a still better source.[3] Vondel, however, in the foreword to the Amsterdam artists mentioned earlier, named sculpture as well as painting each time that he referred to the likeness and relationship between the two sister arts, only failing to do so when he was quoting from antique writers.

In his book on the painting of the ancients Franciscus Junius, using terms which were applied to oratory by Cicero, described the function of painting in this way: 'The opportunity of painters agrees wholly with that of orators and poets, seeing that it allows them equally to teach, to please, and to move'.[4] Thus one of the bonds between poetry and painting, and between these and oratory, was their power to teach and to encourage virtue. It follows that what was written about this function primarily in connection with poetry was also relevant to the art of painting in seventeenth-century Holland, and indeed to sculpture as well in so far as this was used as a means of expressing ideas. Both

---

[1] In a poem on Van Campen's death, 'Uytvaart' [etc.], see Bibliography.
[2] See pp. 47–8 above and p. 79 below.
[3] See Bibliography s.v. Meyster.
[4] *De schilderkonst der Oude* [etc.], Middelburgh, 1641, p. 330. "De gheleghenheyd der Schilders met de gheleghenheyd van d'Orateuren ende Poeten t'eenemael over een komt; aenghesien het hun… ghelijckelick toestaet t'onderwijsen, te vermaecken, te beweghen." Based on Cicero, *De optimo genere Oratorum*, para. 1: "Optimus est enim orator qui dicendo animos audentium et docet et delectat et permovet".

63

Van Mander and Vondel were concerned with the didactic qualities of poetry. Van Mander explained, and Vondel translated, the *Metamorphoses* of Ovid, and in discussing this work both evidently wished to defend it against objections, made on religious grounds, to the untruthful and pagan fables that it contained, and it may well be that Calvinistic objections had the effect of bringing the educative value into prominence. Van Mander took care to point out, as others had done before him, that there was imagery in the Bible as strange as any used in poetry, and to show that Ovid's imagery could not be interpreted literally.[1] Vondel, introducing his translation of the *Metamorphoses* into Dutch verse, quoted St. Augustine as saying that 'When a concept of the imagination is given us to convey any meaning then it is no lie, but a certain flowered kind of truth', and that all that had been said by wise and holy men and even by Our Lord himself would be taken for lies if this were not so.[2] The use of poetic imagery was also liable to be called in question when it was expressed in visual terms. Hans Bontemantel recorded dryly that when in 1660 the city council authorized the burgomasters to provide suitable entertainment for the dowager Princess of Orange and the young Prince Willem III on a state visit to Amsterdam: 'Tulp requested that the burgomasters would please not have such heathen gods and goddesses ride on show on triumphal cars as was done when the House of Nassau was entertained in the previous year'.[3] Happily in this instance tradition was on the side of the gods and goddesses and their defence was easy, for Bontemantel's account continues: 'The burgomasters said that they were resolved to carry out the entertainment in the way in which . . . it was done last year'.[4] It would be interesting to know whether Dr. Tulp approved of the pagan imagery used in the decoration of the new Town Hall, but on that point the records are discreetly silent. Nothing is known about the circumstances in which the symbolic scheme of the building was decided on and it is quite possible that it was never discussed officially by the city council.[5]

Both Van Mander and Vondel drew on Natales Conti in composing their

[1] *Wtleggingh*, fol. *iiij r.

[2] *Werken*, VII, p. 387. "Wanneer ons een gedichtsel tot eenige bediedinge wort bygebragt, dan is het geene logen, maer een zekere gebloemde wyze van waerheit." From *Quaestiones Evangeliorum*, II, 51; see Vondel, *Werken*, VII, p. 890, note, where the passage is quoted.

[3] This and the following quotation are from Bontemantel, MS. *Resolutien*, II, i, p. 411. "Tulp versocht dat Burgemeesteren, geliefde sulcke hydense gooden en godinnen op Triump waegens als gedaen wierde inden voorleeden jaare op de festoyeringe vant huys van Nassauw niet ten toon te laaten om rijden".

[4] "Burgemeesteren syde van voor neemen te syn de onthaelinge te doen in manieren als . . . voorleeden jaere was gedaen."

[5] No record of its discussion either by burgomasters or the city council has been found. Not all the burgomasters' decisions were recorded, see List of Sources s.v. MS. *Res. Burg. and Oud-Burg.*

introductions,[1] and Vondel saw him as having played a leading part in bringing forward the hidden truths and the 'doctrines of virtue and of upright and civil association' that, as Plato had implied, were to be found in fables.[2] He also, for the third time in his published works, quoted from the passage in the *Republic* in which the use of fables in teaching children is described, which reads:

> Don't you understand . . . that we begin by telling children fables, and the fable is, taken as a whole, false, but there is truth in it also? . . . [Suitable stories should be chosen.] And the stories on the accepted list we will induce nurses and mothers to tell to the children and so shape their souls by these stories far rather than their bodies by their hands.[3]

Van Mander, as well as quoting from this passage, defined the function of the poet in ancient times.[4] Poets and wise men, he wrote, clothed the truths they had discovered 'in excellent disguises' to make others eager to learn them and to prevent them from being defiled. The poets were priests and were the keepers and expounders of holy mysteries, they were entrusted with the education of kings, and by their writings 'the laws of cities, just and trustworthy judgements and past sentences were held in honour and preserved'. 'By praising virtues and virtuous forefathers in a very charming and ingenious way [they] fired hearts' to follow after in the way of virtue and 'compelled' their hearers to look with great aversion on the path that leads to hell:

> For poetry, married to and united with the delightful art of song, taught all sciences and arts, and having more power than unembellished naked words without any measure poetry was the mother and nurturer of the happy and prosperous well-being of the community.[5]

After writing this passage Van Mander stressed once again the power of poetry to lead the soul to virtue, and then turned to other subjects.

In the account of the Town Hall that was published by Dapper in 1663[6] the meaning of a large part of its sculptured decoration was explained by passages

---

[1] Vondel, *Werken*, VII, p. 386, note (L. C. Michels).

[2] Op cit., VII, p. 387: "Leerstukken der zeden, en van oprechten en burgerlyken ommegang".

[3] *The Republic*, II, xvii. From the translation by Paul Storey (Loeb Classical Library), London [etc.], 1930-5. For Vondel's citations of this passage see *Werken*, I, p. 502, VII, p. 388, and X, p. 35.

[4] *Wtleggingh*, fol. *iij r. and v. The quotations are from these pages. *Aerdigh* in the original has been translated 'charming and ingenious' since Kilian's definition (see his *Etymologicum*) suggests it combined these meanings in Van Mander's day. 'Fired hearts' and 'compelled' are respectively "maeckten vyerighe borsten" and "dwonghen" in the original.

[5] "Daer toe t'Gedicht met de verheugende Sangh-const ghehouwt en vereenight, leerde alle wetenschappen en Consten: en hebbende meerder vermoghen, als onghemeten en onghecierde naeckte woorden, was de *Poësie* Moeder en Voedster des gheluckighen en voorspoedighen ghemeenen welstandts."

[6] *Beschryving*, pp. 328-77.

65

taken from Van Mander's work on Ovid, as has already been indicated in the case of the relief representing Amphion. It seems likely that parts of the decoration were based either on Van Mander or on the sources of information that he used, although such borrowing cannot be proved conclusively. Where it can be demonstrated that Ripa was referred to for parts of the decoration Dapper's account does not follow his descriptions, so that it cannot be taken as a guide to the sources from which the decoration was drawn. Nevertheless it seems that the use of imagery as it was described by Van Mander and by Vondel, the nature of the decoration of the Town Hall, and that of the early descriptions of its meaning, present a single and a consistent picture, and that by virtue of the relationship between poetry and the pictorial arts which was stressed in Amsterdam at the time when the decoration was made, one of the functions belonging to the poets of antiquity was shared there with sculptors and painters. Their work in the Town Hall was evidently intended, by means of its symbolism and its examples, to serve as a reminder to the beholder, whether magistrate or citizen, and to instruct him. Indeed it was intended to instruct him to some extent in an active way, by 'moving', 'firing', or 'compelling' him to practise the virtues of civic life. Represented scenes and symbolic figures had been placed for the same purpose in town halls earlier, but here all the decoration of the building, planned in a single scheme and with a regularity comparable to that of metre in poetry, took over their function.

The lunette in the western wall of the Burgerzaal, which is above the entrance to the burgomasters' chamber and under the relief of Mercury and Argus mentioned above, is carved with a representation of two children, who bear the fasces which symbolized the authority of the Roman senators (illus. 68). They are accompanied by two eagles, which hold the mirror and serpent of Prudence and Jupiter's thunder and lightening in their claws. Oaken garlands also appear in the design, and it includes grapes and apples, which are represented below a roundel in the centre.

The burgomasters' chamber itself is spacious, measuring thirty-six by rather over twenty feet, and being eighteen feet high.[1] At the end of the room opposite the door which leads from the Burgerzaal it has large windows overlooking the Dam, and in the north wall, to the left as one enters, is the opening through which the burgomasters could look down into the *vierschaar*, with beyond

---

[1] Particulars about the early state of the room and its decoration are from Dapper, *Beschryving*, pp. 370–2, unless otherwise stated.

it a door leading to the publication gallery. Opposite this door is a window which faces south, being in the side wall of the central salient of the front façade, and opposite the opening into the *vierschaar* is the fireplace. There appear to have been plans for a fixed seat for the presiding burgomaster at the centre of the inner wall,[1] with doors, of which the second led to the burgomasters' council room, to either side of it. The table stood on a carpet at the same end of the room,[2] and the four seats round it had green velvet cushions with the coat of arms of Amsterdam embroidered on them in gold and silver thread; on the table was a screw, for use in sealing documents with the city seal. The floor is of marble, and the walls are dignified by marble Corinthian pilasters which support a frieze running round the top of the room. The mantelpiece (illus. 69–72, 133), which consists of a frieze and cornice supported by columns and pilasters all of white marble, is of the same order. The frieze of the mantelpiece bears a carving in low relief which represents 'The Triumph of Fabius Maximus, Burgomaster of Rome'[3] and on the wall above it, as a fixed part of the decoration of the room, is a painting by Jan Lievens[4] that continues the story, showing how Suessa, the son of Quintus Fabius Maximus, demanded as consul of Rome that his father should dismount from his horse in deference to his office. The significance of this scene is explained in a verse by Vondel which is written below it:

> The son of Fabius bids his own father dismount from his horse before the honour and dignity of the city, which recognizes no obligations due to birth and demands that he should approach respectfully. So a statesman honours the office which is laid on him.[5]

The Roman triumph was represented in the room used by the burgomasters, it was recorded, 'to hold continually before their eyes a famous example of the rewards which those who protect their fatherland deserve'.[6] The relief also

---

[1] What appears to be a seat is shown on Vennekool's plan, *Afbeelding*, pl. B. The position of table and tablet show that the president's seat was in this position.

[2] The tablet's position is mentioned in an early edition of *Beschryvinge van het Stadhuis; Description de l'Hotel de Ville d'Amsterdam*, Amsterdam, 1714, p. 58.

[3] H. Quellien, *Statuen*, II, Index, entry for pl. O: "De Thriomph van Fabius Maximus, Borger-Meester van Roomen".

[4] See H. Schneider, *Jan Lievens, sein Leben und seine Werke*, Haarlem, 1932, cat. no. 102, and Van de Waal, *Geschied-uitbeelding*, I, p. 217.

[5] Quoted from the inscription itself:
  De Zoon van Fabius gebied zijn eigen Vader
  Van 't paard te stijgen voor Stads eer en aghtbaarheid.
  Die kent geen bloed en eischt dat hij eerbiedig nader.
  Dus eert een man van staat het ampt hem opgeleid.

[6] *Bouw schilder en beeldhouwkonst*, p. 9, description of pl. LII: ". . . om hun onophoudelyk voor ogen te stellen, een berucht voorbeeld der beloningen, welke de beschermers van het Vaderland verdienen".

heightened the significance of the picture above it, by stressing the greatness of Quintus Fabius Maximus.[1]

On one side of the opening through which one looks into the *vierschaar* the attributes of Justice and Prudence are carved, and two keys, a rudder, an oak-leaf wreath with olive branches woven through it, grapes, and ears of corn are represented on the other. These symbols of good government are linked together by garlands of oak leaves hung from lions' heads by bands of ribbon and are accompanied by the words PRVDENTER and FORTITER, written on scrolls. In the top of the opening a strong hand clasping a spear is shown, within a frame of oak leaves. The ceiling, which was painted by Jan Gerritsz. van Bronckhorst, is divided into two compartments. In the one over the place where the table stood, a woman representing the burgomasters' high office is depicted against a blue sky, holding two keys and a sceptre.[2] To her right is a large Bible and to her left are arms ready for use against the city's enemies. Below her a child seems to fly down into the room with a palm branch and a wreath of oak leaves, ready to reward the burgomasters for virtue. In the second compartment children hover in the air bearing the fasces and the imperial crown which belongs to the city's coat of arms. The divisions of the ceiling were decorated with further symbols in gilded plasterwork, with among them the coats of arms of the burgomasters who held office when the building was first taken into use: Cornelis de Graeff, Joan Huydecoper, Hendrik Dircksz. Spiegel and Joan van de Pol. It may be added that the painting by Pieter Saenredam of the old Town Hall has which already has been referred to, together with one by Van der Ulft representing the new, hung on the north wall. The poem on the inauguration of the building which was addressed to the burgomasters by Constantijn Huygens also hung in the room, written in manuscript and set in an ebony frame. The manuscript continued to hang there when a marble or touchstone tablet bearing the poem carved and gilded by Elias Noski was set up above the presiding burgomaster's seat.[3] It seems as though this tablet replaced a copy of the prayer used before the election of burgomasters and councillors, which hung 'behind the burgomasters'

---

[1] Needless to say Quintus Fabius Maximun arrived on horseback in order to test his son's ability to uphold the dignity of his office; see Dapper, op. and loc. cit.

[2] The subject is given by van Dyk, *Schilderyen op het Stadhuis*, pp. 108–9.

[3] Described in Dapper's account, 1663, as being in the burgomasters' council-room, and in *Beschrijving van 't Stadhuis*, 1782, p. 55, as in the position mentioned here. Purchased by the city only in 1666; MS. *Res. Burg. and Oud-Burg.*, 9 July, 1666. For the poem see p. 38 n. 2 above.

table' when Dapper's description of the Town Hall was written. The prayer contained the following passage:

> Because thou always hast chosen some from among the people to rule as governors and as thy servants in this the world, to punish the wicked and to protect the virtuous, and because we are gathered at present in thy name to choose such persons ... we pray and beseech thee ... that thou wilt so enlighten our hearts ... that we ... may elect godfearing, true and wise men who are enemies to covetousness, whom, O bountiful Father, we mercifully pray, thou then wilt so enable by thy Holy Spirit that they may judge all in righteousness and justice, giving each his due, and that they may govern in all faithfulness, to the magnification of thy holy name, to the edification of thy Christian Church, to the quiet, peace and unity of the citizens and inhabitants of this town, and all others, and to their souls' salvation.[1]

The ideals that found expression in this prayer were those represented in the symbolism that surrounded the members of the city government, both in ceremonial (the rod of justice, it will be remembered, was carried beside the sheriff at the inauguration of the Town Hall) and in the decoration which formed part of their rooms or was directly related to them. Not all of this decoration can be discussed in detail here, but some further parts of it may be described as examples to show its nature.

The decoration of the larger offices and the council-rooms is of a similar kind to that of the burgomasters' chamber, though they have no giant pilasters to add to their dignity. There are paintings over the fireplaces appropriate to the use of the rooms, their subjects taken from the Bible or from the history or mythology of the ancient world, and some of them explained by verses. They have symbolic paintings and plasterwork in the ceilings and there are carvings, some of them also symbolic, in the friezes of the mantelpieces. The burgomasters' council-room had rich hangings on the walls, and both there and in the council chamber – the meeting-room of the city council – the chairs were

---

[1] Referred to as the prayer used 'in taking office' in Dapper's account. Bontemantel, describing the election and taking office of burgomasters and councillors (*De regeeringe*, I, pp. 95–97 and II, pp. 6–15) makes it clear that a prayer was said before the elections but mentions no other; it must have been this to which Dapper refers. Quoted from Bontemantel, MS. *Civ. en mil. reg.*, I, p. 48. (Also given in De *regeeringe*, I, pp. 95–96, with minor variations.) "Dewyle ghy altyt eenige uytten volcke hebt vercooren omme als overhyt ende uwe dinaers in deese de werelt te regeren, de boose te straffe ende de vroome te beschermen, ende wy iegenwoordich in uwen name versamelt syn, om sulcke te verkiese; ... soo bidden ende roepen wy u aen, ... dat ghy onse harte sulckx wilt verlichten ... dat wy ... Godt vreesende, waerachtige verstandige mannen, ende de giricheyt vyant synde, mogen verkiese, den welcken wy u, O goedertieren Vader, dan genadelyck bidden met uwen hyligen Geest, sulx te willen bequamen, dat sy alles in recht ende gerechtichyt, mogen oordeelen, yder het syne geven, ende in alle getrouwicheyt regeeren, tot groot maekinge van uwen hyligen naem, opbouwinge van uwe kercke Cristij, rust, vrede ende enicheyt vanden Burgeren ende inwoonders dese stede, ende alle anderen, ende haerer sielen salicheyt."

provided with cushions embroidered with the city's coat of arms.[1] These two rooms are of great size, each being thirty feet wide and about fourty-five feet long and having a barrel-vaulted ceiling thirty-six feet high. Their decoration if of a corresponding grandeur, for they have fireplaces at either end with mantelpieces so high as to be well above eye level, each supported by four columns and pilasters and surmounted by vast paintings which reach almost to the tops of the rooms. By virtue of their size and their realism these paintings thrust themselves on the spectator's attention. Those in the council chamber show scenes from the Old Testament concerning good counsel and wisdom, as suited the origins of the city council, and these themes are also illustrated in the mantelpiece friezes. The paintings in the burgomasters' council-room (illus. 73–76) represent, in scenes showing the virtues of the Roman consuls Gaius Fabricius and Curius Dentatus, the steadfastness and moderation of the good governor, who cannot be deflected from his duty by bribes or threats.[2] In the frieze of the northern mantelpiece is carved the cog of the city's early coat of arms. It is supported by mermaid children riding on dolphins[3] and accompanied by others who play with swans, seals, and other water creatures. The frieze of the southern mantelpiece of the same room has carved at its centre the city's later coat of arms, with children playing with the symbols of good government to either side of it and others who, in the guise of Hercules, drive away on the one side a harpy with the hind legs of a beast and on the other a griffin.[4] These children have winged companions who fly busily about in the paintings of the coffered ceiling carrying a great garland of flowers, holding wreaths of laurel and oak and other symbols, or playing among birds and butter-flies above the deliberations of the council of burgomasters and ex-burgomasters

[1] The hangings of the burgomasters' council-room were paid for in 1658; Kroon, *Stadhuis*, pp. 73–74. The cushions are mentioned by Filips von Zesen, *Beschreibung der Stadt Amsterdam* [etc.], Amsterdam, 1664, pp. 261 and 282. Kroon, p. 76, mentions a payment for fourty-one cushions, but gives conflicting information as to its date.

[2] Such a comparison with Roman leaders must have been suggested earlier by the decoration of the room used as a council chamber and for feasts in the Doelen, or headquarters of the Civic Guard, of Rotter-dam, which was described in 1634 as having "the burgo-masters' and chief officers' pictures placed in both ends, and the Roman emperors on both sides of the room"; Sir William Brereton, *Travels in Holland . . . England, Scotland and Ireland* [etc.] (Chetham Society), London, 1844, p. 11. In the burgomasters' council-room and chamber in the Amsterdam Town Hall, however, the comparison was made not with emperors, but consuls.

[3] In the *Iconologia* of Ripa *Animo piacevole, trattabile, e amorevole* is represented by a child on a dolphin (ed. 1624, pp. 40–41).

[4] The *Beschryvinge van 't Stadhuis*, 1782, states that the elements are represented in the mantelpiece friezes and implies that the monsters being chased away represent envy and other such vices.

70

who met in the room below.[1] The gaiety and lightheartedness of all these children seems to typify the happiness that must result from good government and it seems that here sea and land (represented in the mantelpieces) and even the heavens above share in and contribute to its harmony. The words LENE CONSILIUM DATIS and STET CAPITOLIUM FULGENS[2] are written on scrolls between the panels of the ceiling, and branches of oak and palm, the sword and sceptre of justice, and shells, which represent wisdom,[3] also appear in it. Pieter de Hooch, in a painting which dates from the 1660s (illus. 73),[4] shows a number of well-dressed visitors admiring this scene, standing by the table at which the burgomasters sat[5] or wandering about the room and so allowing the modern onlooker to sense its spaciousness. The hangings on the walls are of a striped material with red and blue in it, the floor is of black and white marble, and the lower divisions of the small-paned mullioned windows have shutters that open inwards which are also red in colour. This room must have given an impression of warmth and of quiet splendour in the morning light when on the day following the inauguration of the Town Hall, the city council met there at nine o'clock, their own room not being ready, and, 'with the customary unity and sweet harmony'[6] returned to their ordinary business.

The citizen or the foreign visitor whose affairs brought him to the Town Hall, though he may not have had occasion to enter the burgomasters' chamber and the council-rooms, was nevertheless surrounded by imagery that had bearing on the city's government, as has already been seen. He might notice, as he passed though the Burgerzaal, how the figure of Amsterdam took a proud place in the universe that was created there, sitting enthroned above the eastern entrance between the reliefs in which Amphion and Mercury and Argus are

[1] The room was used for the meetings of the council of burgomasters and ex-burgomasters, whose function is described by Bontemantel, *De regeeringe*, I, pp. 162–9.

[2] From Horace, *Carmina*, III, iv. line 41, a passage concerning the inspiration of even [Augustus] Caesar by the wise counsel of the Muses, who are addressed, and from ibid., III, iii, line 42, where Juno prophesies the continuation of Rome's glory so long as Troy remains in ruins. 'Ye give lenient counsel' and 'May the Capitol [or Town Hall] stand illustrious'. Thanks are due to Miss M. Vos for the identification of these quotations.

[3] The shell, which appears elsewhere in the building, was connected in antiquity and in the Renaissance with those who were inspired, and thus with wisdom.

[4] Dreesmann Coll., Amsterdam; *Verzameling Amsterdam, W. J. R. Dreesmann*, Amsterdam, 1942–51,I, p. 8. Dated by the style (that of De Hooch's first Amsterdam period, 1662–70) and by the costumes depicted.

[5] Bontemantel, MS. *Civ. en mil. reg.*, II, p. 25, shows the arrangement of the room for the election of members of the government. When the room was used by the city council the table stood in the same place; Bontemantel, *De regeeringe*, II, p. 9.

[6] MS. *Res. Vroedsch.*, 30 July 1655: "Met de gewoonlijcke eenigheijt ende lieffelijcke harmonie". The city council's own room was ready only in 1660 (MS. cit., 18 Feb. 1660).

depicted, wearing a crown of turrets and city walls, guarded by lions, and holding palms and olive-branches in her hands (illus. 34). She is accompanied by Strength and Wisdom, and the four elements fly down to greet her, represented as children, who bear a rudder, an eye with rays round it on a sceptre, the caduceus and winged hat of Mercury, and a cornucopia, symbols which may also be taken together to denote good and prosperous government.[1] In the frieze of the entrance below her feet are flowers and fruits representing 'The four seasons of the year', which themselves signified 'The rise and decline of the life of man'.[2] These have an hour-glass among them. On one side of them is the sun and on the other the moon, and beyond these there are symbols of day and night and signs of the zodiac (illus. 35–37).[3] Palm branches and crowns of laurel and oak, pairs of intertwined serpents, anchors and crowns made up of ships' prows[4] appear in the bronze bars of the doors and openings of the end walls of the Burgerzaal. In the fillings of the spandrels of the arches of the eastern wall crowns of oak and olive, and palm branches, are carved, and the wall is hung with festoons of oak and olive. Such festoons and fillings, composed of symbols related to the figures near them or made up of fruits and flowers which add to the symbolic scheme in a more general way, serve as links in the design of the building between pictorial decoration and architectural ornament, and such links also bring the various elements of the symbolic scheme into a formal relationship with one another. At one end of the northern gallery, for example, above the arches to either side of the figure of Venus, are carved festoons made up of rushes and weighted down at either end by bunches of apples, reminders of the golden apple given her by Paris, which Venus holds in her hand. Her belt, composed of shells and roses, is wound round the festoons, and pairs of doves making love to each other are perched on them and on rose and myrtle branches in the spandrels of the arches. Beside the relief in which

---

[1] H. Quellien, *Statuen*, II, Index, entry for pl. 4, gives this description: "De Cracht bestaende in de 4 Elementen boven de inkomende Deur". ('Strength, consisting of the four elements above the entrance door'.) The main figure evidently represents Amsterdam since an eagle holds the shield and crown of the city's coat of arms above her. Her strength is emphasized by the figure of Strength at her right hand, by the crown of towers and walls, and by her lions. The sceptre surmounted by an eye is given by Van Mander as a symbol of wise government; *Wtleggingh*, fol. 132 v.

[2] H. Quellien, op. cit., II, Index, entry for pl. M. "De vier getijden van't Iaer . . . het op en afdalen van't Leeven van den Mensch."

[3] In the paintings proposed for the lunettes of the east and west walls (Vennekool, *Afbeelding*, pls. H and R) further signs of the zodiac are indicated, though they do not form a complete series. It seems likely that two sets of the signs of the zodiac were planned, one for each end of the hall (cf. the two sets of the elements) or one for the lower, one for the upper zone. The absence of a series of signs in the frieze above the west entrance, however, breaks into this arrangement.

[4] See *The Cambridge Ancient History*, Cambridge, 1923–39, VII, p. 679.

72

Venus appears, and on the 'pedestal' below her, hanging festoons composed of shells and wet reeds, with roses among them, are carved, reminders of her birth, which ushers in an age of plenty, while in the decoration which fills the panels within the arches such details as the apparatus from her dressing-table, a mirror and comb, tresses of hair, and a little brush are represented (illus. 54, 57–60).

The doors of the Insurance and the Bankruptcy offices are in the same gallery (illus. 61), and their decoration, like that surrounding Venus, makes up part of its formal scheme. The door of the Insurance Office is surmounted by a relief representing Arion, 'who was so insured by his playing that he had himself thrown into the sea and was set on land by a dolphin',[1] and that of the Bankruptcy Office (illus. 62–64) by one depicting the Fall of Icarus. Above Arion is carved a festoon made up of oak leaves with poppy fruits among them, representing, it must be supposed, the material strength and the easy sleep of the man who is safely insured.[2] There are hanging garlands to either side of the relief, made up of poppy fruits and oak and olive branches, and at each side of the door, hanging delicately on a single ribbon, are carved sound locks, with oak leaves and acorns. Above Icarus there hangs a festoon of prickly holly leaves, with broken locks, torn money-bags, and what may be taken for bundles of unpaid bills in a tattered condition and tied up with string. In its centre hangs an open money-box, upside-down and evidently empty, and the festoon, insecurely tied together, hangs on breaking cords and has scavenging rats crawling about in it. Hanging garlands of thistles and bindweed are carved to either side of the relief, and beside the doors there hang open locks and empty purses which, though they seem at first sight to be sound, prove to have had the bottoms cut out of them. These symbols confronted the provident citizen and the bankrupt when they came on business to the Town Hall, while reliefs representing Faithfulness and Silence, festoons and garlands containing locks and keys, pens, pencils, an inkpot, scrolls sealed with the city seal, and tape for tying up papers greeted those who entered the Secretary's office in the southern gallery.

[1] H. Quellien, *Statuen*, II, Index, entry for pl. G: ". . . die op syn spel soo geassureert was dat hy hem liet in zee worpen, en wiert door een Dolphijn aen't lant gezet". The design of the relief is reminiscent of the plate in which Arion is represented in *Parvus Mundus*, Antwerp, 1584, although it was not based on it exactly. This work was republished by Pers with alterations and with rhymes by Vondel as *Den gulden winckel der konstlievende Nederlanders* [etc.], Amsterdam, 1608; see Vondel, *Werken*, I, pp. 266 and 402.
[2] Ripa, following Ovid, gives the poppy as a symbol of Sleep; *Iconologia*, 1624, p. 91 *(Carro della Notte)*: "Ovidio gli cinge il capo con una ghirlanda di papavero significante il sonno". Cf. the symbolism used by Vondel in the passage quoted on p. 60 above.

The city government was concerned with the citizen from his childhood onwards, should he be in need of care. Those concerned with the city's dependents did their business in a room which has over its mantelpiece a painting of Lycurgus adopting his nephew in a palace strongly reminiscent of the new Town Hall of Amsterdam, and in the ceiling a symbolic figure is depicted with the scales of Justice and a book in her hand, who charitably shelters two children, as the *Mater Misericordiae* shelters the faithful, under her ample cloak.[1] There are cherubs among flowers carved in the frieze of the mantelpiece of this room and other cherubs, some of them wearing seventeenth-century childrens' caps, appear with palms, flowers, and birds feeding their young in a nest in the plasterwork in the ceiling. As an addition to this scheme the fragment of the painting of the Nativity by Pieter Aertsz. which had been in the old Town Hall was placed in the same room, where it hung between the windows 'in a very old-fashioned gilded frame'.[2] It was held that St. Joseph was represented in the fragment, and he must have been included at this point in the decorative scheme as the arch-foster-father, for to him was entrusted the upbringing of Christ Himself.

Those who came to register intentions of marriage did so in the Chamber of Matrimonial Affairs, where a pair of right hands being clasped together, a symbol of faithfulness,[3] was carved in the centre of the mantelpiece. The Dutch word *trouw*, which means 'faithfulness', may also signify 'marriage'. After the calling of banns, either in church or from the publication gallery of the Town Hall, the engaged couples returned to be married before the law in the magistrates' court. The magistrate whose turn it was to officiate would say 'Take off your gloves and give each other the right hand', and holding hands the couple would make their promises.[4] The symbol was thus a very familiar one.

Although on Sundays and Tuesdays and occasionally on other days as well marriages took place in the magistrates' court, it was used at other times as a court of justice, where statutes were made[5] and where the more important civil and all criminal causes were heard. There the sheriff sat at the head of the magistrates as the representative of the sovereign authority, on a cushion

[1] Both paintings are by Cornelis Holstein, see Van Dyk, *Schilderyen op het Stadhuis*, pp. 134–5.
[2] See p. 22 n. 3 above. In fact a shepherd, not St. Joseph, is represented.
[3] The symbolism of the joining of hands is discussed by Erwin Panofsky, 'Jan van Eyck's Arnolfini Portrait', *The Burlington Magazine*, LXIV, 1934, pp. 117–27.
[4] Procedure described by Bontemantel, *De Regeeringe*, I. p. 249.
[5] Ibid., I, p. 258

embroidered with the coat of arms of the Province of Holland, and with the rod of justice to the right-hand side above his chair.[1] Justice is represented above the entrance to this room (illus. 77–79), at the western end of the Burgerzaal, as a counterpart to the figure of Amsterdam which ornaments its eastern entrance, where, it will be remembered, she is seen with the figures of Strength and Wisdom beside her and with olive and palm branches in her hands, which symbolize peace and the rewards of virtue. Justice, who brings vice its due reward, sits with Covetousness and Envy under her feet, Death on her right, and Punishment, who turns her face away from Justice,[2] on her left. In the relief behind these figures there hover, above Punishment, harpies, and above Death, two children bearing instruments of punishment, a bunch of birch twigs and the thunder and lightning of Jupiter. In the frieze below these figures is represented, according to the description given by Hubertus Quellien, 'The rewarding of good and the punishment of evil: with the measure with which one measures one shall be measured'.[3] In the centre of the frieze is carved an eye, which must refer to the all-seeing eye of God,[4] surrounded by rays and with wings to each side of it and flanked by two wooden measures of length. To the right of these, as seen from the figure of Justice, is a cornucopia wound round with spring and summer flowers and filled with fruit and ears of corn, from which a hand bearing a palm branch and a crown of laurel emerges. To the left is a horn surrounded by thistles and containing handcuffs, chains, ropes and birch twigs, which has a hand holding a scourge coming out of it. The right-hand end of the frieze is carved with a cherub, what appears to be a shackle, the mirror of prudence, and branches of olive and myrtle, and the left-hand end with the head of a harpy, a watchman's rattle, the serpent of the Fall of Man, an instrument of torture, and a scorpion.[5] On the spandrels of two of the arched openings in the west wall of the Burgerzaal beside the entrance there appear, paired together, palms and lilies, and thistles and roses which

---

[1] Ibid., I, p. 10.

[2] Noticed in *Beschryvinge van 't Stadhuis*, 1782, p. 36. Like Ripa's figure of *Bugia*, 'the Lie', *Iconologia*, 1624, p. 82, punishment is represented as a cripple supported by a wooden crutch.

[3] *Statuen*, II, Index, entry for pl. L. "De Beloningh van de goede en de Straf van de quade, Met de Maet daermen meede meet, salmen gemeten worden." The saying comes from Luke, vi, 38.

[4] According to Van Mander, *Wtlegginghh*, fol. 132 v., a single open eye 'signifies the watchful Father of Lights, God'. The same symbol was placed in a central position in the *vierschaar*, see p. 81 below.

[5] As well as these symbols a star, and a bunch of flowers which may have individual significance appear in the frieze below Justice. These are to her right. To her left are a bat, and a female mask with a serpent twining through it. Possibly the scorpion should have formed part of a series of signs of the zodiac, for which see p. 72 n. 3 above. Van Mander, *Wtlegginghh*, fol. 130 v., gives it as 'an evil or inimical deceit', and Ripa, *Iconologia*, 1624, p. 398 *(Libidine)*, as a symbol of Lust.

have prominent thorns; in those of two further arches symbols of justice appear. The garlands on the wall are of oak, wound round with ribbons or with olive branches, but the garland directly over the door contains lilies and two burning torches, and has carved at its centre a clock face with the hands set at twenty-five minutes past eleven, almost the final moment of the eleventh hour.[1] The spandrels of the entrance arch contain, to the right of Justice a crowing cock and to the left a hooded falcon. The entrance leads to the magistrates' court through a passage on one side of which the sword of justice and a bridle, the symbol of moderation, are carved in a hanging festoon of laurel and oak. On the other side of the passage, in a similar festoon, the lion-skin and club of Hercules appear. Above the entrance to the room itself were painted in gold letters the words "Audi & Alteram partem",[2] and it seems that the scales of justice were to have been painted on the panels of its doors.[3]

The splendour of the room struck the seventeenth-century visitor as he entered: . . . "è vaga, nobile e sontuosa per le tappezzerie, per le dorature e per le pitture, e per i marmi".[4] The room is of great size, measuring about eighty by thirty-two feet, but only its southern half takes up the full height of the first floor of the building, for above the northern half there is a mezzanine, which contained the sheriff's office. The magistrates sat in the northern half, separated from the higher part of the hall by arches which have half-columns set against them on the southern side. These half-columns are made of wood but are painted to represent red marble; they have carved and gilded olive, holly, and oak leaves twisted round them and they support a frieze decorated with cherubs, pairs of doves, and olive-branches. The ceiling of the higher part of the room is vaulted, and in its central panels there are paintings, damaged, and at the time of writing covered, representing Justice flanked by Strength and Prudence. In the panels which surround these paintings the names and the coats of arms of the sheriff and magistrates of the year of the Town Hall's inauguration are depicted in high relief. Over the southern fireplace, which the magistrates must have faced as they sat in the northern part of the room, is a large painting by Ferdinand Bol of Moses descending from Mount Sinai

---

[1] In Dutch 11.30 is called "half twaalf", 'half twelve', and striking clocks sound twelve strokes at this time in anticipation of the hour that follows. The expression 'the eleventh hour' is used in Dutch as well as English and comes from the parable told in Matthew, xx, 1–6.

[2] 'Hear the other side as well'.

[3] Vennekool, *Afbeelding*, p. 8 and Pl. Q, in which the inscription appears, with pairs of scales depicted on the double doors below it.

[4] Quoted from the brothers De Bovio, who saw the Town Hall on 8th December 1677; Brom, 'Reisbeschrijving', *Bijdragen*, 1915, pp. 107–8.

holding the tables of the law.[1] The frieze of the mantelpiece below it adds to the meaning of this scene, for it shows the Children of Israel worshipping the Golden Calf and illustrates their vicious and lawless life before the law was instituted (illus. 80–83). Under the painting was written:

> The Hebrew Moses has received the Law from God, with which he returns from above to the people, who greet him reverently and welcome him eagerly. The free State begins to flourish when the people respect the laws.[2]

The bar at which the prisoner stood when trials were in progress was probably in the southern part of the room, where, as he stood facing the magistrates, he should have seen behind them, above the northern mantelpiece: 'Alexander Magnus, holding one ear shut while two people are pleading a cause, so giving one ear to the one, and keeping its partner for the other party'.[3] Above the arches that divided him from the magistrates he should have seen a representation of the Last Judgement.[4]

After trial the prisoner, unless he was acquitted, would be conducted back to prison by the private stair which linked the magistrates' court with the gaoler's quarters, by which he had come up. If his offence was proved and was of a serious nature, and yet he refused to acknowledge his guilt, he was examined subsequently in the torture chamber in the presence of sheriff, burgomasters, and magistrates.[5] We need not follow him there, but may notice that instruments of torture are carved in the vaulting of the ceiling and that Artus Quellien was paid for 'three heads' for the room as well as for 'a wooden knocker to be cast in bronze for the prisons'.[6]

The sentences passed on those who had committed minor offences were

---

[1] See A. Heppner, ' "Moses zeigt die Gesetzestafeln" bei Rembrandt und Bol', *Oud-Holland*, LII, 1935, pp. 241–51.

[2] Inscription now painted out. Quoted from *Beschryving van 't Stadhuis*, 1782, p. 77:
> Hebreeusche Moses heeft de Wet van God ontfangen,
> Waar mede hy naar 't volk van boven wederkeert,
> Dat hem eerbiedig groet, en welkomt met verlangen:
> De vrye Staat luikt op, als 't volk de wetten eert.

[3] Vennekool, op. cit., p. 8. "*Alexander Magnus,* sijn een oor toehoudende, terwijl 'er twee pleyten; alsoo het eene ghevende aan d' eene, en het toe-gehouwde bewarende voor d' andere Party."

[4] Vennekool, op. and loc. cit. Simply described as "het Oordeel", 'the Judgment'. This representation and the one just referred to are mentioned only in this source and probably they were never executed. Paintings of the Last Judgement in Town Halls are discussed by Georg Troescher, 'Weltgerichtsbilder in Rathäusern und Gerichtsstätten, *Westdeutsches Jahrbuch für Kunstgeschichte Wallraf-Richartz-Jahrbuch*, XI, 1939, pp. 139–205, though neither of those originally planned by Van Campen for Amsterdam are noticed. Only one by Jacob Backer, not part of his design, is mentioned (cat. no. 2).

[5] The description of the course of justice given here is based on Bontemantel, *De regeeringe*, I, pp. 58–68. Wagenaar's account, *Amsterdam*, III, pp. 316–18, has also been used, but only to elucidate Bontemantel's text.

[6] A. Quellien, MS. Papers, no. 14 (an account paid 19 Dec. 1654) and no. 20 (paid 27 Dec. 1656).

announced and carried out without delay, but those who had committed more serious crimes were kept waiting until the next occasion when the scaffold was put up, so that they might be punished publicly, those of them who were to receive the death penalty being told beforehand that they might expect it. On the day of execution the indictments of those who were waiting to receive other public punishments were read out while they stood at the bar in the magistrates' court and they were then taken, after waiting in the chamber of justice while the death sentences were pronounced in the *vierschaar* below, to hear their sentences pronounced from the publication gallery. The City Bell was rung. The sheriff and magistrates filed in from the burgomasters' chamber to the gallery. The rod of justice, 'a thorn branch ... of fair length and thickness',[1] was put out through the window at the sheriff's side. Then the prisoners were led in through the door that links the gallery with the chamber of justice, and stood behind the authorities while the sentences were read out. The decoration in the ceiling of the publication gallery was suited to the occasion and to the other events that took place there, the announcement of peace or war, the publication of new statutes, and the calling of banns of marriage, for the figure of Time is painted in the central panel and Good and Evil Fame in the panels to either side of it, while between the paintings trumpets are depicted in the plasterwork. On one side the trumpets are shown with olive-branches and flowers, among them lilies, twined round them, and on the other they appear with a rose branch with thorns on it, holly, and the thunderbolts and lightning of Jupiter.

The *vierschaar* (illus. 84–97) as has already been stated, was used only for the pronouncing of the death sentence. There too the thunderbolts and lightning of Jupiter are depicted, for they appear, winged, against the great bronze doors by which the court is entered, together with crossed swords, one of which is wreathed in flames. Above these symbols are the city's early and its present coat of arms, and in the solid panels of the lower parts of the doors crossed bones and skulls are depicted in relief, with scrolls in front of them bearing the words of warning which, according to Virgil, Theseus shouted during his agony in hell: DISCITE JUSTITIAM MONITI ET NON TEMNERE DIVOS; 'Be warned; learn to be just, and do not slight the gods'.[2] The bars themselves are cast in the form of strong saplings around which ivy twines, and when the doors are closed their edges together have the form of a tree-trunk, around which the

---

[1] Bontemantel, *De Regeeringe*, I, p. 10.
[2] *Aeneid*, VI, line 620.

serpent of the Fall of Man, with the fateful apple in his mouth, winds himself as though he would keep the doors closed on the prisoner.

When the ground plans of the Town Hall were recorded in the prints of 1648 it was planned that the *vierschaar* should have an entrance flanked by small semicircular niches in each of its end walls, and that there should be three large niches with smaller ones between them in its western wall, and small niches between the windows. There was to be a similar arrangement of niches in the upper part of the room, where the window linking the *vierschaar* with the burgomasters' chamber, which is shown on the first floor plan of 1648, is in the centre of the southern wall. In the plans of 1650 only one of the entrances is shown, the northern one being replaced by a rectangular niche in which a marble seat for the Secretary was placed when the final design was executed, and on all four walls at first floor level, as well as at ground floor level in the eastern wall, the small niches shown in the plans of 1648 still appear. The niches planned for the northern and southern walls at ground floor level, however, have been replaced by openings which, though their proportions were altered, form part of the final design of the room, while the western wall is articulated as it was in the final design. The steps that lead up to this wall, and the bench that is built against it, are also shown in the prints of 1650, and since the wall provides fields for sculptured reliefs and the use of the bench adds greatly to their significance, since, too, the large niches in the wall at first floor level have been replaced in these prints by the spaces in which paintings were to have been put,[1] it is probable that the decorative scheme had been decided on when the prints were made. The first models for it were paid for before 24th October 1651 and the first marble sculptures before 11th April 1652.[2] The decision to ornament the room with two orders of pilasters had been made earlier, for they appear on the plans of 1648.

On the morning of execution cushions were placed along the marble bench against the western wall of the *vierschaar* and, after a prayer had been said and the indictments of the 'ordinary' prisoners had been read in the magistrates' court, the sheriff and magistrates, wearing special black garments with velvet bands over them marked with silver crosses, a heart, and the monogram of Amsterdam, came down to the *vierschaar*. They took their places on the bench, the sheriff sitting in the centre with the rod of justice in his hand, and the nine

---

[1] Shown by Vennekool, *Afbeelding*, pl. K.
[2] A. Quellien, MS. Papers, nos. 5 and 6, which can be taken to date from before the first payments recorded on the sheets following them chronologically; the dates of these payments are those given here.

magistrates ranged in order of seniority to either side of him. Thus seated they faced the waiting citizens on the Dam outside, discernible through the bronze bars of the window openings, and, before them, the figures of Justice and Prudence which stood in the niches of the window wall, confronting them as a reminder of their duties and not visible to the populace.[1]

The public in their turn looked in, so far as they were able, from the Dam, and saw a hierarchy embodied and represented before them. The sheriff and magistrates sat, raised on their bench of marble, in light which streamed in through the upper windows of the *vierschaar* from the publication gallery, while the rest of the lower part of the room, because of the arcades outside, was dark and gloomy. Over these officials there was a heavy projecting cornice supported by the figures of four women, whose plaits of hair are wound into the volutes of the Ionic capitals above them. The wall between these figures is thus divided into five panels, three of which are wide and two narrow, which replace the niches shown in the ground plan of 1648, and in the two narrow panels designs in which oriental tapestries are imitated are carved in low relief. Such designs appear nowhere else in the whole building, and the city's coats of arms, which are carved as though on shields hanging against them, serve to emphasize their strangeness. Vitruvius explains that the inhabitants of Caria, a Peloponnesian state, conspired with Persia against Greece. They were defeated by the Greeks, the men were killed and the women were taken captive:

> Not at one time alone, were they led in triumph. Their slavery was an eternal warning. Insult crushed them. They seemed to pay a penalty for their fellow-citizens. And so the architects of that time designed for public buildings figures of matrons placed to carry burdens; in order that the punishment of the sin of the Cariatid women might be known to posterity and historically recorded.[2]

Thus it was suitable that the figures of female Cariatids should be placed in a hall of justice and that they should be seen by public and prisoner alike when the death sentence was pronounced, and the eastern design of the carvings placed between them might serve as a reminder of the reason for their presence

---

[1] In this description it is not always possible to show by the tense used whether the works mentioned were carried out. The original design for the decoration of the *vierschaar* was followed to the top of the first cornice. Above this some parts were changed and others omitted. The description of parts which were not carried out is based on Vennekool, *Afbeelding*, pls. K, L, M, and N, except where other sources are referred to.
[2] Vitruvius, *De Architectura*, I, i, 6. Quoted, with translation, from Granger. "... non una triumpho ducerentur, sed aeterno, servitutis exemplo gravi contumelia pressae poenas pendere viderentur pro civitate. Ideo qui tunc architecti fuerunt aedificiis publicis designaverunt earum imagines oneri ferundo conlocatas, ut etiam posteris nota poena peccati Cariatium memoriae traderetur".

there. On the under side of the cornice supported by these figures, above the narrow panels, the snake-haired heads of gorgons were carved and, above the wider panels to either side, the rods and axe of justice, which also appear in the bronze bars of the openings in the end walls. Above the central panel, and thus over the place where the sheriff sat, was carved an eye giving forth rays,[1] with an olive wreath round it, a palm branch, and a sword. Similar wreaths and palm branches are carved in the spandrels of a shallow arch which frames the central space. The other arches in the room, over windows, the door, and the Secretary's seat, have holly leaves carved in their spandrels, while the bars of the outer wall are cast in the form of thorn branches, with the serpents of Mercury's staff twisted round the central bar of each window and his winged hat and a large sunflower above them.

In the panel in the centre of the western wall, framed by the shallow arch and with its high relief enhanced by contrast with the tapestry-like panels to either side of it, the judgement of Solomon is represented,[2] carved to look as though it were taking place under and beyond one of the arches of the room. Reliefs illustrating Greek and Roman justice appear to either side of it in the two large spaces at the ends of the wall, showing Zaleucus, the law-giver of the Locrians, having his own eye put out to relieve his son of his full punishment,[3] and Brutus watching the execution of his own sons for treachery.[4] These scenes are set in the open air and appear to be taking place beyond the cornice of the *vierschaar*, and they and the central scene are linked together by forming a single composition, with antique buildings at its outer sides. The perspective of these buildings leads into the distance and is arranged so that it is seen correctly by the spectator as he stands looking in through the central window from the Dam, so that quite clearly the three reliefs, and presumably therefore the rest of the inner wall of the *vierschaar*, were designed to appear to him as a background to the events that took place within the court. As will be remembered the statues of the Counts of Holland were probably arranged in the *vierschaar* of the old Town Hall in such a way that they faced outwards,[5] so that it is likely that there too the decoration was arranged with reference to the spectator rather than the occupants of the court, though in a less elaborate way. The Old Testament scene, in which there is no such illusion of unlimited

[1] See p. 75 n. 4 above.
[2] The story told in I (Vulgate III) Kings, iii, 16–28, is illustrated.
[3] Aelian, *Varia Historia*, XIII, xxiv.
[4] Livy, II, iv and v, and Valerius Maximus, V, viii.
[5] See p. 21 above.

depth, confronts the spectator inescapably in the centre and so is emphasized, and the eye is led to the figure of Solomon, which dominates the scene, by the form of the semicircular niche behind his throne and by the ribs of the shell[1] that is carved within it. This central figure, raised above steps and holding a scepter in his hand, appeared directly above the sheriff as he sat on the bench.

Over these three reliefs, and set forward above them by the projection of the cornice, were to have been placed three paintings, together representing the Last Judgement, with the figure of Christ as Judge in the centre above both Solomon and the sheriff, and souls being taken to heaven and hell in the panels to the right and left, the elect escorted by unarmed angels and the damned being pursued by others bearing flaming swords and driven forward by the devil.[2] The frieze in the lower cornice is decorated with holly leaves, thistles, and skulls, and the lower part of the room is hung with carved festoons made up mainly of prickly plants; among these decorations loathsome serpents crawl. At the level of the painting of the Last Judgement, where the room is flooded with light, children playfully hanging shields on bundles of lictors' staves were to appear in the niches, and the frieze of the upper cornice was to have pairs of cherubs represented in it.[3] In the highest zone of the room, which also is well lit, the figures of prophets and sibyls holding scrolls were to appear, as though bearing silent witness to the events that took place below.[4] They were to be painted in the form of statues placed above the upper cornice, and set against a sky which seems to have been designed as a continuation of the sky shown in the paintings of the Last Judgement.[5] Rays were to have been painted as though shed from a point in the centre of this vaulted heaven, in which the symbols of eternity were to have been depicted,[6] accompanied by a

[1] See p. 71 n. 3 above.
[2] The paintings, as well as being shown by Vennekool, are mentioned in his *Afbeelding*, p. 6, by Meyster, *Land-spel*, II, p. 6, and by Vondel, *Inwydinge*, line 1085. A painting by Van Campen of Christ as Judge, Town Hall, Amersfoort (illus. 90–91), appears to be connected with this scheme; P. T. A. Swillens, 'Jacob van Campen als schilder', *Elsevier's Maandschrift*, XLVIII, July-Dec., 1938, p. 293. Thanks are due to Miss L. Bolleman and Dr. H. E. 's Jacob for arranging for the writer to examine and take photographs of this painting.
[3] This statement is based on the design shown in Vennekool's engravings. The upper cornice was in fact decorated with a slightly different design, which also contained cherubs. The nature of the garlands planned for the upper part of the rooms remains unknown.
[4] Vennekool, op. and loc. cit., mentions the figures as prophets and sibyls and states that they were to be painted in imitation of statues. Meyster, op. and loc. cit., describes them as sibyls and evangelists.
[5] Suggested by Vennekool's engraving of the west wall and by Meyster's description, see following note.
[6] Meyster, op. cit., II, pp. 6–7, in describing the paintings of the Last Judgement, refers to:
 . . . d'Heyligen vol deugd, [die] nae d'eeuwigh' hoogte stijgen,
 Om't zalige gewest van Eng'lenburgh te krijgen,
 Daer d'eeuwigheyt verbeeld, in het verhemelt stond,

82

shower of tulips and other flowers, which would rain down over the judicial hierarchy.

The prisoner who was to receive the death sentence was led through the bronze doors into the *vierschaar* before the sheriff the magistrates took their places there, and stood waiting in the dark part of the room, surrounded by its forbidding ornament and able to see the sword of justice and the gruesome gorgons' heads on the under side of the cornice. When the gentlemen had come in and were seated the sheriff asked each of the magistrates in turn if it was late enough in the day for the court of justice to be held. 'Then', to quote a contemporary account, 'the sheriff looked up to where the burgomasters were leaning out of the window (arranged for the purpose) and said: "What do the burgomasters say on the city's behalf?" '.[1] When the burgomasters in answer had given their consent to the holding of the court the prisoner was placed close to the sheriff, and in front of him, where he would complete the series of exemplary scenes to be set before the public in the *vierschaar* and bring their meaning very near to them. So standing he heard the voice of the sheriff giving an account of his confessed misdeeds and asking the magistrates to declare him a 'child of death'. The magistrates filed out in order of precedence and went up to the burgomasters' chamber where they stood in a half circle, the Secretary a little apart, while the presiding magistrate reported the sheriff's request. This done, and when the burgomasters had given their advice, the magistrates filed back and the sheriff asked them for their verdict. Their president, remaining seated, declared the prisoner a child of death. The sheriff then asked in what manner the prisoner should receive his punishment, and once again the magistrates filed out, this time the most junior first, to ask the advice of the burgomasters. When they had returned and were seated the junior magistrate declared that the sentence was that to be read out by the Secretary.

> Met punts eens Diamants te midden in het rond
> Van een vergulden Slangh, die met den mond gegrepen,
> Het eynd haers starts vast hiel.

('. . . the Blessed, full of virtue, [who] rise to the eternal height, to gain the blessed region of the City of Angels where eternity stood [read 'stands', meaning 'is' in this context, since the tense is evidently changed to provide a rhyme-word] represented in the arched roof, by the point of a diamond in the middle of the circle formed by a gilded serpent, who firmly held the end of her tail gripped in her mouth.') Eternity was clearly to be represented, since the words "stond . . . verbeeld" show that the symbols were not used metaphorically. The diamond was a symbol of hardness *(durezza)*, see Ripa, *Iconologia*, 1624, pp. 44 *(Architettura Militare)* and 146–7 *(Crudeltà)*, hence, presumably, of durability and in this sense eternity as well. The serpent with its tail in its mouth also symbolizes eternity.

[1]   Bontemantel, *De regeeringe*, I, p. 67: "Doen sach den Schout nae bovene, alwaer Burgemeesteren uyt het venster (daertoe geordonneert) laegen, en syde: wat seggen Burgemeesteren van stats wegen?".

The centre of attention changed, and the prisoner was placed facing the Secretary as he sat in his seat at the centre of the north wall of the room, which has a relief representing Silence in front of it to symbolize his office, and a shell carved above the seat itself, together with a festoon of thistles and holly and hanging garlands of oak. The back wall of the niche in which it stands is filled with carved foliage and weeping children, and to each side of it serpents are carved, winding round tree-trunks and with apples in their mouths. Above the back of the Secretary's seat children weeping over a death's-head are carved. If he should raise his eyes so far the condemned man would catch sight of the maliciously grinning faces of the serpents, and would see the children weeping as the Secretary rose to read his sentence.

One part of the decoration that was planned for the *vierschaar* remains to be mentioned.[1] It is referred to in a passage by Everard Meyster, in which he describes how the Serpent 'seems to look laughingly at Adam there on high', who appears 'at the time when he flees from Eden because of the forbidden fruit, with Eve his wife – created too beautiful to gape at an apple in such a shameful way – on the other side';[2] we are not told what Eve is on the other side of. Even allowing for poetic license (for the serpents do not in fact look up, but down), and for the dangers of interpreting a piece of very bad verse, in which the sense is contorted for the sake of the rhyme-words, one must suppose that somewhere in the *vierschaar*, and probably above the level of the serpents' heads, Adam and Eve were to have been represented.

---

[1] For a fuller discussion see Katharine Fremantle, 'Drie modellen voor de vierschaar van het voormalige Stadhuis', *Bulletin van het Rijksmuseum*, IV, 1956, pp. 72–77.

[2] Meyster, op. cit., II, p. 6: The quotation follows in its context:

> De Kind'ren afgebeeld met traenen uyt-gestort,
> Beweenen Dagh en Nacht dien 't quaetdoen heeft verkort,
> Beklagende dat schoon, 't geen d'eersten Mensch belaegden
> Zijnn' eerst' onnoselheyt, die d'Opperheit behaegden,
> Eer d'Appel-beet het goed verbeten had, en 't quaet
> In brogt, door d'alderslimst' en snoodste Slange raedt;
> Die'r kunstigh uytgewrogt, (op d'hoeken van twee boogen
> Met d'appel in de mond) noch lachend schijnt te oogen
> Naer Adam daer om hoogh, waer hy uyt Eden vlugt,
> Met Eva sijn gemael, om den verboden vrught,
> Aen d'ander kant uyt d'Aerd te heerelijck geschapen,
> Om aen een Appel haer zoo schendigh te vergapen.

('The children depicted with [their] tears pouring forth bewail, day and night, those whom the doing of wrong has cut short, lamenting that beauty which lay in wait for the first man [and?] his first innocence, which pleased the Reigning Power before the biting of the apple had bitten away good and brought in evil, through the most cunning and wily serpent's counsel; which [serpent], carved there with art (on the corners of two arches, apple in mouth) still seems to look laughingly at Adam there on high' etc.) The weeping children referred to are those above the Secretary's seat.

84

Three models in the Rijksmuseum at Amsterdam bear out this supposition.[1] They were evidently made in preparation for the casting of a pair of bronze doors, and they can be identified with three models described in 1769 as 'A model of the doors of the *vierschaar* depicting Adam and Eve' and 'Two large wooden bas-reliefs, being models for the doors of the *vierschaar*'.[2] The doors represented in these models were to have had solid panels on which children weeping over death's-heads were to be depicted in relief in a style and with a composition very like those of the sculptures over the Secretary's seat. Above the panels were to have been bars similar to those of the *vierschaar* doors. Adam was to have been represented in the upper part of one of the doors, a serpent was to have been shown winding round the bars, cast in the form of tree-trunks, to close them in the centre, and Eve was to appear 'on the other side' of the central bar. Meyster's indication that such a representation was planned for the upper part of the room suggests that the design was intended for shutters to close the window between the *vierschaar* and the burgomasters' chamber; wooden shutters in this position are mentioned in descriptions of the Town Hall and are consistently referred to as 'doors'.[3] The solid panels would have been high enough to give the burgomasters privacy when the court was not sitting, and in all probability the 'doors' would have been used as well at those tense moments when the magistrates filed in to the burgomasters' chamber to ask for advice and to decide on their verdict. If indeed the doors depicted were intended for this position the reliefs would have provided a silent commentary appropriate to such a moment. The figures of Adam and Eve, representing the Fall of Man, would have formed a symbolic counterpart to the paintings planned for the upper zone of the *vierschaar*, by showing the beginning of the story which ends with the Last Judgement, and these representations of divine justice would together have completed the significance of the scenes of human justice in the zone below, both illustrated and actual, by placing them in their context in the history of human transgression. All alike, together representing the whole

[1] *Cat. beeldhouwwerken*, nos. 282, and 305 (two models).
[2] Dated MS. inventory, *Notitie van boetseersels en pleisterbeelde enz bewaard wordende op de kunstkamer van het Stadhuijs der Stad Amsterdam*, Gemeente-Archief, Amsterdam, Library, H, Stadsmuseum [etc.]; items Q and MM: "een model van de deuren der vierschaar verbeeldende Adam en Eva" and "twee groote houte basreliefven zijnde modellen tot de deuren van de vierschaar".
[3] e.g. Vennekool, *Afbeelding*, p. 6, and Dapper, *Beschryving*, p. 353. It is of course possible that the models represent a rejected design for the entrance doors, but Meyster's evidence, since he mentions only a single representation of Adam and Eve, and that high up, weighs against this. Only the entrance and the window above it would need doors or shutters. Whatever position the design was for it must have been rejected before the *Afbeelding* was published, since the lower doors are shown and the wooden shutters mentioned in it.

range of time, and history, including the present, would have been shown in relation to eternity, symbolised in the vault above.

When the ceremony in the *vierschaar* was over the condemned man was taken upstairs to the room where the other prisoners were waiting, and it was at this point that their sentences were read out from the publication gallery in the manner which has been described. Meanwhile cushions were spread in a circle in the chamber of justice, on the marble floor in which the coat of arms of the city and two great two-edged swords are inlaid. There, when the last of the sentences had been pronounced, the sheriff, burgomasters and magistrates, the Secretary, a minister of religion, and a visitor of the sick, with any others who were present, knelt with the man who was about to go out to the scaffold while a final prayer was said. The end followed swiftly, and after the other prisoners had received their punishments the rod of justice was withdrawn from the gallery window and the crowd went home.

Cornelis Kilian, in his dictionary of the Dutch language, first published in 1574,[1] defines the word *versieren*, which in modern Dutch means 'to decorate', as "Comminisci, fingere, effingere, confingere, commentari: excogitare, ementiri, assimulare", while under the heading *vercieren* he gives the meanings "Ornare, adornare" and others of the same kind. He gives as well nouns related to the two verbs. The two families of words, though differently derived,[2] were not always spelt differently, although in the writings of some authors a distinction was made. Van Mander, writing at the beginning of the seventeenth century, makes use of both meanings. Unconsciously betraying his own enthusiastic and enquiring nature and surely also portraying himself on his journeys in Italy, he describes how travellers in foreign countries, coming to some beautiful building that they find locked up, "verlangen om [te] weten watter voor uyt-nemende heerlijcke wercken en vercieringen inwendich zijn" – or 'long to know what excellent splendid works and *decorations* are inside' – and peer through cracks and crevices to get a view of them.[3] He refers also to the "vreemde versieringhen, hoe dat de lichamen verandert souden zijn ghewor-den" – 'strange *inventions* [of] how bodies were changed' – of Ovid's *Meta-*

---

[1] See Bibliography s.v. Kilian; also A. Zijderveld, 'Cesare Ripa's Iconologia in ons land', *Oud-Holland*, LXIV, 1949, p. 115, n. 3.
[2] E. Verwijs and J. Verdam, *Middelnederlandsch Woordenboek*, The Hague, 1885–1929, s.v. *Versieren* (second definition).
[3] *Wtleggingh*, fol. *ij r.

morphoses.[1] He seems to use this sense more frequently. Yet by 1765 this meaning of *versieren* and of words related to it had disappeared and it had come to mean only "to adorn, trim, deck, garnish, embellish, [and] to set off".[2] Vondel and his contemporaries, in the middle of the seventeenth century, used *versieren* freely in the first sense, but quite as often in the sense of 'decoration'.

These two meanings, both contained in what to the ear is a single word, are beautifully illustrated in the decoration of the seventeenth-century Town Hall of Amsterdam, and their definitions may be used to define its nature. It includes fanciful invention of the most ingenious kind, it has been imagined and shaped and studiously considered, and it includes an element of counterfeit. By virtue of these it embellishes the functions of the city's life with ingenious and edifying imagery. But this embellishment with ideas is only one part of the purpose of the decoration of the Town Hall. It was also created "to adorn, trim, deck, garnish, embellish, [and] to set off" the building's architecture.

[1] Op. cit., fol. *iiij r. The use of the conditional in the Dutch, which has no equivalent in English, implies unbelief on the part of the speaker.
[2] Sewel, *A Compleat Dictionary*, edition of 1766, s.v. *Vercieren*. The spelling 'Versieren' is also given, with a cross-reference.

CHAPTER IV

THE ANTIQUE COLUMN

Hier light hij Marmerloos die soo veel Marmers sleet,
En soo wel slijten leerd', als noch heel Holland weett,
En noch heel Neerland siet, en Neerlands ommelanden:
Die 't Gotsche krulligh mall met staetigh Roomsch vermanden,
En dreef ouw' Ketterij voor ouder Waerheit heen.

HUYGENS, on Van Campen's grave, 1658[1]

The developments in the use of imagery which determined the nature of the symbolism of the Town Hall of Amsterdam have not as yet been studied closely, and it has been necessary, in attempting to define the significance of the building as a whole, to discuss its imagery in relation to the circumstances in which and for which it was created without exploring its origins in detail, for to do this would be a task too large to be attempted here. Evidence about the origins of its architectural forms, however, lies nearer to hand, and much may be found out about them if example buildings of successive phases are examined and if the main factors that combined to produce them are taken into account. In doing this it may prove possible to throw new light on the nature of one of the major achievements of seventeenth-century Dutch architecture, whose most splendid surviving monument is the Town Hall itself. That achievement was the creation for the first time in Holland of a classical style of architecture in which buildings were considered in the round and as a whole, in relation to their setting, and with their decoration an integral part of the design.

In a remarkable passage written in his description of the life of Michelangelo Van Mander commented on the architecture of the Netherlands of his own day, seeing it with a detachment and an understanding of the art of the Italian Renaissance which led him to express himself with an unwonted display of feeling:

> In architecture beside the old common manner of the ancients and Vitruvius he [Michelangelo] has brought forth other new orders of cornices, capitals, bases, tabernacles, sepulchres and other ornaments, wherefore all architects that follow after owe him thanks for his having freed them from the old bonds and knots,

---

[1] From 'Op het graf vanden Heer Iacob van Campen', *Gedichten*, VI, p. 247. There was as yet no monument on the grave. 'Here lies, marbleless, he who used so many marbles, and also taught others to use them, as still all the Netherlands, and the Netherlands' neighbour countries, see; [he] who admonished Gothic curly foolery with the stately Roman, and drove old Heresy away before older Truth.'

and given them free rein, and licence to invent something beside the Antique. Yet to tell the truth this rein is so free, and this licence so misused by our Netherlanders, that in the course of time in Building a great Heresy has arisen among them, with a heap of craziness of decorations and breaking of the pilasters in the middle, and adding, on the pedestals, their usual coarse points of diamonds and such lameness, very disgusting to see.[1]

It may be added that when Van Mander had occasion to show figures in an antique building in one of his paintings[2] he created architecture of a most classical kind, which is quite unlike anything that was built in the Netherlands in his own day and anticipated what was to follow there only many years later.

In the first years of the seventeenth century the towns of Holland, under the pressure of the war with Spain, were still crowded together within their defences, their houses, as has been seen in the case of Amsterdam, packed together on narrow sites, each claiming a share of the street or water frontage by which goods came and went (see illus. 6, 7). These houses were Gothic in form and their ridged roofs ran at right angles to the street or quay. Each façade was simply a gable-end with the wall below it, and it is significant that what in the Latin languages is called 'façade' in Dutch is called *gevel*, for the gable-end and the wall that supported it was usually the only part of a house that could be seen. This being so it was usually built up higher than the structure of the house behind it, to give it added dignity, and it was often decorated. Such a façade was not an essential part of the building's structure, as the young Swedish architect Nicodemus Tessin noticed to his amazement when he visited Amsterdam in 1687 and recorded in his diary "Im bauen habe ich hier eine wunderliche maxime gesehen, dass man die facciade von vorn erst zu letzt aufführt wenn dass hauss schon unter dach ist".[3]

---

[1] Van Mander, *Schilder-boeck*, fol. 168 v. Up to "versieren" the passage is based on Vasari's life of Michelangelo (*Le vite de' più eccellenti pittori, scultori ed architettori*, ed. Gaetano Milanesi, Florence, 1878–85, VII, p. 193). The outburst that follows the borrowing is naturally in no way suggested by Vasari's words, and may be taken to be Van Mander's own. "In der Architecture, beneffens den ouden ghemeenen wegh der Antijcken en *Vitruvij*, heeft hy [Michelangelo] ander nieu ordenen opgebrocht, van Cornicen, Capiteelen, Basen, Tabernakelen, Sepultueren, en ander cieraten, waerom alle naevolgende Architecten hem te dancken hebben, dat hy hun van d'oude banden en stricken verlost heeft, en ruymen toom, en verlof gegheven, van yet beneffens d'Antijcken te versieren: Doch om de waerheyt te segghen, is desen toom so ruym, en dit verlof by onse Nederlanders so misbruyckt, dat metter tijdt in de Metselrije een groote Ketterije onder hun ghecomen is, met eenen hoop raserije van cieraten, en brekinghe der Pilasters in't midden, en op de Pedestalen voeghende hun aenghewende grove puncten van Diamanten, en derghelijcke lammicheyt, seer walghelijck om aen te sien."

[2] In the Christ in the Temple, Kunsthistorisches Museum, Vienna; E. Valentiner, *Karel van Mander als Maler*, Strasburg, 1930, pp. 79–80 and illus. 24.

[3] Gustaf Upmark, 'Ein Besuch in Holland 1687', *Oud-Holland*, XVIII, 1900, p. 128. James Thornhill recorded a similar impression on a visit to Rotterdam: "The Building[s] here lean prodigiously, . . . ye

Architecture could hardly be conceived in the round in these circumstances, and even partly or wholly free-standing buildings were often constructed in the same way and were mainly decorated on their gable-ends. Moreover architects, who at this time were masters of the trades of building, had not travelled far enough to see truly classical architecture for themselves, and can have had little opportunity to read about its theory. They could, however, copy and adapt its motifs, reproduced in two dimensions on the printed page, and it is not surprising that the architectural forms of the Renaissance were for the most part reflected in decoration applied to buildings rather than in their structure at this time in Holland, as they had been in the sixteenth century. Only later, when travelled and scholarly patrons began to be interested in the theory of classical architecture, and could find men capable of carrying out their ideas as architects in the modern sense of the term, could the conception of architecture alter. A degree of wealth and security which was lacking at the beginning of the seventeenth century in Holland was also necessary for this development.

The architecture of Lieven de Key, the city mason and master builder of Haarlem in the early seventeenth century,[1] is of the kind that has been described, and the Meat Market which he built there in the years 1602 to 1603 (illus. 98–99) must have been rising before Van Mander's eyes while he was preparing his book for publication. It is a large free-standing building which is Gothic in form, for like other master builders of his day in northern Europe De Key can only have been trained in Gothic methods of construction and can have known at first hand of no others suitable for a work of this size. The market hall inside, though it is supported by Doric columns, has a shallow vaulted ceiling. The ends walls and the gable-ends are decorated with ornament of the kind that Van Mander described, which was evidently based on the engraved models published in the southern Netherlands by such writers as Cornelis Floris and Hans Vredeman de Vries (e.g. illus. 100), or on works of architecture derived from them. This must largely account for the 'applied' and two-dimensional nature of the decoration of this and other similar buildings, but it must also be remembered that before Renaissance motifs were first used in northern Europe Gothic architectural forms had been applied to buildings merely

Fronts wch. consist generally of Brick and stone, being run up after ye whole Anatomy of ye wooden house is finisht"; MS. diary of his journey to the Netherlands, of 1711, p. 44 (photographic copy, Art History Institute, Utrecht; present whereabouts of MS. unknown).

[1] De Key was born in Ghent at an unknown date, spent some years in London, and afterwards settled in Haarlem, where he became master builder to the city in 1593. See M. D. Ozinga, in *Kunstgeschiedenis*, II, p. 20, where the terms defining his office are quoted.

as ornamental motifs there, and had been elaborated as such. The application of Antique forms, as they were called, to the surfaces of buildings must have followed naturally enough, and indeed this was regarded as their proper use. Each of the gable-ends of the Meat Market at Haarlem is clearly designed to be seen from the front, for such gable-ends when seen from the side or back entirely lose their ornamental quality. It follows that this building, with its decoration, is not intended to be considered as a solid entity, and it probably never occurred to De Key that people living in a later age might try to think of it as such. It is illuminating, though difficult, to walk round such a building as people must have done when it was new, simply taking pleasure in the play of texture on the separate surfaces and delighting in the ingenuity of their ornament; adding up impressions mentally as one goes, and so only forming a total impression of the whole. Generally speaking such an aggregate of surfaces and motifs *was* the architecture of the antique style to the master builders and the ordinary citizens of Holland in Van Mander's day. The characteristics of Michelangelo's architecture and of that of antiquity were seen from too great a distance and through the work of too many intermediaries to be distinguished clearly from each other.

To people thinking in these terms the theoretical treatises of antique and renaissance Italy must have been hard to understand, for one cannot easily grasp the essential nature of classical architecture, its design in terms of solid form and well-proportioned space, by looking at diagrams, and of the treatises of Italian writers on architecture only that of Serlio had been translated into Dutch at the beginning of the century.[1] It was natural that master builders such as De Key should turn to the heavily edited and indeed very fanciful versions of antique art which were published by northern artists, whose problems of use and adaptation were much the same as their own. These writers provided what purported to be classical ornament in a form which was described on a title-page as 'convenient and useful for all ingenious builders, such as brick-layers, stonemasons, and other lovers of the antique Architectures, invented and made according to the teaching of Vitruvius' – in this instance by Hans

---

[1] A Dutch translation of Books I-V of Serlio's treatise was published in Antwerp in 1553 and in Amsterdam in 1606 and 1616, and of Book IV only in Antwerp in 1549. Dutch translations of the treatises of Vignola (Utrecht, 1629, Amsterdam, 1640 and 1642), Palladio (the five orders 'extracted from' his work, Amsterdam, 1646) and Scamozzi (Book IV only, Amsterdam 1640) appeared before 1650. It seems that no Dutch translations of those of Alberti and Vitruvius had appeared by this date. See *Catalogus der Kunsthistorische Bibliotheek in het Rijksmuseum te Amsterdam*, Amsterdam, 1934–6, and Julius Schlosser Magnino, *La letteratura artistica*, Vienna [1956].

Vredeman de Vries.[1] Addressing the Reader of Understanding De Vries explains how his models are intended to be used. He has not, he says, given measurements in his various engravings:

> '... for every person of understanding according to his needs can easily discover the measurements drawn in each piece, or arrange them to his contentment according to the opportunity of his work, always following the order and teaching of Vitruvius.[2]

The models were many and very various, and the order and teaching of Vitruvius were not enlarged upon, so that the reader was in fact given leave to combine and adapt their forms at will. Lieven de Key, it is clear, set about this task with gusto. Yet it has to be emphasized that De Key's architecture, as he saw it, was composed according to the precepts of antiquity, for the gable-ends of the Haarlem Meat Market are decorated with two orders arranged in correct suggestion: Doric, with Ionic above it; and in his design for the façade of the Town Hall at Leiden[3] there are four orders, Doric, Ionic, Corinthian and Composite below the herms at the top. Few precepts, however, were in evidence, and De Key may be imagined turning over page after page of his pattern-books, adapting and fitting their treasures in to his design very much as he pleased. The licence to do so was part of the precious tradition of 'the Antique' as it was handed on to him, and so fancy could be given free rein. Indeed it was essential to antique architecture as it was understood by Dutch builders and their patrons at the beginning of the seventeenth century.

It appears that the reaction which came at the end of what for the purposes of this discussion may perhaps be termed the phase of Mannerism,[4] was very widespread. In the field of painting it is recognizable in the works of the Carracci in Italy and in those of the circle in Antwerp in which Rubens was trained,

---

[1] *Architectura, de oorden Thuschana, in tween ghedeylt* [etc.] , Antwerp, 1578. "... bequaem, en nuttelijck voor alle ingenieuse bouwers, als metsers, steenhouwers ende andere liefhebbers der antiquer Architecturen. Gheinventeert ende ghemaect naer de leeringhe Vitruvij."

[2] Op. cit., Introduction. "... want deser maten can elc verstandighe sulc hem noodich is lichtelijc wt elck stuc geteeckent bevinden oft stellen tot sijnen contentemente naer de gelegentheyt sijns wercks, altijts volghende de oorden ende leere Vitruvij."

[3] A design identified as one paid for in 1595, Gemeente Archief, Leiden; see Georg Galland, *Geschichte der Holländischen Baukunst und Bildernei* [etc.], Frankfurt, 1890, pp. 214–15 and fig. 88, and Vermeulen, *Handboek*, II, p. 286. The design was carried out with alterations and the executed version copied when the Town Hall was rebuilt.

[4] In a lecture given at the Courtauld Institute, London, in 1954 Professor A. F. Blunt distinguished between art in which the precepts of the Italian Renaissance were deliberately, and often wittily, denied, which he called Mannerist art, and that in which they were broken with unconsciously. The term Mannerism has, nevertheless, been used here for want of a better, to refer to the mannered art which followed that of the High Renaissance, whatever form it took.

and its effects can be seen both in Italian and Belgian sculpture and in the architecture of Italy and France. It consisted in a movement towards the ideals of classical art, though these found expression in very various forms, and in the north, where the principles of classical art had not already been embodied in works of the Renaissance, it was a movement not only of reaction, but also of discovery. It must have prepared the ground for the classical art of the middle of the seventeenth century, including that of Poussin, Duquesnoy, and Algardi, as well as for the Baroque. The works of Hendrik de Keyser, both in sculpture and architecture, belong to this intermediate phase in the history of art, and his greatest buildings, those commissioned by the city council of Amsterdam, have a certain unity of form and sense of space which were new in Holland, though they are composed of the same elements as the buildings of Lieven de Key, which we proposed to call mannerist – Gothic construction and 'Antique' decoration. The introduction of such architecture was an individual achievement which heralded a new age, though it did not itself lead further in the development of Dutch art, for the more truly classical form of architecture that took pride of place later was first introduced into Holland in entirely different circles.

De Keyser, who was born in 1563, was the son of a Utrecht cabinet-maker, and was brought up at a time when furniture was loaded heavily with decoration such as that invented with such ingenuity by Hans Vredeman de Vries. He was trained under the engineer and sculptor Cornelis Bloemaert, the father of the painter, and in 1595 he was appointed master sculptor and stonemason to the city of Amsterdam.[1] His status there was no higher than that of the city's master bricklayer and master carpenter, but in 1612 he was mentioned in the burgomasters' minute-book as stonemason and "*architect*",[2] a term which does not appear to have been used earlier in Dutch city records. Even before this time he had been singled out to design the city's most important buildings, and the other master tradesmen, his colleagues, must have worked on them with him, but according to his designs.

In his position as city architect De Keyser had opportunities which were new in Dutch art, and which were due in the first place to economic conditions, for

[1] See biography by De Bray, in Danckerts, *Architectura*, pp. 6–7, and Neurdenburg, *De Keyser*, pp. 5–6, who corrects dates given by De Bray, using the city records.

[2] Vermeulen, op. cit., II, p. 264 and note. Up to this time the term *bouwmeester*, 'master of building', had been used, and it continued in use after the introduction of the word *architect*, the terms being used synonymously. Vermeulen states that De Keyser had not been referred to as *bouwmeester* or as *architect* before 1612 in the official records.

as has already been shown, in the early years of the century, with the increasing prosperity and rapid expansion of Amsterdam, building had to be undertaken on an unprecedented scale. The Exchange was built at this time, as well as the earliest of the churches that were provided for the districts newly added to the city. Of these churches the first to be built was the Zuiderkerk (illus. 101–2, 105–6), which was designed by De Keyser and was begun in 1603.[1] A new, not a borrowed, form was found for it, and for this reason it is important in the history of Dutch architecture.

The problem which faced De Keyser in designing this church was in itself a new one. Hardly any churches had been built in Holland during the troubles of the Reformation, and afterwards pre-reformation churches had been taken over for Protestant use. This was the first large Protestant church to be built there. No altar was needed and no choir, and the attention of the congregation was to be focussed on the pulpit, which naturally was placed in a central position so that the minister could be heard throughout the church. This implied an entirely new conception of church architecture, no longer one in which the building expressed a movement in one direction, towards the altar, and served as a shrine, but one in which it was a meeting-place, in itself unimportant, its emphasis, unlike that of an English Protestant church, alone that of enclosing the meeting. Perhaps this new conception helped De Keyser to arrive at the sense of unity of form and space, rhythmically composed and divided, which is first apparent in Holland in this church. Yet the Zuiderkerk is Gothic in its structure, for it consists of a nave and aisles with sloping roofs, though the gable-ends are masked by a decoration of classical motifs and the roof-beams are hidden by a barrel-vault of planks as they were, for instance, in St. Janskerk at Gouda, the last of Holland's great pre-reformation churches. There are tie-beams both across the nave and aisles, as there sometimes were in earlier buildings,[2] and there are buttresses, unconvincingly disguised by classical pediments, to help carry the thrust of the roof; the flattened roofs of the side aisles, which make the addition of short lengths of balustrade on the skyline possible, represent only a minor concession to renaissance taste, though a significant one. There are, however, no transepts, so that the ground plan is a simple rectangle, and only cross-vaulting and higher windows in the second and fifth

[1] Particulars from Danckerts, op. cit., pp. 12–13.
[2] It is unlikely that these were added later, as E. Neurdenburg suggests, op. cit., p. 43. They appear in Danckerts' prints of 1631, *Architectura*, pl. III, without mention in the text of an addition, and the design of the capitals and arches allows for them.

bays, making what must be described a pseudo-transepts, lighten the church and bring variety into its form. Tuscan columns, though they are not classically used, support the series of rounded arches which separate nave and aisles, and punctuate the composition rhythmically; the balance and unity of the interior are only interrupted by the base of the tower, which is made to take up exactly one bay of the western aisle.

It seems, then, that in designing the Zuiderkerk De Keyser tried his utmost to make a unified building in the classical sense, but that his means were limited. There was certainly no precedent within reach for constructing a hall of the necessary size except on Gothic principles, and it is doubtful whether, even if De Keyser had known how to set about it, it would have been possible to build it in another form. There were probably limitations of weight and cost, for this church, like most Dutch buildings, had to be constructed on a foundation of piles driven into marshy ground, and extra weight would add very greatly to the initial expense. Moreover stone was very costly, for there is no durable stone to be quarried in Holland; stone had to be imported and large blocks in particular were very difficult to get.[1] These factors account for the many wooden roofs, and the very general use of brick, in Dutch architecture. In the ordinary way stone was used mainly for decorative purposes and where it was of advantage for structural reasons, though as the country became more prosperous its use increased.

It is noticeable that the outside of the Zuiderkerk has less unity of form than the interior, which seems to have taken precedence when the plans were made, so that interior and exterior are not entirely in harmony, and that the smaller details of the decoration have been added on to the form of the church, as the decoration was 'added on' in the work of Lieven de Key. Yet, as the balustrades with the flat roof behind them demonstrate, there is in fact an interplay between the more important decorative features and the structure itself such as De Key never arrived at, and this must be the result of an ability on the architect's part to think of his building not as an aggregate of surfaces and motifs, but as a single form seen in the round. A comparison of the tower of the Zuiderkerk with a tower built by Lieven de Key, that of the New Church at Haarlem, brings out this difference clearly (cf. illus. 106, 108). De Keyser's tower is ornamented with niches and columns that are part of its structure, while De

---

[1] De Bray, in Danckerts, op. cit., pp. 5 and 11, discusses these conditions and their limiting effects on Dutch architecture.

Key's pinnacles and arches are simply added to the structure that they embellish.

In the Westerkerk (illus. 103–4, 107), which was built in the area added to the city in 1609, De Keyser brought the interior and exterior of his building into harmony, for the composition of the space within this church is reflected clearly in its external form. The building was begun in 1620, the year before the architect's death, but except for the upper stages of the tower it was completed according to his design.[1] The ground plan is similar to that of the Zuiderkerk, and there are pseudo-transepts, but here there is a clerestory, and the pseudo-transepts are much higher. They have steeply-pitched ridged roofs of the height of the roof of the nave, and are supported by columns set against buttresses below the gable-ends. As in the Zuiderkerk the tower breaks the symmetry of the plan, but here it does not interrupt the interior space, which is symmetrical on each axis. The church is much larger than the Zuiderkerk, as well as higher, and the weight of the upper part is borne by clustered Tuscan columns which, with rounded arches above them, form the arcade of the nave and the pseudo-transepts. Above the columns there are short projecting strips which run up to a cornice. This in turn has Ionic pilasters above it and these run between the windows of the clerestory and support a second cornice below the roof, which is barrel-vaulted and has cross-vaulting where it is met by the vaulting of the pseudo-transepts. Thus the orders, if the intermediate pilasters are left out of account, are used in correct succession as they were by Lieven de Key, while the forms of the decoration are relatively simple and add to the harmony of the structure itself. It is impossible to take a photograph which does justice to this harmony, for this church, like the Zuiderkerk, is composed simply to surround the worshipper, and no movement in a particular direction is implied; indeed the very inadequacy of photographs points to the nature of De Keyser's achievement.

The first buildings of the phase that follows can be discussed only with great diffidence, for if their significance in the history of Dutch, and indeed of European, culture is to be understood, they will have to be considered afresh, and evidence taken into account which till now has been neglected. It will be necessary to see them in their context in the history of European art, and as expressing, in concrete form, ideas that were current internationally among the

[1] Danckerts, op. cit., pl. XI, shows the original design for the tower, and in the text, p. 14, De Bray states that it has been built to about half its height and will be completed to De Keyser's design. Yet the upper half is not as shown in the engraving.

learned of the day, their objective search for scientific and artistic principles, and their detached and critical study of the antique world. It is quite certain that the evidence on which such a revaluation could be based does exist, and that some of it is of major importance, but at the present time much of it has still to be assembled, and, though the main lines of its import are distinguishable, there has as yet been little opportunity to examine in detail even the evidence that already lies to hand. So at this point a picture can be built up only of fragments, and some parts of it will remain unknown to us because pieces are missing or because their significance is not yet clearly seen.

In the year 1635 the Secretary to the Stadholder, Constantijn Huygens, wrote to his friend Joachim de Wicquefort about the building of his new house on the Plein in The Hague, and about his studies in architecture:

Monsieur,

Tout ce que je puis derobber au publiq s'emploije à l'Architecture antique. C'est l'humeur ou m'a porté ce petit bastiment, que j'iroij entamer, s'il plaisoit à ce troisiesme hiver de la saison. J'en suis desià si avant, que je furette soigneusement les choses plus obscures, et prens plaisir à sçavoir en theorie ce que la prattique ne me demandera jamais. Cela me faict rechercher tous les bons textes de Vitruve, et tous les commentateurs *ch'egli s'e serato adosso*, par un stile dur, scabreux, fantasque, et si esloigné de la grace du siecle qu'on luij attribue, que derniermentj'aij osé doubter aveq M. Heinsius, si Auguste l'a jamais ouij parler. Par tant de preface je pretends de vous induire à m'assister de vostre entremise en la recherche de ces livres. Les Italiens m'alleguent un Giovanni Incundo [Giocondo], Caesare Cesariano, G. Baptista Caporali, Daniele Barbaro, patriarcha d'Aquileia, et Bernerdino Baldi, abbate di Garistalla et en parlent aveq bien du faste. De tout cela rien ne se recouvre pardeça les monts. Non pas Léon Baptista Alberti seulement, en son Latin original, que je desire tant conferer aux versions.[1]

By the end of his life Huygens had built up a connoisseur's library of books on architecture, as he had on many subjects, and it can be taken as certain that by then he had to hand at least eleven editions of Vitruvius and the Latin edition of Alberti that he had so much coveted, as well as the works of Serlio, Vignola, Palladio, Scamozzi, Du Cerceau, and many other authorities, a good number of them in more than one edition.[2]

---

[1] 8th March 1635; Koninklijke Bibliotheek, The Hague, Kon. Acad. MS. XLIX, Vol. I, fol. 667 (Worp 1088). On Vitruvius cf. Wotton, *Elements*, Preface, p. vii: "It was in truth an unhappinesse, to exprese himselfe so ill, especially writing (as he did) in a season of the ablest Pennes". The phrase including the Italian quotation means: 'and all the commentators that he has amassed because of' (the qualities of his [literary] style).

[2] P. Leendertsz. Jun., 'Een merkwaardige catalogus', *Tijdschrift voor Nederlandsche taal- en letterkunde* (Maatschappij der Nederlandsche Letterkunde te Leiden), XXIV, 1905, pp. 197–201, has shown that the

When, four years later, Huygens had moved into his new house (illus. 113-15), he sent sets of engravings of it to his friends,[1] and among them he sent a set to Rubens,[2] with whom he had corresponded though they had never met, accompanied by a letter in which he wrote:

> ... voijci le morceau de Brique que j'aij eslevé à la Haije, en un lieu, que j'ose bien nommer des plus illustres du village. Quand je l'entamaij, la main de l'éternel ne s'estoit encor appesantie sur moij; je vivoij doublement, dans la saincte compagnie *di Lei ch'è salita a tanta pace, e m'ha lasciato in guerra* ... C'est ce qui me porta à ceste egalité reguliere de part et d'autre, que vous trouverez en ces departements, que vous sçavez avoir tant pleu aux Anciens, et que les bons Italiens d'aujourd'huij recerchent encor aveq tant de soin: distribuant les quartiers des deux chefs de ma famille en deux Sales, deux Chambres, deux Garderobes, deux Cabinets, et autant de Galeries. Le tout separé par une sale d'entrée ou vestibule, et couplé sur le derriere, par la communication d'un passage privé. Aujourd'huij, ce qui avoit esté destiné pour la Mere, sert aux Enfants et à ceux qui les gouvernent. Ma portion est du costé du jardin, que je decouvre à gauche: à droicte tout ce qui sort et entre par la Bassecour; et sur le devant une excellente Plaine, ceinte de Bastimens, que grands, que mediocres; close de deux rangs de Tilieux au croissant de leur aâge; et rebordée d'un pavé de Ruë de 36 pieds, dont le costé que flanquent les saillies de mes Galeries s'estend en ligne droicte à quelques mil pas.[3]

books left by Huygens to his sons which were sold by Abraham Troyel, The Hague, 15 Mar. 1688 (catalogue reprinted by W. P. van Stockum Jun., *Catalogus der bibliotheek van Constantyn Huygens* [etc.], The Hague, 1903) formed only part of his library, that those possessed by Constantijn Huygens his eldest son, sold by Bauduin van der Aa, Leiden, 26 Sept. 1701 (copies of catalogue in Koninklijke Bibliotheek, The Hague, and in Universiteitsbibliotheek, Leiden), were largely from the father's library, and that other books from the father's library were in neither of the sales. An examination of the two sales catalogues as far as the books concerning the arts is concerned strongly supports the first two of these statements. Although in the catalogue of the second sale some books on antiquities published after the father's death are listed, no such works on architecture are mentioned there; it is not known that the son, who succeeded his father as the Stadholder's Secretary, studied the subject; and so far as architecture is concerned the two lists are almost entirely complementary and appear to describe a single library. It therefore seems reasonable to assume, in the absence of evidence to the contrary, that the son's architecture books came from the father's library, and accordingly the books on architecture listed in the two catalogues have been counted together to provide the particulars given here.

[1] Letters in Huygens' correspondence (Worp nos. 1763 and 2051) show that these are by Pieter Post; a set of five is in the topographical collection of the Gemeente Archief, The Hague. The house no longer stands, and the discussion here is based on these engravings.

[2] Rubens had altered and enlarged his own house in Antwerp, which he bought in 1610, to his own designs; see A. J. J. Delen, *Het huis van Pieter Pauwel Rubens* [etc.], Brussels, 1933, pp. 17–45. Delen shows (p. 26 and note) that while work was in progress Rubens bought copies of Barbaro's and Philander's editions of Vitruvius, and other works on architecture, including that of Scamozzi, and that in the same years he had a copy of Serlio bound.

[3] 2nd July 1639, Koninklijke Bibliotheek, The Hague, Kon. Acad. MS. XLIX, Vol. I, fol. 899 (Worp no. 2149). In the second sentence Huygens refers to his wife's death, which took place in 1637 when he was moving into the new house; J. H. W. Unger, *Dagboek van Constantyn Huygens* [etc.] (publ. Oud-Holland), Amsterdam, 1885, p. 30.

The results of Huygens' researches are evident in the design of his house in a very particular way, for its main rooms at least were planned according to the principles of mathematical and harmonic proportion that Vitruvius and his commentators had laid down and that had been used by the architects of Renaissance Italy, in particular by Palladio, and, at least in a simple form, by Inigo Jones in England.[1] Such proportions, as Professor Wittkower has shown, were comparable to and often based on the relative lengths of sounding strings, or of organ pipes, in making musical notes in harmony with one another.[2] The height of each of Huygens' principal rooms was a third of the length and the breadth one half the length, proportions which represent the division of the octave into a fourth and a fifth in music. The two halls were cubic in form. The external measurements seem also to have been related by proportion, and the various rooms to have been related by proportion to each other. The ambassador and diplomat Sir Henry Wotton, who as a neighbour at The Hague when Huygens was a boy had taught him the English technique of playing the lute,[3] and whose treatise on architecture was translated into Dutch perhaps at Huygens' instigation and certainly with his interest,[4] described "a sound piece of good Art" in building as one "where the Materials being but ordinarie Stone, without any garnishment of Sculpture, doe yet ravish the Beholder (and hee knowes not how) by a secret Harmony in the Proportions".[5] In writing this Wotton was echoing ideas which were latent in the treatise of Vitruvius and had been worked out by the architects of renaissance Italy and their successors in the classical tradition;[6] it was held that to search for perfection of mathematical proportions in architecture, and for such harmony, was to search for truth, as it is revealed in universal principles. Stress had been laid on this conception by Daniele Barbaro in his commentary on Vitruvius, and it must have been a source of inspiration for the researches and the architecture of Palladio.[7]

It therefore appears that when Huygens wrote of "cest egalité reguliere de part et d'autre ... que les bons Italiens d'aujourd'huij recerchent encor

---

[1] These principles have been brought forward and discussed by Rudolf Wittkower in his *Architectural Principles in the Age of Humanism*, London, 1952. Jones' use of simple mathematical proportions is well known but so far as the present writer knows this aspect of his planning has not been investigated in detail.

[2] Op. cit., pp. 89–135.

[3] A. H. Kan, *De jeugd van Constantijn Huygens door hemzelf beschreven*, Rotterdam and Antwerp, 1946, p. 25.

[4] Letter to Huygens of 6 Feb. 1642, Worp no. 2942.

[5] *Elements*, p. 9.

[6] Wittkower, op. cit., esp. p. 100, note; and p. 125, where Wotton is quoted.

[7] Ibid., pp. 60–62.

aveq tant de soin" his meaning was an exact one, and that he applied the principles of 'the good Italians' with all the powers of his careful scholarship in the building of his house. He realized that it was to be an innovation,[1] and he had written to Rubens when he first informed him of his plans for the building, after giving the dimensions of the site: "Vous ne serez pas marrij d'apprendre, que je pretens faire revivre là dessus un peu de l'Architecture anciene, que je cheris de passion, mais ce n'est qu'au petit pied, et jusqu'à ou le souffrent le climat et mes coffres".[2] Jacob van Campen, who was described by a contemporary as a 'clever mathematician'[3] came to him in connection with the project and helped him, as Huygens put it, "en Vitruve tresparfaict".[4] His exact share in the design, however, is not known.

The contrast between Huygens' architecture, planned on mathematical principles and built up of classical forms, and the buildings of De Key and De Keyser does not need stressing, and neither does the change in what was thought of as 'antique' art, for these are clear enough. Yet something more must be said about Huygens himself, for in referring to him we have left the world of merchants and tradesmen and the city councils that they formed, and the master builders who worked for them, and are among men whose knowledge and tastes reached far beyond the borders of their own lands. Huygens corresponded, across Europe, with the learned of his day, Descartes and Lipsius among them. He wrote Latin, French and Dutch poetry, was an expert musician, a student of the classics, and was deeply interested in both science and the arts. In 1618, at the age of twenty-two, he had been to England with Sir Dudley Carleton, then ambassador at The Hague, who a few days after their arrival took him to see the court at Greenwich,[5] and it is likely that they saw the Queen's House, being built there by Inigo Jones, in its early stages. It was England's first truly classical building, planned on the principles

[1] See quotation p. 104 below.
[2] Letter of Nov. 1635, Koninklijke Bibliotheek, The Hague, Kon. Acad., MS. XLIX, Vol. I fol. 623 (Worp no. 1301).
[3] Theodor Schrevelius, *Harlemias, ofte ... de eerste stichtinghe der stadt Haerlem* [etc.], Haarlem, 1648, p. 383: "geswinde *Mathematicus*". Schrevelius was Rector of the Latin School at Haarlem, where Van Campen lived for many years. The Haarlem engraver and print-seller Jacob Matham, in the dedication of a print by his son Theodoor which G. J. Hoogewerff dates 'between 1621 and 1630', also refers to Van Campen's skill in mathematics; see G. J. Hoogewerff, *De Noord-Nederlandse schilderkunst*, The Hague, 1936–47, II, pp. 138–9 and note.
[4] Letter to De Wicquefort, 5 Dec. 1634, Koninklijke Bibliotheek, The Hague, Kon. Acad. MS. XLIX, Vol. I, fol. 502 (Worp no. 1046). Probably Van Campen arrived soon before this date, since in a letter to De Wicquefort of 11 Apr. 1634 (Worp no. 897) Huygens described his proposals for his house without mentioning Van Campen, and in the later letter he tells of his coming as though it were recent news.
[5] Letter of 6 June (old style) 1618, Worp no. 45.

of Italian classical architecture, and its fame, as "some curious devise" had reached Carleton in Holland in the previous year.[1] During this visit to England Huygens also saw "la Galerie a peintures du feu Prince" and Lord Arundel's gallery,[2] with both of which Jones must have been concerned.[3] In 1620 Huygens spent a few weeks with the Dutch ambassador in north Italy, and his diary of the expedition shows that he was deeply impressed by the monuments of antiquity that he saw there, and also by Palladio's theatre at Vicenza, "bastiment moderne, mais à la verité tel qu'en Europe ne se peut voir chose plus belle", as he described it.[4] He paced out the amphitheatre at Verona while his companions were resting in the midday heat, being unsatisfied with the visit made by the ambassadorial party the same morning, and climbed to the top to see the huge pieces of marble that were still in place there. In the years 1621 to 1623 Huygens was in England for a total of seventeen months, on the staff of embassies, moving in court society and often waiting about in London, his work held up while the King was out of town. He knew Cecil, Lady Bedford, and also the Killigrews, in whose house he met Bacon and Donne[5] and he dined several times with the widow of Sir Ralph Winwood in Lord Arundel's house.[6] He was knighted through the good offices of Buckingham.[7] He cannot have met Sir Henry Wotton on these visits, since he was abroad at the time.[8] He saw a number of Masques, wrote a letter seeking the acquaintance of Ben Jonson,[9] and is known to have seen the Royal Banqueting House designed by Inigo Jones when it was first in use.[10] It is not recorded that he met its author, though it seems that in these circles he can hardly have failed to do so, and a single piece of evidence perhaps suggests

[1] Letter from John Chamberlain, of 22 June 1617, quoted by J. Alfred Gotch, *Inigo Jones*, London, 1928, pp. 92–93. The phrase quoted here can perhaps best be translated into modern English as 'some ingenious invention'.

[2] Letter of 4 July 1618, Koninklijke Bibliotheek, The Hague, Kon. Acad. MS. XLIX, Vol. I, fol. 50 (Worp no. 51). The late prince was Henry, Prince of Wales (d. 1612). Huygens had obtained access to the galleries "par l'adresse de certains Gentilshommes Anglois qui m'ont grandement obligé" (stated in the same letter).

[3] Jones was appointed surveyor to Prince Henry in 1611 and to King James in 1615. He was concerned with Arundel's collection and designed alterations to his house, among them to the gallery. See Gotch, op. cit., and James Lees-Milne, *The Age of Inigo Jones*, London, 1953, esp. pp. 35 and 64.

[4] J. A. Worp, 'Constantijn Huygens' Journaal van zijne reis naar Venetië in 1620', *Bijdragen en mededelingen van het Historisch Genootschap*, XV, The Hague, 1894, pp. 62–152. Quotation from p. 118.

[5] See Huygens' letters of these years, Worp, *Briefwisseling*, I, pp. 60–137 and notes.

[6] Letter of 22 Dec. 1636, Worp no. 1512.

[7] Letter of 25 July 1622, Worp no. 164.

[8] *Dictionary of National Biography*, ed. Leslie Stephen, London, 1885–1904, s.v. Sir Henry Wotton, and *Calendar of State Papers*, Venetian, Vol. 1619–21, London, 1910, p. 148 and note.

[9] 18th Oct. 1622, Worp no. 190.

[10] See Rosalie L. Colie, '*Some Thankfulnesse to Constantine*', The Hague, 1956, pp. 31–32.

it – a letter promising prints of his house to a friend in England, in which he wrote:

> ... une taille douce vous ira dire ou j'habite. De mesme (puis que je suis en train d'enrager) Mr. Inigo Johns le sçaura s'il luij plaist, pour apprendre que le Bon Vitruve n'est pas du tout exclú d'Hollande.[1]

The tone of this passage does seem to imply that there had been exchanges over architecture between Inigo Jones and Huygens earlier. If these two scholars did meet it is just possible that Huygens had opportunities for the study of drawings[2] and for discussion which were lacking on his visit to Italy, and whether they did so or not one of Huygens' interests and powers of penetration cannot have failed to grasp the nature of the changes that were being made in English building by Inigo Jones, so that he may well have been fired with new possibilities in the field of architecture on English soil.[3]

If classical forms were used consistently and with understanding in certain works in Holland in the 1630s, no buildings so purely Italian in conception as those built in England by Jones were ever made there, for certain French elements were introduced at about the same time. It is possible that the wings which flanked Huygens' forecourt, and the pitch of his roofs, which suited a northern climate, were French in origin, and though the influence of Italian classical architecture may in part have reached Holland via England it certainly did so, in a modified form, via France.[4]

It appears that Prince Frederik Hendrik was less learned in architectural theory than his Secretary,[5] but he was deeply interested in architecture, even to the details of planning, and he could undertake large works, as his means

---

[1] Letter of 11–21 Nov. 1637, Koninklijke Bibliotheek, The Hague, Kon. Acad. MS. XLIX, Vol. I, fol. 748 (Worp no. 1765).

[2] Inigo Jones had measured and drawn antique buildings in Italy and possessed a collection of architectural drawings, see W. G. Keith, 'Inigo Jones as a Collector', *Journal of the Royal Institute of British Architects*, XXXIII, Dec. 1925, pp. 95–108.

[3] In a book now in preparation Professor A. G. H. Bachrach examines Huygens' English relationships, shows that Italian influence in the field of literature reached him, *inter alia*, via England, and gives further information which has bearing on his interest in architecture. The present writer is much indebted to him for discussing the subject with her and pointing the way to further information.

[4] The possibility of Huygens having received inspiration in the field architecture in England has been enlarged on here because it has not, to the present writer's knowledge, been brought forward before. Yet the importance of possible English inspiration must not be overestimated, and it must be repeated with emphasis that no balanced picture of the factors which combined to create the styles of 17th-century classical Dutch architecture can be formed without further investigation. In order to demonstrate its presence this one element has been arbitrarily, and temporarily, brought forward.

[5] The books on architecture listed in the inventory of the Stadholders' library, compiled under Huygens' supervision in 1686, Koninklijke Bibliotheek, The Hague, MS. no. 78. D. 14, provide evidence of this. Works by the leading authorities are represented, but seldom in more than one edition.

improved with the growing prosperity of the country.[1] He must have been to a great extent personally responsible for the introduction of French taste.[2] In 1598 he had spent a year with his mother, Louise de Coligny, at the court of Henri IV, who was his godfather and was very fond of him, he had visited him again when his architectural and town planning schemes in Paris were under way, and he remained in contact with France afterwards.[3] There can be little doubt that the making of the Plein at The Hague and the planning of the area round it was inspired by the planning of the Pont Neuf area and the conception of the Place des Vosges,[4] which in their turn must have been based on Italian models.[5] By 1630 the Stadholder's position had grown to be comparable in many respects with a royal one in international affairs, and it would not be surprising if the prince emulated the patronage of the arts of the French court, both in improving The Hague as the governmental centre of the country and in the building of his palaces.

It will have been noticed that Huygens, in writing to Rubens, described the position of his house in The Hague with some pride (illus.115-17). It was in an area lying to the east of the Binnenhof, the centre of government and the Stadholder's residence, which itself lies on the southern side of the Vijver, the lake that ornaments the centre of The Hague. This area was occupied earlier by a small wood on the side nearest to the Binnenhof, a triangular strip of land separated from this wood by a canal, and the Stadholder's garden,

[1] See the passages from the letters Worp nos. 897 and 1025 quoted on p. 104 below. Letters written by Huygens to Amalia van Solms during the campaign of 1636 also show the Stadholder's enthusiasm for architecture (Worp nos. 1424 and 1427–8) and a letter written by Brosterhuizen to Huygens (3 Feb. 1639, Worp 2036) shows that he planned a publication of prints of notable buildings.

[2] An English traveller, on a visit to one of the prince's palaces and The Hague in 1634, noted in his diary: "The ladies and gentlemen here all Frenchified in French fashion"; Sir William Brereton, *Travels in Holland . . . England, Scotland and Ireland* [etc.] (Chetham Society), London, 1844, p. 33.

[3] See F. W. Hudig, *Frederik Hendrik en de kunst van zijn tijd*, Amsterdam, 1928, pp. 4–5. Frederik Hendrik's other godfather was Christian IV of Denmark. Through both, as well as through Princess Amalia van Solms, he had connections with the English and the Bohemian courts, in which the arts were also patronized. From 1621 the ex-king and queen of Bohemia lived at The Hague, and there was a close friendship between the ex-queen Elizabeth, daughter of James I of England, and Princess Amalia, who had been at the Bohemian court.

[4] Pointed out by Hudig, op. cit., p. 20.

[5] It seems likely that the immediate source for the schemes of Henri IV was the planning of the new town of Leghorn, built by Cosimo I de' Medici from 1571. The description of the city by Jan Martensz. Merens, in A. Merens, 'De reis van Jan Martenz Merens door Frankrijk, Italië en Duitschland', *Mededelingen van het Nederlandsch Historisch Instituut te Rome*, Second Series, VII, 1937, pp. 116–17, shows the similar purpose of its planning. Except for the making of the Pont Neuf (an inherited project) the Paris schemes date from after the king's marriage, and the idea of such planning may well have been brought to France by Maria de' Medici, whose interest in architecture is evident, when she arrived as his bride in her golden ship from Leghorn (see Merens p. 117). For the Paris schemes see Anthony Blunt, *Art and Architecture in France, 1500 to 1700* (Pelican History of Art), London [etc.], 1953, pp. 113–17.

which was more extensive. To the north of the wood was the eastern end of the Vijver, and beside this, to the north of the garden, lay land belonging to St. Sebastian's Company of the Civic Guard of The Hague, on which they had shooting ranges. Their headquarters was to the north of these, beside the north-east corner of the Vijver, and there was a narrow path along the water's edge. During the years 1631 and 1632 a proposal to sell the Stadholder's garden in plots for building was considered by the States of the Province of Holland and West Friesland, to whom the land belonged, with the intention that this valuable property should be made to pay for alterations carried out in the Binnenhof.[1] Prince Frederik Hendrik pressed them to use the ground as an open space, and, evidently in consideration of his services to the country, they agreed to do so in spite of the financial loss and to make the arrangements in consultation with him. Later, at his own request, he was given the disposal of the triangular strip of land to the west of the garden, and this he made over to Constantijn Huygens for the building of his house: Huygens wrote less than a month after the transfer had been made that he had designed it, "le tout à l'instance de S. Ex.e qui, par affection naturelle qu'il porte à l'Architecture, ne cesse d'animer un chascun à l'embellissement de la Haije, et à mesme intention m'a honoré de ce beau present".[2] Six months later Huygens described how the Stadholder was spurring him on, "desirant veoir ma maison sur pied: pour y avoir contribué beaucoup de son ordonnance et pour estre ... assez nouvellier en bastiments".[3] A site at the northern end of the wood was sold to Prince Johan Maurits of Nassau, whose house, the Mauritshuis (illus. 115, 118-19), was planned and built at the same time as that of Huygens and in a similar style.[4] The canals that bordered the Stadholder's garden were filled in, a double row of lime trees was planted at its edges, and wide roads were constructed all round it, that on the north side, which was made on what

[1] Information from J. K. van der Haagen, 'Het Plein, Huygens en Frederik Hendrik', *Die Haghe, Jaarboek*, 1928-9, pp. 6-38, except where other references are given. Maps in the Algemeen Rijksarchief, The Hague, nos. 3305-9, show proposals for the use of the land, including that finally adopted.

[2] Letter of 11 Apr. 1634; Koninklijke Bibliotheek, The Hague, Kon. Acad. MS. XLIX, Vol. I, fol. 597 (Worp no. 897).

[3] Letter of 17 Oct. 1634; Kon. Bibliotheek, The Hague, Kon. Acad. MS. cit., fol. 520 (Worp no. 1025).

[4] The design of the Mauritshuis may have resulted from a collaboration similar to that which produced Huygens' house. In a letter to Huygens Prince Johan Maurits referred to his own house, "de quoy ... vous et Monsr. van Campen en tirez la plus grand part de l'honneur"; Koninklijk Huisarchief, The Hague, Inv. 27/2, I, Collectie Huygens, 9 (Worp no. 2996, giving the date, whose last figure is not clearly legible, as 9 May 1642). Anslo, in 1648, ascribes one of Huygens' houses (probably that on the Plein) and also the Mauritshuis to Van Campen. Houbraken, 1721, attributes Huygens' houses both on the Plein and in Voorburg to him as well as the Mauritshuis ('Het gekroonde Amsterdam', in *Olyf-krans*, 1750, p. 173, and *Schouwburgh*, III, p. 381, respectively).

had been part of the garden itself, being extended to give access to the Binnen-hof, where a stone bridge and entrance gates wide enough for carriages were made to lead into the inner court. Previously the Binnenhof had been linked with the Stadholder's garden, which itself had been enclosed, by small gates, a wooden bridge, and a narrow track, and the change transformed the court from a self-contained, castle-like, complex of buildings into an integral part of a larger scheme which was planned as a whole. The northern edge of the former garden, beyond the road, was divided into plots which were sold for building, with the stipulation that only one house should be built on each plot and that the work should be finished quickly. Good houses already stood on the east and south of the new square, and these were not interfered with.

Other changes were made at the same time, for in 1632 or early in 1633 St. Sebastian's Company of the Civic Guard requested the States of Holland and West Friesland that in view of the making of streets and selling of property in the Stadholder's garden, which would 'serve particularly for the adornment' of The Hague, they would grant permission for plots of land belonging to the Guard to be disposed of for building, to be carried out immediately and uniformly, and that the road along the end of the Vijver on which the proposed houses would stand should be constructed in conformity with the streets that were to surround the new square, To this project 'his Excellency [Prince Frederik Hendrik] showed himself particularly inclined, and had already had various maps and drawings made of it, of the houses and the street to be made there'.[1] This request too was granted. The end of the Vijver was filled in and straightened, and the road on the west side of the Stadholder's garden was carried across it. This was the paved road thirty-six feet wide that Huygens later described, on which his house stood.[2] The old headquarters of the Civic Guard was replaced by a modern building paid for by Prince Frederik Hendrik,[3] which was designed in a style similar to that of Huygens' house and the Mauritshuis by the architect Arent 's Gravesande, who had worked for the Stadholder on other buildings.[4] The foundation-stone was laid by the young Prince Willem, later the Stadholder Willem II, in 1636.[5]

---

[1] Quotations from Van der Haagen, op. cit., pp. 23–24. "... zijne Excellentie hem toonde zonderlinge mede genegen te wezen, ende hadde albereijts daer van doen maeken verscheijde caerten ende aftekeningen van de huijsen en straet aldaar te maeken."
[2] See quotation p. 98 above.
[3] The St. Sebastiaansdoelen, surviving as no. 7 Korte Vijverberg. Hudig, op. cit., p. 21, states that it was a gift from the Stadholder, and Vermeulen, *Handboek*, III, p. 111, that he largely paid for it.
[4] Vermeulen, op. cit., III, pp. 110–11.
[5] See inscription on main façade.

There can be little doubt that the Prince himself inspired these changes made in the centre of The Hague, and that they were thought out as a single scheme, and though these improvements to the city were not the only ones with which he was concerned[1] they were of particular significance. No such large and costly piece of town planning had been undertaken in Holland before except in the interests of transport and defence, for only now could such a project be afforded. Moreover the scheme provided a notable example, introduced on the best authority, of architecture planned in a new style and in relation to its surroundings. The exact nature of this relationship cannot be defined without further investigation, but it is interesting to notice that the height to the upper cornice of Huygens' house was thirty-six feet, the same measurement as the width of the road outside his gate, which he took care to specify in describing his house to Rubens, and that the depth from the front to the back of the Mauritshuis is just double this measurement. If these correspondences were thought out deliberately it is quite possible that the two houses were conceived not as objects complete in themselves and placed in ornamental positions, but as being extended in space beyond their own confines by formal harmonies. Such a conception cannot in any case have been understood very generally, but very soon buildings in which the new style was emulated were commissioned by patrons outside the Stadholder's circle[2] and the reshaping of the centre of The Hague may well have been pointed to as a precedent for measures taken later at Amsterdam, when the buildings round the Dam were brought into a single complex and much valuable property was destroyed to provide space and a suitable setting for the new Town Hall, while further inspiration for the new Town Hall might be drawn from the Stadholder's palaces.

The Palace of Honselaarsdijk[3] (illus. 120-1, 123) was built by the Prince on the site of an old house between The Hague and the sea, which had been used as a centre for hunting. It was begun in 1621, four years before Huygens became his secretary, so that Huygens can have had no share in the early part of its design. By 1631 the main body of the new building was completed. It consisted of a *corps de logis* with octagonal turrets, later altered into square

---

[1] H. E. van Gelder, *'s Gravenhage in zeven eeuwen*, Amsterdam, 1937, p. 130, describes another scheme which he supported and in part inspired.

[2] The Cloth Hall at Leiden, commissioned in 1638, is outstanding among these buildings, being very early in date, and having features in common with both Huygens' house and the Mauritshuis. Discussed by Vermeulen, op. cit., III, pp. 243–6.

[3] Now destroyed. Information from Slothouwer, *Paleizen*, pp. 39–88 and Appendices.

pavilions, at its front corners,[1] wings with square end pavilions towards the garden, which was large and eleborately planned, and a low open gallery which joined these wings to form a court. The plan was in fact French in type, though what one would expect to be entrance court here faced the garden, perhaps owing to the exigencies of the site. The roofs were very steeply pitched, in the French manner, and varying pitches were used, so that the end pavilions, though they were square in plan, had ridges to their roofs. There were galleries in the side wings, and sets of apartments arranged in the square pavilions in the French style.

In view of these facts, and since no drawings are mentioned in the accounts for the building for before 1630, when the greater part of the structure was already built, the possibility that plans were obtained from France cannot be ignored[2] and at least it is evident that the Stadholder was following the latest developments in France, and built his palace accordingly. Its simple form seems to reflect the restraint and unity brought into French architecture in the Paris schemes of Henri IV and in the works of Salomon de Brosse, and the plan has a number of features in common with that of the Luxembourg Palace, begun by Salomon de Brosse for Maria de' Medici in 1615,[3] though Honselaarsdijk was simpler and smaller (cf. illus. 122, 123). The apartments in the pavilions were planned in a similar way, there were galleries in the side wings, and the staircase was in the same position in relation to the general form of the building and to the court.

In 1633 Jaques (or Simon) de la Vallée, who was the son of Maria de' Medici's master of works, and French garden experts arrived at Honselaarsdijk to work for Prince Frederik Hendrik.[4] De la Vallée was appointed his architect in 1634 and stayed in Holland until 1637.[5] At Honselaarsdijk he built a grand stone staircase in place of the original wooden one, with an oval dome above it. In 1643 Huygens wrote on the Stadholder's behalf to the Dutch ambassador in Paris asking for the advice of French 'architects and gardeners separately'[6] on projects for further extensions, and for plans by French architects for a chapel. It seems, in fact, that at every stage of the design French taste was followed.

[1] The change was made during the 1640s. The triangular pediment in the centre of the front façade, replacing an earlier gable, dated from the 1630s (E. H. ter Kuile, in *Duizend jaar bouwen*, II, p. 123).
[2] Slothouwer, op. cit., p. 44, suggests this.
[3] For the works of Salomon de Brosse see Anthony Blunt, *Art and Architecture in France, 1500 to 1700* (Pelican History of Art), London [etc.], 1953, pp. 120–3.
[4] Slothouwer, op. cit., pp. 50 and 52.
[5] He was the first to be appointed architect to the Stadholder. For the record of his appointment and dismissal see Slothouwer, op. cit., p. 325.
[6] Letter of 16 Feb. 1643, Worp no. 3220.

In discussing the nature of the buildings of the Stadholder and his circle patrons have been referred to rather than architects, for evidently it was they, and not the architects themselves, who determined the form that these buildings took; indeed architects had to be sought for who were capable of working to their patrons' ideals, even if it meant going abroad to find them. Jacob van Campen, however, seems to have had a share in creating the new style that these patrons developed, even in the initial stages. He had not been trained as a master builder like his predecessors in Holland, but as a young painter of some means he went to Rome, where he studied antique sculpture and buildings and took up architecture.[1] He had had some practical experience of building before he came to help Huygens with his house,[2] and he evidently knew his Vitruvius, which, only two years later, he possessed in Barbaro's Italian edition.[3] It is possible indeed that it was his knowledge that inspired Huygens to study the theory of antique architecture in detail for himself. Soon after he came to Huygens Van Campen was working for the Stadholder,[4] though he was never his official architect; we know that he was responsible for parts of the decoration of the palaces,[5] but his share in their architecture remains unknown. His work for the Stadholder, Huygens, and Prince Johan Maurits must have given him exceptional opportunities for applying and developing his knowledge of the theory of classical art; it also enabled him to work on large schemes of decoration and brought him into contact with French ideas. Though the form of architecture that was introduced on the

---

[1] Filippo Baldinucci, *Notizie de' professori del disegno da Cimabue in qua*, Florence, 1681–1728, VI, p. 380, says of him: "il quale essendo in sua gioventù passato a Roma, vi fece grandi studj dall' antiche sculture e fabbriche, tantochè ritornatosene alla patria, ebbe lode di avere in Olanda ricondotto l'ottimo gusto dell' architettura". Apparently Baldinucci received this information on good authority, for at the end of the life he says that Matthias Withoos was a pupil of Van Campen, and that Withoos taught Gaspar van Wittel. At the time when Baldinucci must have been collecting information for his biographies Van Wittel was living in Italy.

[2] Houbraken, *Schouburgh*, III, p. 382, states that Van Campen had worked as an architect in Italy: "Hy won de gunst van een Kardinaal die hem aanleyding tot de Boukonst gaf, waar van het begrip hem zoodanig toeviel dat hy verscheide roemwaarde werken voor den zelven deed maken". ('He won the favour of a Cardinal, who gave him encouragement to [take up] architecture, the understanding of which came so naturally to him that he made various works for this same [Cardinal] which are worthy of renown.') Though these particulars are given as part of a story concerning a soothsayer the available evidence suggests that other details of Van Campen's stay in Italy given in the story are based on fact, and Houbraken's statement may be accepted provisionally. Van Campen had certainly worked as an architect in Holland before joining Huygens. The foundation-stone of the house which he built in Amsterdam for Balthazar Coymans (No. 177 Heerengracht) is dated 14th March 1625 – see A. A. Kok, *Amsterdamsche Woonhuizen* (Heemschutserie), Amsterdam, 1943, p. 94 – documentation kindly pointed out by Professor M. D. Ozinga. The design of this house was published as Van Campen's by Danckerts, *Architectura*, pl. XLIII, in 1631.

[3] Mentioned in a letter from Bannius (Jan Albert Ban) to Huygens of 11 Aug. 1636, Worp no. 1417.

[4] He was working for him by 6 Aug. 1636, see Slothouwer, *Paleizen*, pp. 267-8.

[5] Documents showing this are quoted by Slothouwer, op. cit., Appendices.

Plein at The Hague and in the palaces underwent many adaptations and modifications during the rest of the century, it perhaps reached its most remarkable developments, and those most consistent with its origins, in Van Campen's hands.

The New Church in Haarlem (illus. 109-12) was built by Van Campen on the site of a Gothic building and beside the church tower by Lieven de Key that has already been referred to.[1] It was designed in 1645 and finished in 1649. The outside, it is evident, had to be built in such a way that the tower would not look out of place beside it, and so it gives an impression of length, although in fact the church is square. The interior, however, has perfect symmetry, which was only to have been broken by two shallow bays opposite each other which accommodate the porch and organ. The roof has crossed barrel-vaults, and low coffered ceilings fill the spaces between them, supported by Ionic pillars at the inner corners and pilasters against the walls, and though some of the beams resting on these columns and pilasters are supported in the centre by further columns and others are not it has been shown that this was due to a modification, made for economy, of the architect's first proposals.[2] The design is an extraordinarily neat one, and the space of the interior is, as it were, built up of the simple forms of semicircles and squares. No sources of inspiration for the arrangement can be pointed to with certainty,[3] and it may very well have been Van Campen's own invention, arrived at in an attempt to provide a truly classical church design, for it seems clear that, so far as his powers and the exigencies of his commission would allow him, he brought 'the good Vitruvius' to Holland in the beautiful spatial harmony of this composition.

In the Town Hall of Amsterdam the two elements whose entry into Dutch architecture have been outlined here, pure Italian classicism and classicism adapted in France to northern needs, were combined and used with great splendour to express with a full voice, not the ideals of a prince, but of a merchant city's government, for, as has already been shown, this building was planned to correspond with the city's new status. It could be built of very large

[1] See M. D. Ozinga, *De Protestantsche kerkenbouw in Nederland van hervorming tot Franschen tijd*, Amsterdam, 1939, pp. 59–66.
[2] Ibid., p. 60.
[3] Ozinga, op. cit., p. 63, notes a relationship of the plan with those of certain Venetian 16th-century centrally planned churches such as S. Giovanni Chrysostomo, which, as he points out, has barrel vaults, but has a central cupola and smaller cupolas above the corners. Further suggestions as to its derivation are made by John Summerson, *Architecture in Britain 1530 to 1830* (Pelican History of Art), London [etc.], 1953, p. 130, and E. H. ter Kuile, in *Duizend jaar bouwen*, II, p. 135.

blocks of stone, although these had to be imported at great cost and required a forest of tree-trunks to support them, streets which at the time in Amsterdam were exceptionally wide could be made to either side of it, and it was given not only the scale but also the form of a palace.

The general arrangement of the Town Hall is reminiscent of that of Honselaarsdijk (cf. illus. 123, 125). There are square corner pavilions containing sets of apartments, here to be used as government offices, a grand stair in the centre behind the entrance, and long galleries. Yet if the arrangement of this civic palace was perhaps based on that of the Stadholder there were modifications to suit its very different use. The *vierschaar*, as has been seen, was given its traditional position in the front of the building, taking the place of the entrance hall, and equal entrances were provided to either side of it to lead to the stair behind. The Burgerzaal was built across what would otherwise have been the central courtyard, so that two smaller courts were formed. The four ranges of building surrounding the courts are of equal height, so that the Town Hall when it is seen from the outside appears as a single block-like construction of great size and weight. In this respect, as well as in the horizontal emphasis of its cornices, it resembles many of the renaissance palaces of Italy, and in particular the Farnese Palace in Rome, a free-standing building of great size, which, like the Town Hall, takes up the whole of one side of an open space in a crowded city, towering above the houses that surround it, and though the Town Hall has a sloping roof, which was a necessity in the northern climate of Holland, this too is horizontal in emphasis; the roof-line is virtually unbroken, so that the apparent solidity of the building remains undisturbed. Moreover the four ranges are of equal width. The Town Hall does not consist of a body with limbs attached to it, as did the Palace of Honselaarsdijk, but each range contains a suite of rooms with windows looking out into the city and a gallery on the court side which gives access to them, an arrangement very common in Italy, where the galleries are usually open. In the Farnese Palace, however, the first floor galleries, which run round three sides of the central court and give access to the main rooms, are closed and are lit from the court by windows, so that in this respect they are very similar to those of the Town Hall.[1] In addition to this likeness the arrangement of the entrance to the large room at the back on the first floor of the Farnese Palace,

[1] Although the galleries of the first floor were open in the earliest designs for the Farnese Palace it seems clear that they were entirely closed by the seventeenth century. See Herbert Siebenhüner, 'Der Palazzo Farnese in Rom', *Westdeutsches Jahrbuch für Kunstgeschichte Wallraf-Richartz-Jahrbuch*, XIV, 1952, pp. 144–64.

that decorated by Annibale Caracci, is similar to that of the entrance to the magistrates' court (cf. illus. 124, 125).

The roof-line of the Amsterdam palace is broken by one large feature only, the 'tower', with its cupola, and it will be remembered that a tower was a necessity to give a prominent position to the city's principal timepiece and to house the City Bell. No tower of traditional design would have been thinkable as an adjunct to a classical building of this kind, and it is not surprising that a form of dome that had been used both in antique temples and renaissance churches was adapted here to a new use. Bramante's Tempietto beside San Pietro in Montorio in Rome, the only renaissance building which was included by Palladio among his illustrations of antique architecture, may well have provided a model for the cupola, which is hemispherical,[1] although by the time it was designed this form had been used by other architects not only in Italy but also in France. The 'drum' on which the cupola rests is arcaded, so that the carillon inside it can sing out unhindered over the city to mark the hours.

It is likely that works by Palladio himself provided Van Campen with inspiration for the great triangular pediments which form part of the east and west façades of the Town Hall and give the rooms of the upper floors extra height at the centre of the building. Such a pediment seems to have first been used in Holland at Warmond Castle, in a wing which appears to have been designed by Salomon de Bray in 1629 and has since been destroyed.[2] The way in which this feature was used in the architecture of the Stadholder's circle and of the Town Hall of Amsterdam, and its decoration (in the north façade of the Mauritshuis, in the façade of the Palace of Noordeinde in The Hague, and in the Town Hall itself) with sculptural scenes in which a number of figures are shown, suggest that there the inspiration came direct from the

[1] Palladio, *Quattro libri*, Bk. IV, pp. 64–66. The dome as shown by Palladio is hemispherical and has sixteen ribs. Three different versions of the Town Hall's cupola are shown in early records. In the prints of 1650 it is without ornament, has straight sides of a height equal to the projection of the cornice below it, and is hemispherical above them. In the model in the Waag Museum, Amsterdam, it appears to be hemispherical, and it has eight ribs very similar in form to those of Bramante's dome. In Vennekool's prints its general form is hemispherical, but its lower part is stepped, as are the domes of the Pantheon, illustrated by Palladio (Bk. IV, pp. 74–84) and of Bramante's design for St. Peter's, Rome (see Sebastiano Serlio, *Tutte l'opere d'Architettura, et prospetiva, di – – Bolognese* [etc.], Venice, 1619, Bk. III). The dome as it was finally constructed, after Van Campen's withdrawal, is plain and appears to be hemispherical.

[2] The design is recorded by Pieter Saenredam in two drawings in the Gemeente Archief, Haarlem, which are dated 1632, on one of which the tympanum bears the name and date S. Bray, 8. 3. 1629. See P. T. A. Swillens, *Pieter Janszoon Saenredam, Schilder van Haarlem 1597–1665*, Amsterdam, 1935, cat. nos. 58 and 59, illus. 26–27 (as designs for Haarlem Town Hall) and E. H. ter Kuile, *De Nederlandsche monumenten van geschiedenis en kunst*, VII, i, The Hague, 1944, p. 223 and illus. 447–8.

classical architecture of antiquity and from Palladio.[1] It is perhaps worth noticing that Van Campen's design for the lantern which contained the city bell also has features in common with Palladio's designs, among them that of the lantern which surmounts the dome of the chapel of the Villa Barbaro at Maser.[2]

It seems that the interior of the Town Hall was most carefully designed, like the exterior, on the principles of antique and later classical architecture. It was not only planned with great symmetry, but the rooms were evidently designed on a system of measurements based on mathematical units, different units being used in the corner pavilions from those used in the main suites of rooms.[3] It has not yet proved possible to discover the principles on which this system was based, but it is clear that it was worked out in theory with great refinement since many of the measurements given on the plans contain fractions of inches so small that they are meaningless for the practical purposes of building. The Burgerzaal, whose measurements appear to have been based on the same units as those used in planning the main rooms, is 120 feet long and almost 60 feet wide from wall to wall. The central part of Vitruvius' basilica at Fano, the only one of his buildings whose actual measurements he recorded, had a ground plan of 120 by 60 feet.[4] The height to the upper cornice is 90 feet, that is, half the sum of length and breadth, the proportion laid down by Vitruvius for the height of all oblong rooms.[5] The section of the vault above it is semicircular.

The architectural members are also as antique as Van Campen could make

---

[1]   See further pp. 182–4 below.

[2]   The scrolls of the Town Hall's lantern as shown in the engravings of 1650, and the eight-sided cupola of that of the model, Waag Museum, Amsterdam, are somewhat similar in form to the scrolls and cupola of the lantern at Maser. This, however, has rectangular openings, where that of the Town Hall, in all versions of the design, has rounded openings corresponding in form with those of the arcade of the drum below (cf. illus. 5, 183). Lanterns similar in type are illustrated on a very small scale in Palladio's *Quattro libri*, Bk. II, pp. 19 and 60. There is no documentary evidence that Van Campen saw architecture by Palladio when he was in Italy, though the style of the works with which he was connected strongly suggests that he did so.

[3]   Evident from the nature of the measurements given by Vennekool in his ground and first floor plans, *Afbeelding*, pls. A and B. Since in the measurements of the rooms in the corner pavilions thirds of inches are involved, and fractions involving seventeens and their multiples appear in those of the other rooms, it seems that different units were used for these parts of the building. There is evidence that Inigo Jones' pupil John Webb worked out architectural plans in terms of units, referred to as "spaces"; see Margaret Whinney, 'John Webb's drawings for Whitehall Palace', *The Walpole Society XXXI, 1942–43*, London, 1946, p. 98. The measurements in Vennekool's plans of the Town Hall of Amsterdam have been discussed in an article by C. Wegener Sleeswijk, 'De maten van het Paleis op den Dam te Amsterdam', *Architectura*, 1940, pp. 338–41.

[4]   *De Architectura*, V, i, 6. For a further parallel see p. 39 n. 2 above.

[5]   Op. cit., VI, iii, 8.

them – antique, that is to say, in a scholarly sense of the term – and in place of the fanciful use of printed pattern-books which has already been described, here borrowing of a very different kind may be discerned. Van Campen modelled the architectural ornament throughout his building, even that of doors and fireplaces, on the engravings which illustrate Scamozzi's treatise on architecture,[1] copying with exactness and where it was necessary adapting his models with restraint and wisdom to serve new purposes (illus. 126-7, 131-4). Every particular was followed, usually with only very small variations where an inadequacy might be suspected in the engraving,[2] and indeed at some points the sculptured ornament seems to have taken over something of the style of the engravings, so meticulously were the models used.[3] No detailed comparison to show the nature of this borrowing can be made here except with the aid of photographs, and to these the reader is referred, but it can be stated with certainty on the basis of many such comparisons that the borrowing is unquestionable, and that it is consistent throughout the work; moreover Van Campen had a precedent for it, since it was recorded by an excellent authority that the architectural ornament of one of the principal rooms of the Mauritshuis was taken from the same source.[4] Only a few details such as the fluted pilasters, with which the Corinthian order is presented in its richest and gayest form in the Burgerzaal and galleries, are lacking in Scamozzi's illustrations, and for the pilasters Van Campen turned to the next authority further back in the Italian tradition of research on antique architecture, to Scamozzi's master Palladio, and used his illustration of the Corinthian order

[1] Vincenzo Scamozzi, *L'idea della archittettura universale* [etc.], Venice, 1615. The engravings used are those in Pt. II, Bk. VI.

[2] There is, for example, a leaf carved above the forward scroll of the door-tops in the north and south galleries which is absent in Scamozzi's engraving of a Corinthian door-top, from which the design was clearly taken. There the leaf appears only above the scroll set against the side of the doorway, and its design was copied for Van Campen's forward scroll. There is a similar small variation in the design of the Corinthian cornice.

[3] Thanks are due to Dr. D. E. Strong for bringing this to the writer's notice. It appears in the foliage of capitals and other ornaments, where a certain linear quality is noticeable, particularly in the divisions between the fronds of the leaves. In some cases, however, where the execution is less skilful, small variations occur, and part of the lower cornice in the Burgerzaal had four beads to a reel in a bead and reel ornament instead of two, but part is correctly copied from Scamozzi's engraving.

[4] Book of drawings of the Mauritshuis, Koninklijke Bibliotheek, The Hague, MS. no. 128, A. 34, entry in index for nos. 9–12, where the note is added: "De Pijlasters van dese Voor-sale met haer gevolgh sijn van de ordine Romano beschreven door Vinc. Scamozzi" ('The pilasters of this entrance hall with what is derived from them are of the *ordine Romano* described by Vincenzo Scamozzi'). The book was made for Prince Johan Maurits by Pieter Post, who was himself concerned with the building; see his letter to Huygens of 31 Oct. 1640, Worp no. 2562. Here it is not known whether Van Campen was responsible for the borrowing, but for that in the organ-case at Alkmaar, also earlier than the Town Hall, he must have been; see pp. 167–8 and notes below.

of the portico of the Pantheon as his model (illus. 128-30).[1] It was reasonable that he should refer to this building for the completion of the design, since Scamozzi's version of the order is similar to that of the Pantheon, and may well to a great extent have been based on it.[2] The pilasters of the porch of the Pantheon have an unusual feature, a rounded rib at each of the outer corners, and the form of the ends of this rib is not clearly explained in the engraving. It appears that Van Campen misunderstood Palladio's meaning, for the fluted pilasters in the Town Hall are designed as those of the Pantheon porch appear to be in his illustration and not as they are in the building itself, and by this misunderstanding Van Campen's use of the engraving is virtually proved.[3]

The consistent borrowing from Scamozzi's engravings for the architectural ornament of the Town Hall, and the compact and symmetrical forms of each part and of the building as a whole, together create the harmony of its formal design, while the use of the different orders, and variations in the way in which they were applied, in materials, and in representational sculptural ornament, exclude all possibility of monotony, and though there were what we may now call baroque features in the planning as well as in the decoration of the Town Hall – the strong effects of weight and mass, contrasts between light and shadow and between deep and limited space, and the necessity of the spectator both to give scale to the whole composition and as a focussing-point within it that have been referred to in an earlier chapter – these cannot at the time have been thought of as being in another style, and the classical harmony, though it was enlivened, is not broken by them. The careful borrowing that contributed to the creation of this harmony cannot be dismissed as unimaginative and slavish imitation. Rather it was a matter of keeping honestly to certain principles which might contain the essence of universal truth, and to design a building so large and so intricate in accordance with these principles was in itself a work of imagination and of skill. Van Campen, it will be remembered, was not only a student of antiquity, but was also an artist and a mathematician; here art and science were both essential to a single process of creation, and the imagination was harnessed, in the search for truth and reason that had taken fancy's place.

Van Mander's verdict on Dutch architecture has already been quoted. Salomon de Bray, writing about 'modern architecture' in 1631 with the works

---

[1] *Quattro libri*, Bk. IV, p. 80.
[2] In his book on the orders Scamozzi does not mention the sources from which his version was taken.
[3] The design is still less clearly given in the copied illustrations which appear in some later editions of Palladio's work, and from these Van Campen could not have drawn the same conclusions.

of De Keyser foremost in his mind saw, as he put it, 'the true [that is, Roman] architecture as resurrected' in Holland in his own day.[1] Philips Vingboons, writing in 1648, the year in which the Town Hall of Amsterdam was founded, praised Roman architecture, and beside it that of France, which 'might almost be compared with the Italian', and he took the Louvre and the Luxembourg Palace 'out of all the Royal buildings' as examples to illustrate his meaning. Pious antiquity, as he saw it, had been 'fetched up out of the dark' in many countries and in Holland among them, for there, 'in a few years, in spite of the tempests of war, . . . many changes have been seen, not only in large and prominent, but also in ordinary buildings, both in the towns and in the countryside'.[2]

There had indeed been many changes since Van Mander raised his cry of protest at the beginning of the century, and only a few of them have been considered here. Yet what may perhaps be described as a metamorphosis of the Antique has been seen taking place in Dutch architecture, and it is clear that an essential change in the nature of seventeenth-century thought was recorded in its monuments, the Town Hall of Amsterdam among them, in visible form.

---

[1] Salomon de Bray, in Danckerts' *Architectura*, p. 5: "de waerachtige *Bouw-konst* . . . als errysen". The context makes it clear that Roman architecture is referred to.

[2] Philips Vingboons, *Gronden en affbeeldsels der voornaamste gebouwen van alle die – – geordineert heeft*, Amsterdam, 1688 (first published 1648), Intro. [p. ii]. ". . . men in korte jaren, onaengesien d'Oorloghs onstuymicheden, . . . veel verandering heeft gesien, niet alleen in de groote en uytstekende, maer oock in de ordinarise gebouwen, soo in de Steden als ten platten Lande."

CHAPTER V

THE SCULPTURED BUST

FIRST PART

For the greater part of the sixteenth century the southern and northern provinces of the Netherlands formed a single region, whose cultural centres were Brussels, which contained the court of the Governor of the Netherlands, and Antwerp, then the most important trading city of the world. The division of the two countries, which began with the revolt of the northern provinces against Spain in the 1570s, was first only due to political chance, though by the beginning of the seventeenth century it had come to stand for religious as well as political differences. Because of the blockading of the river Scheldt, on which Antwerp's trade depended, and because of the great cost of measures taken to further the long war against the Dutch, she became impoverished. Rubens described her condition vividly when he wrote in 1627: 'this city . . . languishes like a consumptive body, declining little by little. Every day sees a decrease in the number of inhabitants, for these unhappy people have no means of supporting themselves either by industrial skill or by trade'.[1] In 1628 he gave a further description: 'Our city is going step by step to ruin, and lives only upon its savings; there remains not the slightest bit of trade to support it'.[2] Amsterdam, meanwhile, took over Antwerp's position as the leading centre of world trade and, as has already been seen, expanded with amazing rapidity. New centres of culture arose or became important as a result of the republic's growing wealth and security, in the Stadholder's circle in The Hague, in Leiden, where the first university of the United Provinces had been set up in 1575, in Amsterdam, and in other cities.

The growing differences between the Southern Netherlands and the United Provinces gave rise to profound differences in the forms of their art, which diverged, during the course of the century, very widely. It was typical of the Dutch Republic that portraits and paintings of everyday scenes, of landscapes, or of still life, usually small in size, and carried out with the patient observation of nature that was characteristic of the native tradition of painting in the Low

---

[1]   Magurn, *Letters*, p. 185. This and further quotations from Rubens' letters are given in Magurn's translation unless it is stated otherwise.
[2]   Magurn, op. cit., p. 279.

116

Countries from early times, were in constant demand. They provided a form of investment that was treasured and enjoyed in daily life by the members of every class of Dutch society,[1] and they could easily be moved about and bought and sold. De Lairesse, writing in the first years of the eighteenth century, may have been right in attributing the small demand for works of sculpture in the United Provinces not only to the expense of marble (which all came from abroad) but also to the difficulty of rescuing them in case of fire, and of transporting them when moving to new quarters.[2] Dutch paintings had none of these disadvantages. It was also typical of the Republic, where the familiar objects of everyday life were valued and cherished and where each city had a great measure of independence and of local pride, that domestic and civic architecture should flourish, and that care should be lavished on them. When Rubens published engravings of the merchant city of Genoa in 1622 he hoped to see the rebirth of antique architecture in the private houses of gentlemen in northern cities,[3] and his home city of Antwerp, where he had just completed his own house in the form of a small renaissance palace, must have been in the forefront of his mind. Yet it was not so much in the impoverished city of Antwerp as in Amsterdam that his hopes for the architecture of northern countries were fulfilled, for the style of classical architecture which was brought into being in Huygens' and Prince Maurits' houses in The Hague in the early 1630s was being skilfully adapted to the needs of Amsterdam merchants very shortly afterwards,[4] and by the end of the seventeenth century many hundreds of houses that were classical in design had been built in the areas added to the city. Even before Prince Maurits' house was finished the new style was also being applied to Dutch civic architecture,[5] with the result that has now been seen: that the Amsterdam Town Hall was built in this classical style – one arrived at in Holland although the elements that went to make it up for the most part came from abroad.

Antwerp, meanwhile, remained the outstanding centre for religious and decorative painting and for sculpture. The refurnishing of the churches of the Southern Netherlands, which had been denuded by the iconoclasms of the Reformation, provided work for generations of artists, painters and sculp-

[1] See E. S. de Beer, *The Diary of John Evelyn*, Oxford, 1955, II, p. 39 and note.
[2] G. de Lairesse, *Groot Schilderboek* [etc.], Haarlem, 1740, II, pp. 232–3. (First published 1707.)
[3] P. P. Rubens, *Palazzi di Genova* [etc.], Antwerp, 1622, Introduction.
[4] The series of classical houses built by Philips Vingboons for these patrons began with two country houses designed in 1637 and an Amsterdam house designed in 1638; Vermeulen, *Handboek*, III, p. 176.
[5] See p. 106 n. 2 above.

tors alike, in spite of the troubled times, while the churches of the Dutch Republic, now in the hands of Protestants, remained almost bare.[1] Moreover Rubens' presence in Antwerp, with his numerous pupils, gave a new impetus and direction there to the development of these arts. His scholarly enthusiasm for antiquity was comparable with that of Huygens, and like Huygens he had the text of Vitruvius to hand when he was designing his house.[2] Rubens, however, could put his scholarship to use in the design of comprehensive schemes of decoration, for which, as a painter, he had a preference.[3] A contemporary described him as 'the most learned painter in the world',[4] and the commentary written by his friend Gevaerts on the decorations which he composed for the entry of the Cardinal Infante Ferdinand into Antwerp in 1635[5] shows the way in which his learning was applied to such designs; classical instances are quoted, and Roman coins on which details of the formal design and the symbolism were ultimately based are illustrated. Rubens' knowledgeable use of antique ideas and motifs in decoration is to a great extent analogous to their use in architecture by Huygens and Van Campen,[6] and in this respect his decorative schemes form a counterpart to the architecture which Huygens and Van Campen evolved. Moreover Rubens conceived his designs (in whatever medium they were to be carried out) as Huygens and Van Campen did, in terms of space and solid form, and (whatever their complexity) as unified compositions. Since his works and theirs had these features in common – outstanding ones at the time in the art of the Low Countries though they would not have been remarkable in Italy – it perhaps is not surprising that decoration of the kind that Rubens developed in Antwerp was combined with the new Dutch style of architecture in the Amsterdam Town Hall.

The design of the Town Hall's decoration and the style of its sculpture have still to be considered if the formal nature of the building as a whole is to be understood. It will be convenient to examine them together, and to view them, like the architecture, in the perspective of history, for by these means

[1] Their embellishment was usually confined to the ornamentation of pulpits and of seats for important members of the congregation, to organ-cases, and to monuments.
[2] See p. 98 n. 2 above.
[3] Expressed in a letter of 1621 referring to the project for the ceiling of the Royal Banqueting House, London; Magurn, op. cit., p. 77.
[4] From a letter written by Philippe Chifflet on Rubens' death; Magurn, op. cit., p. 508.
[5] C. Gevartius, *Pompa introitus . . . Ferdinandi* [etc.], Antwerp, 1641.
[6] Rubens and Huygens both wished to revive classical architecture, as has been shown. Of the painters of antiquity Rubens wrote that he followed them 'with the profoundest veneration', though their works could not be taken as models, being so little known; see his revealing letter to Junius, Magurn, op. cit., pp. 406–8. For a description of his learned versatility see Evers, *Peter Paul Rubens*, p. 378.

the advent and nature of the baroque element which has already been noticed, though only in passing, may be clearly seen. In the decorative scheme this element predominates, for the relation of the spectator to the decoration is governed by it. It is this relationship which determined the nature of the Town Hall as it fulfilled its purpose, form and symbolism together. It is a baroque Town Hall although, as has been demonstrated and implied, its architecture and its symbolism are infused with a learned classicism. A comparable classicism will be seen to form an ingredient of the style of its sculpture.

At the beginning of the seventeenth century the architectural style that was current in the Southern Netherlands was similar to that of the United Provinces. Its structural forms were usually Gothic, and its ornament, applied additively and ingeniously to its surfaces, was sometimes derived from Serlio but as often from pattern-books such as those of Cornelis Floris and Hans Vredeman de Vries. The sculpture of the whole of the Netherlands was in keeping with such architecture, for, although the work of Giovanni Bologna was known and emulated, the sculptural style developed by Floris in the sixteenth century and spread widely by his pupils and his prints was still dominant in both countries. Sculptural decoration was composed additively and ingeniously like architectural ornament, it was antique only in intention, and rather than forming part of the structures it embellished it was applied to them. Individual works of sculpture in their turn, though they might be designed in emulation of antiquity, were composed limb by limb and feature by feature; they stood uneasily, and their proportions and gestures were often exaggerated in a mannered way.

Sculpture of this kind was used to ornament the free-standing tabernacle, dated 1604, which was made by Jerome Duquesnoy the Elder for St. Martin's church, Alost (illus. 140).[1] It is built of wood and painted to look like marble, and it stands between the ambulatory and the choir, filling one of the high arches of the arcade between them. Its general form is Gothic, but it is composed entirely of details borrowed from renaissance art, and it is ornamented on both sides, and on every available surface and foothold, with sculptured decoration and with figures. The sculpture, though it was evidently designed in emulation of antique art, is composed feature by feature, the figures are strangely proportioned, and they seem to stand unsteadily. At the centre

---

[1] The attribution is confirmed by records of payments; G. Sobotka, in Thieme-Becker, s.v. Jerôme Duquesnoy d. Ä.

of the choir side, above the doors behind which the Sacrament was kept, is a relief representing the Last Supper, and in the corresponding position on the other side the Passover, its antetype, is represented. The tabernacle is supported by caryatid virtues and evangelists, and below the reliefs are children, imprisoned in strapwork decoration such as Floris designed, who seem to have no place in the symbolic scheme.[1] Figures of the Fathers of the Church flank the reliefs, and above there are many smaller figures, some of them holding the symbols of the Passion, and some, at the centre, being grouped to form narrative scenes. Two further figures, in niches high up on the central pinnacle, represent St. John the Baptist and, on the choir side, the Risen Christ. A pelican in her piety appears at the summit, perched with her young above a strapwork basket of fruit, which is set on a dome supported by infant caryatids. The parts of this composition are separately designed; they may best be seen from different viewpoints, and not all of them from the ground. This would prove, should any proof be needed, that it was additively composed. Moreover the symbolism of the tabernacle is additive like its architecture and sculpture, for the programme is set out before the spectator as it might be in a written chronicle, its episodes following one another, so that the whole must be 'read' and the parts put together in the reader's mind before their significance can be fully understood.

The Alost tabernacle was based on a more splendid tabernacle made by Cornelis Floris fifty years earlier,[2] it is a retardative work, and it is not of outstanding quality. Yet it is significant, for it is the principal surviving work of the elder Jerome Duquesnoy, the father of François Duquesnoy and the younger Jerome, and it shows how whole-heartedly Floris' style, like the pattern-book style of architecture spread and nurtured by the prints of Hans Vredeman de Vries, could still be used at the beginning of the seventeenth century. Van Mander in his *Schilderboeck*, which appeared in the year in which Jerome Duquesnoy's tabernacle was finished, described that 'filthy modern' style of architecture, which he so much detested, as one which would be shaken off with difficulty.[3] He might have described Floris' sculptural style in the same way, for it had similar tenacity.

Nevertheless in certain works of sculpture which date from the years that

[1] Similar children are also carved on large scrolls below the relief on the ambulatory side. The scrolls on the choir side have evidently been altered.
[2] In St. Leonard's church, Léau, made in 1550 to 1552. See R. Hedicke, *Cornelis Floris und die Florisdekoration*, Berlin, 1913, pp. 64–72 and pls. XXVI-XXXI.
[3] In the Life of Pieter Coecke van Aelst, *Schilderboeck*, fol. 218 v.

followed, developments were made which correspond with the changes that took place in Dutch architecture. In part they were due to the same author, Hendrik de Keyser, and perhaps they are most clearly evident in his major sculptural works, which date from the end of his career. Among them is the tomb of William the Silent (illus. 141-3), which was commissioned by the States General in 1614.[1] When De Keyser died in 1621 it was almost finished, and all the figures on the tomb are by his hand.

This monument is of particular importance, since it commemorates the first liberator of the United Provinces. Marble was shipped for it from Italy, and six large bronze figures and an effigy carved in white marble form part of it. It stands in the place of honour in the New Church at Delft, where before the Reformation the high altar stood, and, since both church and grave are orientated correctly, the head of the tomb is towards the nave, which must have added to the problems faced by the designer. The tomb has some likeness to sixteenth-century state monuments designed by Cornelis Floris, and to tombs in France; perhaps it most closely resembles the tomb of Henri II in S. Denis by Primaticcio and Pilon.[2] Yet though the underlying idea is the same there is no evidence that De Keyser went to see any of these works, and the tomb of William the Silent is not based closely on them. A new form of monument had to be devised for the founder of a Protestant republic. The traditional figure kneeling in prayer would be unsuitable, for members of the Dutch Reformed Church do not kneel to pray, but sit, and, perhaps to take the place of such a kneeling effigy as well as to suit the monument's unwonted position, the Stadholder is represented as a victorious field-marshal, sitting in a commanding posture at the head of the tomb and looking down the church. Behind this seated figure, which is of bronze, is the marble effigy in which the body of the prince is represented, lying on a sarcophagus at the centre of the monument. At the feet of the dead prince there is a bronze Fame, who seems to move forward swiftly over him, blowing the trumpet which she holds in her right hand. Seen from the centre of the nave this figure appears behind the seated effigy, as though blazing forth the glory of the prince's military deeds. Above these figures is a vaulted marble canopy, and standing virtues cast in bronze are set in niches at the corners of the tomb.

[1] See Danckerts, *Architectura*, p. 22, Neurdenburg, *De Keyser*, pp. 115–21, and R. F. P. de Beaufort, *Het Mausoleum der Oranjes te Delft*, Delft, 1931.
[2] For these tombs see Hedicke, op. cit., pp. 38–42, 55–63, and pls. XXIII and XXV, and J. Babelon, *Germain Pilon*, Paris, 1927, pp. 9–15, 59–61, and pls. 5–20 and 22–24. The possible derivation of the Delft tomb from these sources is discussed by De Beaufort, op. cit., pp. 57–62.

Among De Keyser's works of architecture his churches in particular were noticed, since a strong movement towards classical unity can be seen in them. The structure of the tomb, which has the parts of broken pediments facing outwards at its corners and is surmounted by four obelisks, is unlike them in its architectural forms. Motifs taken from classical art were used in it with great plasticity, and its classical solemnity was mingled with what may perhaps be called mannerist wit: a wit that may also be seen in De Keyser's more decorative architecture – his designs for entrances and his house façades.[1] The tomb's sculptured figures are composed with similar versatility, and in designing them De Keyser used the whole range of the forms that were to hand, playing on their differences very skilfully. Forms such as those used by Giovanni Bologna, clearly, were suitable for the rushing figure of Fame, while only a figure of classical dignity was appropriate to the most precious virtue of Liberty; not officially one of the theological or the cardinal virtues, but in the tomb of a national liberator of the utmost importance, so that she is given the place at the Stadholder's right hand. This figure has an apparently classical unity which may well be compared with that of De Keyser's church designs, a unity which in general is set off by the drapery. Moreover, though it has a certain degree of elongation, in common with sixteenth-century sculptured figures, it is idealized and simplified. The other virtues have a similar unity and simplification, but their drapery is more elaborate, and, appearing as though it were blown against them, it obscures their forms, partly disguising these qualities. The effigies, in contrast to the virtues and the Fame, have the particularized realism which was traditional in the native art of the Low Countries, and this realism has been given an immediacy of a new kind, by being made to take its place as part of representations which, rather then being built up piece by piece, seem to have been conceived each as a unified whole.

The same characteristics of unity and immediacy may also be seen in De Keyser's bronze figure of Erasmus at Rotterdam (illus. 145), which was commissioned for the chief market-place of the city in 1618.[2] The scholar is shown as though walking forward, holding an open book in his hands, turning its pages and absorbed in thought. The design of his robe is wholly in keeping with

---

[1] Many of the plates in Danckerts, op. cit., illustrate such designs. Halves of broken pediments turned outwards are used in that shown in pl. XXXI.

[2] See Neurdenburg, *De Keyser*, pp. 123–6. Metal was bought for the casting six months before De Keyser's death, and it may be assumed that the final model was by his hand. The statue was set up by Pieter de Keyser in 1622. It is to some extent based on a woodcut of Erasmus by Holbein (illus. Aloïs Gerlo, *Erasme et ses portraitistes*, Brussels, n.d., pl. XVI).

his posture, and it expresses the form of the body underneath. The robe, which is lined with fur, hangs heavily and in thick folds and it is portrayed with a realism based on close observation of form and texture. The face and hands are represented with similar realism. Here, in a figure shown in quiet action, there is no overstatement of gesture or of form. Indeed the implied movement is shown with such restraint that from the front it can scarcely be noticed.

Sculpture with similar characteristics was developed in the Southern Netherlands at about the same time, but there it is harder to point to its authorship because the making of sculpture amounted almost to an industry and commissions were often carried out by families whose members worked together. The innovations must have been due at least in part to the Colyns de Nole, then a leading sculptor family in Antwerp, and a figure was made in their workshops in the years round about 1620 whose style resembles that of De Keyser's Erasmus – a figure described as St. Gommarus, though it must represent St. Bavo, which is in St. Gommarus' church in Lierre (illus. 144).[1]

In 1614, when a commission given to Rubens for a triptych for the high altar of St. Bavo's cathedral, Ghent, fell through on the death of the bishop who ordered it, Rubens wrote to his patron the Archduke Albert, governor of the Netherlands: 'The present bishop . . . has allowed himself to be persuaded to erect a most preposterous high altar, without a picture of any sort, but only a statue of St. Bavo in a marble niche with some columns'.[2] The sculpture for this marble altarpiece, which has now been dismantled, was made by the Colyns de Nole in 1615 and the years that followed, and three alabaster figures from it are now in Lierre, the St. Bavo, patron saint of the church in Ghent, included. The design was changed during the making of the altarpiece, and in 1623 it was made to include Rubens' painting of the Conversion of St. Bavo which is still in the church, but by that time the statue of the saint had been carved; we do not know for what position its author designed it. Since it was the principal figure of an important and costly work it may be assumed that it was made either by Robert, then head of the family workshop, or by Hans his brother, and both its history and its style make it clear that it was not designed by Rubens, though the Colyns de Nole were working to his designs at the same time or very shortly afterwards.[3]

[1] For particulars see A. Jansen and C. van Herck, 'De Antwerpsche beeldhouwers Colyns de Nole', *Jaarboek Koninklijke Oudheidkundige Kring van Antwerpen*, XIX, 1943, pp. 62–65.
[2] Magurn, *Letters*, p. 56.
[3] On the high altar of Antwerp Cathedral and most probably also on the Jesuit Church, Antwerp; for references see p. 127 n. 2 and p. 131 n. 2 respectively.

The St. Bavo has the unity of form and particularized realism which have already been seen in De Keyser's sculpture. He is shown wearing a Roman breastplate and sandals, a tasselled and fringed cloak which, like Erasmus' robe, hangs heavily, and an ermine tippet, for he was a king. He stands with his weight on one foot, with the other foot a little forward, and with his left hand slightly raised, so that his stance and his gestures reinforce the suggestion that he is in prayer or sees a vision which is given by his upward glance. He is portrayed consequently, the folds of his drapery explaining the underlying forms, and neither these nor the gestures are exaggerated. Like De Keyser's Erasmus he is represented with an observant realism, as though he were seen at a particular moment, by a spectator who is unobserved. There is something tentative, however, about both these figures, as though their stance, even though they balance easily, is precarious, and as though their unity was in part due to the very restraint by which they are so convincingly portrayed; an immediate realism of this kind had yet to be achieved in figures portrayed in strong action, and no longer bound by the form of a block of wood or stone, and they had yet to be related to the observer.

When Rubens was first in Rome, in 1601 and 1602, Annibale Carracci was painting his great scheme of decoration in the Farnese Palace, and in 1605 to 1608, when he was there again, it was the most resplendent recent work of decoration in the city – one which must have been much talked of, the more so because it demanded comparison with Michelangelo's Sistine ceiling. Figures painted to look like sculptured decoration – caryatid herms, antique heads from which garlands are hung, and putti – were to be seen there behaving in a most unwonted way, the herms turning to embrace each other or to shift the weight of the loads they carry, the heads showing their delight or their boredom by grins and yawns, and the putti wriggling and playing with the pleasure of naughty children, glancing mischievously at each other across the room.[1] Indeed one child draws his companion's attention to another's behaviour. Many years later Rubens made a drawing of part of this decoration,[2] and in it the turn of the head of one of the herms is altered. The herms in Carracci's ceiling have no connection with the figures represented below

[1] The relation of these figures to each other was pointed out by Mr. Michael Kitson in a lecture first given at the Courtauld Institute of Art, London University, in 1956.
[2] Cat. exh. *Tekeningen van P. P. Rubens*, Rubenshuis, Antwerp, 1956, no. 116, pl. LII. In the Victoria and Albert Museum, London.

them, but seem to exist in a stone world of their own. Rubens' herm, however, whether by chance or intention (and his original may have shown a different version of the design) looks down towards the nude figure gazing upward who sits below him.

Rubens is known to have visited Florence, in 1600, and again a year after he was first in Rome,[1] and it is likely that he saw Michelangelo's Medici Chapel in the church of S. Lorenzo, where sculptured figures are related to each other similarly.[2] There the seated figures of the dead princes look towards the centre of the east wall, where a group representing the Virgin and Child is placed. The priest saying mass for the two princes at the altar at the west end of the room could see the relationship between the figures, and he himself, also looking to the east, completed the formal and the symbolic design. In this chapel of the dead no nave is necessary, and there is no place for a further participant or for a witness of the scene.

It seems likely that in certain of his decorative and symbolic works, carried out in painting or in sculpture, Rubens, building on the knowledge which he had of renaissance and mannerist decoration in North Italy, made use of ideas taken from the Farnese Gallery and from the Medici Chapel, making figures look at each other across space that was either fictive or was real, making them take part in a single action, or including the spectator in his scheme. In his designs for tapestries depicting the life of Achilles, which date from the 1620s, some of the herms that flank the different scenes look across at each other as though commenting on them, and seemingly sculptured figures participated in his decorations of 1635 for the triumphal entry of the Infante Ferdinand into Antwerp in a similar way. There the screens and arches each expressed a single theme as a complex work of art, but one which was formally and symbolically unified. On the screen which showed the Prince being welcomed to Antwerp, for example, Public Rejoicing and the Spirit of the City of Antwerp, painted to appear as statues to either side of the central scene, turned towards it as though taking part in its action (illus. 153). On that showing Mercury deserting Antwerp the statue-like figure representing Industry, striking fire from a stone to symbolize the citizens' attempt to save themselves from ruin by their own labours, turned away from the central scene, dejected.[3]

---

[1] H. G. Evers, *Rubens und sein Werk, neue Forschungen*, Brussels, 1943, pp. 12 and 18.

[2] Their arrangement is described by J. Wilde, 'Michelangelo's designs for the Medici Tombs', *Journal of the Warburg and Courtauld Institutes*. XVIII, 1955, p. 64.

[3] Gevartius, *Pompa*, pls. pp. 11 A and 147 A and text pp. 148–9. It may be noted in connection with the Achilles designs and with these decorations that there are male figures which look across at each other

Rubens made painted figures look across real space in a much earlier design, that of his paintings in the choir of Sta. Maria in Vallicella, which date from his second visit to Rome,[1] when he was commissioned to provide a setting for the miracle-working painting of the Virgin and Child which was to be placed above the high altar. In the first version of the design the picture was set in a single painting placed above the altar, in which it appeared above an arched gateway, surrounded by child angels, who decked it with garlands, and with saints standing below, looking at it, or glancing away in thought. Its setting in the second version of the design is different. In a central painting, placed above the altar, child angels who hover in the air hold up the picture of the Virgin and Child as though showing it to the congregation, while other angels, who look up at it, kneel below in worship. The saints appear in paintings placed on the walls of the choir to either side, at an angle to the altar. They are represented, as they were before, the principal figures as though they were looking at the miraculous picture and the others as though they were discussing it or were in deep thought, but now the saints are related to the picture and the altar in the real space of the church; they stand at a distance, though they are nearer to them than the congregation is.[2]

From the examples whose designs are known, and from his letter about the altarpiece that he designed for St. Bavo, Ghent, in which he wrote that he had put 'considerable effort into drawing up the plan of the entire work, as much for the marble ornamentation as for the picture',[3] it is evident that Rubens planned his altarpieces for high altars in the Netherlands on similar principles, and that he designed them each as a single composition in which architecture, sculpture, and painting were used together. In the altarpiece which he began in 1610 for the high altar of the church of St. Walpurgis in Antwerp,[4] from which the principal paintings are now in Antwerp Cathedral, the Christ in the Raising of the Cross looked up at a figure of God the Father which appeared

flanking the arches of a grotto in the Jardin des Pins, Fontainebleau, by Primaticcio, see A. F. Blunt, *Art and Architecture in France, 1500 to 1700* (Pelican History of Art), London [etc.], 1953, pl. 37.

[1] See Evers, *Peter Paul Rubens*, pp. 51–60, where illus. 23 shows the relative positions of the side paintings and the altar. Evers discusses the development of the design in his *Rubens und sein Werk, neue Forschungen*, Brussels, 1943, pp. 107–19.

[2] The writer is grateful to Professor J. Wilde for pointing out this relationship.

[3] Magurn, op. cit., p. 56.

[4] See Rooses, *Leven*, pp. 127–35, where a sketch from the painting which records the form of the altarpiece is given (copied by Evers, *Peter Paul Rubens*, p. 128). It is not known to what extent Rubens was responsible for this altarpiece's general form. Since its angels were painted, and were evidently similar in composition to angels on altarpieces which he is known to have designed and to other figures by him, it is likely that these were by Rubens.

in a painting above. This upper picture was flanked by angels with *mouvementé* drapery, which were painted and cut out round the outlines,[1] and above it there was a pelican, represented in gilded wood. No further details of the design of this alterpiece are known from the surviving records, but it is clear that not only the paintings of the surviving triptych but also these and the upper ones were closely interrelated, and formed one scene.

The arrangement of the altarpiece representing the Assumption of the Virgin which Rubens designed in 1618 or 1619 for the high altar of Antwerp Cathedral (illus. 146)[2] is known more precisely, and its great painting is still there. Sculptured angels, resting on a broken pediment above the frame of the picture, leant down with palm branches and with wreaths in their hands, as another angel does within the painting, proffering them to the ascending Virgin depicted below, while Christ was represented in sculpture in a niche in the centre of the pediment, looking down towards her and offering her a crown which, as she ascended, she held steadily in view. The crown was evidently the most firmly established point in the painting's turbulent composition, though it was outside the picture itself. Above the figure of Christ – which seems to have been slightly larger in scale than the figures in the painting

---

[1] Mentioned by Jacobus de Wit, who knew them in the early eighteenth century; De Bosschere, *Kerken*, p. 137. Some at least of the free-standing parts of the Triumphal Entry decorations were painted on board and were so cut out; Evers, *Peter Paul Rubens*, p. 376.

[2] Known from the engraving in *Théâtre des plans de toutes les villes des Pays Bas*, Amsterdam, n.d.; see Rooses *Oeuvre*, II, pp. 173–80. The altarpiece's unity suggests that it was designed by one artist and it is planned on the same principles as the painted parts of the St. Walpurgis' church altarpiece and as Rubens' altarpiece of the high altar of the Antwerp Jesuit Church (see pp. 128-130 below). No other artist made designs of this kind in Antwerp at the time and the whole design must be by Rubens himself. This conclusion is supported by the 18th-century writer Mols in his notes on De Wit's MS. on Antwerp churches (though Mols' belief as to the sculptor who executed the design was wrong): "DEN AUTAER is oock van de ordonnantie van *Rubens*, & geloove uytgevoert door *Jan van Mildert*" ('The altar is also designed by Rubens , and I think carried out by Jan van Mildert'); De Bosschere, *Kerken*, p. 27. Moreover in the *Acta Capitularia* of the church a meeting held in 1618 is referred to at which the church authorities met Rubens. They saw two models and decided to show them to the bishop and to take whichever he preferred. The painting for the altar is not mentioned in the entry. Further, in the contract for the painting, signed in 1619, the picture is described as "een paneel daerop de historie van onse Lieve Vrouwen hemelvaert, oft Coronatie"; 'a panel bearing the story of Our Lady's assumption, or Coronation'. (Documents quoted by Rooses.) It is not likely that the exact subject was undecided when the contract was drawn up and, rather than being alternative subjects, the Assumption and Coronation may well be alternative titles, used to set down the subject of a design which was hard to describe; the painting shows the assumption, but in the design of the whole altarpiece, including the painting, the Coronation of the Virgin was also implied, and the crown was emphasized (see text). Records concerning the marble parts of the altarpiece, which were commissioned by the Colyns de Nole in 1621, are given by A. Jansen and C. van Herck, 'De Antwerpsche beeldhouwers Colyns de Nole', *Jaarboek Koninklijke Oudheidkundige Kring van Antwerpen*, XIX, 1943, pp. 66–67, where further literature is quoted. P. Visschers, *Iets over Jacob Jonghelinck . . . Octavio van Veen . . . en de gebroeders Colyns de Nole*, Antwerp, 1853, pp. 55–59, quotes a contract for these parts. It mentions a large painted model and a drawn one, and shows that the festoons and the figures of God the Father, Christ, and the dove representing the Holy Spirit were sculptured in white marble, and that the angels, also of white marble, were carved in the round.

but would have been in keeping with them when seen from below – the Holy Spirit appeared in the form of a dove, and higher still, in the tympanum of the pediment which surmounted the centre of the altarpiece, God the Father was represented, holding his hands open and outstretched as though in a gesture of welcome. Here it is clear that architecture and sculpture were used not as frame for a painting but as an integral part of a unified composition; the meaning of the painting was emphasized and completed by the sculpture and by the architectonic arrangement of the altarpiece as a whole, and the assumption of the Virgin was shown not simply as a take-off for heaven (as, looking at the painting only, one might assume) but in its entirety, and as though it were taking place not in fictive space beyond a picture-frame, but in the very presence of the worshippers in the church.

In the altarpiece of the high altar of the Jesuit Church, St. Charles Borromeo, at Antwerp, the only one of Rubens' major altarpieces whose architecture and sculpture have survived, though his paintings have been separated from it (illus. 147-9, 174),[1] the worshipper is related by glance and gesture to the design, and indeed, because of this relationship, he is necessary to the composition and completes it. The decoration of the church, which was dedicated in 1621, was designed by Rubens,[2] and the arrangement of the choir, which is apsidal, is so similar to that of the apsidal sculpture gallery in Rubens' house

[1] Rooses, *Oeuvre*, I, pp. 31–52, and II, pp. 264–6 and 289–91, discusses the paintings done for the church and their documentation. The appearance of the church and of its altarpiece, as they were before the church was damaged by fire in 1718, is recorded in paintings, see C. van Herck and A. Jansen, 'Archief in beeld' (2e deel), *Tijdschrift voor geschiedenis en folklore*, XI, 1948, pp. 86–87. The earliest of these is by Sebastian Vrancx (d. 1647), Kunsthistorisches Museum, Vienna (illus. Evers, *Pieter Paul Rubens*, p. 221). In these paintings the details of the altarpiece are indicated rather than described, and there are variations even in paintings by the same hand, yet taken together they suggest that its design has not been materially altered though it has been restored (Ferdinand Peeters, *Une visite a l'Eglise Saint-Charles d'Anvers*, Antwerp, 1924, p. 25). Further, the style of the sculpture appears to be of the seventeenth century, and a drawing by Rubens related to the angels has survived which shows a similar style though there are variations of detail (Kupferstichkabinett, Berlin; illus. Gustav Glück and Franz Haberditzl, *Die Handzeichnungen von Peter Paul Rubens*, Berlin, 1928, no. 132). On these grounds it is assumed here that the whole work, except for the removal of the paintings, has remained substantially unchanged.

[2] There is ample evidence of this in Rubens' own works; see cat. exh. *Tekeningen van P. P. Rubens*, Rubenshuis, Antwerp, 1956, nos. 67–71, and Michael Jaffé, 'Rubens' drawings at Antwerp', *The Burlington Magazine*, XCVIII, 1956, p. 314 and note, where Rubens is described as "master decorator" of the church. This evidence is supported by written records. Of the high altar De Wit wrote in the eighteenth century (De Bosschere, *Kerken*, p. 60): "Den HOOGEN AUTAER is geordonneert door *Rubens*. waer van de Schetse, elders int' Professie Huys, in syn geheel is, de Belden daer boven op synde syn appaert door Rubens geschildert geweest". ('The high altar is designed by Rubens; the sketch of it, elsewhere in the House of Profession, is of the whole. The sculpture that are at the top of it were painted separately by Rubens.') De Wit's commentator Mols could not find the sketch of the whole in the monastery in 1771, but this does not disprove the statement. Further evidence of Rubens' authorship of the church's decoration cannot be discussed here, though it must be noted that where the original decoration survives its design is in keeping with that of documented works by Rubens.

that it is tempting to suppose that he gave advice on at least this part of the church's architecture; a good and even light falls on the altarpiece, as it did on Rubens' sculpture, from side windows and from a lantern in the half dome of the apse, so placed that they do not dazzle the spectator.[1] The paintings of the altarpiece, which were displayed successively at different seasons, were set in a frame flanked by two pairs of columns, with above it a broken pediment. Immediately above the centre of the frame two child angels point to and support a tablet which now bears the monogram of the Virgin, large angels in fluttering drapery, who formerly held out wreaths as well as palm branches above the Jesuit Saints of the paintings below, seem to hover above the ends of the broken pediment, and over the outer columns there are standing angels bearing torches. Surrounded by these sculptured figures, in a niche at the pediment's centre, there is a statue of the Virgin and Child, and above this statue, carved in high relief, is a dove representing the Holy Spririt. In the miracle-working picture of the Virgin and Child in the church of the Vallicella, which in Rubens' first setting was placed, within the painting, in an equivalent position, Christ was depicted with his hand raised in blessing, and staring forward. The Christ of the Jesuit Church altarpiece, standing on his mother's knee, likewise raises his hand in blessing, but as he does so, quite unmistakably, he looks down at the members of the congregation, making it clear that, in particular, he is blessing them. This small figure, placed high above the altar, cannot escape notice because of its position and its gesture, and because the outstretched arms of the hovering angels follow and emphasize the surrounding curves of the half dome, concentrating the attention on this central point within it. The proportions of the group, moreover, though they are ungainly when it is seen from a higher position, appear correct when it is seen from the ground. It must also be noticed that in the great arch which leads to the apse of the church there are four niches (see illus. 150), which evidently formed part of Rubens' scheme[2], and it may be presumed that he intended them to be filled with figures. Although certainly two, and very likely all four, of the

---

[1] In one of the two engravings by Harrewijn which record the appearance of the house (reprod. Evers, *Peter Paul Rubens*, p. 155) light is shown falling from the top of the half-dome and from one side window of the sculpture gallery, which is shown as a chapel. It cannot be determined whether in Rubens' day there was a window in the corresponding position on the other side (information kindly given by Mr. F. Baudouin).

[2] Shown in their present form in a drawing for the decoration in the church archives; C. van Herck and A. Jansen, 'Archief in beeld' (2e deel), *Tijdschrift voor geschiedenis en folklore*, XI, 1948, cat. no. 35 and pl. I. This drawing was attributed to Rubens in the eighteenth century though it is not by his hand.

statues of Jesuit saints which they contain date from after Rubens' death[1] it seems probable that he suggested the arrangement at least of the two lower ones.[2] These are in a position analogous to that of the saints in the side paintings in the Vallicella choir, and, like them, are related to the altar and its setting, in the real space of the church. They turn, however, not towards the altar but towards the congregation, and one of the two lower figures points emphatically to the cross he carries, the other towards the centre of the choir.

As well as illustrating the way in which Rubens made use of real space in planning decorative compositions, the main altarpiece of the Jesuit Church at Antwerp, together with the church's façade, shows that he was responsible for the development of a new sculptural style, one whose immediate realism forms the counterpart of that of his spatial planning, and that under his inspiration feats were performed in sculpture which before had seemed possible only in painting. The manner of gesticulating and the fluttering draperies of the angels of the altarpiece might be described as identical with those of figures in Rubens' paintings for the church, and it is as though the force of gravity was ignored in them. Moreover the inner pair of angels, as has been noticed, appears to hover over the pediment rather than rest on it. The child angels which support the monogram are carved almost in the round, and with detailed and particularized realism. They are plump and dimpled creatures, as lively as the seemingly sculptured children that play in Carracci's ceiling, and the well-fed Flemish babies who fly about in Rubens' paintings are their close relations. Like these they behave as though they had no weight, though their appearance belies it. On the church façade angels of the same kind (though they are a little more grown-up, and are carved by a different hand) support the monogram of the Holy Name (illus. 151) above the door, for which a drawing by Rubens survives,[3] and it is clear that these and the child angels of the altarpiece, both sculptured and painted, were similarly designed. They are composed consequently, each is seen both as a whole and as part of a larger

[1]   Two were set up and paid for in 1659 (see Gabriels, *Quellien*, p. 157) and the coat of arms accompanying the upper figures connects them with the payment. The niches are shown empty in the painting by Vrancx referred to p. 128 n. 1 above.
[2]   17th and 18th-century inscriptions on what are clearly preparatory drawings in the archives of the church indicate that the lower figures were part of the original design, and in two cases connect the drawings with Rubens; see Van Herck and Jansen, op, cit., cat. nos. 35 (where it may be added that the appropriate saint's name is written in the drawing of one of the lower niches), 36, and 37. Moreover the lower figures bear no coat of arms, so that they may well have been paid for by the Jesuits themselves as part of the original scheme.
[3]   In the British Museum, London; Arthur M. Hind, *Catalogue of Drawings by Dutch and Flemish Artists ... in the British Museum*, II, London, 1923, no. 41.

composition, and the individual personality of each one, as well as its particular features, forms part of the general scheme. There is a similar consequence and individuality, and a certain sense of movement, in the garlands of both the altarpiece and the façade, some of which hang quite freely, and the whole of the altarpiece was so unified, in its style and its implied movement, that it was possible for the group of the Virgin and Child to be distinguished from the rest, and thus emphasized, not only by its position, but also by a difference of style,[1] and by its apparent stillness. It is not known with certainty who executed these various sculptures, though both Hans van Mildert and the Colyns de Nole seem to have had a share in them.[2] A large number of sculptors must in fact have worked on Rubens' scheme, but in the present connection it is the nature of the work, rather than its execution, that is of interest.

It is evident that in the designs of these altarpieces (and it must be supposed in others of the same kind) Rubens introduced a way of planning symbolic decoration into the Netherlands which had been unknown there before, and gave it an immediacy of a new kind, by adding a northern element of particularized realism to it, and by making architecture, sculpture, and painting speak with one voice.[3] Moreover he gave northern sculpture a new unity of form, though he was not himself a sculptor, and he applied a painterly freedom to sculpture for the first time, using it, as Giovanni Bologna and others had done, as though it were not bound by the force of gravity or by the nature of its materials, yet designing it to be seen from a particular viewpoint, and with the traditional realism of northern art. The contrast, both in planning and style, between his unified and naturalistic works and the additive and somewhat artificial compositions of the followers of Floris does not need stressing, and Rubens' clearly-made formal statements make even the carefully planned relationship between the main figures of De Keyser's state tomb, and the

[1] This effect may well have been calculated even if the sculptor who carved the group was responsible for its details.

[2] Attributions are summed up by A. Jansen and C. van Herck, 'De Antwerpsche beeldhouwers Colyns de Nole', *Jaarboek Koninklijke Oudheidkundige Kring van Antwerpen*, XIX, 1943, pp. 65–66 (façade) and 76–77 (high altar). These writers show, p. 67, that the De Noles may have been working on St. Aloysius' altar in the church at the same time.

[3] It must be noted that only the revolutionary qualities of Rubens' decorative works have been touched on here. His designs were also strongly traditional, though their traditional elements were transformed. So, for example, traditional representations, formerly additively arranged, were welded together and given a new immediacy in his designs for the Triumphal Entry (Evers, *Peter Paul Rubens*, pp. 370–82) and the winged figures holding out crowns which were rife in the spandrels of arches in renaissance decoration and were evidently based on the Victories of antiquity, became hovering angels with similar, though more specific, functions on the Jesuit Church altarpiece and façade and the Cathedral altarpiece.

considerable unity and immediacy of his statues, seem tentative. In their unified planning and use of materials, in their inclusion of the spectator, and in the use of sculpture which appears to have no weight and which must also be seen from a principal viewpoint Rubens' schemes can only be closely compared to those of Bernini in the art of his own time.[1] Rubens, however, was the forerunner, for Bernini's baroque schemes are all later in date than the altarpiece designs that have been mentioned and his statue of David, the first of his works in which the spectator was essential to the design,[2] was not begun till after the Jesuit Church in Antwerp was dedicated. Bernini is likely to have been inspired by the same models as Rubens though he must have arrived at the new decorative principles very nearly if not quite independently.[3] In his very long working life he carried their use much further than Rubens did, and applied them with the greatest grandeur and with such sureness of planning that he could add to his schemes without disturbing their unity. He combined these principles with sculpture that gives the impression of idealized forms and expressions of emotion rather than describing particularized ones, with a heightened realism of texture, and often with an exactly calculated distortion, even in details, which, when the work is seen from the right viewpoint, perfects the impression that he desires to give. This form of idealized realism, whose immediacy is intense, differs from the particularized form of immediate realism which Rubens evolved, and though Rubens used distortion in his altarpieces, as has been noticed, it seems that he did so only to adjust the relations between his figures, and their proportions, to the observer's view.

Both Rubens and Bernini were devout Catholics.[4] It was natural that the new form of decoration that they evolved should be used in the service of

[1] The characteristics of Bernini's sculpture are summed up by Wittkower, *Bernini*, pp. 7–8.

[2] The spectator looking at this work is brought into relationship with the figure by its scale and its immediate appeal to his emotions, and feels that he is about to have a stone slung over his head, aimed at a point above him. The figure is represented as aiming at a giant, but the giant is not portrayed; it is the presence of the spectator which, by virtue of the work's realism, gives it scale and so conveys the meaning. See also Wittkower, op. cit., p. 6 and illus. 13. In the Galleria Borghese, Rome.

[3] Chantelou records Bernini's very great admiration of Annibale Carracci; e.g. *Journal du voyage en France du Cavalier Bernin par* – (Collection Ateliers), Paris, 1930, p. 62. Wittkower has drawn attention to Bernini's use of paintings by Carracci in the Farnese Gallery in designing one of his early works (op. cit., pp. 5–7). Bernini is likely to have known Rubens' Vallicella paintings, but there is no evidence that he was inspired by them. His patron Cardinal Scipione Borghese, however, had been strongly in favour of Rubens' commission for the church; Magurn, *Letters*, p. 39.

[4] Both had connections with the Jesuits. Rubens appears to have been in close touch with d'Aiguillon, the head of the Jesuit College in Antwerp, not only (as may be assumed) in connection with his designs for the Jesuit Church there, but also in the discussion of scientific matters. For this information the writer is indebted to Professor C. Parkhurst. The General of the Jesuit Order, Father Oliva, was the 'particular friend' of Bernini, see Chantelou, op. cit., p. 20.

religion, and that the propagandist spirit of the Counter-Reformation should give them both their greatest opportunities for developing it. Its secular application in the seventeenth century is overshadowed by the emphatic religious statements that were made by its means. Yet one of the works which seems to have inspired it, as has been seen, was the decoration of the Farnese Gallery, whose main themes were taken from antique mythology, and Bernini applied the new principles in the fountains and other secular ornaments that he designed for the city of Rome, and doubtless also in his stage settings.[1] Rubens made use of them in his designs for tapestries and for the Triumphal Entry, and also in the scheme of painted decoration that he carried out for Maria de' Medici at the Luxembourg Palace.[2] Decoration planned in a baroque way could thus be introduced into the protestant republic of the United Provinces and used there for secular purposes without modification, and, as might be expected, it made its entry in the Stadholder's circle, where French fashions were followed and where there were also close connections with the English court.[3] It is likely, however, that it arrived only after some delay.

When, from about 1635, Prince Frederik Hendrik was decorating his newly-built palaces[4] artists experienced in large schemes of decoration were hard to find in the United Provinces. There had been no occasion there for such works, since they were not needed for churches, and since till that time secular patrons there had not been able to commission works of art on a large scale. There were however, a few Dutch painters who were familiar with Italian or Flemish decorative works, and these the Stadholder employed: among them were Gerrit van Honthorst, of Utrecht, who had made his name in Italy and by then had worked for the English and the Danish courts,[5] Paulus Bor of Amersfoort and Christiaen van Couwenberch of Delft, both of whom had been to Italy, and a group of painters from Haarlem. This group included Pieter Soutman, a pupil of Rubens, and both Pieter de Grebber and his father

[1] Wittkower, op. cit., p. 32, discussed the relationship between baroque stage settings and other decoration such as Bernini evolved.
[2] This may be concluded from preparatory sketches for the series. The writer is indebted to Dr. E. Haverkamp Begemann for this information; see also his 'Rubens schetsen', *Bulletin Museum Boymans*, V, 1954, p. 8, where the subject is touched on.
[3] For these connections see p. 103 and note, above. Rubens had carried out a large scheme of decoration for Charles I at Whitehall, see p. 138 below .
[4] Information on the decoration of the palaces is based on the documents and inventory quoted by Slothouwer, *Paleizen*, Appendices, except where other references are given. The conclusions drawn here sometimes differ from those given in his text.
[5] Jay Richard Judson, *Gerrit van Honthorst* [etc.], The Hague, 1959, pp. 112–22.

Frans, who had been trained in Antwerp and had acted as Rubens' trusted agent in negotiations with Sir Dudley Carleton in 1618, and who in addition was known to Jacob van Campen's father and probably taught the young Van Campen.[1] It also included Van Campen himself, who not only had been to Italy, but also was described by Baldinucci, whose sources of information were sound, as *discepolo*, thus either a pupil or a follower, of Rubens.[2] Dutch sculptors were also employed, although since Hendrik de Keyser's death in 1621 there had been none in Holland who were more than mediocre. In addition both paintings and sculpture were ordered form Antwerp artists, among them from Gonzales Coques, Van Dyck, Artus Quellien, and Willeboirts Bosschaert, whose allegorical style was based on that of Rubens. A painting for a chimney-piece was also commissioned from Rubens when his activities as a political agent for Spain were over.[3]

Normal commerce between the United Provinces and the Southern Netherlands had been possible during the truce of 1609 to 1621, and the Stadholder had many paintings from Antwerp, among them works by Rubens and Van Dyck, when an inventory of his possessions was made in the early 1630s.[4] Clearly he had a taste for Flemish works of art, and this may have been encouraged by Constantyn Huygens after he had joined him as his Secretary. Huygens' admiration of Rubens was profound, and he reiterated his regrets that the events of the times prevented their meeting.[5] In view of this taste, and of the dearth of decorative painters and of sculptors in Holland, it is not surprising that Flemish artists were employed on the decoration of the palaces even while the war with Spain was going on and that Van Campen, whose ideas at least at a later stage in his career were qualified by developments that had been made in Flemish art as will be seen, was entrusted with many of the arrange-

[1] For Frans de Grebber and Rubens see Magurn, *Letters*, esp. p. 59. For possible links between Van Campen and Rubens see P. T. A. Swillens, 'Jacob van Campen als schilder'. *Elsevier's Maandschrift*, XLVIII, 1938, ii, pp. 290–2. Rubens' visit to Holland in 1627 must have been too short to be of consequence for the history of Dutch painting.

[2] Filippo Baldinucci, *Notizie de' professori del disegno da Cimabue in qua*, Florence, 1681–1728, VI, p. 380. His entry concerning Van Campen is headed: "JACOPO VVAN CAMPEN, ARCHITETTO E PITTORE, Discepolo di Pietro Paulo Rubens" [etc.].

[3] Letters by Huygens of 2 July and 14 Nov. 1639, Worp nos. 2149 and 2272 respectively.

[4] S. W. A. Drossaers, 'Inventaris van de meubelen van het Stadhouderlijk kwartier met het Speelhuis en van het Noordeinde te 's-Gravenhage', *Oud-Holland*, XLVII, 1930, pp. 193–236 and 241–76. See also J. G. van Gelder, 'Rubens in Holland in de zeventiende eeuw', *Nederlandsch Kunsthistorisch Jaarboek*, 1950–1, pp. 103–50.

[5] A. H. Kan, *De Jeugd van Constantijn Huygens door hemzelf beschreven*, Rotterdam and Antwerp, 1946, p. 74; letter by Huygens of Nov. 1635, Worp no. 1301. Huygens' view of, and relations with, Rubens are discussed by Van Gelder, op. cit., pp. 140–4.

ments for the decoration. He supplied paintings himself and transmitted payments for both paintings and sculpture, and it is likely that in some cases he was also responsible for their design. There is evidence which suggests that he designed the sculpture made in 1636 for the great tympanum on the front façade of Honselaarsdijk Palace, whose putti, which played about among garlands and held up the Stadholder's coat of arms, were to be carved 'half round' and 'pinned into the wall to the depth of ten Rhineland inches'.[1] The style and arrangement of the putti that appear in the surviving records of the design, which however are scanty,[2] are perhaps more reminiscent of the painted and sculptured putti of Rubens than of any to be seen in sculpture at that time in Italy.

There is no complete description of the palaces built by the Stadholder, which have been destroyed, but it is clear that there were concerted schemes of painted decoration in some of their rooms. There were galleries both at Honselaarsdijk and Rijswijk whose decoration may have been comparable with that of the Galarie des Rois in the part of the Louvre constructed by Henri IV[3] and may possibly have been inspired by it. In that at Honselaarsdijk there was a series of portraits of members of the royal houses of Europe and of the Stadholder's family, with allegorical scenes and views of their castles under the windows between them. In that at Rijswijk there were portraits of sovereign princes and their consorts, with their victories below the windows, and each accompanied by a painted coat of arms.[4] In other rooms there were schemes of painted decoration of another kind. In the entrance hall at Honselaarsdijk, which housed De la Vallée's great stair, there were a number of 'very large' paintings, among them 'sloping pieces',[5] which suggests that the paintings, although they were on stretchers, covered the walls. They showed Flora and Venus, who appeared as counterparts, as well as quantities of children, some flying, and some also with festoons. It seems that the decoration also

---

[1] See p. 166 and note below. The passage there quoted continues: ". . . welverstaende dat ijder kind binnen den muer gesteert sal wesen ter diepte van thien rij[n]landtsche duijmen".

[2] Details are shown on the model of the building (probably of the eighteenth century), Koninklijk Archief, The Hague, and in a drawing by Abraham Beerstraten, Rijksprentenkabinet, Amsterdam.

[3] Described in detail by Henri Sauval, *Histoire et recherches des antiquités de la ville de Paris*, Paris, 1724, II, pp. 37–40.

[4] De la Serre, *Histoire de l'entrée de la Reine Mère du Roi Tres-Chrétien dans les villes des Pays-Bas* [etc.], Amsterdam, 1848, adds to our knowledge of the gallery in his description of the visit made by Maria de' Medici in 1638.

[5] Quotations from the records given by Slothouwer, op. cit., pp. 278 and 271 respectively. John Evelyn described the ceiling painting, which he saw in 1641, as representing "the rape of Ganymede. . . and other pendent figures" *(The Diary of John Evelyn*, ed. E. S. de Beer, Oxford, 1955, II, p. 56).

covered the ceiling, for 'two painted figures seen from below on the vault of the staircase' (it was in fact a shallow dome) were paid for with other paintings for the room.[1] This part of the scheme, however, was to be superseded. In the great hall which lay behind the staircase on the first floor and was the principal apartment of the palace hunting equipment and scenes showing Diana resting or at the chase were depicted, for Honselaarsdijk was in origin a hunting castle. The decoration of the ceiling of this room was clearly of a North Italian kind and it is likely that that of the staircase hall, carried out at the same time and by the same group of artists, was like it. The ceiling of the great hall showed a painted 'gallery', or balustrade, running round the room, apparently ornamented with pots of flowers, and there were shepherds and shepherdesses walking or playing (we may suppose that they were making music) who must have appeared as though they were behind the balustrade. Honthorst decorated the ceiling of the great hall at Rijswijk with a similar painting at about the same time, and he may have introduced this form of decoration into the Stadholder's circle.[2] Yet it is by no means certain that he did so, for Van Campen transmitted payments for the ceiling at Honselaarsdijk to Bor and Pieter de Grebber, who painted it, and he himself contributed one of the hunting scenes. It is possible that it was he who invented the decorative scheme both of the great hall and of the staircase. He, like Honthorst, in all probability had visited northern Italy, where Veronese, working in a tradition that Mantegna had founded, had created decoration of much the same kind in Palladio's Villa Barbaro at Maser, a building in whose architecture Van Campen may well have been interested.[3]

Allegorical scenes painted after the manner of Rubens, and the decoration of ceilings in a North Italian manner with flying figures seen against a blue sky, were used together as elements of a baroque scheme at the end of the 1640s in Princess Amalia van Solms' country pleasure-house outside The Hague, the Huis ten Bosch. They may have been combined in this way in the palaces earlier, but there is no proof of it, and it is likely that, in spite of the interest in Rubens that is evident, a taste for schemes of decoration such as

---

[1] Slothouwer, *Paleizen*, p. 270. Substantial payments were made at the same time for the painting of the 'piece going round' in the staircase hall. This may well have formed part of the decoration of the ceiling, cf. the description which follows of the ceiling of the great hall.

[2] Joachim Sandrart, *Teutsche Academie der edlen Bau- Bild- und Mahlerey-Künste*, Frankfurt, 1675-9, p. 304, describes this painting in some detail, and it appears in an engraving (reprod. Slothouwer, op. cit., p. 119). The accounts show that is was painted from June 1638 to May 1639, and that the Honselaarsdijk ceiling was well under way by March 1638 and was thus the earlier. A small ceiling painting by Honthorst of a similar kind, however, is dated 1622 (cat. *Mostra del Caravaggio*, Milan, Palazzo Reale, 1951, no. 120, pl. 89).

[3] See p. 112 above and pp. 182-3 below.

136

he designed was acquired in the Stadholder's circle only when the main part of the decoration of the palaces had been completed. The paintings by Rubens that were known and emulated in Prince Frederik Hendrik's time in the United Provinces were almost entirely those which dated from before the end of the Twelve Years' Truce in 1621,[1] the year in which the principal decorations of the Jesuit Church at Antwerp had been finished, and it was only in the next year that work on Rubens' first great secular scheme had been begun: the scenes from the life of Maria de' Medici for the Luxembourg Palace.[2] Rubens' baroque planning in composite works carried out for churches might have been known in the United Provinces; Van Campen, among others, might have seen works by him of this kind,[3] and Soutman, who stayed in Antwerp till 1624, may have seen work being done on the Medici scheme in addition to them. Yet Dutch patrons in the 1630s must have known of Rubens' court decoration mainly by hearsay.[4] It perhaps is not surprising, this being so, that the painted decoration of the Stadholder's royal galleries, though it was begun after the Luxembourg gallery had been completed, was of an earlier kind.

Possibly Theodor van Thulden was the first to bring a technical knowledge of Rubens' later decorative schemes to the United Provinces and arrived at a time when a taste for such decoration had already been formed. He made the official engravings of Rubens' designs for the Triumphal Entry which were published with Gevartius' description in 1641, and he settled in 's Hertogenbosch soon afterwards. He had probably been one of Rubens' pupils, and he is known to have worked in the 1630s on one of his decorative schemes.[5] It must have been after his arrival, and was perhaps after the prince's death in 1647, that he ornamented the ceiling above the Honselaarsdijk stair, evidently replacing the figures that had been painted there earlier, with 'Triumphs and ceremonial entries etc. of his Illustrious Highness Prince Frederik Hendrik . .

[1] J. G. van Gelder, op. cit., pp. 106–7.
[2] Now in the Louvre. See Rudolf Oldenbourg, *P. P. Rubens* [*etc.*] (Klassiker der Kunst), 4th ed., Stuttgart and Berlin, n.d., pp. 243–63.
[3] Van Campen became a master in the Haarlem painters' guild in 1614 and went as a young man to Italy (Weissman, 'Jacob van Campen', *Oud-Holland*, XX, 1902, p. 119; Houbraken, *Schouwburgh*, III, p. 381). He therefore probably went south during the Twelve Years' Truce. Through his connections with De Grebber he may well have been encouraged to visit Antwerp on this journey or at some other time.
[4] No 17th-century engravings of the Medici Cycle (c. 1622–5) are known. Prints of the Triumphal Entry (1635) were published only in 1641. Rubens' decorations had been set up in Inigo Jones' Banqueting House at Whitehall by March 1636 (H. G. Evers, *Rubens und sein Werk, neue Forschungen*, Brussels, 1943, p. 85) and Dutch visitors could have seen them there. It seems that prints of this decoration were not made until some time afterwards.
[5] He worked on the paintings for the Torre del Parada (see H. Schneider in Thieme-Becker, s.v. Theodor van Thulden).

gained both by land and sea'.[1] This painting, or series of paintings, must have formed a substantial piece of baroque decoration, planned and carried out in a Rubensian style,[2] and it may well have been comparable with Rubens' ceiling at Whitehall, set up in 1636, in which the career of James I was glorified. On the occasion of the wedding of the Stadholder's son Prince Willem and Princess Mary Stuart in 1641 a number of visitors from the Dutch court must have seen this work for the first time,[3] though news of it must have reached the republic earlier. The substitution of Van Thulden's design for the earlier composition, itself painted two years after the Whitehall ceiling had been put in place, is perhaps another indication of a belated change of taste in the United Provinces, and of the tardy arrival there of great schemes of decoration such as Rubens devised.

Our knowledge of the decoration of the palaces still remains to a great extent conjectural, but the decoration of the Huis ten Bosch has survived and can be described.[4] The house is symmetrically planned, in the manner of a Palladian villa, and its main feature is a central hall which takes up most of its height. The ground plan of this hall has the form of a shallow-armed cross whose inner corners are sloped off, and it has an intricate vaulted roof surmounted by an octagonal lantern and a dome. The structure was nearly completed when Prince Frederik Hendrik died in 1647, and his widow had the hall decorated as a monument to him, Huygens suggested that it should be named the Oranjezaal, the Hall of the House of Orange, and it was he who devised its symbolic scheme, designed to record the dead prince's glory. His work was the result of painstaking research and elaborate organization, as Rubens' great schemes had been,[5] and when it was finished he was clearly satisfied, feeling that it surpassed "beaucoup d'autres entreprises illustres qu'on rencontre dans les plus grandes cours de la Chrestienté";[6] he would have published

[1] From an inventory of 1758 given by Slothouwer, op. cit., p. 287. "Triumphen en Inhalingen etca. van zijne Doorl: Hoogheid Prins Frederik Hendrik . . . zoo ter land, als ter zee behaeld."
[2] The description, and Van Thulden's style, which was closely modelled on that of Rubens, make this evident.
[3] Neither the Stadholder nor Huygens, however, was present; letter from Huygens of 9 May 1641, Worp no. 2704.
[4] The house was built by Pieter Post and was begun in 1643. For its original appearance and the arrangement of its decoration see P. Post, *De Sael van Orange*, Amsterdam [1654] (façade altered and wings added in the eighteenth century). For information and illustrations see Slothouwer, op. cit., Appendices, and J. G. van Gelder, 'De schilders van de Oranjezaal', *Nederlandsch Kunsthistorisch Jaarboek*, 1948–9, pp. 119–56; these have been referred to here.
[5] Magurn, *Letters*, p. 83.
[6] Information and quotation from Huygens' own account, *Mémoires de Constantin Huygens*, ed. T. Jorissen, The Hague ,1873, pp. 135–6.

engravings of the decoration with an explanation in Latin, for all the world to read, if he had not been prevented from doing so by the high cost.

Huygens' comparison suggests that when he thought out the scheme he had works by Rubens in mind, and both the choice of the painters who contributed to it and its formal and symbolic composition bear this out. He went to Antwerp in 1648 to witness the proclamation there of the Peace of Munster,[1] by which normal relations with the Southern Netherlands were restored, and he went again in 1649. On that occasion he saw sketches for the decoration of the Oranjezaal,[2] for important parts of it were ordered from Antwerp artists as soon as the war was over. Jordaens, Rubens' most eminent successor, was commissioned to paint the main piece and one of the paintings that was to flank it, and Willeboirts Bosschaert and Gonzales Coques, both living in Antwerp, contributed further paintings. Other parts of the scheme, including the decoration of the ceiling, were carried out by artists in the United Provinces, among them Honthorst and Van Thulden, and it was Van Campen who, in collaboration with Huygens, planned and co-ordinated the paintings, sending sketches and detailed instructions to the artists who carried them out and having their preliminary designs sent in for approval or correction. At this point, in fact, a Dutch painter undertook the formal planning of a Rubensian scheme, and fed back ideas that originated in Antwerp, as will be shown, to Antwerp artists.

The decoration is consistently lit as though from the windows, and its perspective is designed to be seen from the centre of the hall, where the visitor witnesses the prince's glory and the splendour of his career as he looks about him. A triumph appears in the lowest range of paintings, represented as though its participants had halted to form symbolic tableaux in triumphal arches round the room which seem to form part of the actual architecture, and the procession culminates in Jordaens' great painting (illus. 152), in which Prince Frederik Hendrik appears on a triumphal car, surrounded by other princes of the House of Orange. His wife, in a picture set at right-angles to this vast canvas, looks towards her approaching husband, while Destiny, at her side, points out Death, the bringer of change, who appears in the picture opposite her. In this way these figures are related to each other in the space in which the spectator stands, while the spectator himself provides the focal point of the scheme and links its parts together. Above the triumph episodes from the prince's life are

---

[1] J. H. W. Unger, *Dagboek van Constantyn Huygens* (publ. Oud-Holland), Amsterdam, 1885, p. 47.
[2] Letter from Huygens to Princess Amalia, 16 Aug. 1649, Worp no. 4969.

depicted, from his phoenix-like birth, represented above the fireplace,[1] to his apotheosis. Both the tableaux and these upper paintings are interspersed with mythological scenes which reinforce their meaning, and there are other symbolic paintings on the ceiling, where children hold up a portrait of the sorrowing princess, or fly busily about in a cloudless sky as their counterparts did at Honselaarsdijk and Rijswijk. These children, however, are not accompanied by painted musicians like those of the palaces, for in the Oranjezaal there is a balustraded gallery below the lantern in which real musicians played,[2] and they, looking down, completed the decoration.

The planning of the decoration of the Town Hall of Amsterdam is of the same kind, for there, as has been shown, figures and whole scenes were related to each other in space and reinforced each other's meaning, the spectator was essential to the design, and he also defined its scale as he walked about the building or paused to look down from its balustraded openings. It is in the Huis ten Bosch, however, slightly the earlier of the two schemes, that the origins of Van Campen's baroque planning are most evident. There the Rubensian nature of the scheme cannot be questioned, for though in theory he could have arrived at such planning for himself echoes of Rubens in the composition show that in fact he did not do so.[3]

It seems that Huygens, searching for a fitting form for the memorial to his dead master, found an admirable model in Rubens' scenes from the life of Maria de' Medici in the Luxembourg Palace, and although at that time there were no engravings of those paintings the scenes from the life of Prince Frederik Hendrik in the Oranjezaal contain details as well as ideas which appear to have been taken from them.[4] To these scenes Huygens added a Roman triumph, making the victories of antiquity illuminate those of modern times, and in designing this, as well as other parts of the decoration, Van Campen evidently turned to another work by Rubens – one which had appeared in engravings – and used it a number of times. He echoed, rather than borrowed, but the echoes ring clear, and similar echoes may be discerned in other compositions by him.[5] It was to Gevartius' *Pompa Introitus Ferdinandi*, with

---

[1]   The fireplace has been removed, so that the placing of this scene no longer adds to its symbolism.
[2]   Journal des voyages de M. de Monconys, Lyons, 1665–6, II, p. 143: "Au tour de la courniche de laquelle ['la lenterne de la voute'] regne une Tribune pour mettre des Musiciens, & qui regarde au bas de la sale".
[3]   Van Campen left Italy too early to come under the influence of Bernini's schemes: he must have been back before Coymans' house in Amsterdam was begun in 1625.
[4]   J. G. van Gelder, op. cit., p. 153, n. 1; Jay Richard Judson, *Gerrit van Honthorst* [etc.], The Hague, 1959, p. 125.
[5]   In his design for the monument to Admiral Tromp in the Old Church, Delft (the authorship is given by

its illustrations engraved by Van Thulden from Rubens' designs, that he referred – Huygens had a copy, and there was another in the Stadholder's library, so it was readily accessible[1] – and he made use of it in the designs of paintings carried out by different artists. The doors of the Oranjezaal were decorated with a *trompe l'oeil* painting by Van Couwenberch of a kind reminiscent of Veronese[2] in which Minerva and Hercules appear to be pushing open the doors of this hall of fame, and its composition has the character of a version-in-reverse of Rubens' Temple of Janus, where Discord pulls one of the doors open and both Peace and Princess Isabella of Austria do their best to push the other shut (illus. 156-7).[3] Jordaens' painting in the triumph[4] strongly resembles Rubens' antique Triumph of the Infante Ferdinand[5] in its general composition and in a number of its features, although it is a great deal more elaborate (illus. 152-3). Van Campen's own painting of Prince Frederik Hendrik Crossing the Three Rivers[6] echoes Rubens' representation of Prince Ferdinand at the Battle of Nordlingen,[7] where he appears, baton in hand, as the Stadholder does in the Oranjezaal picture, similarly mounted, and dominating the composition in much the same way (illus. 154-5). Other echoes, though fainter ones, may be suspected,[8] but it is in these instances that Van Campen's interest in Rubens' decoration is proved.

In the decoration of the Town Hall itself, although its purpose was different, there are further reminiscences of the Triumphal Entry,[9] but there is no need

Dirk Evertsz. van Bleyswyk, *Beschryving der stad Delft*, Delft, 1667, p. 182), where the tritons on the cornice are strikingly similar to those above the decorative screen representing Mercury deserting Antwerp, Gevartius, *Pompa*, pl. p. 147 A. For further references to Rubens see n. 9 below.

[1] This assumes that the book was bought when it first appeared, as is probable; the lists mentioning it are of later date: *Catalogus der bibliotheek van Constantyn Huygens* [etc.], The Hague, 1903 (reprint by W. P. van Stockum of sale catalogue of 1688), Libri miscellanei in folio, no 313; Inventory of the Stadholders' library, 1686, Koninklijke Bibliotheek, The Hague, MS. no. 78 D 14, no. 2146.

[2] Cf his *trompe l'oeil* painting of a figure on a door in the Villa Barbaro at Maser, illus. Bernard Berenson, *Italian Pictures of the Renaissance, Venetian School*, London, 1957, II, fig. 1050.

[3] Gevartius, *Pompa*, pls. p. 117 A and B.

[4] In this case it is recorded that Van Campen sent a detailed sketch for the composition to the artist (letter from Jordaens to Huygens of 23 Apr. 1651, Worp no. 5132) and it may be assumed that he also provided a sketch for the painting by Van Couwenberch just mentioned.

[5] Gevartius, *Pompa*, pls. p. 108 A and B.

[6] The subject and the painter are convincingly identified by J. G. van Gelder, op. cit., p. 131.

[7] Gevartius, *Pompa*, pls. p. 99 A and B.

[8] Possibly there are general references to the Triumphal Entry decorations in the captives and trophies in the Oranjezaal triumph and in the armour etc. painted on the walls between its scenes, cf. Gevartius, *Pompa*, pls. pp. 99 A and 108 A. There is also some resemblance between the Apollo in Van Campen's Aurora and that of Gevartius' title-page, which Rubens himself designed.

[9] In some cases the likeness may be due to chance, but the list is nevertheless formidable: [1] Apollo in the upper painting proposed for the east wall of the Burgerzaal, Vennekool, *Afbeelding*, pl. R, cf. that on Gevartius' title-page where the figure, chariot, and horses more closely resemble Van Campen's than those

to discuss them. For already it is clear that a form of baroque decoration evolved by Rubens was used in the Town Hall as it had been in the Huis ten Bosch very little earlier. In both it was used with only slight modification, the admixture of a decorative element taken from North Italian renaissance painting, which Rubens also had used, but which, in the hands of Dutch artists, was moulded into a baroque form rather differently. That, at least, is true of the planning of the decorative scheme of the Town Hall and of the style of the paintings that formed part of it. In its sculptural style, however, a further element appears: the classicism which has already been referred to.

in possible prototypes in Italy. [2] Painting showing Neptune proposed for the same wall, cf. Rubens' Neptune Stilling the Waves, *Pompa* pls. pp. 11 A and 15 (painting formerly at Dresden; see also p. 44 n. 1 above). [3] Painting showing Victory and Fame proposed for the inner wall of the council chamber of the Civic Guard, *Afbeelding*, pl. X, in which the Janus' Temple motif appears again (for authorship see Bibliography s.v. Vennekool). [4] Groups of prisoners with trophies set up above them proposed for the same wall, cf. *Pompa*, pls. pp. 99 A and 108 A. [5] Sculptured lions over doors accompanying Cybele in north-east gallery, cf. those above the main painting on the back of the Arcus Ferdinandi, *Pompa*, pl. p. 108 A (cf. illus. 67, 153). [6] Flying children and harpies above entrance of the Magistrates Court, cf. those above the door of the temple of Janus (cf. illus. 77, 156). [7] Miners working with picks and carrying baskets of ore carved on west tympanum, cf. those represented on the back of the Arcus Monetalis, *Pompa*, pl. p. 155. A further reminiscence of Rubens, though not of the Triumphal Entry decorations, is described on pp. 177-9 below. The use in the Town Hall of certain symbols applied so far as their meaning is concerned in accordance with their use by Rubens (as described by Gevartius) was unhappily noticed too late for discussion here. The author hopes to consider this subject in a separate publication.

CHAPTER VI

THE SCULPTURED BUST

SECOND PART

The style of the Town Hall's sculptural decoration originated both with Rubens in Antwerp and with François Duquesnoy in Rome, and to understand its complex nature the historical survey begun in the last chapter must be completed. Some features of the sculptural style inspired by Rubens have been noticed but only his manner of planning decoration has so far been followed to Holland; the arrival there of a Rubensian sculptural style has yet to be seen. The style of Duquesnoy's sculpture and its appearance in the Southern Netherlands must also be considered, for this style was grafted on to the Rubensian one and was transferred to the soil of Amsterdam, where the two combined bore decorative fruit of an unwonted kind.

When Jerome Duquesnoy the Elder finished his intricate tabernacle for St. Martin's church, Alost, in 1604 his son François[1] was seven years old, and it was only in 1618, when he was twenty-one, that François left for Italy. He received his first training in his father's workshop in Brussels, and his journey south, made 'in order to exert himself further in his art',[2] was paid for by the Archduke Albert, Governor of the Netherlands, to whom he had presented a work in ivory. Evidently he was a promising sculptor before he left the Netherlands. He left before the innovations made by Rubens in the decoration of the Jesuit Church at Antwerp can have been evident, trained in a tradition which was becoming outdated and was based on the piecemeal emulation of antique art. This being so it is not suprising that Duquesnoy's mature style was formed in Rome,[3] where he studied and copied antique sculpture with the deepest interest, joined early in 1624 by Poussin, with whom he also drew and made models from the putti in Titian's Feast of Venus.[4] There were hardly any works by the young Bernini to be seen when Duquesnoy got his first impressions of Italy, and though he worked from 1626 on Bernini's decorative

---

[1] See Mariette Fransolet, *François du Quesnoy, sculpteur d'Urbain VIII, 1597–1643* (Académie royale de Belgique), Brussels, 1942, and the early biographies mentioned there.

[2] "Pour s'esvertuer davantaige au faict de son art." From François Duquesnoy's request to the Archduke, quoted by Fransolet, op. cit., p. 39, n. 9.

[3] This is clear from his style. Works made before he left Brussels have not been identified.

[4] Oskar Fischel, *Tizian* (Klassiker der Kunst), Stuttgart and Leipzig, 1911, p. 41. Now in the Prado, Madrid.

schemes and must have adapted his style to them it seems that he based his own personal style on antique and renaissance art. If he referred to the sculpture of his own era it must have been to the figure of St. Cecilia made in the last years of the sixteenth century by Stefano Maderno for the church of S. Cecilia in Trastevere, or to other works, in painting as well as in sculpture,[1] in which the movement towards classicism which followed the mannerist era was represented. Duquesnoy's St. Susanna in the church of S. Maria di Loreto (illus. 169), of the 1630s, is remarkably similar to Maderno's St. Cecilia in its restraint and its classical unity. Yet it has a simplification of form which was not to be found in the sculpture of the time and which must have come from antique sculpture, and in spite of its great suppleness it has a classical steadiness of posture.

François Duquesnoy did not return to the Netherlands, and it was left to his brother, Jerome Duquesnoy the Younger,[2] and to other followers, to bring his style to the Low Countries. Jerome, who was five years younger than François, joined him in Italy as soon as his apprenticeship was over, and his style too was formed in Italy. He returned to the Spanish Netherlands after François died in 1643 and his works there show to what an extent he shared his brother's interest in antique and renaissance art. His tomb of Bishop Triest (illus. 158) in St. Bavo, Ghent, which had been commissioned from François,[3] has three principal figures: a Christ based on Michelangelo's Risen Christ in S. Maria sopra Minerva, a figure of the Virgin which is skilfully adapted from François' St. Susanna, and the effigy of the bishop, which except for the portrait head is almost a copy of the sixteenth-century effigy of Bishop del Monte by Ammanati in S. Pietro in Montorio. The Virgin implores her Son to have mercy on the bishop, as the inscription proves, putting her hand out towards him, while the bishop himself looks in the direction of the altar, to all appearance unaware of her petition. The tomb is not related to the spectator and is self-contained, and there is little, except for this interplay between the figures, to suggest that it dates from the mid-seventeenth century. When Lucas Faydherbe[4] referred to this work in designing the tomb of Archbishop

---

[1] G. P. Bellori points out that a composition by him representing Divine and Profane Love formed a variant on that of Annibale Caracci in the Farnese Gallery; *Le vite de' pittori, scultori, et architetti moderni*, Rome, 1672, p. 271.

[2] See Georg Sobotka in Thieme Becker, s.v. Jerôme Duquesnoy d. J.

[3] François had sent the project for the tomb and two putti that were to form part of it from Italy; see Mariette, *Abécédario* (Archives de l'art français), Paris, 1851–60, II, p. 141.

[4] For Faydherbe and his works see Br. Libertus, *Lucas Faydherbe, beeldhouwer en bouwmeester*, Antwerp, 1938.

Cruesen (illus. 159) for Malines Cathedral in 1660 he made use, as might be expected, of its arrangement but not of its style. There the Risen Christ is based on a painting by Rubens. The archbishop prays fervently to him, and a Rubensian figure representing Time, who takes the place of the Virgin, turns away from the archbishop, powerless. The combination of Rubens' baroque style in the flanking figures with elements derived from Bernini in the gestures and glance of the effigy is clear, and there is no reflection of the Duquesnoys' classicism.

Faydherbe, who was born in Malines in 1617, had finished his training as a sculptor in Rubens' studio, and when he left him in 1640 he did so with a testimonial from his master: 'Because of the affinity that there is between our arts of painting and sculpture, with my instruction and his diligence and intelligence, [he] has profited very greatly in his art'.[1] The episode is revealing, for it shows how deeply Rubens was concerned with sculpture, even at the end of his career. Yet Faydherbe was by no means the only sculptor who learnt from Rubens.[2] It would not be an exaggeration to say that more than a generation of Antwerp sculptors came under his influence, and through his designs a baroque sculptural style was developed in the north earlier than it was in Italy, as has been seen. This style became general in the Southern Netherlands in the second quarter of the seventeenth century, and when François Duquesnoy's classical style was introduced in the 1640s in an uncompromising form it must have been too foreign to be easily assimilated.[3]

In the cathedral church of Ste Gudule, Brussels, where figures representing Christ, the Madonna, and the twelve Apostles were set up on the pillars round about the 1640s,[4] works of the tradition inspired by Rubens and of that of Duquesnoy may be seen together. Both Faydherbe and the younger Jerome

[1]   Max Rooses and C. Ruelens, *Correspondance de Rubens* [etc.], Antwerp, 1887–1909, VI, p. 262 (translated by the present writer). ". . . door de ghemeynschap die onse consten van schildery en beldhouwery t' saemen hebben, met myne instructien ende syne neerstigheyt ende goeden gheest, seer veel gheprofiteert heeft in syne conste."

[2]   In addition to Faydherbe Robert and Hans Colyns de Nole, Hubert van den Eynde, Hans van Mildert, Sebastian de Neve, Erasmus Quellien the elder and other masters are known to have executed sculpture to Rubens' designs. For documented instances see A. Jansen and C. van Herck, 'De Antwerpsche beeldhouwers Colyns de Nole'. *Jaarboek Koninklijke Oudheidkundige Kring van Antwerpen*, XIX, 1943, pp. 67–68 and 71–72 and Rooses, *Oeuvre*, II, pp. 307 and 324. References concerning Artus Quellien's relationship with Rubens are given below; p. 149, n. 6.

[3]   At the beginning of the eighteenth century, however, Michiel van der Voort the Elder followed François Duquesnoy's style closely in works carried out in the Southern Netherlands: see Mark Edo Tralbaut, *De Antwerpse "Meester const-beldthouwer" Michiel van der Voort de Oude* [etc.] (Koninklijke Vlaamse Academie voor Wetenschappen, Letteren en Schoone Kunsten van België), Brussels, 1949.

[4]   See Henri Velge, *La collégiale des Saints Michel et Gudule à Bruxelles*, Brussels, 1925, pp. 259–65.

Duquesnoy contributed to the series, and in their figures of St. Simon and St. Thomas (illus. 162, 163) the characteristics of the two traditions can be recognized. Faydherbe's St. Simon stands firmly and majestically, yet the power of strong movement is implied in this figure as it is in figures by Rubens. The head and beard are of a type that he painted, and both these and the enormous hands are portrayed with the particularized realism of form and texture that he developed – one in which tactile qualities are emphasized. Because of this, and because of the figure's implied ability to move, which is shown as movement might be shown in a 'still' from a film, it has great immediacy. It might almost be a painted figure by Rubens translated into stone, were it not for a certain hesitance in the proportions and an incomplete co-ordination between the stance and the arrangement of the drapery. Jerome Duquesnoy's figure of St. Thomas, on the other hand, has not this immediacy. It is static and wistful, and the right hand is open and held up with an arrested gesture which suggests that the saint is shown at the moment when his doubt was changed into belief. The individualized realism of the St. Simon is absent and instead the figure is idealized and has a certain dryness of form and texture. It is clearly an adaptation of François Duquesnoy's St. Andrew (illus. 161), which forms part of Bernini's scheme in St. Peter's, Rome, and must largely have been based on antique art;[1] presumably Jerome used some model or drawing made by his brother.[2] The head is so similar that the wind that blows in St. Peter's disturbs the northern figure's hair and beard and the stance is identical, though the strong gesture of the St. Andrew, by which, in the position for which it was designed, it would have been linked into Bernini's scheme, has been eliminated.

Faydherbe remained as consistent a follower of Rubens as Jerome Duquesnoy did of his brother. Indeed in later works, and in particular in his great reliefs in Notre Dame d'Hanswijk, Malines, he not only emulated those qualities of Rubens' style which Rubens himself had applied to sculpture; he also adapted Rubens' manner of pictorial composition to sculptural designs – brilliantly, if with a lack of discernment. He never went to Italy, and it is natural that the works of his master Rubens, which remained pre-eminent in the Southern Netherlands, should continue to be his main source of inspiration.

Artus Quellien, the sculptor of the Amsterdam Town Hall, whose Ara Coeli Madonna formed part of the St. Gudule series, was in a more fortunate

[1] The torso appears to have been based on that of the Laocoon, which Duquesnoy is known to have studied.
[2] Jerome brought works by François to the Netherlands.

146

position and elements derived from Rubens and Duquesnoy are combined or appear successively in his works, sensitively modified and adapted according to the requirements of each commission. His education as a sculptor enabled him to achieve this synthesis, which remained beyond the reach of Jerome Duquesnoy and Faydherbe, the one trained in an outdated northern tradition and turning exclusively to Italy and the other without a first-hand knowledge of Italian art. Moreover Quellien was less close to François Duquesnoy than Jerome was, and less close to Rubens than Faydherbe, yet had excellent opportunities for understanding the works of both these masters. From this ideal position he could view the works of both objectively and without fanaticism and could draw on the styles of both without compromise.

Quellien was born in Antwerp in 1609 and must have received his training there in the 1620s.[1] In the years that followed he carried out works in his own city and for Prince Frederik Hendrik, for whom he made a Pallas and other figures, and who paid him for over-life-size figures of Mars and Venus in 1634.[2] He went to Italy only after these works had been made, so it is clear that he was an accomplished and successful sculptor before he left Antwerp and that his style was first formed, unlike the styles of François and Jerome Duquesnoy, in the immediate neighbourhood of Rubens. Growing up in that environment and as a sculptor's son[3] he must have been well aware of the changes in both painting and sculpture which Rubens inspired. His brother Erasmus was trained in Rubens' studio in the early 1630s, so that at that time he probably had inside knowledge of what was going on there. It is not known whether he himself was in contact with Rubens, and the dated works in which they perhaps collaborated were made after Quellien's return from Italy, but it may be assumed that he came under Rubens' influence early,

---

[1] Information concerning Quellien is based on Gabriels, *Quellien*, and on sources quoted there (the more important of which are here referred to separately), also on an important biographical passage in a letter from Michiel le Blon to Huygens of 27 Jan. 1646 (Worp no. 4259) which may be quoted (in translation from the Dutch original) here: 'The bearer of this letter, Artus Quellien, is the famous and skilful Antwerp sculptor who, earlier, made the Pallas, life size, and several other statues for his Highness [Prince Frederik Hendrik] before he went to Italy, where he practised his art for some years with great profit, and returned to Antwerp. There he has made various excellent works, both in churches and for private persons, and even also some statues for the late Heer Hellemans which I understand his Highness has obtained, as well as two marble children, life size, for the Heer Kletscher, etc. And since he is working on four similar children for the Heer Kabouw, and, one being finished, wished to bring the same over himself to see and get to know the country and these art-lovers, I did not wish to refrain . . . [from recommending him to Huygens and through him to his Highness]'.

[2] Entry in the Stadholder's accounts for that year, quoted by Slothouwer, *Paleizen*, p. 265.

[3] A short account of Artus' father, Erasmus Quellien the Elder, known as a wood carver of standing who had many pupils, is given by Gabriels, op. cit., pp. 72–75.

and that he went south with a style, now unknown, which had developed accordingly.

Although he spent some years in Rome Quellien is unlikely to have worked as a pupil in Duquesnoy's studio[1] for he arrived there aged about twenty-five and as an experienced sculptor. Sandrart, who was there at the time and who knew Duquesnoy, gives an account of Quellien's activities: 'Through the assistance of François Duquesnoy, who was well disposed to him, he got the right insight in every respect. Moreover he did not neglect to apply himself diligently to the academies of antiques, through which he made marked improvement'.[2] Quellien's adherence to the antique is likely to have been due to Duquesnoy's advice, and he was certainly influenced by him. The style of a sleeping child which Quellien carved in ivory in 1641 is very close indeed to that of works by Duquesnoy (cf. illus. 170, 171).[3] He made a number of other figures of children after his return from Italy[4] – there is no record that

[1] Gabriels' theory that he probably met Van Campen there for the first time (op. cit., p. 28) is untenable, since Huygens' correspondence shows that Van Campen was in the United Provinces throughout the time that Quellien was in Rome.

[2] Joachim von Sandrart, *Teutsche Academie der edlen Bau- Bild- und Mahlerey-Kunste*, Frankfurt, 1675-9, I, p. 351. The quoted passage follows in its context: "Arthus Quellinus, von Antorf bürtig, wurde von der Natur gleichsam zu der Bildhauerey beruffen, und liesse vielfältige Proben dieser seiner Wissenschaft, in seiner Geburts-Stadt, von sich sehen. Woraufhin er nacher Rom gezogen, und vermittelst des *Francisci Quesnoy*, als welcher ihm wolgeneigt gewesen, in allem das rechte Liecht überkommen, auch ihme sich bey denen *antichen Academien* steif zu halten, fleissig angelegen seyn lassen, wordurch er dann merklich zugenommen, und wieder nacher Haus gekehret, auch sich allda mit gutem Ruhm und Lob niedergelassen, also dass seiner Arbeit viel nach Amsterdam begehret worden, woselbst er auch das Welt-berühmte Rahtshaus mit allen Statuen und *Basso-relieven*, ... über sich genommen [etc.]". The term 'academies of antiques' presumably refers to the study of antique sculpture which formed an important element in the work of Academies of Art in Italy, see Nikolaus Pevsner, *Academies of Art Past and Present*, Cambridge, 1940, Chs. II and III. The correspondences between the accounts given by Le Blon and Sandrart strongly suggest that both are accurate.

[3] In the Walters Art Gallery, Baltimore, 11.6 cm. long, signed and dated. Its style resembles in particular that of Duquesnoy's putti in SS. Apostoli, Naples, and on the tomb of Van den Eynde in S. Maria dell' Anima, Rome. Its composition is of the same kind as that of works connected with Duquesnoy and listed by Fransolet, op. cit., p. 176. The present writer is grateful to Professor J. G. van Gelder for drawing her attention to this work, which is not discussed in the literature on Quellien. Georg Sobotka perhaps knew some such works since he considered Quellien "in seinen kleinplastischen Arbeiten dem Fiammingo [Duquesnoy] oft zum Verwechseln änlich"; *Die Bildhauerei der Barokzeit*, Vienna, 1927, p. 94. Christian Scherer, *Elfenbeinplastik seit der Renaissance* (Monographien des Kunstgewerbes), Leipzig, n.d., p. 34, and Otto Pelka, *Elfenbein*, Berlin, 1924, p. 325, mention no works in ivory which are certainly by Quellien.

[4] See the quotation from Le Blon, p. 147 n. 1 above. Some of the figures were for Dutch patrons as Le Blon implies. The Heer Kletscher was probably Thomas Kletscher, goldsmith and jeweller in The Hague, for whom see H. E. van Gelder, 'Een Haagsch Burgermeesterspaar door Daniël Mytens', *Mededelingen van de Dienst van Kunsten en Wetenschappen*, VII, 1940, pp. 33-36; the present writer is indebted to Professor J. G. van Gelder for this identification. The Heer Kabouw was the Dutch Cornelis Nobelaer, Heer van Cabouw. The Heer Hellemans was perhaps Don Franciso Hellemans who lived in the Southern Netherlands and whose daughter Eleonora had married P. C. Hooft. For these see Worp, *Briefwisseling*, IV, p. 276, notes 4 and 5. A payment for two modelled children made for 'Segers living in Holland', until now unidentified, was due to Quellien's father's heirs in 1642; Stadsarchief, Antwerp, Weeskamer 1642 (477). It is not im-

he made such figures earlier – and it is probable that these too were of the kind that Duquesnoy had developed and brought into vogue.[1] Though Quellien cannot have failed to see works by Bernini in Rome both Sandrart's account and his own sculptural style show that his main interest there was in antique art and in works in which it was emulated. Only one clear echo of Bernini can be distinguished in his sculpture: the inclusion and arrangement of the sitter's hand in two of his portrait busts,[2] in which he adapted a theme used by Bernini in his bust of Thomas Baker.[3] Except in this one instance the baroque element in Quellien's style seems to have come from Rubens.

By 12th August 1639 Quellien was back in Antwerp and had carved the printer's mark of the Plantin press which is above the door of the Plantin-Moretus Museum (illus. 164). Its style is Rubensian though one may suspect that for the narrow folds of Constancy's drapery Quellien was indebted to Duquesnoy or to antique sculpture; in Rubens' drawing for the printer's mark (illus. 165) and in the engraved and woodcut versions of the design this drapery is different.[4] The Hercules, although the posture is changed, is of exactly the type derived from the Farnese Hercules which appears in Rubens' drawing, which he often represented, and which may be seen in the St. Christopher of the wings of his triptych of the Descent from the Cross in Antwerp Cathedral.[5] The composition of the relief, though the figures sit instead of standing, corresponds closely with the drawn and printed designs and must have either been due to Rubens himself or derived from them.[6]

possible that these too were by Artus, and the futher connection with the United Provinces is interesting. A life-size cupid by Duquesnoy had reached the Dutch court earlier, see Fransolet, op. cit., pl. IX and p. 180.

[1] See Fransolet, op. cit., pp. 186-7, where works by Duquesnoy in 17th-century collections are listed.

[2] In the busts of Andries de Graeff, 1661 (Rijksmuseum, Amsterdam), and of Johan de Witt, 1664-5 (Dordrecht Museum).

[3] See Wittkower, *Bernini*, cat. no. 40. The bust was being carved in 1638. The likeness to Bernini's Vigevano (cat. no. 5) is slighter and it may be concluded that Quellien left Rome after the Baker bust had been designed. The placing of the hand is likely to have been planned by Bernini; see Cecil Gould, 'Bernini's Bust of Mr. Baker: the Solution?', *The Art Quarterly*, XXI, 1958, p. 172.

[4] Drawing by Rubens of c. 1627 in the Plantin-Moretus Museum, Antwerp; Gustav Glück and Franz Martin Haberditzl, *Die Handzeichnungen von Peter Paul Rubens*, Berlin, 1928, no. 167. For the engraving, by Cornelis Galle, and woodcut, by Jan-Christoffel Jeger, see Herman F. de Bouchery and Frank van den Wijngaert, *P.P. Rubens en het Plantijnsche huis* (Maerlantbibliotheek), Antwerp and Utrecht, 1941, pls. 82 and 110.

[5] Rudolf Oldenbourg, *P. P. Rubens* [etc.] (Klassiker der Kunst), 4th ed., Stuttgart and Berlin, n. d., p. 53.

[6] It is possible that in 1639 or not long afterwards Quellien carved the monument, now destroyed, which Rubens designed for the grave of Johan Gevartius (see Gabriels, op. cit., pp. 81-82) but the attribution rests solely on the 18th-century account of De Wit, who is not always reliable. Further works, now lost, designed by Rubens and attributed by De Wit to Quellien, were too early in date to have been by him. Quellien may have worked to designs by Rubens for the Jesuit Church, Antwerp, since, with a member of the Van den Eynde family, one of the Quelliens carved the communion-rails for the high altar (*Klaegende-Dicht over het onverwacht en schrickelyck verbranden . . . van den . . . Tempel Godts van het Huys der Professien van de Societeyt*

Quellien worked in the same manner after Rubens' death in 1642 and on occasions where there is no reason to suppose that the design was connected with him. In both his group representing the Virgin and Child, St Joseph and St. Anne in St. Paul's church, Antwerp (illus. 172-3), of 1644, and in his Ara Coeli Madonna (illus. 160),[1] which is undated, the Virgin is of a type common in Flemish painting and in Rubens' work. In the group of 1644, which is set against a pillar in the Gothic church, the St. Joseph and St. Anne are also like figures in Rubens' paintings and are portrayed with a particularized realism comparable to that of his style.[2] The Virgin leans down to show the child Christ to the congregation, supporting him and helping him to hold the heavy orb, as though she were placing him in their presence, while St. Joseph and St. Anne, who stand to either side, draw back in awe and reverence, sharing in the congregation's reactions. The Ara Coeli Madonna, which originally was set up on one of the first pillars of the chancel in Ste Gudule, though in what position is not known, is related to the spectator in a similar way. She seems to float above her crescent moon, withdrawn from the ordinary world. Yet from whatever angle one sees her she also seeks contact with the spectator in spite of her remoteness, reaching her hand out gently to link the sinner in the church into the unseen world of which she forms part.

Between the making of the Plantin printer's mark and of the group representing the Holy Family Quellien carved the sleeping child in ivory, which but for his signature might be taken for one of Duquesnoy's works. This suggests that in sculpture carried out in the Southern Netherlands Quellien as it were expressed himself in his mother tongue – the language of forms and relationships in space that was spoken around him and that he was expected to speak – but that on occasion, communing with himself or with some particular patron, he enjoyed using a language which he had learnt in Italy and spoke equally well. Rubens himself might have been such a patron. His admiration for Duquesnoy's putti is recorded,[3] and his own painted and sculptured putti, though they were descended from real children in Antwerp whom he

Jesu binnen Antwerpen [etc.], Antwerp, 1718, p. 2). The date of this lost work is unknown. Since it formed a prominent and important feature of the church's decoration Rubens is likely to have designed it. Quellien may also have carved two of the figures in the niches of the chancel arch, though the evidence on this point is conflicting. These too may have been carved according to Rubens' indications or designs (see p. 130 n. 2 above).

[1]   The dating of other figures in the series suggests that the madonna was carved after Quellien's return from Italy.

[2]   The parallels are in type rather than pose, and are many. The likeness of Quellien's St. Anne to that of Rubens in his Virgin with the Lamb, Pitti Gallery, Florence, is particularly striking.

[3]   Magurn, *Letters*, pp. 413-14.

saw and knew, were also descended from those of Titian. His putti and those of Duquesnoy, by this reckoning, were cousins. The distance, which has grown with the centuries, between the styles of northern baroque art and of seventeenth-century classical art in Italy, was bridged over, as in this instance, by likenesses between them: by baroque elements in Duquesnoy's works – the behaviour of his putti has a baroque immediacy which brings them close to the spectator though their forms are idealized – and by the tremendous classicism of Rubens. Rubens' St. Christopher, the movement and the drops of sweat taken away, would become the Farnese Hercules.

The two languages were used together, perfectly suitably, in the Town Hall of Amsterdam, where the Rubensian Baroque of Quellien's sculptural style matched that of Van Campen's decorative scheme, and where his Duquesnoy-esque classicism, which seems to have come to the fore at this point in his career, matched the studied classicism of Van Campen's architecture. The sculpture of the pediments has been justly described as 'following the antique closely in its details [and] extremely painterly and colourful in its general effect'.[1] Yet there is no duality. The Baroque of Rubens and his followers, though it is painterly and colourful to a marked degree, has an underlying architectural quality which is classical in its nature and is allied to that of antique art, and this suited it for use in a building whose architectural forms in themselves are classical. This quality, whose presence distinguishes Rubensian baroque art from that of Bernini and his followers (where the structure is of a different kind) is the ground bass which links the varied harmonies of the Town Hall's decoration together.

It is important to examine this basic element in the Baroque of Rubens and of the Amsterdam Town Hall, since in comparing Rubens' sculptural works with those of his predecessors it could not easily be seen, being overshadowed, in that view, by his innovations. Seen from another viewpoint it is evident. For this reason the present attempt to plot the position of the architecture and decoration of the Town Hall in the landscape of their surrounding history must be completed by taking bearings on the Baroque of Rubens, and on the style of Van Campen and Quellien, from another direction, confronting works by these artists in which both architecture and sculpture are involved with closely comparable works by their successors. Rubens' Jesuit Church altarpiece has already been considered, but it will be useful to compare it at this point

[1] "In den Einzelheiten stark antikisierend, in der Gesamtwirkung höchst malerisch und farbig." Georg Sobotka, *Die Bildhauerei der Barokzeit*, Vienna, 1927, p. 94.

with the setting of the high altar of S. Jacques' church, Antwerp, which dates from 1686 to 1698,[1] and since no later Dutch building is closely comparable with the Amsterdam Town Hall the case of the great organ in the New Church, Amsterdam, by Van Campen and Quellien, may be compared for this purpose with the eighteenth-century organ-case of St. Bavo's, Haarlem.

The altarpiece in S. Jacques' (illus. 175) was made by Artus Quellien the Younger,[2] a member of the generation of Flemish sculptors trained soon after Rubens' death in whose works the Baroque of Bernini, in a modified form, took hold in Antwerp. It is made entirely of marble and consists of an open-work screen of columns against which the church's patron, St. James the Less, is seen ascending to heaven. The columns, which support a heavy cornice, are for the most part twisted, and the movement of these twisted columns, upward and towards the centre, is one with the movement of his ascent, while swirling clouds and flying cherubs raise him. The cornice does not support an architectural structure but is surmounted by a glory lit from the clerestory of the Gothic choir in which the altar stands, and within this glory the Trinity waits to receive him.

In this altarpiece architecture and sculpture are fused and form a pictorial composition. The spectator's reason is set at a disadvantage and his emotions are appealed to directly as they are in Bernini's Cornaro Chapel,[3] whose altar setting in some respects is similar. The curves of the screen of columns and of the cornice are so subtle that it would be hard to draw a plan of them, and the figure of the saint is placed within a curved niche of columns, before whose sides other columns stand so that its depth cannot be determined. The proscenium formed by these columns separates the figure of the saint from the congregation and yet reveals him, and his position in actual space is not defined. It is the emotional impact of the composition and not its spatial arrangement which brings the saint, at the moment of his ascent to heaven, into the worshipper's presence.

Rubens' altar setting (illus. 147-50, 174), in contrast with this work, is an architectural composition, and it speaks to the reason as well as to the emotions.

[1] A closer comparison could be made with Rubens' setting for the high altar of Antwerp Cathedral, whose narrative element is similar to that of the St. Jacques altar and may have been a source of inspiration for it, but it seems better to compare it with a work which can still be seen.
[2] Artus Quellien the Younger (Arnoldus Quellien) was a relative of the Artus Quellien of the Amsterdam Town Hall and was his pupil; this was recorded by Erasmus Quellien, Theodor Levin, 'Handschriftliche Bemerkungen von Erasmus Quellinus', *Zeitschrift für Bildende Kunst*, 1888, p. 175. See further Marguerite Devigne, Thieme-Becker, s. v. Artus II Quellinus.
[3] In S. Maria della Vittoria, Rome; illus. Wittkower, *Bernini*, pl. 67.

The form and position of each part of the design and the way in which the parts are related are clear to the observer as they are in antique architecture and sculpture though here the terms are different: as with the St. Christopher the antique, by the addition of movement and immediate realism, has been transformed. Though the angels on the broken pediment defy the laws of gravity it is quite clear where they hover, and the whole of the structure behind the altar, set within the semicircular curve of the apse, is composed in a series of parallel planes whose transitions can be grasped easily; indeed they are summed up by an enormous pair of hanging garlands. The whole setting of the altar is built up logically and understandably, the relation of the spectator to it is clearly defined, and architecture, sculpture, and painting remain distinct though they are used together.

In Van Campen's organ-case in the New Church, Amsterdam, which was constructed while the Town Hall was in building,[1] there is a similar clarity of definition, and this is strikingly evident when, in imagination, a later organ such as that in Haarlem (illus. 177) is placed beside it. The Haarlem organ, which was built from 1735 to 1738,[2] has great depth. It is set against the west wall of the church but projects some distance from it, and it appears as a sculptural composition. Its surface heaves and billows and is broken by sharp angles, so that a painterly interplay of light and shadow is added. The architecture which supports the organ gradually gives way to the sculptural decoration of the player's tribune above it, and the projections of the organ-case are veiled so that they flow into one another and their forms cannot be analysed. The sculptured figures and leafy decoration of the organ-case seem to take part in its implied movement. They are represented, one might almost say sketched in, in a way which is perfectly satisfactory to the spectator as he stands in the church but without further definition, for the emphasis is on the pictorial effect of the whole scheme and not on any of its details.

The unity of Van Campen's organ (illus. 176, 178-9) is of a different kind. It results from the classical harmony of the architectural scheme and from the concerted action and symbolism of the sculptural decoration, which takes its

[1] A. J. M. Brouwer Ancher, 'Een paar aanteekeningen betreffende de Nieuwe Kerk te Amsterdam', *Amsterdamsch Jaarboekje*, 1897, pp. 18-19, shows that work was begun in 1650 or earlier and finished in 1655. There are contemporary records of Van Campen's authorship in Meyster, *Land-Spel*, I, pp. 55-56, and in the title of the anonymous satirical poem 'Eerplicht aan mijn Heer en Meester Jacob van Campen' [etc.] quoted by A. W. Weissman, 'Jacob van Campen in 1654', *Feestbundel Dr. Abraham Bredius* [etc.] (publ. Oud-Holland), Amsterdam, 1915, p. 285.

[2] See F. Allan, *Geschiedenis en beschryving van Haarlem*, III, Haarlem, 1883, pp. 328-73. The sculpture of the organ-case itself is by Jan van Logteren, that of the niche below it by J. B. Xavery.

place as part of the archtectural scheme and yet remains distinct from it. The case is faced by a plane surface ornamented by ranges of pipes, which is broken by the traditional projections that make it possible to accommodate a number of ranges. Here, however, the projections are semicircular or have angles which are not sharp enough to destroy the sense of the organ's surface, which echoes the surface of the end wall of the church at no great distance behind it.[1] The organ is surmounted by a triangular pediment, above whose corners carved figures stand, there are putti in the tympanum, and on the *rug-positief*[2] there are half-reclining figures. The whole structure rests on pillars bearing carved reliefs, and on pilasters, columns, and half-columns of a Corinthian order copied from Scamozzi like the architectural orders of the Town Hall.[3] The frieze and cornice above them and the central door leading to the uncompleted tower and the tribune were also taken from Scamozzi's treatise. Renaissance models and precepts, based on those of the ancient world, were in fact adapted in the organ's architecture to a purpose unknown in antiquity, but one in which the use of proportions based on musical harmonies would be singularly appropriate.

In the design of the organs' sculpture, nevertheless, Van Campen or Quellien,[4] or the two together, applied more recent principles, for though the sculptural motifs that have been mentioned might appear in antique or renaissance architectural designs these provide no precedent whatever for the behaviour of these figures. One of the musicians on the pediment is singing, and follows the rhythm of the music with her outstretched hand.[5] Another, on the *rug-positief*, echoes her song and gesture. Two swans perched on this part of the instrument join in the chorus, and a large sphere in the centre, carved with signs of the zodiac, may be presumed to add celestial music. The other figures on the pediment and the *rug-positief*, who hold instruments in their hands, pause

---

[1] The difference in depth between the two organ-cases in part is due to technical changes in the design of organs.

[2] The part of the organ behind the player's seat. The Dutch term is used since there is no equivalent in English.

[3] The engravings used are those in *L'idea della architettura universale* [etc.], Venice, 1615, Pt. II, pp. 135, 138, 152, 155, and 163.

[4] Quellien's responsibility for the sculptural decoration may be considered certain on stylistic grounds. Moreover he was paid the large sum of 1600 gulden by the city authorities for 'two flat pilasters for the organ' of a church which is not named. The account recording this, A. Quellien, MS. Papers, sheet 11, can be dated between 18 Sept. 1652 and 1 Aug. 1653. No other large organ was being made or repaired in Amsterdam at this moment (see Joachim Hess, *Dispositien der merkwaardigste kerk-orgelen* [etc.], Gouda, 1774, pp. 6-12) and there is every probability that the 'pilasters' were the piers bearing reliefs which support the New Church organ.

[5] This figure and the one forming a pendant to it are variants of the figures of Prudence and Justice in the corresponding positions on the eastern pediment of the Amsterdam Town Hall (cf. illus. 178, 180).

in their playing to listen attentively.[1] The song is accompanied by an angel choir, for on the upper part of the organ-case are cherubs, formally the supporters of its architectural projections, who sing for all they are worth. The central projection ends in a miniature organ in the pediment which is played by a small winged organist and is surrounded by a band of cherub musicians: a band which appears thoroughly disorganized, so realistically are these angel children portrayed. Children in the great reliefs below the tribune busy themselves with other instruments, while pipes and horns, kit fiddles and bells decorate the central doorway and in addition a swarm of cherubs plays below the *rug-positief*, which rests on the wings of angels. Some of these cherubs make a great noise with recorder and flute, tambourine and cymbals. In the paintings on the organ shutters the theme of music-making is reiterated.[2] Finally, and perhaps to the present-day spectator unexpectedly, a row of raucous parrots carved in high relief on the otherwise Corinthian frieze sums the matter up. Like the rest of the decoration they are portrayed with a particularized realism which thrusts their seeming presence on his notice, for they hold up heavy garlands and peck at them, as though irritated by their bands. The parrot symbolized eloquence.[3] The organ itself has a *vox humana*, which was justly famous. While this voice sounded the seventeenth-century audience, who usually promenaded, showed their respect by halting to listen attentively.[4] As has been noticed the adult players represented by Quellien on the organ-case do the same. Only the obstreperous cherubs, who perhaps know no better, presume to accompany the choir of voices.

What may be seen in little in the organ of the New Church may be seen on a grand scale in the Amsterdam Town Hall, where real musicians played from the windows.[5] There the sculptural decoration takes its place as part of Van

[1] At the summit of the pediment is King David, with harp and sceptre. The other figures do not appear to represent individuals. Those which sing take precedence, being to the right as seen from the organ.
[2] They are by Jan van Bronckhorst and depict, with great realism, scenes from the life of David. For a vivid description see Vondel, *Inwydinge*, lines 355-84.
[3] See Van Mander, *Wtleggingh*, fol. 131 v., and Ripa, *Iconologia*, 1624, p. 200 *(Eloquenza)*.
[4] An account is given by the brothers De Bovio, who heard an organ recital, apparently in the New Church, in Amsterdam in 1677: "In quest'organo vi è un registro, che toccato imita la voce umana, in maniera che pare agli orecchii di chi sente, che canti un bel concertato coro di diverse voci. Al suono di quest'aria tutti cessarono di passeggiare, et ognuno attentissimo stava rivolto all'organo"; Brom,'Reisbeschrijving', *Bijdragen*, 1915, p. 115.
[5] Concerts were given from eleven till twelve every morning by the city musicians; Vondel, op. cit., lines 511-15; Melchior Fokkens, *Beschrijving der wijdtvermaarde koop-stadt Amstelredam* [etc.], Amsterdam, 1662, p. 146; Filips von Zesen, *Beschreibung der Stadt Amsterdam* [etc.], Amsterdam, 1664, p. 259. Vondel mentions their playing music by Orlando [di Lasso], and Fokkens that there were six players.

Campen's classical architectural scheme as it does in the organ-case. It is comparable with the decoration of antique and renaissance architecture in its placing and in many of its details. Yet its represented figures, literal and symbolic, are made relevant to each other and to the spectator in the way which Rubens devised, which takes the structural logic of antiquity as its starting-point but goes so far beyond it as to create a new style. In this sense, quite literally, the achievements of antiquity were surpassed in the Amsterdam Town Hall. Van Campen and Quellien must have been well aware that the building, with its decoration, was not the equivalent of an antique one. Yet they may have felt that what had been begun with great magnificence in antiquity was brought to its logical conclusion in the modern world. Poussin, who took the greatest care to model his works on those of antiquity, developed a spatial organization within his paintings which was in essence classical though it was not known in the art of antique times.[1] That perhaps to some extent provides a parallel.

Van Campen designed the Town Hall's sculptural decoration in considerable detail, as his arrangements for the paintings in the Oranjezaal might lead one to suppose. The evidence on this point is formidable. Two drawings which show early versions of the reliefs in the pediments can be attributed to him,[2] and Vennekool's prints of the building, which illustrate Van Campen's intentions, show the decoration of the façades, the *vierschaar*, Burgerzaal, and galleries in detail and in almost every respect as it was carried out.[3] There are moreover likenesses to other works by Van Campen which seem to indicate his authorship, though here caution must be used, for there are also many resemblances which could be due to separate borrowings from the same source, notably from antique works and from the works of Rubens, which Quellien as well as Van Campen would have been likely to draw on. The likeness of the arrangement of the stage set of the theatre Van Campen designed for Amsterdam to the arrangement of the reliefs showing scenes of justice in the *vierschaar*, however, is so strong as to suggest common authorship.[4] In the

---

[1] For example see Anthony Blunt's analysis of Poussin's painting The Ashes of Phocion, 'Heroic and Ideal Landscape in the Work of Nicolas Poussin', *Journal of the Warburg and Courtauld Institutes*, VII, 1944, pp. 163-4.

[2] Fremantle, 'Some Drawings', *Oud-Holland*, 1953, pp. 73-90.

[3] See Bibliography s. v. Vennekool.

[4] In the arrangement of the central sections of the stage setting and of the inner wall of the *vierschaar*, both of which show a throne in the centre and outdoor scenes to either side, elements from the traditional settings for *tableaux vivants* and from mediaeval art are combined. See George R. Kernodle, *From Art to Theatre*, Chicago, 1944, p. 167.

relief showing Brutus and his sons there is a figure, admittedly echoing figures in antique sculpture,[1] which also appears in a painting by De Grebber in the Oranjezaal[2] and in Van Campen's painting of Christ in Judgement which was probably destined for the *vierschaar* of the Town Hall (cf. illus. 90, 93).[3] This figure might have been used independently by the two painters and by Quellien but it is unlikely, for it is used consistently in the three instances. In the Oranjezaal it represents Jupiter, who is carried on a car in Prince Frederik Hendrik's triumph, in Quellien's relief it appears as a statue of Jupiter, and in the Christ in Judgement there is an allusion to Jupiter's supreme power; for here as well the figure holds his thunderbolts and lightning. At the west end of the Burgerzaal another motif which seems to have been a favourite with Van Campen may be noticed: the dish carried by Fire, which is of the same form as one in a scene in the Oranjezaal which Van Campen himself painted,[4] and as another in one of the paintings by him which decorated a house on his property at Amersfoort and are now in the museum there.[5] Having thus shown that large parts of the Town Hall's sculptured decoration were indeed designed in detail by Van Campen himself it may be added that the likeness in design between different parts of the scheme suggests that Van Campen was the author even where there is no further proof of it. The scheme may nevertheless have been worked out to some extent in collaboration, for Van Campen and Quellien were well acquainted.[6] Moreover Quellien's fine technique and his understanding may have encouraged the burgomasters and Van Campen in the first instance to embark on such an elaborate and detailed project.

Quellien's main contribution, however, was made in his realization of Van Campen's designs in terms of sculpture, which he carried out with a brilliance and originality which match these qualities in Van Campen's scheme and also, one may suspect, make up for its defects. The artists working on the decoration of the Oranjezaal found Van Campen's sketches hard to follow,[7]

[1] For presiding figures of this type see Salomon Reinach, *Répertoire de la statuaire grecque et romaine*, Paris, 1906-8, II, pp. 13-20.
[2] See Slothouwer, *Paleizen*, illus. 111.
[3] See p. 82 n. 2 above.
[4] The attribution cannot be doubted. It is made by J. G. van Gelder, 'De schilders van de Oranjezaal', *Nederlandsch Kunsthistorisch Jaarboek*, 1948-9, pp. 134-40.
[5] See R. van Luttervelt, 'De schilderingen van Jacob van Campen uit het Hoogerhuis bij Amersfoort', *De Gids*, 1946, second quarter, pp. 153-9, and Van Gelder, op. cit., pp. 138-40.
[6] In 1654 the city authorities paid Quellien 300 gulden for living expenses incurred by Van Campen, which implies that he had lodged with him, in total for a considerable time; Kroon, *Stadhuis*, p. 51.
[7] Letter from Huygens to Princess Amalia of 3 Sept. 1649, Worp 4974. "Van Campen, qui pretend qu'on suive exactement ses ordonnances, les marque si obscurement, que ceux qui les doibvent executer, sont obligez d'en faire nouveaux modeles de leur main, pour veoir s'ils s'entendent." Here Worp is quoted.

and though they are small in scale the surviving drawings for the sculpture of the Town Hall pediments (illus. 185) suggest that Quellien was faced with the same difficulty. He may well have had to bridge gaps in the instructions that he received. Yet he did more than fill gaps: it might be true to say that, like Aaron, he acted as a mouthpiece for a prophet who was inarticulate. In Van Campen's decorative paintings – his Christ in Judgement, his Oranjezaal scenes, and his wall paintings at Amersfoort – the figures and other subjects as it were adhere to each other because of a lack of subtlety in the drawing and the tonal values (e.g. illus. 90-91). His figures are stocky, with limbs just a little too short for their bodies, and they have a certain awkwardness of movement and articulation as well as a curious and inexplicable charm. His males are ruddy and unbeautiful and the dark eyes of his females (one can hardly express it otherwise) are set in their bland faces like the currants in a bun. In following nature Van Campen's drawing was sensitive[1] but it seems that when he was working from imagination his delicacy of draughtsmanship and his power of differentiation to some extent deserted him. The reliefs in the *vierschaar* have characteristics in common with these independent works. The figures are grouped together in the foregrounds, the middle distance is suppressed, and the backgrounds are only lightly indicated. Yet here the proportions of the figures are finely calculated and each is fully characterized (e.g. illus. 92-93). The 'drawing' is detailed and delicate and the relative positions of the different parts of the composition are indicated by gradations from very full to very low relief as though by a formal shorthand. The relations between the figures are explained in the same way so that there is no feeling that they cling together. This clarification and refinement of the scenes, and the characterization which heightens their drama, must be due to Quellien.

The *vierschaar* reliefs were carried out, doubtless at Van Campen's instigation but by means of Quellien's skill, consistently and to the finest detail in classical terms as befitted scenes from antiquity. The style is based on that of antique sculpture and both in the figures and their setting there are references to antique and renaissance art. The executioners are reminiscent of figures in Roman reliefs representing sacrifices.[2] The figure of Brutus' son, bound and kneeling

[1] This may be concluded from his drawings of Constantijn Huygens the younger as a child (Teyler's Museum, Haarlem) and of Pieter Saenredam (British Museum, London), and also from his painted portrait of Leendert Nicasius (Town Hall, Amersfoort); see H. E. van Gelder, *Ikonografie van Constantijn Huygens en de zijnen*, The Hague, 1957, illus. 35, and P. T. A. Swillens, 'Jacob van Campen als schilder', *Elsevier's Maandschrift*, XLVIII, 1938, July-Dec., pp. 289-99, illus. 2 and 7.

[2] That on a sarcophagus in the Uffizi, Florence (used by Raphael in his Sacrifice at Lystra) may be borrowed, turned round so that it is seen from behind. Illus. Strong, *Scultura Romana*, II, p. 420.

to receive his punishment, perhaps contains some memory of the reliefs of the Sacrifice of Isaac made by Brunelleschi and Ghiberti[1] as well as of a painting by Rubens of the same subject[2] The head of the agonized Saleucos is based on that of the Laocoon and the faces of the onlookers are clearly inspired by Roman portraits. Yet the classical motifs are not copied exactly but are echoed very much as Rubens' motifs are echoed in Van Campen's decoration, and the distant world to which they belong is brought close to the beholder by the baroque means that have been described.[3] The Caryatid women of the *vierschaar*, unlike ancient caryatids, bend their shoulders under the weight of the architecture and the citizen who looks in from the Dam witnesses their humiliation.

The sculpture of the *vierschaar* in its entirety may be regarded as an anthology of classical decoration chosen to illustrate a complex theme and translated into terms current in the seventeenth century. The reliefs, seen separately and each as a whole, are reminiscent of the great reliefs on the Arch of Constantine and may have been inspired by them. Yet their composition is freer and the setting of each scene is more fully explained. Elsewhere in the *vierschaar* children climb among acanthus-leaves like the occupants of the 'peopled scrolls' of antiquity[4] though they are northern children, who weep miserably for the sentenced prisoner. The figures of Justice and Prudence in the niches between the windows look like statues although they are carved in low relief,[5] and painted statues of prophets, it will be remembered, were to have appeared above the upper cornice. These seeming statues were designed to give the impression of antique decoration, but the use of one means of representation to simulate another, itself bringing a symbolic figure as it were into the spectator's presence, was a refinement developed in modern times. The figures ornamenting the apparent architecture of Rubens' Triumphal Entry decorations, painted as statues representing living beings who witnessed and responded to the various scenes, are very closely comparable; Justice and Prudence actively make use of their attributes, they do not merely hold them, and the prophets

[1] Those made in 1401-2 in competition for the commission for the doors of the Baptistery in Florence, now in the Museo Nazionale there.
[2] In the Garbáty collection, Scarsdale, U.S.A.. The painting was engraved in 1614 and the figure in the *vierschaar* relief faces in the same direction as that in the engraving; see J. G. van Gelder, 'Rubens in Holland in de zeventiende eeuw', *Nederlandsch Kunsthistorisch Jaarboek*, 1950-1, p. 102.
[3] See the description of the *vierschaar*, pp. 78-86 above.
[4] For these see J. M. C. Toynbee and J. B. Ward Perkins, 'Peopled Scrolls: a Hellenistic Motif in Imperial Art', *Papers of the British School at Rome*, XVIII (New Series Vol. V.), 1950, pp. 1-43.
[5] The classical drapery of these two figures is reminiscent of that of Duquesnoy's statue of St. Susanna, which Quellien may have had in mind.

were designed to appear as though watching the events taking place below, turning to their companions as though making some comment, or looking appealingly towards the symbol representing God at the centre of the vault above.

The anthology in translation is continued in the decoration of the rest of the great building. In the galleries the planets, like Justice and Prudence, are represented as statues though they are carved in low relief: Quellien referred to the panels below them as 'pedestals' perhaps for this reason.[1] Had they been carved in the round these statues would have been able to stand, for their attributes are arranged as if to support them. Mercury indeed is provided with the treetrunk which prevents the legs of many marble figures from breaking though he has no need of it. Here too there are echoes of classical works which, appropriately, are statues.[2] The carvings above the doors in the northern and southern galleries not only take the form of, but also look like reliefs, and in one of them there is a representation apparently drawn from a recent source though it illustrates an ancient fable.[3] Such a major interpolation from a modern source appears to be unusual. Yet the design of the semicircular doortops beside the planets may have been based on a work by Rubens[4] and the figures above the doors of the Burgerzaal are not grouped in an antique way, nor do there seem to be classical prototypes for the way in which the attributes of the personified elements on the Burgerzaal arches are strung up above them.[5] The Elements themselves are ultimately derived from figures on the spandrels of Roman triumphal arches though their symbolism was taken from Ripa, and here the Arch of Trajan at Benvenuto, with its representations of the seasons in the spandrels of the smaller arches – figures which turn towards the spectator – was perhaps the main prototype. In the Town Hall the figures do not remain behind the surface of the arches they decorate, however, as they would in a Roman work, but project far beyond them, and they not

[1]   A. Quellien, MS. Papers, nos. 12 and 13. Correctly the term was applied to the free-standing or projecting block on which a statue or architectural member rested (Cornelis Danckertsz., *Grontregulen der bow-const, ofte de uytnementheyt van de vyf orders der Architectura van Vincent Scamozzi*, Amsterdam, 1658, pl. 1).

[2]   The gesture of Apollo, who holds his hand behind his head, and Mercury standing nonchalantly with his legs crossed, as he does in the Town Hall, may be seen in a number of classical statues; see Reinach, op. cit., pp. 241-3 and 363-5. The figure of Saturn eating his child is clearly reminiscent of antique statues of Satyrs with children. (Mars incongruously wears trousers, the costume of barbarians in Roman times, with his military clothing.)

[3]   See p. 73 n. 1 above.

[4]   See p. 141 n. 9 [5] above. The arrangement of the lions resembles that in Rubens' work and the other door-tops are arranged similarly.

[5]   The compositions most closely resembling them are perhaps those shown by Agostino Mitelli in some of the plates in his *Freggi dell'architettura*, Bologna, 1645.

only seem to face the spectator but in some cases they also seem to move towards him.

Details from the decoration of the other rooms need not be examined, for it was of a similar kind, and further description would be repetitive. Yet in order to show how the manner of composition and style that Van Campen and Quellien evolved in their sculpture were applied even in the smallest detail it will perhaps be useful to consider the mantelpiece friezes in the burgomasters' chamber and the magistrates' court. There the nature of the sculpture is summed up very neatly and its range can be seen.

The frieze in the burgomasters' chamber, as was stated earlier, represents the triumph of a Roman burgomaster (illus. 69-72). The figures it portrays wear classical garb and there are countless quotations from antique works.[1] Yet the translation into modern terms is a free one. The victory parade is of a surprising kind and contains some unwonted elements: it includes for example, a number of dogs representing faithfulness, an urchin who has donned a helmet and sword too big for him, and animals associated with Roman sacrifice. On the front of the mantelpiece one sees the main part of the procession, preceded by trumpeters one of whom turns to blow his instrument towards the hero (a trumpeter on the Arch of Titus does the same) and followed by a man on horseback, his drapery blowing. The gradations of the relief are very fine and in the background flags and trophies are indicated so that there seems to be a crowd behind the foremost figures. These figures are carved in relief as high as the small scale of the work allows and show a very great variety of postures – one suspects that in some cases motifs from antique reliefs are seen from new points of view.[2] Two soldiers in the procession ride energetically towards the spectator, a man raises his arm to give a prisoner a blow,[3] and two further figures struggle to lift jars containing booty. A woman with a basket on her head, familiar in the art of the Renaissance, steps lightly across the path of the horses which draw the triumphal chariot. The effect given by the broken groups of figures, which are seen in a raking light, is painterly and the carving creates depth with a suddenness unknown in antique sculpture. Quintus Fabius Maximus rides, like the emperor Titus in the relief on his Arch in Rome,

---

[1] Here, as with the sculpture already described, it is usually impossible to point to single prototypes, but the allusions to groups of works in antique and sometimes in renaissance art are clear.

[2] E. g. the child carrying a box of incense. Such a figure appears, seen from the front, in a relief on the Arch of Constantine, and here is seen from the side. It appears front view on the western tympanum, see p. 178 and p. 181 n. 2 below.

[3] The prisoner has the clothing worn by Dacian Prisoners in Roman reliefs.

in a tublike chariot hung with garlands and drawn by four neatly pacing horses. Yet these horses are not spread out, like the horses of Titus, by a convention which allows them all to be seen, but appear in sharp perspective. The procession as a whole is portrayed with realism of the same kind, for at its head, at the left-hand end of the mantelpiece, the spectator seems to stand in the excited crowd by the city gates and to watch it approaching, accompanied by a group of women and the symbolic river god and Roman wolf with her children. At the other end of the mantelpiece the last horses of the procession are seen from behind, receding. In referring to this frieze the writer of the eighteenth-century guide-book to the Town Hall commented on the naturalness of the figures and their clever arrangement,[1] and in these features the works of antiquity were certainly outdone.

The frieze in the magistrates' court, according to the same author, represents 'the Israelites who in Moses' absence set up the golden calf and hold a Bacchic feast round it' (illus. 80-83).[2] Here events from Bible history are portrayed in what might be regarded as Roman terms. The golden calf appears in the centre on a pedestal which is hung with garlands like a Roman altar. On a tripod beside it Aaron, in the clothes worn for Roman sacrifices, is burning incense on a tripod and beasts for a sacrifice are being led up. A family of Israelites, who wear Roman dress only slightly modified,[3] kneel before the image and worship it, the youngest child instructed by his father. A group behind the image makes music and to the right dancers, their antique drapery flowing behind them, drunkenly perform a figure with linked hands.[4] Near to them a feast is in progress at which even the children and a small dog have wine in plenty and another dog gnaws in a homely manner at a bone. The girl with the basket on her head brings a load of fruit to the table, here turned round so that she is facing us.[5] To the left soldiers are gaming with cards and dice in the state

[1] *Beschryving van 't Stadhuis*, 1782, pp. 53-54.
[2] Ibid., p. 77. "Het Israëlitische volk, welke in afzyn van Moses, het gulden kalf oprechte; en daar rondtom een Bachusfeest vieren."
[3] Here one of the women wears a tight bodice over her Roman clothes. The contesting mothers in the relief of Solomon's Judgement in the *vierschaar* wear similar garments, which presumably indicate that the scene is not one from Greek or Roman antiquity. The dress of some other figures in the mantelpiece relief, notably of those in the scene on its left-hand end, is based on clothes worn in the Low Countries in the sixteenth and seventeenth centuries.
[4] The figure, in which dancers with linked hands go under the arms of others, appears frequently in renaissance and 17th-century art. Poussin, in his painting of the Worship of the Golden Calf in the National Gallery, London, uses the theme in the context in which it is used here.
[5] In this instance the designer's ability to free motifs from the viewpoint from which they are traditionally shown, thinking of them 'in the round' and turning them, is demonstrated.

162

of unpreparedness described in the Bible,[1] a woman stops her spinning to make love, and a drunkard lies sleeping with his mouth open, his cup still in his hand, in the posture of an antique Endymion. Beyond him there is a herdsman, also asleep, with his neglected flock, and a small figure in the furthest distance can be distinguished as Moses on Sinai, receiving the Law from God, unaware of what is going on. In the scenes of lawlessness that take place in the foreground there is very little that the spectator is spared; at one end of the mantelpiece frieze theft and murder are being committed in spite of the loud protests of the ever-faithful dog, and at the other, which appropriately is in a dark corner, one witnesses the most disgusting effects of drunkenness. Here the tents of the Israelites are indicated in the background though, for some unknown reason, the background of other parts of the relief are incompletely carved. Yet whatever the setting these Biblical figures in (for the most part) Roman costumes provide in symbolism the prototype for the crudest Dutch genre scenes, and in form must be derived from them. The meaning of the relief, emphasizing that of the painting above it, was conveyed to the magistrates who sat opposite it with the recommendation of classical ancestry but also with the force of familiar terms. Here, to suit the occasion, the antique phrases were translated more freely than anywhere else in the Town Hall.

Terracotta models for much of the Town Hall's sculpture survive, together with a number of reduced copies, for which there must have been a fashion in Amsterdam.[2] In many cases the models can be recognized by their free style, which is combined with a great cogency of drawing both of form and texture. Some parts of the terracotta version of the design of the front tympanum, moreover, which was baked in a number of separate pieces, have a grid of lines marked on them which was added before they were baked, for the transference of the design to a later model or to the blocks of marble (see illus. 20).[3] Lines are also indicated on the model for the lower part of the relief showing the story of Brutus, but here the indications were touched in before

[1] Exodus, xxxii, 25.
[2] The greatest number of these pieces, many of which are evidently preparatory models, are in the Waag Museum and Rijksmuseum, Amsterdam, and belong to the city. There are others in the Lakenhal Museum, Leiden, the Print Room of the British Museum, London (in the top of a Dutch bookcase), and the Van Herck collection, Antwerp; Professor J. G. van Gelder kindly drew the writer's attention to the two last mentioned. As yet there is no detailed study of these works and of the many references in early inventories to works of the same kind. These references (and the appearance of another such work in a painting by T. Regters of 1754, see E. Pelinck 'Een Amsterdams familiestuk Jeronimo de Bosch en zijn kinderen', *Jaarboek Genootschap Amstelodamum*, XLVI, 1954, pp. 105-9) demonstrate their popularity.
[3] This work is in the Waag Museum, Amsterdam. The markings are evident on the sections showing sea horses, a winged Triton, a crocodile, and a swan, towards the right-hand end as one faces it.

the baking very lightly indeed, presumably so that members of the city government or others to whom the model was shown should not notice them.[1]
For the Atlas surmounting the back pediment two models survive which show
very slight variations, and two models for this figure, the second made 'for
greater improvement', are mentioned in Quellien's papers.[2] Quellien mentions
many other models, the majority of which correspond to surviving terracotta
pieces in the city's possession.[3]

Most of the pieces which can be identified with certainty as models are
clearly by a single hand, which must be that of Quellien, His thoughts
are directly recorded in them in visible form so they are specially revealing.
They are strongly reminiscent of Rubens' painted sketches in their organization
and in the brilliance and precision with which even details are represented and
with which textures are indicated. The sense of light and colour in them,
which is inimitable, also resembles that in Rubens' sketches. In the model for
the back tympanum,[4] for example, the border and fringe of Africa's drapery
are shown summarily but clearly and even the decoration on the bangle that
she wears is indicated, the water which pours from the jars of the river-gods
seems to glide and the fish to glitter in it, and the warm roughness of the
fishing-net which the river IJ wears is conveyed so vividly that one seems able
to feel it (illus. 192, 195). Such details, it must be added, were carried over into
the marble sculpture of the Town Hall, though they are not portrayed there
with the speed and the precise impressionism of the clay models. Close inspec-
tion reveals that even in the vast carvings on the pediments the details of the
models were followed with great delicacy though it must have been clear that
except on very rare occasions they would not be visible.[5]

If the models show Quellien's indebtedness to Rubens with particular

[1] In the Rijksmuseum, Amsterdam. These markings imply lines as follows: horizontal (1) touched in
behind ear of dog, on background to left of corner of cloak held by child, on executioner's left leg
below knee and on his right leg at knee level, (2) on drapery over Brutus' arm at elbow level, on inside
of cloak below other arm, below shoulder of boy next him, on sleeve and arm above elbow of soldier,
across stomach of Brutus' third son and on executioner's body at top of hip, (3) marked on background
and across knees of statue of Jupiter at level of top of third son's head: vertical (1) touched in between
shoulder-blades of body of first son, on Brutus' knee, and on inside of his cloak close to his body, (2) on
second son's thigh, on soldier behind him, on right arm and breast of third son and (3) on executioner's
left leg, on breast of child bearing cloak, and at top of executioner's right shoulder.

[2] MS. Papers, no. 5. Both are in the Rijksmuseum, Amsterdam.

[3] Most of these pieces came from the *Rariteitenkamer* of the Town Hall via the Academy founded by Louis
Napoleon in the building (then Palace), later moved to the Oudemannenhuis, Amsterdam, and thence to the
Stadhouderskade. Thanks are due to Mr. J. Leeuwenberg for this information.

[4] In the Rijksmuseum, Amsterdam, *Cat. beeldhouwwerken*, no. 177, 3.

[5] The writer is greatly indebted to Jhr. Ir. P. F. O. R. Sickinghe for the opportunity of seeing the pediments
from scaffolding erected for repairs in 1957.

vividness (and the likeness is too strong to be due to chance) they also illustrate his indebtedness to François Duquesnoy. The form of decoration chosen for the lunettes over the doors beside the planets in the eastern and western galleries may have been derived from one of Rubens' inventions, but the pairs of putti which form part of the designs and which appear in each case to either side of a central roundel remind one of the pairs of child angels on Duquesnoy's tombs in Rome[1] in their style and in their most natural behaviour. In the Town Hall this theme is deliciously applied. The children beside Diana play with the fish which are among her hunting trophies, trying to hold these slippery monsters and to swarm up a cornucopia by their aid, while those who accompany the ferocious wolves of Mars weep fearfully (illus. 43-45, 53, 166). The arrangement in all probability was Van Campen's[2] but Quellien must have been responsible for the likeness of style, which is clearly evident in both the final sculpture and the models (cf. illus. 43, 166, 167).[3] It may be seen in particular in their delicate representations of the small bodies, in the types portrayed, and even in the expressions on some of the children's faces.[4] At the same time these models, like those already described, have the warmth and colour of Rubens' sketches and their 'drawing' is much more forceful than that of Duquesnoy in many of the details.

A further reference to Duquesnoy must be mentioned: that in the great bronze figure of Justice on one of the corners of the front pediment, which is clearly based on his statue of St. Susanna (illus. 168, 169). The likeness here is most evident in the terracotta model,[5] and, although the miniature Justice on the model for the Town Hall's architecture is comparable in its general design, there are here more specific borrowings which must have been due to Quellien. The Justice has the same lissomeness as the St. Susanna, and the drapery is of the same kind as hers though it is rather more elaborate. The head has the same clear oval form and similar classical features, gently portrayed. Yet the

---

[1] The tombs of Adrian Vryburch and Ferdinand van den Eynde in S. Maria dell' Anima, Rome (illus. Fransolet, *Duquesnoy*, pls. XXVI and XXVII).
[2] Models for the lunettes beside Apollo and Diana are mentioned in the earliest of Quellien's surviving accounts, A. Quellien, MS. Papers, no. 5, which was paid at various dates in 1651, thus long before Van Campen's withdrawal.
[3] There are models for lunettes in the Waag Museum and Rijksmuseum, Amsterdam.
[4] Compare for example the left-hand child in the lunette to the right of Diana, and that in the model for this lunette in the Rijksmuseum, Amsterdam, with the left-hand child in Duquesnoy's monument to Van den Eynde (see illustrations). The type, the tilt of the head, and the expression are almost the same.
[5] In the Rijksmuseum, Amsterdam. The companion model, for the Prudence, which is also there, is more massive and does not appear to be derived so directly from Duquesnoy. The nose in this model is a replacement; the features of the model for the Justice are well preserved.

likeness, though it is strong, is not an exact one, for once again a translation into Rubensian terms has been made. Duquesnoy's saint stands upright, gracefully poised, while Justice has rounded shoulders which, in the most natural manner, suit the figure to the position, high above the spectator, in which the bronze version stands, by bringing the head slightly forward. The proportions of the classical figure on the pediment are thus seen from the Dam undisturbed by the effects of perspective.[1]

It is likely that Quellien made his models direct from Van Campen's drawings and probably, till his withdrawal, Van Campen approved them before the works themselves were carried out. The only direct evidence on this point is Quellien's mention, in an account paid in 1654, of three models for festoons 'of which two were made to the satisfaction of Mons. van Campen';[2] these festoons, like other sculpture for the outside of the building, were to be carved in the city stonemason's yard.[3] Indirect evidence is added by the contract, dated 1636, for the sculpture of the front pediment of Honselaarsdijk Palace, which was apparently designed by Van Campen. This document clearly lays down the procedure that was to be followed on a comparable occasion:

> Mr. Jan Vos, living at Haarlem, has undertaken to deliver to Honselaarsdijk . . and to set up in the great pediment there, twelve children carved in half relief in suitable Bentheim stone, according to the drawing of this [work] to be delivered to him at the. . . Heer van Campen's, to whose approval he the contracting party shall first be obliged to model each one of the said children in clay, and further to put the work together to the approbation of the same.[4]

About the organization of Quellien's studio there is no evidence at all except that which is provided by the styles of the sculpture. It is tempting to suppose that his methods were like those of Rubens; that he made the models himself, for his patrons' approval and for use in laying out the final work, that the

[1] The other figures on the pediments are similarly adjusted, though both Prudence and Peace appear with their heads thrown back. Adjustments of proportion to suit the viewpoint, though not such modifications of posture, were made in antique times.
[2] A. Quellien, MS. Papers, no. 13. " . . . waer van 2 g[e]mackt waren tot contentement van de Mons. van Kampen."
[3] Models made for the yard are mentioned in four entries in Quellien's MS. Papers nos. 12 and 13. Those mentioned in two of them are clearly for festoons on the outside of the building, and probably also that mentioned in a third. In the fourth entry the pieces are not specified.
[4] Archieven van de Nassausche Domeinen, no. 7146, Algemeene Rijksarchief, The Hague. The Dutch text, first published by Slothouwer, reads: " . . . heeft Mr. Jan Vos woonachtich tot Haerlem aengenomen . . . tot Honsholredijck te leveren ende in de groote frontispice aldaer to voegen twaelff kindertjens halff rond gehouwen in bequamen Bentemer steen volgens de teeckeninge hem daer van te leveren, bij den . . . Hr. van Campen, tot genoegen van den welcken hij aennemer yder een derselver kindertjens alvoorens van aerde sal hebben te boetseren, ende vorders ter approbatie van den selven op te maecken". The contract is dated 11 Jan. 1636.

enlarging was done by pupils under his supervision, and that he 'retouched' the most important parts with his own hand. Yet this explanation, though it would account for the consistent carving of much of the sculpture, would not explain the differences that are evident even between important pieces.[1] On many occasions assistants and pupils must have been entirely responsible for carrying out parts of the work, as Rombout Verhulst's signature on three of the principal reliefs indicates.[2] Evidently a number of assistants worked on the marble carvings,[3] and without their help Quellien could not have completed the vast scheme of decoration in the fourteen years or so that he spent in Holland.[4]

Quellien's training of assistants, but still more perhaps the example of his works in Amsterdam, made a very large contribution to the development of Dutch sculpture, for just as the master builders trained in native traditions were not able to help create the new classical style of architecture of the 1630s, so the master masons and figure carvers of the United Provinces[5] were not versed in sculpture suitable for its decoration. They could do little more than follow the drawings that the designers provided, carrying them out in the terms that they already knew, while, as has been seen, Quellien could make a contribution of his own. The garlands on the Mauritshuis façades were evidently designed to appear as though the wind had set them swinging, and as though they were, in reality, hanging against the walls,[6] but they seem flattened out against them (illus. 118-19). Those on Van Campen's organ-case at Alkmaar, which was made before Quellien's advent, are composed of fruits and leaves

---

[1] It is clear for example that not all of the series of the planets and Cybele are by the same hand, nor are the imposts of the arches in the galleries. Concerning the authorship of three of the planets see the following note, and p. 48 and note, above.

[2] He signed the Venus and the reliefs representing Silence and Faithfulness above the doors of the Secretary's office.

[3] Quellien's assistants and pupils are discussed by Gabriels, *Quellien*, pp. 49-62. The younger Artus Quellien, Bartholomeus Eggers (probably from Amsterdam), Rombout Verhulst (from Malines) and perhaps also Ludovicus Willemsens and Frans de Jaggere worked there. Of these Verhulst and Eggers continued to work in the United Provinces after Quellien left, becoming leading sculptors.

[4] Though the earliest surviving accounts were paid only in 1651 Quellien's MS. Papers suggest that his work in Amsterdam had begun in 1650; see List of Sources s. v. A. Quellien. He applied for permission to return to Antwerp in 1664; MS. *Requestboek*, Stadsarchief, Antwerp, fol. 82 v., 8 Sept. 1664.

[5] S. de Bray, *Architectura*, p. 6, describes Hendrik de Keyser as being 'as skilful a sculptor as architect', but though the term sculptor *(beeldhouwer)* was in use it denoted a skill rather than a separate profession. It seems that those practising sculpture in the United Provinces in the first half of the seventeenth century were either master masons or figure carvers *(beeldsnijders,* i.e. those who carved figures and other ornamentation in wood, usually on furniture). Professional sculptors in the modern sense seem to have appeared (or reappeared, after the Reformation) only after the middle of the seventeenth century in the Northern Netherlands, and for this too Quellien must have provided an example and an incentive.

[6] These are compatible with Van Campen's style though there is no direct evidence that he designed them.

which seem pressed together as they may have done in Van Campen's drawings, and are not individualized (illus. 135, 138).[1] These ornaments have not the clarity of classical garlands, though it is clear from their context that they were intended to appear as such.[2] Nor have they the freshness of form and delicacy of execution which may be found in antique sculpture and in that of Quellien; his garlands in the Amsterdam Town Hall, but for the greater depth of their relief, their less crisp cutting, and the larger units of which they are built up, are closely comparable in style with, for example, those of the Ara Pacis (cf. illus. 136-7, 139). Again, in the tympana of the pediments at the back of the Maurits-huis and of the Palace of Noordeinde[3] the figures are, as it were, pressed together as they are in the earliest designs for the pediment sculptures of the Town Hall (cf. illus. 118, 185-7). Quellien, thanks to Duquesnoy's assistance when he was in Rome and his study of the antique there, was able to add a classical clarity in the individual forms to the staccato effect of a classical relief seen in light and shadow which is present in the earlier tympana. It was above all this clarity of form in representational designs that suited his decoration to the classical planning and orders of Van Campen's architecture.

If a sculptor with a personal knowledge of antique art, and one who in his own right was a highly skilful artist, had to be sought for from the start for the worthy decoration of Van Campen's work, by the time the Town Hall was built there was a second requirement, an understanding of the Rubensian form of decoration which by then was in demand in the United Provinces. This too, so far as the making of sculpture was concerned, Quellien imported and estab-lished, though there was no further opportunity for it to be used there so grandly. The combination of baroque and classical elements in the sculptural decoration of the new architecture and to the glory of Amsterdam, nevertheless, was achieved by Quellien and Van Campen together.

[1] For particulars about this work, which is documented as Van Campen's, see J. W. Enschedé, 'Gerardus Havingha en het orgel in de Sint Laurenskerk te Alkmaar', *Tijdschrift der Vereeniging voor Noord-Nederlands Muziekgeschiedenis*, VIII, 1908, pp. 181-261. The specification for the organ is of 1638 and it was finished in 1645.

[2] In the architecture supporting the organ, where the garlands appear, Vincent Scamozzi's Corinthian and Ionic orders are copied; cf. his *L'idea della architettura universale*, plates illustrating these orders in Pt. II, Bk. VI. It is likely that Palladio was referred to, both for the decoration of the bases of the Corinthian columns and pilasters and, as in the Town Hall, for the ribs at the corners of the pilasters; cf. his *Quattro libri*, Bk. I, p. 43, and Bk. IV, p. 80.

[3] A comparison of the sculpture in these two pediments with the early designs for those of the Town Hall very strongly suggests that both were designed by Van Campen.

CHAPTER VII

ARGO SAILS HOME

On the reverse of the medal that was struck to commemorate the inauguration of the new Town Hall of Amsterdam (illus. 1b) the ship Argo, bearing the golden fleece, is shown sailing quietly into the city's harbour. The scene is represented with the careful realism that characterizes the many 'profile' views of Amsterdam that were made in the seventeenth century, as though it were the most natural thing in the world that she should arrive there. The evident ordinariness of the event is symbolic, for it shows, as the Town Hall itself does both in its symbolism and in its architecture and sculpture, to what a great extent elements taken from a distant, antique world had come to form part of the modern and familiar world of seventeenth-century Amsterdam. The antique world, an imagined one although the image was built up painstakingly and with the help of scholarship, provided a pattern for the modern one and in some respects seemed to have been reborn in it. Hooft's histories had already been published,[1] and an engraving showing his portrait in the form of a Roman bust and inscribed with the words ALTER TACITUS had been made.[2] Vondel's plays, based in their structure on antique models, were being performed in a classical theatre belonging to the city. Rembrandt had not yet carried the union of the imagined antique world with that of reality to a point which, as it seems, gave offence to his contemporaries, by painting the one-eyed Claudius Civilis as he must have been, surrounded by barbarian Batavian tribesmen.[3] A close union between the two worlds had been established and as yet remained undisturbed. Round the representation on the medal is written a quotation from the *Argonautica* of Valerius Flaccus: PELAGUS QUANTOS APERIMUS IN USUS; 'To what great profit are we opening the sea'.[4] The knowledge of antiquity illuminated the history of Amsterdam. Trade, one of the most conspicuous features of her history, and philosophy, were united.[5]

Argo sails home into harbour of Amsterdam, an antique ship with the rigging

---

[1] First editon 1642.

[2] F. W. H. Hollstein, *Dutch and Flemish Etchings, Engravings and Woodcuts ca. 1450-1700*, Amsterdam, 1949, XI, Janus Lutma the Younger, no. 7. Presumably made before or soon after Hooft's death.

[3] See p. 186 n. 3 below.

[4] *Argonautica*, I, line 169.

[5] The union of Mercury and Minerva had been discoursed on by Barlaeus in 1632, see p. 46 n. 4 above. Vondel also alludes to it; *Werken*, III, p. 805.

of a seventeenth-century trading vessel, bearing treasures from the antique world and from far-off lands, to be seen through the eyes of Dutch citizens, to be adapted to their needs, and to be used according to their customs and in their hands. The image was perfectly suited to the inauguration of the new building, in which, as has been seen, treasures from ancient times and from many countries, the symbols and the forms of which it was composed, were combined with each other and with traditional elements and were put to a new use, that of expressing in visual terms the glory of the city's history and in doing so of confirming and shaping it; although in the Town Hall many symbolic figures appear Fortune, who is famous for her fickleness, is notably absent, so confidently could this visible statement be made. A similar combination of elements may be found in Dutch literature of the seventeenth century, and there are parallels in both the literature and visual arts of other countries. It is surely significant that Huygens, who evidently to a large extent inspired the scholarly emulation of antiquity in Dutch architecture, had many learned friends abroad and that he and Hooft, in whose work the literature of antiquity was emulated in a similar way, belonged to the same humanist circle. It is clearly also significant that Anslo, in describing the present glory of Amsterdam in his poem on the foundation of the new Town Hall, mentioned the theologian and classical scholar Vossius, who 'declares antiquity ageless' and lamented the deaths of Hooft and of Barlaeus, 'who set Minerva to the service of trade'.[1] These scholars must have had a large share in the creation of the intellectual setting in which the Town Hall was conceived and brought into being.

The way in which treasures borrowed from antiquity were combined with other elements, both foreign and traditional, in the building's imagery has yet to be considered. So far their combination has only been seen in its architectural and sculptural forms, and in these, though they are certainly symbolic of the city's history, pictorial symbolism in not involved. Not only material forms but also images from different sources are combined in the Town Hall's decoration whether it is carried out in sculpture or in painting, and to complete this survey the constitution of its decoration, form and symbolism together, must be examined. In making this examination it will be convenient to consider

[1] Anslo, 'Het gekroonde Amsterdam', in *Olyf-Krans*, 1750, pp. 178-9. Hooft died on 24 May 1647. Since the Town Hall's design was accepted in its final form on 18 July 1648 and the plans of that year do not show fields for reliefs in the *vierschaar* and galleries, neither Hooft nor Barlaeus can have been concerned with detailed plans for the decoration; Vossius, who was Professor of History in Amsterdam's Athenaeum Illustre may have been consulted.

one part of the decoration in some detail, and the relief in the tympanum of the western pediment has been chosen for discussion since the development of its design is well recorded, and since a fair number of its elements can be recognized. The significance of the relief as a whole and its place in the symbolic scheme of the building have already been indicated,[1] and it may be added that since Hubert Quellien's engraving of it bears the inscription "Artus Quellinus invenit et in marmore sculpsit"[2] it is possible that the sculptor was responsible for the final version of the design, as he may have been after Van Campen's withdrawal for that of other parts of the decoration.

Two Italian travellers who recorded their impression of the Town Hall not long after it was completed, after commenting on the "torre di disegno bizzaro" that surmounts the façade on the Dam, went on to describe the relief in the pediment below it in the following words: "L'armi della città si vedono al di setto [sotto] in basso rilievo di marmo con figure e trofei".[3] The description is remarkable, for the coat of arms that is held by the figure of Amsterdam in the centre of the relief is by no means a prominent feature of the design, and although it provides a key to its symbolic content by explaining the identity of the central figure it might easily escape notice. Nevertheless it evidently featured so largely in the explanation that was given to the two travellers[4] that while they may have failed to remember, and certainly failed to record, what scene was represented, the coat of arms was not forgotten.

It has already been seen that the city's old and new coat of arms appear as counterparts within the building,[5] and they were placed in important positions there, as though they were to emphasize that both the city's history and its position in present times were relevant to the main functions of the city government. The two coats of arms were also planned to appear as counterparts on the outside of the building, for not only is the shield bearing three crosses represented on the pediment which overlooks the Dam, but the ship of the early coat of arms appears in a central position in the western tympanum, if only in the background, and in drawings by Van Campen which show his design

[1]   On p. 55 above.
[2]   H. Quellien, *Statuen*, II, pl. 2. See also Bibliography s. v. H. Quellien.
[3]   Diary of the brothers De Bovio, in Brom, 'Reisbeschrijving', *Bijdragen*, 1915, p. 107.
[4]   They were shown the building by Giovanni da Verazzano, an Italian merchant resident in Amsterdam; identified in the diary of Prince Cosimo III de' Medici's visit to Holland; Hoogewerff, *De twee reizen*, p. 36.
[5]   See pp. 70, 78, and 80 above.

for the pediments in an early stage of development[1] both the new coat of arms and the ship are given prominence and indeed are emphasized (illus. 185). In many of the renaissance palaces of Italy the owner's coat of arms is placed proudly above the entrance, and in Palladio's design for villas where there is a pediment there is also, in almost every instance, a shield placed against the tympanum to bear a coat of arms.[2] The shield and the ship of the city of Amsterdam were therefore placed in a position which accorded with the traditions of the renaissance on the façades of the new Town Hall. They did not, however, provide the main feature of the decoration, flanked by figures whose only duty was to support them or hung up with fluttering ribbons like the coats of arms of Italy, but each was made to form part of an elaborate scene whose symbolism, though its general import might be understood at a glance, had a complex meaning.

In Van Campen's drawing of the west tympanum Amsterdam sits enthroned in its centre, a cornucopia in her lap and the ship of the city's early coat of arms held high in her right hand. In the drawing for the eastern tympanum, and in the relief of that tympanum in the building itself, she wears the imperial crown which by grant of the Emperor Maximilian should surmount the shield that she holds in her hand, but in the drawing for the western tympanum she wears Mercury's winged hat, as befits the supporter of a trading vessel, and instruments of navigation are piled up at her feet. These features remain the same in the relief modelled in clay which adorns the western tympanum of the model of the building (illus. 187), a relief which appears to have been based very closely on Van Campen's drawing and may well be by his hand.[3]

In the design shown in the prints of 1650 (illus. 191) certain changes have been made. The cog, represented on a much larger scale, is placed in a central position, supported by kneeling figures on whose shoulders it is raised. Small figures, its traditional occupants,[4] appear inside it, while the much larger

---

[1] For the identification of these drawings, which are in the Rijksprentenkabinet, Amsterdam, see Fremantle, 'Some drawings', *Oud-Holland*, 1953, pp. 73-95.

[2] See his *Quattro libri*, Bk. II.

[3] Statement based on a close comparison of the reliefs on the pediments of the model in the Waag Museum, Amsterdam, with drawings and paintings by Van Campen, which show a similar stockiness and what may perhaps best be described as 'blobbiness', in the handling of the form. The interpretation of the drawn design in the model shows an understanding of the thought of Van Campen, as expressed in the drawing, so precise that it would be surprising in a relief made by another artist from the design.

[4] They appear from the fourteenth century on the city's seal (illus. W. H. F. Oldewelt, 'De stadszegels van Amsterdam', *Jaarboek Amstelodamum*, XXXIII, pp. 25-27). In the seventeenth century they are often accompanied by a dog, presumably representing faithfulness, who looks over the edge of the vessel, but this cannot be distinguished for certain in the design of 1650 for the west tympanum of the Town Hall.

figure of Amsterdam, still wearing Mercury's hat, towers behind them, enthroned in the background. Her arms are outstretched and are supported by figures which stand beside her, while cornucopias of generous proportions, whose position is ill defined, appear to flank both her throne and the supporters of the vessel in front of it. The ships' instruments are omitted, or perhaps may may be presumed to remain at the feet of Amsterdam, here hidden by the cog and its supporters.

If the first version of the design was unsatisfactory in showing a small vessel raised in the City's hand, too delicate an object to be satisfactorily portrayed in sculpture which is in extremely high relief, the second clearly did not give a worthy place to Amsterdam, and it appears that for her sake the prominence of the coat of arms had to be sacrificed, since it was impossible, in a realistic relief, to represent both in the centre at the same time and to give both equal prominence. In the final version of the design (illus. 181, 192-200, 203-4, 205b) the ship was accordingly placed in the background, and its supporters were banished, to become, as it seems, the symbolic figures which support the ship in the design for the fountain that was to be placed in the Town Hall's southern court (illus. 189).[1] Amsterdam was brought back to her original position, and appears there with her arms outstretched, but no longer supported. Ships' instruments have been laid before her feet, she uses the globe as her footstool, and still she wears the winged hat, while the only cornucopia in the composition is held by Europe, who stands beside her.

In the final version of the design for the relief on the western pediment, it will be remembered, the four continents pay their tribute to Amsterdam, and although they are not represented in the relief as it is shown in Van Campen's drawing the significance of the scene represented there was very much the same. This is made clear by Everard Meyster, who in composing his description of the building evidently referred to this or to some similar version of the design. He describes how in the pediment 'a dragging swarm of packs and sacks on sledges (unloaded from barge and boat) is being carried into the lap of the ever-generous Amstel-maiden from all over the globe'.[2]

In Van Campen's drawing the goods are shown arriving, and it is left to

[1]   See p. 40 n. 2 above.
[2]   *Land-spel*, I, p. 29:

> . . . een *sleepende geweemel*
> Van *pack*, van *sack* op *sleens* (geloost uyt *Schuyt* en *Boot*)
> Den *Amstel-maeght* steets milt van 's heele Werelts-kloot
> Wort in 'er *schoot* gevoert.

the cog and the ships' instruments at the city's feet to suggest that they have been brought from overseas. Amsterdam is surrounded by sturdy figures dragging, pushing, and carrying bales, sacks, and other luggage, such as might be seen at work on the city's wharves and quays. To either side of the group of figures there are horses pulling sleighs such as those used to transport goods in the narrow streets that surrounded the Town Hall, and these sleighs, heavily loaded with the packages and sacks that Meyster mentions, would conveniently fill the low corners of the pediment.[1] In style the design has the staccato accents and the active confusion of movement which characterizes reliefs carved in imperial Rome,[2] as might be considered suitable to the decoration of a great building founded in a new Augustan age. Yet the style was also suited to the subject, which is portrayed circumstantially and with a truthful realism which is not disturbed by the representation, for the sake of antiquity, of very nearly all the figures as nudes. Only the women wear what must be regarded as antique drapery, and one small figure in the right-hand foreground is provided with a tunic which is belted at the waist and with a hat. Since this figure was copied faithfully in the relief on the pediment of the model it is unlikely to have been included by mistake, and it is just possible that a master or foreman directing operations is represented, who in Rome in contrast to the workmen (there slaves) might be distinguished by a hat,[3] and who, having one, would have to be clothed if only in a tunic which, although it may have been intended to be Roman, was in fact a mediaeval one.

By the time the prints of 1650 were made the design had been changed, quite clearly, to show the continents bringing their treasures in person to Amsterdam, whose hands, as has been seen, were by then stretched out as though ready to receive them. The continents, which can be recognized by their attributes, stand to either side of Amsterdam. Europe and Asia take their place in order of precedence, and they are followed by America, while Africa,

---

[1] This motif and a similar one on the back pediment of the Mauritshuis (illus. 118) may be adapted from a representation, now lost but known from drawings and descriptions, of the pediment of the Temple of Jupiter on the Roman Capitol. This formed part of a sculptured relief which was in Rome in the seventeenth century. The chariots of the Sun and Moon, drawn by horses towards the pediment's centre, were shown carved on the tympanum. See A. J. B. Wace, 'Studies in Roman Historical Reliefs', 1, Reliefs from Trajan's Forum, *Papers of the British School at Rome*, IV, 1907, pp. 229-59 and pl. XX. Thanks are due to Mr. H. W. van Helsdingen who drew the writer's attention to the lost representation and to Professor J. H. Jongkees who provided further information. For another possible borrowing from the relief see p. 43 n. 2 above.

[2] Reliefs such as that on a Hadrianic sarcophagus representing the Vengeance of Orestes, in the Museo Laterano, Rome (illus. Strong, *Scultura Romana*, II, p. 283) are referred to here.

[3] See p. 3 n. 2 above.

probably by some error, comes last.[1] Europe, who thus stands at Amsterdam's right hand, may be recognized by her crown, and by the bull and horse which accompany her. Asia, who stands to her left, is distinguished by her camel and an ostrich. Africa, who is beside Asia, stands with her back to the spectator, in her arm a cornucopia. A lion is beside her, accompanied by a number of other animals, among them a rhinoceros, an elephant, a large crocodile, and a turtle or tortoise. America, on the other side of the central group of figures, also has a crocodile with her, as well as an ant-eater and two fish, perhaps from tropical rivers. The figures are thus distinguished in the first place by symbols commonly associated with them: Europe by her crown, horse, and bull, Asia by her camel, Africa by her lion and her cornucopia, and America by her crocodile. All these symbols are made to take their places quite naturally in the composition, and all are mentioned by Ripa in his descriptions of the continents.[2] In addition he associates the elephant with Africa by describing her as wearing an elephant's trunk on her head, and that is perhaps why an elephant appears behind her. Other symbols are added to these, apparently suggested by descriptions brought home by travellers: descriptions of ostriches to be found in desert country, and so to be associated with the camel, of the rhinoceros and other strange animals to be found in Africa, and of ant-eaters to be seen in the New World.

In this changed version of the design for the relief Europe and Asia are balanced against each other in the composition, as supporters to the figure of Amsterdam. Both face the spectator, like the saints standing to either side of the Madonna in a *Sacra Conversazione* of the High Renaissance. Asia and America, who are also balanced against each other, nevertheless face one towards and one away from the spectator, and this form of *contrapposto* is to be found elsewhere: in works by classically-minded artists not of the High Renaissance, but of the seventeenth century. The pairs of children in the door-top lunettes of the galleries of the Town Hall are many of them arranged in this way, and a notable example of this form of balanced composition is to be seen in the Church of S. Ignazio in Rome. There, in a frieze in relief which runs round the interior of the building, carefully-balanced pairs of children appear; they hold up coats of arms and garlands, and either both face the spectator, or, still posed with considerable symmetry, turn one towards him and one away.[3]

[1]   In this engraving, and in that by H. Quellien of the final version, the designs are shown in reverse.
[2]   For these, which will be discussed without further references, see his *Iconologia*, 1624, pp. 437-43. Quotations are from this source, and in each case the principal description is referred to unless it is stated otherwise.
[3]   Hans Posse, in Thieme-Becker, s. v. Algardi, states that the frieze is derived from this artist.

This form of symmetry was introduced into the arrangement of the principal figures in the design for the western tympanum of the Town Hall between the making of the drawing and the model, and the publication of the prints of 1650, and, as has already been shown, the arrangement of its central elements was also changed at this point. In other respects, however, the design was altered very little. Boats bringing goods to Amsterdam were substituted for the loaded sledges without any further alteration being made in the main lines of the composition, two nude figures kneeling near the centre of the relief remained in the same places and in similar poses, and a third figure, seen carrying a large and shallow basket on her head in the earlier design, was retained with her basket to become the figure of America.

In the final version of the design[1] the main figures remain in the same balanced pattern, although the order of precedence has been corrected so that it is America who turns her back to the spectator, displaying a feathered headdress, while Africa wears a broad-brimmed hat to protect her from the equatorial sun: a hat which takes the place previously occupied in the composition by the shallow basket that was carried by America. As is natural in a work of very much greater scale the composition has been elaborated by the addition of a number of subordinate figures, and, as has been indicated in discussing the representations in the centre, other alterations have been made. In addition to those already mentioned the nude figures to the side of those in the centre have been replaced by personified rivers. The boats have been omitted; the corners are filled instead with other figures associated with the continents. As might also be expected the symbolism too has become more complex, and it seems that in planning it Ripa's account was very extensively used, although it was by no means slavishly followed, as will be shown. Once again embellishments taken from other sources were added to the accepted imagery, although some of the strange animals which accompanied Asia and Africa in the earlier design are no longer to be seen.

Ripa's Europe, a woman wearing a crown and dressed in royal clothing, sits between two crossed cornucopias, one filled with all kinds of fruits and corn and the other with blue and white grapes. She holds in her right hand a beautiful temple, to show that 'the perfect and most true religion' has its seat there, and she points to kingdoms, crowns, sceptres, garlands and, as it appears in the illustrations and in the explanation of the figure, to the tiara of the pope.

---

[1] Faithfully represented in H. Quellien's engraving, *Statuen*, II, pl. 2 (here illus. 205 b).

These are to one side of her, and to the other there is a horse, and with it flags, shields, and arms, an owl on a book, musical instruments, and artists' equipment, to show that she excels in war, in letters, and in the liberal arts.

This figure had clearly to be modified before it could appear in a scene in which the City itself was depicted, and as part of the decoration of the Town Hall of Amsterdam. When Amsterdam herself was present the arrangement implied by Europe's being seated on crossed cornucopias and having attributes to either side of her would be quite inappropriate, for she would have to take second place; the subservience of even the planets to the departments of the city government within the building makes this evident. She accordingly stands, although she is clad royally, beside the seated Amsterdam, holding one of her cornucopias in her hands (that filled with fruit and corn) while at her feet a child carrying two large bunches of grapes (presumably blue and white ones) hurries in the direction of the City to present them to her. The temple is omitted, and with it the symbols of spiritual and temporal sovereignty, as must be expected in a Protestant republic. Moreover there are no arms; in a Town Hall founded in the year of the Eternal Peace they too would be inappropriate. Two horses, however, accompany Europe, not now symbolizing supremacy in war, but, as it seems, the art of agriculture, for a herd of cattle appears behind them, bringing to mind certain early maps of Amsterdam, in which in the fields surrounding the city cows are to be seen grazing peacefully. The bull, mentioned by Ripa in two additional descriptions as carrying Europe, which here stands beside her, cannot but be at home in these surroundings, and the representation of Europe has in consequence an unexpected homogeneity. The literary and the liberal arts, which remain to be mentioned, are represented by a pile of books so heavy that the very young child to whom they are entrusted has let them fall.

In the relief on the Town Hall Ripa's figure of Asia, as well as being embellished with additional images, has been modified in another way, by being combined with a figure which represents the East in an entirely different context. In Ripa's description Asia wears on her head a garland of fruit and flowers, she is richly dressed, and she wears ornaments of gold, with pearls and jewels. She carries the branches and fruit of spices in one hand, and in the other holds a censer, while a camel kneels beside her 'or [is depicted] in another manner, as seems best to the discreet and discerning painter'. The Asia of the Town Hall relief is accompanied by a standing camel and by an ostrich, as she was in the design of 1650. She holds the chain of a censer in one hand, as

Ripa advocates, while a child beside her, holding the censer by the foot and the chain, blows into it so that the spectator may know that the incense within it is burning. With the other hand Asia holds the camel's bridle and on her head she wears, not a garland, but a turban with a jewelled band, in keeping with the finely-worked clasps that are to be seen on her oriental clothing. Her spices, as we may assume, are carried in a treasure-chest by a second child who, instead of Asia herself, has a garland of flowers round his head, while a third child who appears in Asia's company seems to have no function but that of bringing a bunch of tulips to Amsterdam. By the middle of the seventeenth century the tulip, which was first brought to Europe from Asia, had become a spectacularly profitable commodity in Holland's trade.

Counterparts of the children who stand to either side of the turbanned figure of Asia, one blowing into the censer and one with the treasure-chest, are to be found in the picture of the Adoration of the Magi (see illus. 201) which was painted by Rubens in 1609 for the city council of Antwerp, to be hung in their town hall, and which in 1612 was sent to Spain, where it now hangs in the Prado.[1] In this picture the swarthy turbanned king who, representing the East, brings precious spices to the infant Christ as he lies in the manger, stands facing the spectator, and his camel, which has carried him on his journey, can be seen waiting in the background. He has beside him two children who are strikingly like those of the relief in Amsterdam, for they are similarly posed, and similarly clad. One blows into a bowl of burning spices, which he holds in his hands; the other, and attendant of the white-haired king who stands to his other side, carries a treasure-chest in the manner of an acolyte at a Roman sacrifice (see illus. 202), holding it open with the box facing away from him so that his master may reach what lies inside. His counterpart in the relief on the Town Hall opens his box in a similar manner, but only when a comparison is made with such Roman scenes or with Rubens' painting does the reason appear.

Although the children to either side of the oriental king have exchanged positions in the relief, and although the position of one of them is reversed, the likeness between the two groups of figures is striking, and there can be little doubt that here symbolism belonging to a specifically religious theme was brought to the service of a merchant city together with many of its connota-

[1] Rudolf Oldenbourg, *P. P. Rubens* (Klassiker der Kunst), Stuttgart and Berlin, 4th ed., n. d., p. 26; preparatory sketch in the Gemeente Museum, Groningen. Although in much of the borrowing discussed here the subjects are reversed there appears to have been no engraving of the composition.

tions. It had overtones which might suggest to the discerning spectator the travel of strangers from distant lands to acknowledge their sovereign, an ancient world coming to pay tribute to what was newly born, and the bringing of untold wealth to be presented in homage. To convey these ideas forms were borrowed which had already been used to express such symbolism, although in another context, with special grandeur, and for the decoration of another town hall. As though to make it quite clear that the borrowing was made there is a reminiscence in the relief of another of the figures in Rubens' picture, that of a man seen crouching down to lift one of the heavy gifts that is brought by the eastern kings, for a man struggling with a heavy bale of goods in the train of Africa is depicted in a position which is very similar, and once again there is a likeness not only of form, but also of meaning.[1]

Ripa describes Africa as an almost naked woman, black skinned and with loose and curly hair, who wears, as well as the elephant's trunk on her head, a coral necklace and earrings, and who carries a scorpion in her right hand and a cornucopia containing ears of corn in her left. On one side of her is a most ferocious lion and on the other are vipers and venomous serpents. This figure was not altered essentially in the relief on the Town Hall, although like those already considered it was modified. Africa is depicted there as a Moorish woman, who is clothed and ornamented as Ripa describes, except that her hair is neatly tucked into the broad-brimmed hat whose origin has already been noticed, and an elephant stands behind her, hanging his trunk over her lion's back in a friendly way, so that it may be noticed by the spectator. She holds no scorpion, but as has been seen a lion accompanies her, which, as befits one in such a peaceful scene, appears to be very gentle. Snakes, however, fight on the other side of her at her feet, and a salamander, another venomous animal and one which is also associated with fire,[2] is carried by a boy in her train. Another child who accompanies her carries a parrot, here evidently not a symbol of eloquence, as Van Mander and Ripa describe,[3] but simply a souvenir of tropical countries. In the corner of the pediment near to Africa negroes are busy with the transport of bales, barrels, sacks, and tusks of ivory, and it may be noticed that although she now carries no cornucopia containing ears of corn – for two adjacent figures in the composition each in possession of a horn of

---

[1] The figure also appears in Rubens' Abraham and Melchisedech, c. 1615, Caen Museum (Oldenbourg, op. cit., p. 110). There are similar figures in the mantelpiece friezes of the burgomasters' chamber and the north fireplace of the council chamber, where a child is represented in the same position.
[2] See Ripa, Iconologia, 1624, pp. 464-5 (Nocumento) and 194 (Fuoco) respectively.
[3] See p. 155 n. 3 above.

plenty might be deemed monotonous – a sheaf of corn appears among the sacks to make it clear that the corn is within them.

America, the youngest and the last of the four continents, is said by Ripa to have a frightening face, but in the relief on the Town Hall pediment she looks with a kindly expression in the direction of Amsterdam. She is described as wearing a feather headdress and a cloth which hangs from her shoulders; in the relief the cloth is tucked round her waist. She holds a bow and an arrow, and she carries a full quiver, which alone is to be seen, and under her foot is a human head shot through by an arrow, a gruesome detail which the sculptor has left out. Behind her on the ground there is a man-eating lizard 'of immeasurable size', which is in fact a crocodile, and this is represented in the position that Ripa indicates.

At this point Ripa's knowledge of the New World was exhausted, but, when the Town Hall was built, fifty years had passed since his book was first published, and Dirck Pietersz. Pers, its translator, who sold his books 'On the water, opposite the Corn-market'[1] in mid-seventeenth-century Amsterdam, knew more of America than the tales of ferocious savages and terrifying beasts that had reached Ripa's ears. He had seen the ships of the West India Company riding at anchor in the harbour, and must have known well what was contained in their holds. He evidently thought in terms of trade, and as Ripa's account was, to his personal knowledge, inadequate, he ceased for a moment to be a translator, and completed the description with his own words:

> In order to express the fruitfulness of this land one may add to this image that she has with her a bunch of sugar-cane and some rolls of tobacco, which the ingenious painter, among many known animals and fruits, may add according to his fancy.[2]

The artist who designed the relief on the Town Hall of Amsterdam, who, because of his subject, was bound to think in the same terms, may well have used Ripa's work in the Dutch translation, for he included both sugar-cane and tobacco, as well as other additional figures: fire, as a bald-headed youth with a flame-like lock of hair on his head holding up a bowl with flames emerging from it[3] to represent America's tropical heat; mine-workers, for

---

[1] See the title-page of his edition of Ripa; *Iconologia* (Dutch version), 1644.

[2] Ripa, op. cit. (Dutch version), p. 605. "Men kan by dit beelt, om beter de vruchtbaerheyt deses Lands uyt te drucken, daer by stellen, datse een bos Suycker-riet, en eenige rollen Toback by haer heeft; 't welck de geestige Schilder, uyt veel bekender dieren en vruchten, kan tot zijne vercieringe toestellen."

[3] In this figure details from Ripa's first and second versions of the element of Fire are combined, see *Iconologia*, 1624, pp. 194 and 196.

in the cellars below the city bank great quantities of silver and gold from Peru lay hidden,[1] an armadillo, and two monkeys who, in the corner of the relief, play with tropical fruits beside a cactus plant. To represent tobacco an elderly Red Indian sits on a hamper containing rolls of tobacco smoking a long clay pipe, and the sugar-cane is shown in the hand of a small child who fearlessly pushes it into the mouth of the delighted crocodile.[2]

Only the Rivers now remain to be described. They are seated at the feet of Amsterdam, and in Hubertus Quellien's engraving they bear the names of the Amstel and the IJ. The Amstel is to the left of Amsterdam and the IJ to the right, and they are clearly differentiated. The first is reminiscent of an antique river god, perhaps being in part derived from the Marforio and the giant figures of rivers on the Roman Capitol;[3] the second is modelled on one of Giovanni Bologna's river gods in Florence.[4] The Amstel, wearing a crown of bulrushes and other freshwater plants, leans on his pitcher with the greatest dignity. He has beside him a boat-hook and a rudder, and is accompanied by an animal noted for building dams in streams, the industrious beaver, which is also a symbol of peace.[5] From his pitcher water in which fishes swim pours out to mingle with the waters of the IJ. The IJ, although he has the position of honour, is by no means so splendid. He is portrayed, perhaps as a reminder of Amsterdam's early beginnings, as a poor fisherman, who huddles over his water-pot, itself of a less noble form than the Amstel's pitcher. He is scantily clothed in fishing-nets, and wears the prows of ships as a crown round his head, perhaps a reminder of the many vessels that sailed on his waters as well as a symbol of victory.[6] An anchor and a very large fish, the kindly dolphin,[7] may be seen with him, and a smaller fish, of some flat variety, is to be seen in the water

[1]   Referred to by Vondel, *Inwydinge*, lines 955-9, and others. Miners are represented very similarly on the arch by the Mint designed by Rubens for the Triumphal Entry of Prince Ferdinand, see p. 141 n. 9 [7] above.
[2]   The child with a casket in Rubens' Adoration, on which that accompanying Asia in Quellien's relief is based (both the pose and the association with other borrowings show that it is not merely from the same source) is evidently inspired by the figure holding a box of incense in Roman sacrificial scenes such as that in an Aurelian relief showing a sacrifice, on the Arch of Constantine (illus. Strong, *Scultura Romana*, II, fig. 156). The designer presumably recognized Rubens' reference and may well have designed this child bending over the crocodile with the Aurelian relief in mind, for there an attendant with a sacrificial animal is in a very similar posture (cf. illus. 202, 204).
[3]   In particular the tilt of the head is likely that of the Marforio, which already formed part of a fountain, and there are points of resemblance to the other statues.
[4]   This figure forms part in the Ocean Fountain in the Boboli Gardens, see E. Dhanens, *Jean Boulogne, Giovanni Bologna Fiammingo*, Brussels, 1956, cat. no. XXVI, and illus. 71 and 73. The author is indebted to Professor J. Wilde for pointing out the derivation.
[5]   See Ripa, op. cit., 1624, pp. 494-5 *(Pace)*.
[6]   See p. 72 and note above.
[7]   See p. 70 n. 3 above.

which streams from his pitcher, a final, humble, tribute which is poured out at the city's feet.

Although the first design for this relief, whose origins have now been seen in detail, could be compared with reliefs carved in ancient Rome it would be harder to make comparisons between such a piece of sculpture and the design in its final form. The design has been given an organization in space which at first was missing. In the early design the figures of people carrying goods to Amsterdam seem to tumble against each other, and although those in the centre form a circle round Amsterdam their positions in depth are not defined. In the final version an arrangement of figures in space has been established; by their movements and their glances the continents furthest from Amsterdam lead the eye to the centre and into depth to where she is sitting, while the Rivers act as *repoussoirs*, defining her position, and at the same time as barriers which keep the spectator, in imagination, at a respectful distance from her. Such an arrangement in depth and the impression that the figures are moving freely that results from it, are foreign to Roman sculpture, although there backgrounds are often indicated and the relief may be extremely high. There the sense of the surface of the relief is never lost, while here, by the attention being directed to a figure set within a represented space and seemingly beyond the surface, it is contradicted. To the detriment of its strict antiquity, but to its great enrichment, the relief on the Town Hall's west pediment has the wealth of form, the solid figures set and moving as though in a continuation of actual space, and the strong particularized realism which links the spectator to the scene, of the Baroque of Rubens.

Nevertheless the model for this sculptured relief is likely to have been an antique one. As has been stated Van Campen went to Rome, and it is evident that he made a stay there.[1] Quite likely, therefore, he went to Naples, where the ruined temple of Castor and Pollux was still to be seen, probably the only antique building in Italy of which a pediment entirely filled with figures carved in relief had survived, though there are many representations of such pediments in antique sculpture.[2] Palladio had published a reconstruction of this temple in which the relief was schematically shown,[3] and he had revived such ornament at Maser, in the pediments of the front façade and of the chapel

[1] See p. 108 and note above. "Passato a Roma" implies a stay, but not one of great length.

[2] Representations such as that mentioned on p. 174 n. 1 above must have been known to both Palladio and Van Campen.

[3] Palladio, *Quattro libri*, Bk. IV, pp. 95-97. The temple is also mentioned by Vincenzo Scamozzi, *L'idea della architettura universale* [etc.], Venice, 1615, Bk. VI, Ch. XII.

of the Villa Barbaro (illus. 183). The remains of the antique temple were destroyed in an earthquake in 1688, but very fortunately their appearance was recorded, apparently with great care, in a drawing made on the spot by Francisco d'Ollanda (illus. 182, 184).[1]

The portico, which is of the Corinthian order, is of great size, and the tympanum itself is approximately sixty feet wide; this can be deduced from the height of a figure in the drawing. The figures which ornament it are considerably over life size, and they appear to be carved in high relief, as would be necessary if they were to be distinctly seen since they are at a great height from the ground. The relief is damaged at the centre, so that some of its figures have been lost, but enough remains to show that the figures represented appeared as though in a single scene. There was a central group of figures, which cannot be identified, and a group consisting of two figures to either side. In each of these side groups there is a seated figure, to the left a woman holding a cornucopia, who would have been recognized as an earth-goddess and possibly as Italy,[2] and to the right a river god reclining in the traditional posture, his arm on a pitcher, while in each of the outer corners of the relief there is a water-creature, half man half fish, who reaches up with some object in his hand towards the head of the seated figure beside him. The likeness to the reliefs in the tympana of the Town Hall, both in form and content, is remarkable. The works are comparable in scale[3] and both ornament pediments of the Corinthian order. The reclining figures in the western relief on the Town Hall are comparable with those of the relief that was at Naples, land and water are represented as counterparts in both design (the two reliefs at Amsterdam, as was intended, being considered together) and the actions and poses of the mermaids on the eastern tympanum are very similar to those of the antique mermen. These likenesses could of course have arisen by chance, for the subject portrayed in the Town Hall pediments would suggest itself in Amsterdam and the seated figures at least are very usual in Roman sculpture. Moreover the idea of filling these and other pediments in Holland with sculptured scenes could have come simply from Palladio. Yet it would be in keeping with Van Campen's view of antiquity and its revival if he evolved his design with an actual model from the antique world in mind where one was available, and on this

[1] See A. Trandelenburg, 'Der Dioskurentempel in Neapel' (Archäologische Gesellschaft), *Archäologischer Anzeiger*, 1911, columns 54-57. Drawing in the Escorial, Library, Codex Francisco d'Ollanda, fol. 45 v.

[2] Cf. Ripa, *Iconologia*, 1624, pp. 337-42 *(Italia)*.

[3] H. Quellien states that the Town Hall relief is 82 ft. long; *Statuen*, II, pl. 2.

occasion he may well have done so. In Palladio's reconstruction of the Naples temple the figures are different, and if details from Naples were borrowed for the Town Hall tympana this must have been due to some other intermediary of whom nothing is known, or to the range and intensity of Van Campen's own studies.

However this may be it is clear that the formal design of the relief in the western pediment of the Town Hall was in the first place conceived in classical terms, and that the antique forms that were used in it were modified and enlarged upon so that movement in space was expressed in it, and so that the spectator was brought into relationship with what was portrayed, in the manner of baroque art. In its symbolic scheme antique imagery, or images modelled in the Renaissance on those of ancient times by Ripa, Palladio's counterpart in this field, were modified and enlarged upon in a similar way; they were given an immediacy and a realism which made them speak directly to the spectator. In the representation of Asia associations with a well-known symbolic figure from another context were put to use. The monkeys and cactus plants and armadillos that accompany America must have been brought home from trading expeditions or vividly described by travellers, and they would bring lively and immediate impressions to the spectator's mind. He had probably smoked tobacco himself and had tasted the sugar, and he may have handled silver brought from the Peruvian mines. The meaning of the figures was thus enriched for him by his own experience and by the life of his immediate surroundings, which was reflected in them. Further, the homeliness and understanding gentleness with which the elements of the design were portrayed and were related to each other must have brought them closer to him. These qualities, characteristic of the native traditions of art in the Low Countries from early times, added warmth and vitality to the complex scene and invited the attention of the beholder. The child with the censer handles it with great care, afraid that it will burn him. The crocodile, in the presence of Amsterdam, has the docility of a domestic animal, and it is natural that a child should feed it. The monkeys pursue their own amusements as though they were unobserved, and so we are encouraged to observe them.

History, tradition, and use remain to be mentioned as elements of the design, and they are essential to it, for they provide the starting-point of its symbolism, whose origins are to be found in the history, the traditions, and the actual life of Amsterdam: in the ship of the city's first coat of arms, which was her early trading vessel, and, as an extension of the same theme, in a scene from

184

her markets and quay-sides which showed the goods that had been brought home. Its purpose was to exemplify and illustrate the trade of the city, and so to extol her greatness. The symbolism was elaborated and enriched by the addition of ideas which embellished the main theme and which were drawn from many sources. It was expressed in a wealth of different terms: forms and symbols borrowed from antiquity and from the modern world. Yet the sources were drawn on and the terms were used for this single purpose, and only in so far as they could be made to serve it. The forms of antique sculpture alone could not provide the thundering oratory that was needed to blaze forth the modern glory of such a city as Amsterdam, the symbolism of antiquity and of renaissance Italy had to be brought up to date to meet changed circumstances, and a new figure, both formally and symbolically, had to be made the central one.

What is true of the relief on the western pediment is true, point by point, of the building as a whole, and of all the decoration which was planned to form part it. The Town Hall was designed, in its entirety, to meet the needs of the civic life of Amsterdam, itself formed by history, tradition, and present circumstances, which determined its character. Thus the main features of the old Town Hall, as has been seen, were carefully preserved in the new, although they were given a new form which was suitable to the city's glorious past and its present nature. Antique forms and imagery, with their historical associations, were adapted to the city's purpose and were modified and enriched in the ways that, in the case of the relief on the western pediment, have been described.

The symbol that came into being as a result is a very complex one, and it is difficult to hold in mind its grandeur and its delicacy at the same time, and to see it as a whole now that the use of the building has altered. Each part fitted with precision into its place in the whole scheme, both formally and symbolically, and the city departments were part of the great symbol. The spectator could not view the Town Hall with detachment. He was related to it from the Dam outside and from the waterway that lay behind it, where goods from all parts of the world were brought in, in reality, below the sculptured representation of the trade of Amsterdam. He could walk through the universe that was created within the building, viewing it from different angles and so defining his relationship to all its parts more and more precisely. He could 'read' the meaning of its wealth of details, expressed in their language of imagery, in so far as he had the patience and the skill. He himself was included in the symbol as he walked across the Burgerzaal or did his business in the various rooms. Indeed, with the councillors and commissioners, the messengers and the clerks, the sentenced prisoner in the *vierschaar* and the sheriff himself, he was necessary to the building, to set the scale of the whole structure, to populate the world-in-little that was created in it, and to complete the parallels that it drew. Even the traffic outside on the Dam, and the little orphan whose papers were kept, neatly docketed, in a cupboard decorated with "festonnekens" by Quellien[1] were important to the Town Hall, which was a symbol extended in space far beyond its own walls.

The spectator is related to only very few Dutch works of art in a comparable way. In the traditional painting of Holland one generally looks as it were through a window, deliberately cut off from the world that seems to be beyond it by a painted curtain or by a frame. Yet Rembrandt, from his very early years, made the spectator join spiritually into the scene that he depicted, as he did in his Judas Returning the Pieces of Silver.[2] Later he also organized the relationship formally. In the painting of the feast of the Batavians which he carried out for the series in the Town Hall (see illus. 39, 40,)[3] the spectator was made a witness of the event, for he was drawn by the perspective of the composition to stand at a point where he could look at it undisturbed by the light from the windows, and from there he could see the scene as though it were taking place in reality before him, under arches which were a continuation of the building in which he stood; it was the presence of the descendants of the Batavians in the gallery below that gave the scene its full significance. In Rembrandt's Syndics[4] a similar relationship was created, and there the intrusion of the spectator produces the scene that is depicted, so that he is the centre through which the whole composition is linked up and is extended into space.

In the schemes of the Oranjezaal and of the Town Hall as a whole (expressing the ideas of two distinct worlds though of a single moment) the same methods were used, but of these the decoration of the Oranjezaal was confined to a single room, if one of special magnificence. Only the Amsterdam Town Hall, of all Dutch buildings, seems to have spoken this baroque language in its

---

[1] *Beschryvinge van 't Stadhuis*, 1782, p. 69, and A. Quellien, MS. Papers, no. 18. Quellien's term, which has a Flemish diminutive ending, means 'little festoons'.
[2] Collection of the Marchioness of Normanby; see Seymour Slive, *Rembrandt and his Critics,* The Hague, 1953, p. 15 and pl. 1.
[3] Fragment in the National Museum, Stockholm. See *Konsthistorisk Tidskrift*, XXV, 1956, pp. 3-39.
[4] Rijksmuseum, Amsterdam; Jakob Rosenberg, *Rembrandt*, Harvard, 1948, II, illus. 126.

entirety, as an organized whole, from its total form to details of the decoration.[1] Bernini made a complex symbol of a similar kind in and around St. Peter's Basilica in Rome, including the pope in the Benediction Loggia and the pilgrim in the crowd in the piazza below in such a way that they are both essential to the scheme, [2] and other such symbols are to be found where the religious fervour resulting from the counter-reformation gave opportunities for their invention.

The scheme of the Town Hall had features in common with these compositions: the use of the expressive value of great size, the use of strong contrasts of light and shade both in interior planning and in the high relief of the sculpture, the welding of the arts of architecture, painting, and sculpture into a single means of expression, and the necessity of the spectator's presence – all characteristic of baroque art. Yet as has been shown the architectural forms used in the building are in themselves classical and they have symmetry, regularity of form, and harmony of proportion of a classical kind. There are no *trompe-l'oeil* effects other than those provided by an honest realism. The participant is related to what is represented as though it were in his presence, but he is not led in a particular direction as he is in the Church's architectural and decorative schemes, whose first effect is in many cases reached by an appeal to the emotions. Instead he remains free to wander in and about the building at will, and, being confronted by what is represented there, to draw his own conclusions.

[1] There is no record of an all-embracing scheme in any of the Stadholder's palaces, which were designed before such decoration was in demand or could be carried out in the Dutch Republic.

[2] The Benediction Loggia is in the centre of the façade. Above it, surmounting the end of the basilica, is a figure of Christ, with figures of the apostles to either side of it. Above the colonnade encircling the piazza and above the buildings flanking the approach to the basilica itself are figures of the saints. All these figures together form a hieratic representation of the Church, which is only completed by the pope in the loggia, as head of the Church on earth, and the faithful assembled in the piazza. The piazza is oval, perhaps as nearly circular as the site allowed, and was to have been surrounded by the colonnade except on the side of the basilica. The plan, with that of the approach to the basilica and of the building itself, thus has very nearly the form of an orb surmounted by a cross. This must have been intended as a symbol, for the blessing "Urbi et Orbi" is given from the Benediction loggia; see Rudolf Wittkower, 'A counter-project to Bernini's "Piazza di San' Pietro"', *Journal of the Warburg and Courtauld Institutes*, III, 1939-40, p. 104, where the mediaeval origins of such a conception are mentioned (illustrations there and id., *Bernini*, pls. I-III). The pope sees before him a crowd of the faithful, representing the city and the world. The pilgrim was led forward and made attentive by the statues of the Angels of the Passion on the Ponte S. Angelo as he entered the City of the Vatican. He then made his way through the narrow streets which led to the basilica, through the colonnade, and out on to the great piazza, where he found himself surrounded by the figures of the saints and was included in the symbolic representation of the Church. The lines of the architecture make it difficult to leave the piazza through the colonnade, and the attention is directed firmly towards what was intended to be the only open side of the piazza and to the façade beyond it, where, below the figure of Christ, the pope appears. The starting-point for the description given here was Professor R. Wittkower's explanation of parts of the scheme given in a seminar in London in 1949. It was further worked out in discussion with Mr. K. Downes, to whom the writer is also indebted.

What his senses perceived might demonstrate the greatness of the city to him, and might 'move' or 'compel' him to practise the virtues of civic life, but it did so by appealing in the first instance not to his emotions but to his reason. It was natural that this form of symbolism should be developed in the United Provinces, a Protestant republic in which humanist learning flourished in the age of the Baroque, and that it should appear in the town hall of a merchant city whose government had brought about the peace by which liberty had finally been secured.

Contemporary learning and the Protestant philosophy of the United Provinces were undoubtedly of importance in the Town Hall, but it had other elements which were peculiar to Amsterdam, for as has been seen the city's world-wide trade, her position in history, her traditions, her corporate life, and the everyday life that was lived in her houses and on her quay-sides all contributed to it. The nature of the city's culture at its greatest moment was thus put on record for future generations in the building as its designers intended, and with a completeness of which they can hardly have been aware. If they had been aware of it they would indeed have been satisfied.

EPILOGUE

In a poem on the medal that was struck to commemorate the Town Hall's inauguration[1] Vondel pointed out that it was not easy to win the golden fleece and that not everyone could have done it. He mentioned the many trials that were undergone in obtaining the fleece, and stated that Argo was famous in ancient times because it was the first vessel to whose lot such treasures fell. Yet, he continued, the cog of Amsterdam[2] is a much better trading vessel, and he ended: 'Wherever one takes the field, on water or land, the city of Amsterdam produces money'.[3]

It is suitable that, before leaving the subject of Amsterdam's seventeenth-century Town Hall, now the Royal Palace, we should be reminded once again, by this quotation, of the immense wealth that was brought in by the city's trade, which made the construction of the magnificent building possible and which had a large share in the achievement of the Peace of Munster, whose conclusion the Town Hall symbolized. Vondel's poem ends with a shout of triumph, which, quite appropriately, is expressed in mercenary terms. It is possible, nevertheless, in interpreting the symbol of the entry of the ship Argo into the harbour of Amsterdam, to place the emphasis rather differently, for according to Natales Conti, whose *Mythologiae* has been referred to before, the ancients believed that Jupiter put the ship Argo in the heavens as a memorial of the benefits that she had conferred on the Trojan heroes in bringing them safely home.[4] When the inauguration took place Amsterdam had come safely and triumphantly through the eighty years' rebellion against Spain, the attempt of Prince Willem II to take the city into his power, and the war of 1652 to 1654 with England, whose Navigation Act passed by Cromwell's parliament provided a new threat to Dutch trade, and in these circumstances the inauguration of the Town Hall must have brought feelings of thankfulness for the city's safe passage through the trials of the past years into many minds. The representation on the medal, therefore, may well have been intended not only to symbolize the mighty trade of Amsterdam, but also to be, like the constellation Argo, a memorial of other benefits that had been given and received.

---

[1] See Vondel, *Inwydinge* (ed. Kronenberg), pp. 73-74 The part of the poem referred to is entitled "Maghtige neering", 'Mighty trade'.

[2] The cog appears on a shield on the medal above the scene showing Argo's arrival.

[3] "Men treck' te water of te velt,
De Stadt van Amsterdam schaft gelt."

[4] Conti, *Mythologiae*, p. 544.

On the morning of the inauguration, it will be remembered, the minister Melchior Johannes preached a sermon in the New Church which struck Hans Bontemantel as 'neat and edifying'. Bontemantel did not remember from which psalm the text was taken, but he remembered its context, and the lines can be identified.[1] They formed part of a song of thankfulness written by the prophet David for a feast of the dedication of the temple, and his gratitude to God was expressed in them, for giving protection, and for deliverance from his enemies:

> I will extol thee, O Lord; for thou hast lifted me up, and hast not made my foes to rejoice over me.

These were the words with which the ceremonies of the day began, and it was only after thanks had been expressed in this manner that the gentlemen of the city government, preceded by the mounted guard and the city messengers and followed by the secretaries and the clerks, crossed the ancient market-place by the dam at the city's centre in order of precedence, and took possession of their new Town Hall.

[1] See p. 2 n. 1 above.

Den 29 Julius 1655, wesende donderdach, s'morgens syn twee predicatien gedaen, een inde oude en d'ander inde nieuwe kerk.

In de nieuwe kerck predicte, domine Melscher Johannes hebbende den Texst psalm [30] het eerste ende tweede vers, waer op een seer nette en stichtelycke predicatie gedaen wiert; waer den Conincklycke Phropheet david van syn soon Absolon, vervolgt wordende, daer over den gemelden Absolon ongecoemen wesende, is david weder te Jerusalem gecoemen, ende den Tempel weder ingewijt.

Nae de predicatie, syn de magistraeten uyt de kercken opt princen hof gecoemen, daer het stadt huijs seedert den brant vant oude stadthuys gehouden is geweest, ende alsoo in volgende ordre nae het nieuwe stadthuys gegaen.

de ruyter wacht, (dat is die het stadthuys bewaecken) alle met nieuwe hellebaerden ....
de steede boeden of roedraegende boeden, alle blootshooft.
myn heer de schout, gaende alleen, aen wiens syde de roede van Justitie gedraegen wierde.
de regeerende Burgemeesteren
de regeerende scheepenen
de out Burgemeesteren
de Tresoriers
de weesmeesters
den Raet sonder onderschyt of Out Scheepenen waren of niet
de secretarissen
de klercken . . .

In ordre voorschreven opt Raet huys gecoemen wesende ende int ronde staende int groote vertreck van Burgemeesteren heeft Burgemeester Graef als presideerende. een clyne aenspraecke gedaen; ende syn daer meede in haer ordenares camer gegaen, en scheepenen, in een Camer by provisie (naest haer ordenares Camer die noch niet gereet lach) daer toe geprepareert; en Tresoriers en weesmeesters inde haere, en den Raet is geschyden.

Burgemeesteren in haer Camer gecoemen en geseeten weesende, syn gecomitteerde uyt den kercken-raet soo vande publique, france, engelse, hoogduytse en andere publique kercken, geassisteert met eenige Ouderlingen, gecoemen en haere Ed. Achtb. geluck gewenscht.

ende syn de predicanten yder een vaetge rinsewyn t'huys gesonden, te weeten alle de predicanten die in kercken dienst syn.

Nae de middach syn de heeren int vertreck van Burgemeesteren, sittende aen taffel in de rang als voor de middach gegaen hadden seer deftich getracteert.

de Burgery optreckende, te weeten ses compaignie vant geele Regiment in seer schoone en bequaeme ordere, de selfde in slach ordere staende, syn de Capiteinen en Luijtenants ofte haer plaets presenteerende, versocht opt stadthuys te coemen, ende inde Justitie Camer gelyt wesende syn aldaer met eenige schroeven, en fluyten wyn beschoncken, ende nae dry salvo scharges met musquetten gedaen weesende, syn de schutterije vertrocken omtrent seven euren savons, gelyck de Magistraeten gedaen hebben, omtrent half negen euren. ende is alles in soete vrolickeyt op de maeltyt toe gegaen.

CRITICAL LIST OF SOURCES

Non-literary and manuscript sources referred to frequently in the text and those requiring comment are listed here.

NON-LITERARY SOURCES

Prints of 1648. Prints of the ground and first floor plans of the town Hall as they were first designed, Gemeente-Archief, Amsterdam, Topografische Atlas. These designs have been discussed and illustrated by Arnoldus Noach, 'Een vergeten ontwerp' (q.v.). For their dating see text, p. 34, where they are also described.

Prints of 1650. A set of six prints of the design of the Town Hall. One bears a privilege of 1650 issued to Daniel Stalpaert. This mentions a number of prints. It is possible to identify the complete set, of which there is a copy in the Koninklijk Huisarchief, The Hague, nos. K. I. 6/16 to K. I. 6/21.

Prints by Hubertus Quellien. See Bibliography s. v. H. Quellien.

Prints by Jacob Vennekool. See Bibliography s. v. J. Vennekool.

Model of the Town Hall. A wooden architectural model for the building, in the Amsterdams Historisch Museum, St. Anthonieswaag, Amsterdam. It may be taken to date from 1648 or very soon afterwards. See further Katharine Fremantle, 'Some Drawings' (q. v.).

MANUSCRIPT SOURCES

Resolutien der Burgemeesteren en Oud-Burgemeesteren. Gemeente-Archief, Amsterdam. The minutes of the council of Burgomasters and Ex-Burgomasters of Amsterdam. It is clear that only some of the discussions and decisions made by the burgomasters are recorded in these minutes; many recommendations and decisions made by the burgomasters which are not referred to in them are mentioned in the minutes of the treasurers and in those of the city council, and the discussion of matters on which decisions were obviously made is not always recorded.

Resolutien der Thesaurieren Ordinares. Gemeente-Archief, Amsterdam. The minutes of the treasurers of the city.

Resolutien der Vroedschap. Gemeente-Archief, Amsterdam. The minutes of the city council of Amsterdam. The resolutions concerning the development of the site of the Town Hall have been published by A. Boeken in an appendix to his article 'Over de voorgeschiedenis' (q. v.). His transcripts of these have been referred to and quoted here, though references to the article have not been given on each separate occasion.

BARGRAVE, ROBERT. *A relation of Sundry Voyages and Journeys made by mee– –.* Bodleian Library, Oxford, Rawl. MS. C. 799. Here the original is referred to and quoted, though extracts have been published by A. Rode, 'Robert Bargrave (ein englischer Reisender des XVII Jahrhunderts)' [etc.], *Jahresbericht Oberrealschule und Realschule in Einsbüttel zu Hamburg*, XIII, 1904–5, pp. 1-29.

BONTEMANTEL, HANS. This writer was a member of the city council of Amsterdam from 1652 to 1672. He made copious notes, including many about the events and procedure of the city government, which are now in the Gemeente-Archief, Amsterdam. Of them the following are of interest in connection with the Town Hall itself: [1] the manuscript *Resolutien van den Raad der Stad Amsterdam*, which gives an account, apparently written from day to day, of the proceedings and decisions of the city council. [2] Volumes I and II of the manuscript *Civiele en militaire regeering der Stad Amsterdam*, which contain a later account of the same proceedings, apparently based on the day to day account but with some additional information. These documents sometimes tell more about the proceedings than the minutes of the city council and in other cases, by variations of wording, add to their significance. [3] Volume III of the same manuscript, published by G. W. Kernkamp, *De regeeringe van Amsterdam soo in 't civiel als crimineel en militaire*, The Hague, 1897. This is an account of the city government illustrated by the relation of events which Bontemantel had witnessed, and is largely based on his earlier notes (see introduction by Kernkamp, Vol I. p. clxxiv).

QUELLIEN, ARTUS. Papers written in his own hand, concerning work done for the city of Amsterdam. Gemeente-Archief, Amsterdam, Thes. Ord. 150. The papers, which bear various early numbers, have also been numbered in a later hand, and this later numbering has been referred to for convenience here though it does not indicate their chronological order. Some of the papers bear accounts of work done and payments made, and others lists of work delivered, some repeating the information given in others. The accounts are not complete, though they record payments for the greater part of the sculpture of the Town Hall and for many of the models made for it. Differences in style between some of the pieces mentioned show that not all the works referred to were made by Quellien's hand. One of the accounts was dated by Quellien, and the approximate dates of the rest can be worked out from the dates of payments recorded in them. Comparisons show that on sheet no. 11 the sculptor made a list of work completed, repeating information given in a number of the surviving accounts. This list opens with three items which are not mentioned elsewhere in the papers, and except for one not connected with the Town Hall the remaining items on it are repeated from the earliest of the accounts, taking these in chronological order and with no omissions. The entries themselves are given in similar wording, none are omitted, and they are very seldom rearranged. Since all the items for the Town Hall which are listed, except the first three, were taken from these accounts, and since there are no large gaps between the dates of the payments recorded in them, it can safely be concluded that they form an unbroken series. The sheets bearing these accounts are, in chronological order, nos. 5, 6, 4 and 8 (which two were receipted on the same date and together form a single list), 3, 10, 2 and 9. It follows that both this series of accounts and the summary on sheet no. 11, which is itself undated, give complete and roughly chronological lists of work delivered between 6th January 1651, when the earliest payment recorded on no. 5 was made, and 4th November 1652, when the items listed on no. 9 were paid for. The descriptions of the first three items mentioned on no. 11, and the prices recorded, make it almost certain that they were all models for the exterior of the building. From the items that follow in the list it can safely be concluded that no sculpture and probably no models for the interior had been made before those mentioned in the dateable papers. The later accounts do not appear to be complete, and there are no later summaries. It must be added that Kroon's arrangement and dating of the information contained in Quellien's papers, in his *Stadhuis* (q. v.), pp. 107–15, is misleading.

194

CRITICAL BIBLIOGRAPHY

This list includes only those published works (books, periodicals, articles, and in a few cases single items in compilations) which for convenience have been referred to in the notes by shortened titles. Comments and explanations have been added where it seemed desirable. The list is not intended as a complete bibliography on the artists and subjects mentioned. For fuller bibliographies the reader is referred to the Catalogus der Kunsthistorische Bibliotheek in het Rijksmuseum te Amsterdam, Amsterdam, 1934-6. *For bibliographies on Dutch subjects see also the following publications of the Nederlandse Oudheidkundige Bond :* Repertorium van boek-werken betreffende Nederlandse monumenten van geschiedenis en kunst *[etc.],* The Hague, 1950, *and (mainly for articles in periodicals)* Repertorium betreffende Nederlandse monumenten van geschiedenis en kunst *[etc.],* The Hague, 1940-3.

★ ★ ★

Amsterdam in de zeventiende eeuw. By A. Bredius and others. The Hague, 1897-1904.

Beschryvinge van 't Stadhuis van Amsterdam, met een verklaaringe van de zinnebeeldige figuren, schilderwerken en beelden, enz. die zo wel binnen als buiten dit heerlyk gebouw gevonden worden. Amsterdam, 1782. One of a long series of guide-books to the Town Hall published in Dutch, English, French and German during the eighteenth century The earliest of those of which there is a copy in the Library of the Gemeente-Archief, Amsterdam, is a French one, quite clearly a translation, dated 1714; the latest are Dutch and English ones of 1782. The texts apparently vary very little. The Dutch edition of 1782 has been referred to except where it is stated otherwise.

Bouw schilder en beeldhouwkonst, van het Stadhuis te Amsteldam. vertoont in CIX figuuren : waarin niet alleen de vier buiten gevels van dat prachtig gebouw verbeeld, maar ook alle de sieraaden van binnen, vertoond worden . . . Met eene geschichtkundige uitlegging van ieder figuur, tot het verstaan der verscheidene onderwerpen, waar van de meesten uit de aêloude geschiedenissen en verdichtselen getrokken zyn. Amsterdam, n.d. In this work, whose style suggests that it is of the eighteenth century, the engravings of the architecture and sculpture of the Town Hall made by Jacob Vennekool and Hubertus Quellien (see under these names) were republished in a single volume, with an introductory description of the plates which is of unknown authorship. In this introduction what is portrayed is described in some detail, and in many cases explanations of the symbolism of the sculpture are given. The work was presumably first published early in the century since an edition published in French, Amsterdam, 1719, contains what appears to be an exact translation of the description of the plates.

Catalogus van de beeldhouwwerken in het Nederlandsch Museum voor Geschiedenis en Kunst te Amsterdam. Amsterdam, 1915. Compiled by A. Pit. At the time of writing no more recent catalogue of the sculpture has been issued.

Catalogus der Nederlandsche en op Nederland betrekking hebbende gedenkpenningen. Koninklijk Kabinet van Munten, Penningen en Gesneden Steenen. The Hague, 1903-6.

Duizend jaar bouwen in Nederland (Heemschut Bibliotheek). By S. J. Fockema Andreae and others. Amsterdam, 1948-57.

Hollantsche Parnas, of verscheide gedichten. Collected by T. van Domselaar. Vol. I. Amsterdam, 1660.

Kunstgeschiedenis der Nederlanden. Edited by H. E. van Gelder and J. Duverger. Utrecht [etc.], 1954–6.

Nieuw Nederlandsch biografisch woordenboek. Edited by P. C. Molhuysen and P. J. Blok. Leiden, 1911–37.

Olyf-krans der vreede, door de doorluchtigste geesten, en geleerdste mannen, deezes tijds, gevlochten. Amsterdam, 1649; and a later edition of the same work: *Olyf-krans der vrede, door de doorluchtigste geesten en geleerdste mannen van dien tyd gevlochten* [etc.], Amsterdam, 1750. An anthology of works on the Peace of Munster, 1648. The edition of 1750 is very largely a reprint of the earlier one. The text of the peace treaty is given, in Dutch, in the 1649 edition only. All other items referred to and quoted here are given in both, and for these the edition of 1750 has been used. A similar reprint appeared in 1748.

'Trompet of Lofrede over den Eeuwigen Nederlantschen Vrede. Aen de Edele en Grootmogende Heeren Staten van Hollant en Westvrieslant', in *Olyf-krans* (q. v.), 1750, pp. XXI-XLVIII. It is stated that this oration was translated from the Latin original by "D. A.", but the name of the author is not given, and is unknown to the present writer.

Zeven eeuwen Amsterdam. Edited by A. E. d'Ailly. Amsterdam, n.d.

ANSLO, R[EINIER]. 'Het gekroonde Amsterdam, met het nieuw Stadthuis, gegrondtvest door Gerbrandt Pankras, Jakob de Graaf, Sybrandt Valconier, Peter Schaap, der Burgemeesteren zonen en neven, onder 't gezag derzelve heeren', in *Olyf-krans* (q. v.), 1750, pp. 163–82; also printed in the edition of 1649. A poem written on the laying of the foundation-stone of the new Town Hall.

ASSELIJN, T[HOMAS]. [1] 'Broederschap der schilderkunst', in *Hollantsche Parnas* (q. v.), pp. 17–33. The poem first appeared in a separate publication in 1654, but since this edition has no pagination the later one has been referred to here. Thomas Asselijn, a minor poet, was in all probability a relation of the painter Jan Asselijn. Jan was a connection by marriage of the artist Nikolaes de Helt Stocade, who made paintings for the Town Hall and was a friend of Artus Quellien and Stalpaert (E. W. Moes in Thieme-Becker s. v. Asselijn; A. Bredius, 'Het schildersregister van Jan Sysmus', *Oud-Holland*, VIII, 1890, p. 231); both Jan and Thomas Asselijn came originally from Dieppe (E. W. Moes and J. A. Worp in *Nieuw Nederlandsch biografisch woordenboek*, Vol. I, s. v. Jan and Thomas Asselijn). Thomas had made poems on, and probably as part of, the decorations for the feast held by the artists and poets of Amsterdam to celebrate St. Luke's day in 1653 (see Katharine Fremantle, 'Cornelis Brisé and the Festoon of Peace', *Oud-Holland*, LXIX, 1954, pp. 222–4 and n. 21). His 'Broederschap der schilderkunst' was written on the occasion of the artists' feast of 1654, at which a 'brotherhood of painting' was set up, as the full title in the original edition demonstrates. It reads: "Broederschap der schilderkunst, ingewydt door schilders, beeldthouwers en des zelfs begunstigers; op den 21 van Wynmaent 1654, op St. Joris Doelen, in Amsterdam" ('Brotherhood of of painting, inaugurated by painters, sculptors and the well-wishers of the same; on the 21st of October 1654 in St. Joris' Doelen, in Amsterdam'). It is thus likely that Asselijn was familiar with the views held in artistic circles in Amsterdam, and that his poem to some extent reflects the ideas of the artists who were present at the feast, some of whom were already working and others about to work on the decoration of the Town Hall (the names of a number of artists who attended the feast given by Jan Vos, 'Strydt tusschen de Doodt en Natuur', *Gedichten*, Vol. [1], pp. 140–1). Its decoration was the great artistic undertaking of the moment in Amsterdam and cannot have failed to be in Asselijn's mind when he wrote in the artists' honour. He does not describe the Town Hall, but his view of the rise of the city and her present glory, of the significance of her new buildings, including this 'show piece' which vies with antiquity (p. 29), and of the activities of her brotherhood of artists who are raising temples to the glory of Pallas and Apollo on the banks of the IJ (p. 31) is, because of the circumstances in which he wrote, of exceptional significance. [2] 'Uytvaart van den heer Jakob van Kampen, Heer van Ranbroek, vermaart bouwmeester en schilder, tot Amersvoort, den 22 September in 't jaar 1657', in *Hollantsche Parnas*, 1660, pp. 419–20. The poem, as it appears in Abraham van Bemmel's description of Amersfoort of 1760, has been noticed in connection with Van Campen, but there it is reprinted anonymously. The evidence it provides about him is strengthened by the earlier date of publication and the identity of the author, which have recently come to light.

BOEKEN, A. 'Over de voorgeschiedenis van den bouw van het voormalige Amsterdamsche Stadhuis', *Jaarboek Amstelodamum*, XVII, 1919, pp. 1–30. See also list of Manuscript Sources s. v. *Resolutien der Vroedschap*.

BONTEMANTEL, HANS. See list of Manuscript Sources.

BOSSCHERE, J. DE. *De kerken van Antwerpen (schilderijen, beeldhouwwerken, geschilderde glasramen, enz.) in de XVIIIe eeuw beschreven door Jacobus de Wit. Met aanteekeningen door– – en grondplannen.* (Uitgaven der Antwerpsche Bibliophilen.) Antwerp and The Hague, 1910.

BRAY, SALOMON DE. See s. v. Cornelis Danckerts.

BROM, GISBERT, 'Een Italiaansche reisbeschrijving der Nederlanden (1677–1678)', *Bijdragen en mededelingen van het Historisch Genootschap*, XXXVI, 1915, pp. 81–230.

CONTI, NATALIS. *Mythologiae sive explicationis fabularum, libri decem* [etc.]. Pavia, 1637. First published in 1551.

DANCKERTS, CORNELIS. *Architectura moderna, ofte bouwinge van onsen tyt . . . gedaen by den zeer-vermaerden en vernuften Mr. Hendrick de Keyser* [etc.]. Amsterdam, 1631. Danckerts was master builder to the city of Amsterdam and worked with De Keyser on buildings for the city. The text is by Salomon de Bray.

D[APPER], O[LFERT]. *Historische beschryving der Stadt Amsterdam* [etc.]. Amsterdam, 1663. This is one of the earliest of the descriptions of the city in which the seventeenth-century Town Hall is included. The descriptions of the buildings of Amsterdam given in this work, in the third edition of the description by Fokkens, 1664, and in Van Domselaer's description, 1665, vary only slightly, and it is stated by Van Domselaer that the account given by Dapper was written by I. Commelin (see Wouter Nijhoff, *Bibliographie van Noord-Nederlandsche plaatsbeschrijvingen tot het einde der 18de eeuw*, 2nd ed., The Hague, 1953, under these writers). Since for this study it has not been possible to analyse each of the early descriptions of the Town Hall in detail the version given by Dapper has mainly been taken to represent them. The probable authorship of the account he gives is not mentioned in the references in each case separately. Measurements too fine to have been taken from the building itself are given in the description; they do not always agree with those of Vennekool in their details, and the source from which they were taken remains unknown. In describing the symbolism of the Town Hall's decoration it appears that the writer borrowed extensively from the *Wtleggingh* of Carel van Mander, and at times added details given by Van Mander which are not to be seen in the decoration itself; e. g. he states that Apollo's cloak is purple and has Medusa's head depicted on it *(see Wtleggingh*, p. 126 r. and *Beschryving*, p. 361) although no Medusa's head is to be seen and the relief of Apollo is of white marble. In one passage which Van Mander himself had taken from the *Mythologiae* of Conti it is clear that it was Van Mander, not Conti, whose work the writer relied on (see text, p. 59 n. 3).

DYK, JAN VAN. *Kunst en historiekundige beschryving en aanmerkingen over alle de schilderyen op het Stadhuis te Amsterdam.* Amsterdam, 1758. This writer cleaned and repaired many of the paintings in the Town Hall. His information about the paintings is in general reliable.

EVERS, HANS GERHARD. *Peter Paul Rubens.* Munich, 1942.

FRANSOLET, MARIETTE. *François du Quesnoy, sculpteur d'Urbain VIII, 1597–1643* (Académie Royale de Belgique). Brussels, 1941.

FREMANTLE, KATHARINE. 'Some Drawings by Jacob van Campen for the Royal Palace of Amsterdam', *Oud-Holland*, LXVIII, 1953, pp. 73–95.

GABRIELS, JULIANE. *Artus Quellien de Oude, "Kunstryck belthouwer".* Antwerp, 1930.

GEVAERTS, CASPER. See s. v. Casperius Gevartius.

GEVARTIUS, CASPERIUS. *Pompa introitus honori Serenissimi Principis Ferdinandi Austriaci Hispaniarum Infantis . . . a S.P.Q. Antverp. decreta et adornata* [etc.]. Antwerp, 1641.

GEYL, P. *Geschiedenis van de Nederlandse stam.* (Revised edition.) Amsterdam and Antwerp, 1948–.

HOOGEWERFF, G. J. *De twee reizen van Cosimo de' Medici Prins van Toscane door de Nederlanden (1667–1669).* Amsterdam, 1919.

HOUBRAKEN, ARNOLD. *De groote schouburgh der Nederlantsche konstschilders en schilderessen.* Amsterdam, 1718–21.

HUYGENS, CONSTANTIJN. [1] *De gedichten van– –.* Edited by J. A. Worp. Groningen, 1892–9. [2] Correspondence, see s. v. J. A. Worp.

KERNKAMP, G. W. See list of Manuscript Sources s. v. Hans Bontemantel.

KILIAN, CORNELIS [Cornelis van Kiel]. *Etymologicum Teutonicae linguae sive dictionarium Teutonico-Latinum . . . studio et opera Cornelii Kiliani Dufflaei . . . curante Gerardo Hasselto Arnhemiensi. Quiet suas adnotationes adiecit.* Utrecht, 1777. This work, the earliest dictionary of the Dutch language, was first published in Antwerp in 1574, although it was given the title "Etymologicon theutonicae linguae" only with the third edition, in

1599 (Geyl, *Geschiedenis*, Vol. I, p. 338). In the edition of 1777, which has been used here, it appears that the annotations of Gerard Hasselt are given separately at the foot of each page; all references here are to what is apparently the text of Kilian himself.

KROON, A. W. *Het Amsterdamsche Stadhuis (thans Paleis), 1625–1700. Zijne geschiedenis naar onuitgegeven officiele bronnen bewerkt door– –.* Amsterdam, 1867. The author states (Intro. p. ix) that he has taken from the documents only so much 'as was absolutely necessary to explain' his subject, i.e. the history of the Amsterdam Town Hall. His pioneer account of the information in the city records, which has been relied on by a number of later writers, is incomplete, very many of his references are inaccurate, and some of his transcriptions are hard to recognize. Not all the statements made by Kroon could be checked by the present writer, and more information may come to light later. His work has been referred to as sparingly as possible here, but it has been of great importance as a pointer to other information.

LEDERLE, URSULA. *Gerechtigkeitsdarstellungen in deutschen und niederländischen Rathäusern.* Philippsburg, 1937.

LOON, GERARD A. VAN. *Beschryving der Nederlandsche historiepenningen* [etc.]. The Hague, 1723–31.

LUTTERVELT, R. VAN. *Het Raadhuis aan de Dam* (Heemkennis Amsterdam). Amsterdam, n.d.

MAGURN, RUTH SAUNDERS. *The Letters of Peter Paul Rubens.* Harvard, 1955.

MANDER, CAREL VAN. [1] *Het Schilder-boeck* [etc.]. Alkmaar, 1603–4; general title-page: Haarlem, 1604. The books of artists' lives which form part of this work are referred to here under the general title. [2] *Wtleggingh op den Metamorphosis Pub. Ovidij Nasonis* [etc.]. Haarlem, 1604. This and the *Uvtbeeldinge der figueren* [etc.], which is paginated with it, are referred to under *Wtleggingh*. They from part of the *Schilder-boeck* but later appeared separately.

M[EYSTER], E[VERARD]. *Het eerste deel der goden land-spel om Amersfoort, van 't nieuw Stad-huys binnen Amsterdam. Gespeelt en vertoont aldaer. Anno 1655. Wel eer door Jor. E. M. gerijmt. Met uytleggingh verlicht en verciert door D. v. W. Den tweeden druck.* Amsterdam, n. d. [And the second part of the same work:] *Hemelsch land-spel, of twede deel der goden land-spel om Amersfoort, van 't nieuw Stad-huys binnen Amsterdam. Gespeelt, en aldaer vertoont. Anno 1655. Door E. M. in Nimmer Dor.* Amsterdam, 1655. Although the edition of the 'first part' referred to here is designated 'The second edition' no official first edition is known. A pirated edition of both parts, less accurately printed and without notes, was published in 1655. A programme for a performance in the present writer's possession dates from the same year. "D. v. W" remains unidentified. The writer and poetaster Everard Meyster was a neighbour of Van Campen's at Amersfoort, they both had properties there, and by 1655 both were Roman Catholics; there appears to be no further evidence about their relations except that contained in Meyster's play, which was clearly written to extol Van Campen and his masterpiece. In the course of the action the shades of a number of artists and architects of the past are summoned by Jupiter to give their opinion of the new Town Hall, and in doing so they describe it. It can be shown, since there are strong verbal reminiscences as well as a likeness of theme, that

199

Meyster's work was largely based on Asselijn's 'Broederschap der Schilderkunst' (q.v.), of 1654, in which Apollo, Pallas and Mercury visit Amsterdam and Apollo cross-questions his companions about the city and its buildings, including the Town Hall, very much as Jupiter cross-questions the artists in Meyster's play. There does not appear to be any connection with Vondel's *Inwydinge* (q. v.) of 1655, which also contains a description of the building. Vondel's work is differently constructed and has only such likenesses of wording as might arise by chance. The two writers mention different features of the building's design, and their sources of information about it were evidently different; in describing the western tympanum, whose design was changed considerably during the course of its preparation (see text, Ch. VII), Meyster mentions the sledges which appeared in the version shown on the model in the Waag Museum, Amsterdam, and in the drawings connected with it, and Vondel mentions the four Continents bringing their gifts who appear in the prints of 1650 and in the final design (lines 875–86). Vondel was shown the building by Stalpaert, who told him about it (lines 1169–70), and he appears to have seen the scheme as it was proposed, and partly executed, in 1655. The sources used by Meyster, whose account is more detailed than Vondel's and who appears to lampoon Stalpaert (Pt. I, p. 43) remains unknown, but a comparison with what was executed and with other information about the design suggests that they were authoritative. It is possible that he had access to drawings or other records at Amersfoort, some of which were outdated when he wrote. His enthusiasm for Van Campen suggests that he would use his sources of information carefully in order to do him justice, but the task of describing an intricate three-dimensional scheme, and of doing so in verse, seems to have been beyond his powers and his account of the building, though informative, is a confused one. His account of the *vierschaar*, in which he describes details not known from other sources, has therefore to be used with caution. The work is of value in explaining the significance of some of the features described, and the notes added to the 'second edition' of the first part by "D. v. W." add to this information. The description of the building is incomplete. In the printer's foreword to the first part, in which the exterior of the Town Hall is described, second and third parts describing respectively the lower and upper parts of the interior are promised, but of these only the 'second part' appears to have been published, that referred to here, and this breaks off abruptly and for no evident reason in the course of the first act, after the *vierschaar* alone has been described. The *Land-spel* has been discussed by Kroon, *Stadhuis* (q. v.), pp. 127–31, and by A. W. Weissman in 'Daniel Stalpaert', *Oud-Holland*, XXIX, 1911, pp. 72–77 and later writings, for its evidence about the circumstances of Van Campen's withdrawal from the building of the Town Hall. Meyster's bitter references to jealousy and to the claims of others to credit for the building (see esp. Pt. I, pp. 26–27, 42–43 and 83) can only be connected with this event, which took place in or after December 1654 (see text p. 25 n. 1). The play appears to have been written in Van Campen's defence and at this point. It may therefore be presumed that all that Meyster describes belonged to Van Campen's own projects for the building. Yet the play does not provide evidence for the date of any part of his scheme because, as has been indicated, part of Meyster's information was out of date before he used it, and because he described work that had yet to be carried out.

NEURDENBURG, ELISABETH. *Hendrick de Keyser, beeldhouwer en bouwmeester van Amsterdam.* Amsterdam [1930].

NOACH, ARNOLDUS. 'Een vergeten ontwerp voor het Paleis op den Dam', *Jaarboek Amstelodamum*, XXXIII, 1936, pp. 141–54.

PALLADIO, ANDREA. *I quattro libri dell' architettura* [etc.]. Venice, 1570.

QUELLIEN, HUBERTUS. *Van de voornaemste statuen ende ciraten, vant konstrijck Stadthuys van Amstelredam, tweeste in marmer gemaeckt, door Artus Quellinus, beelthouwer der voorseyde stadt.* Amsterdam, 1665–9. The author of this work, a draughtsman and engraver, was a brother of Artus Quellien the elder. His engravings record the main parts of the sculptural decoration of the Town Hall as it was carried out, and show in addition a few designs for sculptured panels which must have been intended for the building and are otherwise unknown; the positions for these designs are not indicated. The inscriptions on the engravings are not consistent and so do not give a certain indication of the authorship of the sculpture. Many are initialled "A. Q.", while only two engravings, both of works in the *vierschaar* made before Van Campen's withdrawal, bear in addition the letters "INV." These are the relief depicting the Judgement of Solomon, which was seen in 1653 by Robert Bargrave (MS. A *Relation*, fol. 91 r.) and that showing Medusa's head, mentioned as having already been made in A. Quellien, MS. Papers, no. 12, an account which can be shown to date from before 28th March 1654. In the engraving of the west tympanum, Vol. II, pl. 2, the design is attributed to Quellien (see p. 171). Vennekool, who claimed to represent the building as Van Campen designed it, shows, in plates D and E of his *Afbeelding*, the reliefs of both pediments as they were executed and a rather different version of that of the west pediment only in plate G, which either shows an otherwise unknown stage in the development of the design or else, because it appears at an angle in this engraving, was inaccurately drawn. Moreover either H. Quellien or his publisher took the liberty of describing Artus on their title-page as sculptor to the city of Amsterdam, an office that he never held, and it is possible that exaggerated claims were made for him elsewhere in the publication.

RIPA, CESARE. [1] *Della novissima iconologia di Cesare Ripa Perugino... arrichita... dal Sig. Gio: Zaratino Castellini Romano.* Padua, 1624. [2] The translation of Ripa's work by D. P. Pers: *Iconologia, of uytbeeldingen des verstands... verrijckt... door... Giov. Zaratino Castellini Romano.* Amsterdam, 1644. The Italian edition referred to has been used except where addition made by Pers may be of significance for the decoration of the Town Hall, but a note on the translation may be added here. In his introduction (p. *3 v.) Pers states that among the later editions of Ripa's work he knew of those published at Padua in 1611, 1615, 1618, 1625 and 1630, adding that he had examined that of 1630, "il piu che novissima Iconologia", and had enlarged his own work 'after' it. He evidently referred to *Della piu che novissima iconologia di Cesare Ripa Perugino... ampliata dal Sig. Cav. Gio. Zaratino Castellini Romano, in questa ultima editione di imagini, e discorsi, con indici copiosi, e ricorretta,* Padua, 1630, of which there is a copy in the Library of the British Museum, London. It seems that Pers took his list of editions, in an abridged form, from that given in the introduction to this work, although, unless a misprint has to be reckoned with, he added to it. It seems, on comparing the text of Pers with the more readily available edition of 1624, that he translated with care, omitting only detailed references, some quotations, and an occasional further version of a figure already illustrated. He made occasional additions, as he himself stated: 'sometimes I have... added what I had noticed in various writers, and distinguished the same with little stars★★★ in some places' (p. *4 v.). In other places, however, he did not distinguish them; his addition to Ripa's description of America (see text p. 180) is not so marked.

ROOSES, MAX. [1] *L' oeuvre de P. P. Rubens*. Antwerp, 1886–92. [2] *Rubens' leven en werken*. Amsterdam [etc.], 1903.

SEWEL, WILLIAM [and Egbert Buys]. *A Compleat Dictionary English and Dutch, to which is added a Grammar, for both Languages. Originally Compiled by William Sewel; but now, not only Reviewed, and more than the Half Part Augmented, yet According to the Modern Spelling, Entirely Improved; by Egbert Buys*. Amsterdam, 1766. Sewel's dictionary was first published in 1691. The edition of 1766, the only one that has been readily available to the present writer, has been referred to, though unfortunately there is no means of distinguishing Buys' additions from the original text.

SLOTHOUWER, D. F. *De paleizen van Frederik Hendrik*. Leiden, 1945. Among the many documents given by Slothouwer in the appendices to this work are letters from Huygens' correspondence which have bearing on architecture, some of which are among those quoted here. It has not been considered necessary to give separate references to his quotations.

STALPAERT, DANIEL. See List of Sources s. v. Prints of 1650.

STRONG, EUGENIA. *La scultura Romana da Augusto a Costantino*. Florence, 1923–6.

THIEME, ULRICH, and Felix Becker (editors). *Allgemeines Lexikon der bildenden Künstler von der Antike bis zur Gegenwart*. Leipzig, 1907–50.

VENNEKOOL, JACOB. *Afbeelding van 't Stadt Huys van Amsterdam, in dartigh coopere plaaten, geordineert door Jacob van Campen en geteeckent door Iacob Vennekool*. Amsterdam, 1661. Vennekool was Van Campen's draughtsman. The writer of the dedicatory letter that prefaces this work mentions Van Campen's wish that the Town Hall should be completed to his designs, together with his own wish to complete the publication of the plates depicting it projected by his, the author's, father, as his reasons for the production. This as well as the wording of the title-page, suggests that the plates show Van Campen's design unaltered. All the plates, except for pls. X, Y and Z and pl. Q, which seems to have had alterations made on it, are consistent with each other except in minor details. Plates X, Y and Z, which represent the council chamber of the Civic Guard, are consistent with each other but show an alteration in the design which is recorded in pl. C with the words: 'This wall was not made in the building, but in order to give the war council chamber more space [it was] removed as one can see in the figure Y, yet according to Van Campen's plan [it was] arranged like this'. Hence these plates, though they may well show an adaptation of Van Campen's design for the room (the proposed paintings seem to reflect his style) cannot be taken to record his intentions for it. Some parts of the introduction to the plates, as M. E. Kroneberg has pointed out in her introduction to Vondel's *Inwydinge*, pp. 7–8, are based on Vondel's poem. There are, however, some independent passages of description, and these add to the information provided in the plates. The author of the introduction to this work remains unknown.

VERMEULEN, F. A. J. *Handboek tot de geschiedenis der Nederlandsche bouwkunst*. The Hague, 1928–41.

Vitruvius Pollio, M. *De Architectura.* The edition, with an English translation, by Frank Granger, London and New York, 1931-4 (Loeb Classical Library), has been referred to and quoted.

Vondel, Joost van den. [1] *De werken van Vondel* (Wereldbibliotheek). Edited by J. F. M. Sterck and others. Amsterdam, 1927-40 [2] *Inwydinge van 't Stadthuis 't Amsterdam.* Edited by M. E. Kronenberg. Deventer, 1913. The first has been used except for the poems 'Inwydinge van 't Stadthuis t' Amsterdam', 'Matige regeering', and 'Maghtige neering', for which the edition by Kronenberg has been referred to and quoted. The 'Inwydinge' was published in 1655 and was dedicated to the Amsterdam burgomasters. For information about Vondel's description of the Town Hall see s. v. Everard Meyster.

Vos, Jan. *Alle de gedichten van den poëet- -.* Collected by J[acob] L[escaille]. Amsterdam, 1662-71. Jan Vos was by profession a glazier, who worked on buildings belonging to the city of Amsterdam, including the Town Hall (MS. *Res. Thes. Ord.* 28 Feb. 1657). He designed pageants, was concerned with the Amsterdam theatre, and wrote much verse. Three of his works are referred to here, all of which appear in the *Gedichten.* They are: [1] 'Beschryving der vertooningen; die, op't sluiten der vreede, tusschen zijne Majesteit van Spanje, en de Staaten der Vereenigde Neederlanden, in 't jaar 1648, door order der Wel-Eed. Groot-achtbaare Heeren Burgermeesteren, t' Amsterdam op de Markt vertoont zijn', [Vol. I] pp. 579-86. [2] 'Strydt tusschen de Doodt en Natuur, of zeege der Schilderkunst', [Vol. I] pp. 123-41. [3] 'Inwyding van het Stadthuis t' Amsterdam', [Vol. I] pp. 333-52. [1] In the 'Beschryving der vertooningen' Vos gives the verses composed to describe the show which he devised for performance on the Dam during the peace celebrations of 1648, the last of the three shows given on that occasion by order of the burgomasters. The verses appear in *Olyf-krans* (q. v.) but here have been referred to in Vos' collected works. [2] The 'Strydt tusschen de Doodt en Natuur' was written on the occasion of the dinner held in celebration of St. Luke's Day 1654 by the artists of Amsterdam (Katharine Fremantle, 'Cornelis Brisé and the Festoon of Peace', *Oud-Holland*, LXIX, 1954, pp. 225-6). It consists of a long description of a struggle between Death and Nature, in which Art comes to the rescue of Nature and saves her from death, at the end of which there is a short but informative passage about the feast (see also s. v. Thomas Asselijn). [3] The 'Inwyding', written on the inauguration of the new Town Hall, is dedicated to the burgomasters and treasurers of Amsterdam who held office in 1655, so that it unquestionably dates from that year. In comparing it with Vondel's *Inwydinge* one suspects that Vos covertly took a number of ideas from this work, notable the mention of a series of catastrophies introduced by Envy and culminating in the fire of the old Town Hall, out of whose ashes the new one rises like a phoenix. In view of Vondel's genius it cannot be supposed that the borrowing was on his side rather than on that of Vos. Vos mentions some parts of the Town Hall and its decoration that are not mentioned in Vondel's work.

Waal, H. van de. *Drie eeuwen vaderlandsche geschied-uitbeelding, 1500-1800 een iconologische studie.* The Hague, 1952.

Wagenaar, Jan. *Amsterdam in zyne opkomst, aanwas, geschiedenissen, voorregten, koophandel, gebouwen, kerkenstaat, schoolen, schutterye, gilden en regeeringe, beschreven door- -, historie-schryver der stad.* Amsterdam, 1760-88. Wagenaar's information about the city government is based on the city records, to which he gives detailed references. He designates himself 'writer of history to the city' on his title-page, and [H.] Brugmans, *Nieuw Nederlandsch biografisch woordenboek*, s. v. Jan Wagenaar, describes the work as 'semi-official'.

WEISSMAN. A. W. 'Jacob van Campen', *Oud-Holland*, XX, 1902, pp. 113–27 and 154–69.

WIT, JACOBUS DE. See s. v. J. de Bosschere.

WITTKOWER, RUDOLF. *Gian Lorenzo Bernini, the Sculptor of the Roman Baroque*. London, 1955.

WORP, J. A., ed. – HUYGENS, CONSTANTIJN, *De briefwisseling (1608–1687) Uitgegeven door J. A. Worp*. The Hague, 1911–17. (Rijks Geschiedkundige Publicatiën.) Passages quoted have been taken from the manuscripts themselves. Those merely referred to have been seen in Worp's published version.

WOTTON, HENRY. *The Elements of Architecture, Collected by – – Kt. from the Best Authors and Examples*. London, 1943. First published in 1624.

ZOET, JAN. 'De Zaale van Oranje, gebouwd by haare Hoogheid Amelie van Solms, Princesse Douarire van Oranje', in *d'Uitsteekenste digtkunstige werken door– –*, *Amsterdammer* [etc.], Amsterdam, 1719, pp. 177–89. This poem was first published after the writer's death, in the first edition of Zoet's works, 1675. The third edition is referred to here. The poem was commissioned by Amalia van Solms (P. Geyl, in *Nieuw Nederlandsch biografisch woordenboek*, Vol. I, s. v. Jan Soet) and was to be about the Oranjezaal in the Huis ten Bosch, but in the course of a lengthy description of the new Town Hall of Amsterdam (pp. 182–9) the poem breaks off before the Oranjezaal is reached. The date at which the work was given up is not evident, though the poet mentions three other poems (p. 179), of which the latest, Cats' 'Zorgvliet', appeared in 1658. Zoet's work contains particulars about the meaning of parts of the decoration of the Town Hall, though it adds no new details to what is known of the scheme itself. In the absence of more exact dating it can yield no evidence about the development of the scheme.

INDEX

The following are indexed: (1) subjects, themes, and motifs of the Amsterdam Town Hall's decoration, (2) other topics and representations discussed, (3) persons mentioned, (4) early sources of information.

Italics Entries concerning representations are given in *italics*. Unless it is stated otherwise they refer to those in which the Town Hall and its setting are recorded, or to parts of its decorative scheme.

* Asterisks refer to the List of Sources and Bibliography.

[ ] Sources of information about the main subjects are indicated in square brackets.

The titles of literary sources are referred to by catchwords. For Dutch works a short title in English is added.

INDEX

ILLUSTRATIONS

1. Medal commemorating the Town Hall's inauguration. By G. Pool. 1655. (a) Obverse: The Inaugural Procession Crosses the Dam. (b) Reverse: Argo Sails Home.

2. Amsterdam in 1536. Painting by Cornelis Anthonisz. Historisch Museum De Waag, Amsterdam.

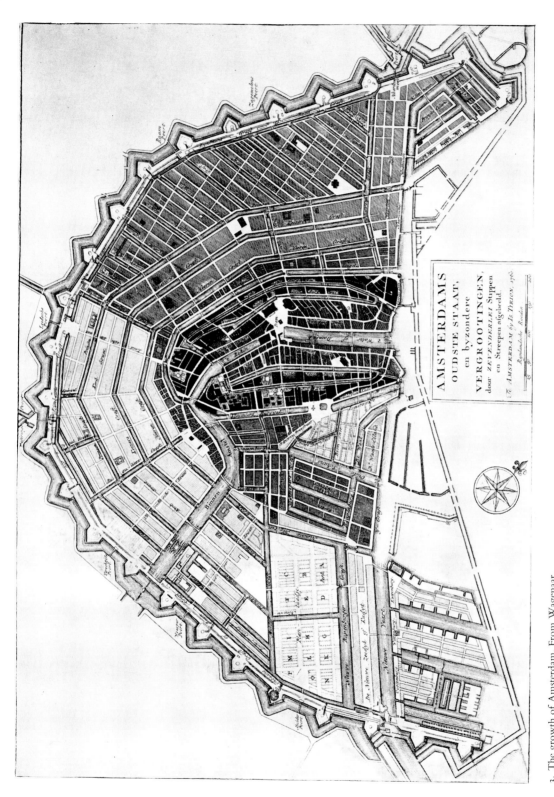

AMSTERDAMS
OUDSTE STAAT,
en byzondere
VERGROOTINGEN,
door ZALZENDERLEI Stippen
en Streepen afgebeeld.

TT AMSTERDAM by IS TIRION 1760.

3. The growth of Amsterdam. From Wagenaar.
  The darkest shading shows the mid-sixteenth-century city, all except the lightest that of 1650. Outer defences completed in 1662.

4. Amsterdam's mediaeval Town Hall in 1641. Painting by Saenredam. Rijksmuseum, Amsterdam.

5. Model for the seventeenth-century Town Hall. c. 1648. Historisch Museum De Waag, Amsterdam.

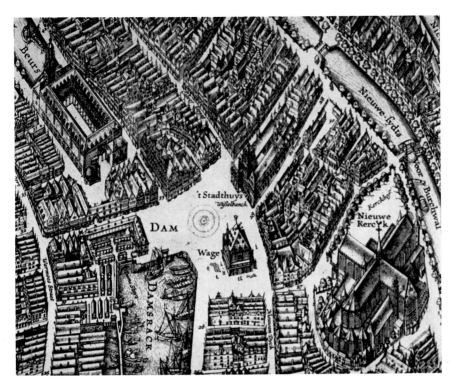

6. The city centre with mediaeval Town Hall. From map by Balthazar Florisz. 1625.

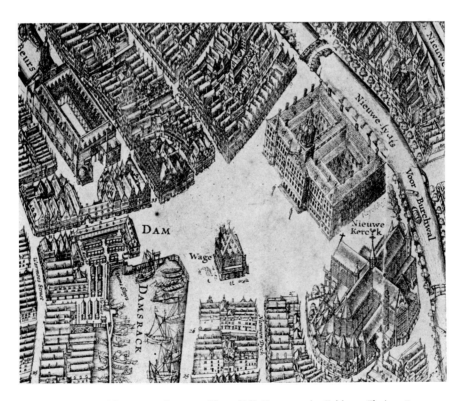

7. The city centre with seventeenth-century Town Hall. From map by Balthazar Florisz. 1657.

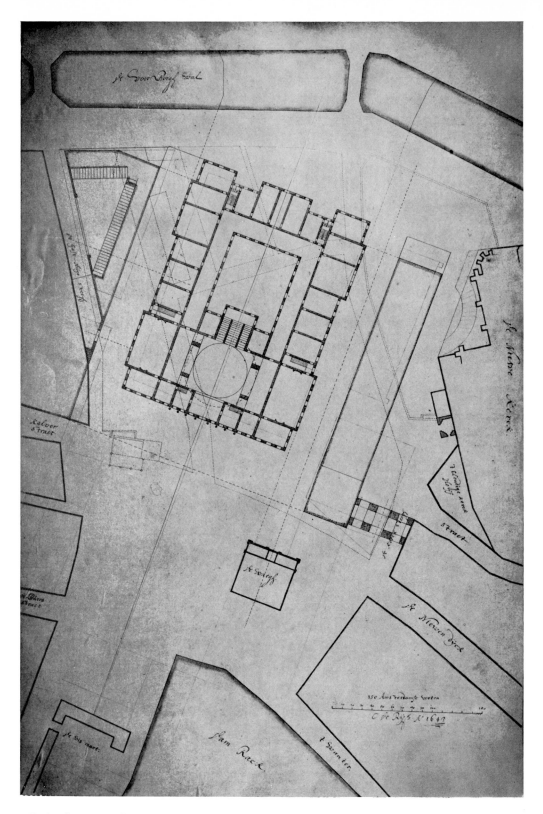

8. Project for Town Hall and Dam. 1643. Tracing of map by Danckerts. Gemeente-archief, Amsterdam.

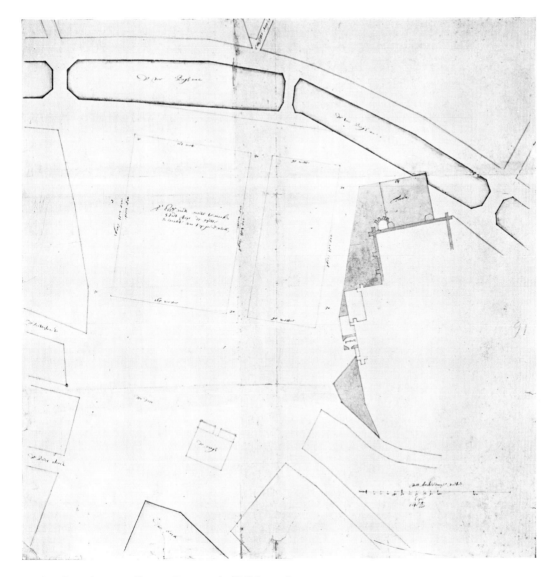

9. Plan of site of Town Hall. 1648. Gemeente-Archief, Amsterdam.

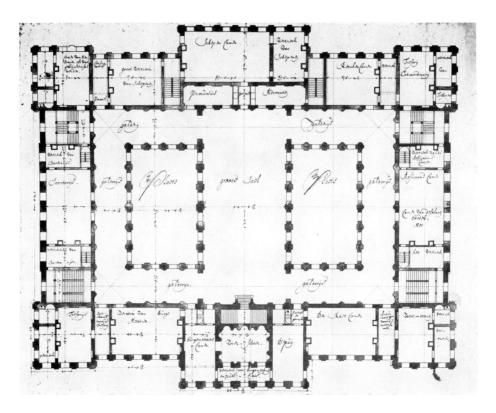

10. First floor plan of Town Hall. Project, 1648. Gemeente-Archief, Amsterdam.

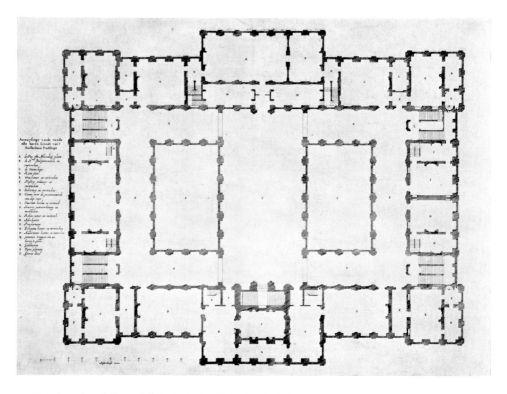

11. First floor plan of Town Hall. Project, 1650. Published by Stalpaert.

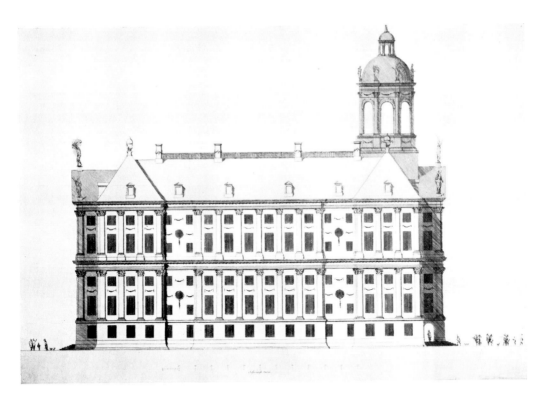

12. South elevation of Town Hall. Project, 1650. Published by Stalpaert.

VOOR-GEVEL VAN 'T AMSTERDAMS STADT HUYS

13. Front elevation of Town Hall. Project, 1650. Published by Stalpaert.

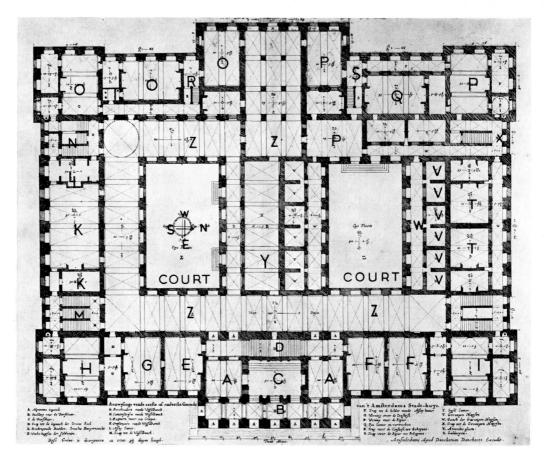

A	Public Entrance
B	Gallery in front of Vierschaar
C	The Vierschaar
D	Stair leading to Burgerzaal
E	Messengers; at night Civic Guard
F	Soldiers' Guard-rooms
G	Book-keepers of City Bank
H	Commissioners of City Bank
I	Suitable for a College
K	Receivers of City Bank
L	Assayer's Chamber
M	Stair to City Bank
N	Stair to Cellars of Assayers' Chamber
O	Caretaker's Quarters
P	Gaoler's Quarters
Q	Torture Chamber
R	Caretaker's Stair to Magistrates' Court
S	Gaoler's Stair to Magistrates' Court
T	Room for Scourging
V	Prisons
W	Passage to Prisons
X	Stair to Prisons
Y	Ammunition Store
Z	Galleries

14. Ground floor plan of Town Hall. After Vennekool.

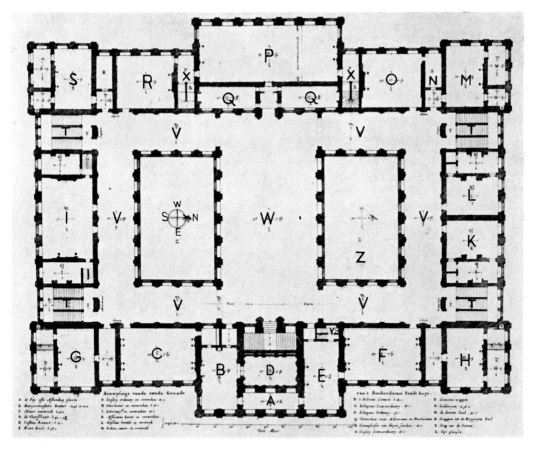

A Puy or Publication Gallery	N Sheriff's Chamber
B Burgomasters' Chamber	O Magistrates' Chamber
C Burgomasters' Council-room	P Magistrates' Court
D The Vierschaar	Q Rooms for Advocates and Prosecutors
E Chamber of Justice	R Commissioners for Petty Affairs
F Council Chamber	S Treasury Extraordinary
G Treasury	T Public Stairs
H Office of Trustees of Orphans	V Galleries
I Secretary's Office	W The Burgerzaal
K Chamber of Insurance	X Stairs to Council Chamber of Civic Guard
L Bankruptcy Office	Y Stair to Tower
M Accounts Office	Z Open Courts

15. First floor plan of Town Hall. After Vennekool.

16. The Cupola. From Vennekool.

17. Cupola from roof of Burgerzaal.

18. Front pediment. Detail.

19-20. Model for front pediment. Details. Historisch Museum De Waag, Amsterdam.

21. Front façade. Capitals.

22. Front façade. Festoon.

23. West pediment from Nieuwezijds Voorburgwal.

24. View from roof, looking towards west pediment.

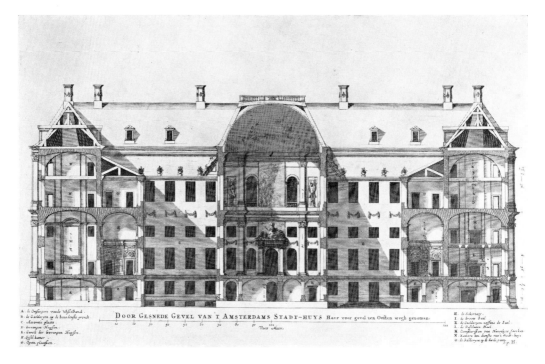

DOOR GESNEDE GEVEL VAN 'T AMSTERDAMS STADT-HUYS Haer voor gevel ten Oosten wegh genomen.

25. The Town Hall. Section, showing west end of Burgerzaal.

26. The Burgerzaal. Floor. From Vennekool.

27. The Burgerzaal, looking east. (All but ceiling shown in reverse.) From Vennekool.

28. The Burgerzaal. Design for ceiling. From Vennekool

30. The Burgerzaal. Design for east wall (in reverse). From Vennekool.

29. The Burgerzaal. Design for west wall. From Vennekool.

31. The Burgerzaal. Air and Fire.

32. The Burgerzaal. Earth.

33. The Burgerzaal, looking east.

34. The Burgerzaal. East entrance. Upper part.

35. The Burgerzaal. East entrance. Frieze: Moon and Stars.

36. The Burgerzaal. East entrance: Waterman.

37. The Burgerzaal. East entrance: Heavenly Twins.

38. North-east Gallery. From Vennekool.

39. Rembrandt. The Conspiracy of Claudius Civilis. Drawing of painting formerly in the South Gallery. Grafische Sammlung, Munich.

40. South Gallery, looking towards lunette formerly filled by Rembrandt's painting.

41. South Gallery. Diana.

42. South Gallery. Panel below Diana.

43. South Gallery. Door-top to right of Diana.

44. South Gallery. Door-top to left of Diana.

45. Model for door-top. Detail. Historisch Museum De Waag, Amsterdam.

46. South Gallery. Apollo.

47. South Gallery. Panel below Apollo.

48. South Gallery. Door-top to left of Apollo.

49. South Gallery. Door-top to right of Apollo.

50. South Gallery. Panel below Apollo: Musical Instruments.

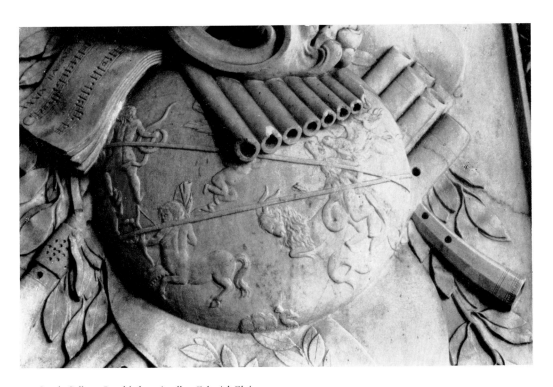

51. South Gallery. Panel below Apollo: Celestial Globe.

52. North Gallery. Mars and Venus.

53. North Gallery. Door-top to left of Mars.

54. North Gallery. Festoon beside Venus.

58. North Gallery. Venus. Detail.

57. North Gallery. Panel below Venus. Detail.

61. North Gallery, showing doors of Offices.

64. North Gallery. Door of Bankruptcy Office. Detail of decoration.

63. North Gallery. Door of Bankruptcy Office. Detail of frame.

65. The Burgerzaal. East wall. Amphion.

66. The Burgerzaal. East wall. Mercury and Argus.

67. North Gallery. Door-top beside Cybele.

68. The Burgerzaal. East wall. Entrance to Burgomasters' Chamber. Door-top.

De Zoon van Fabius gebied zijn eigen Vader
Van 't paard te ftijgen voor Stads eer en aghtbaarheid.

69. Burgomasters' Chamber. Mantelpiece frieze. Front.

70. Burgomasters' Chamber. Mantelpiece frieze. Left-hand end.

Die kent geen bloed en eischt dat hij eerbiedig nader.
Dus eert een man van staat het ampt hem opgeleid.

71. Burgomasters' Chamber. Mantelpiece frieze. Front (continuation).

72. Burgomasters' Chamber. Mantelpiece frieze. Right-hand end.

74. Burgomasters' Council-room. Ceiling. Detail.

73. Burgomasters' Council-room. Painting by De Hooch. Dreesman Collection.

Op 's Burgermeesters waght nagh 'Rome veinigh hoepen.
Als Markus Kurius, het aenseboden gout

75. Burgomasters' Council-room. South mantelpiece frieze. Detail.

Fabricius houdt stant, in Pyrrhus legertenten,
Het gout verzet hem niet, door schandelijcke zucht.

Noch el
Zoo z

76. Burgomasters' Council-room. North mantelpiece frieze. Detail.

79. Entrance to Magistrates' Court: Attributes of Hercules.

78. Entrance to Magistrates' Court. Detail.

80. Magistrates' Court. Mantelpiece frieze. Front. (a) Left, (b) central, (c) right-hand sections.

83. Magistrates' Court. Mantelpiece. Painting and frieze.

81. Magistrates' Court. Mantelpiece frieze. Left-hand end.

82. Magistrates' Court. Mantelpiece frieze. Right-hand end.

DE VIERSCHAER ten Zuyden.

84. The Vierschaar. South wall. From Vennekool.

DE VIERSCHAER ten Westen.

85. The Vierschaar. West wall. From Vennekool.

87 The Vierschaar Caryatids

86 The Vierschaar looking north

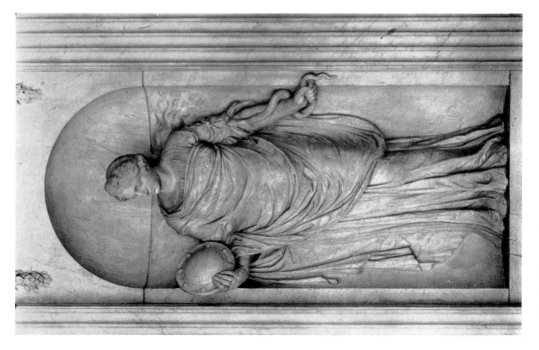

89. The *Vierschaar*. Prudence.

88. The *Vierschaar*. Judgement of Solomon.

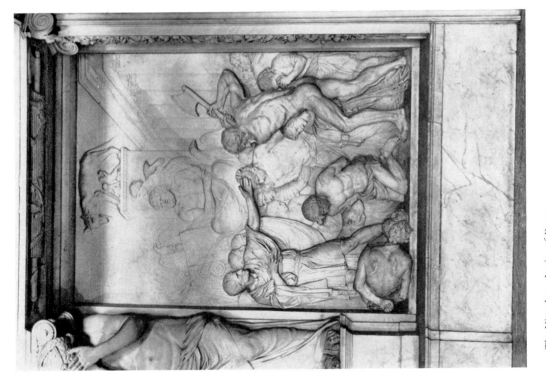

93. The Vierschaar. Justice of Brutus.

92. Justice of Brutus. Detail.

95. Model of 'doors' for the Vierschaar, Rijksmuseum, Amsterdam.

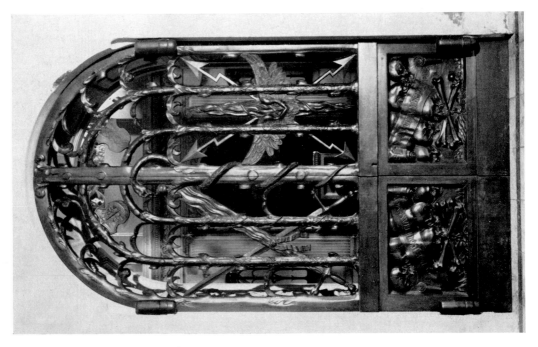

94. The Vierschaar. Doors.

97. The Vierschaar. The Secretary's Seat.

96. The Vierschaar. The Serpent of the Fall.

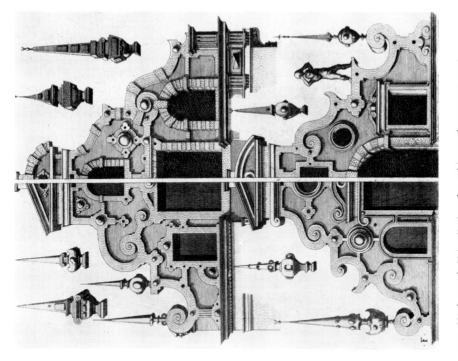

100. Vredeman de Vries. Designs for architectural ornament. 1578.

99. De Key. Meat Market, Haarlem. Detail.

101. De Keyser. Zuiderkerk, Amsterdam. Begun 1603. Engraving from Commelin.

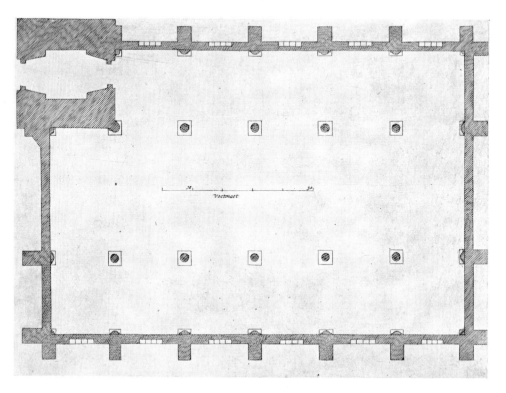

Voetmaet

102. De Keyser. Zuiderkerk, Amsterdam. Plan. From Danckerts.

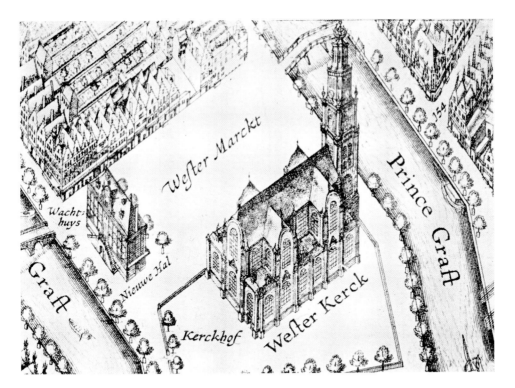

Wester Marckt

Wacht-
huys

Graft

Nieuwe Hal

Kerckhof

Wester Kerck

Prince Graft

154

103. De Keyser. Westerkerk, Amsterdam. Begun 1620. From map by Balthazar Florisz., 1625.

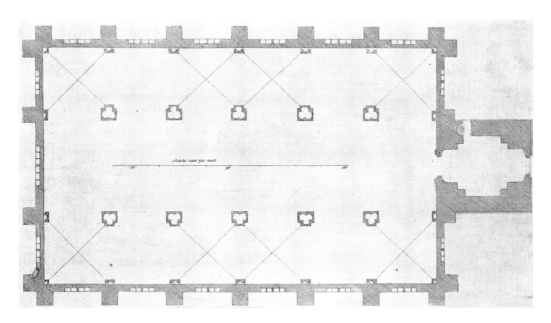

Aacte van 100 voet

104. De Keyser. Westerkerk, Amsterdam. Plan. From Dankerts.

126. De Keyser, Zuiderkerk, Amsterdam. Tower

111. De Keyser, Zuiderkerk, Amsterdam. Interior

108. De Key. Tower of New Church, Haarlem. 1613. Detail.

107. De Keyser. Westerkerk, Amsterdam. Detail of transept.

109. Van Campen. New Church, Haarlem. Interior. Drawing by Saenredam. Gemeente-Archief, Haarlem.

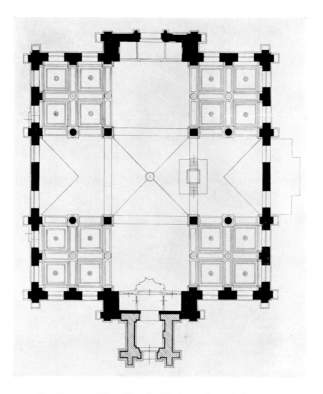

110. Van Campen. New Church, Haarlem. Ground plan.

111. Van Campen. New Church, Haarlem. Begun 1645.

112. Van Campen. New Church, Haarlem. Interior.

113. Huygens and Van Campen. Huygens' house, The Hague. Begun 1634. Section. Engraving by P. Post.

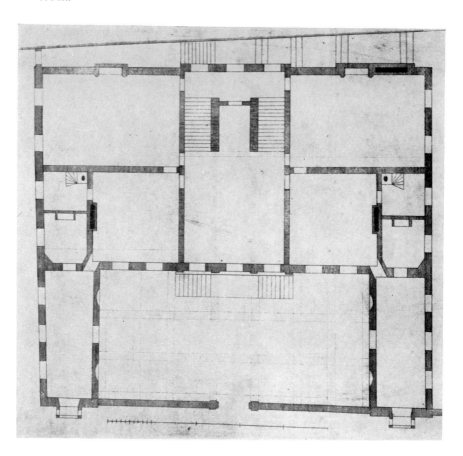

114. Huygens and Van Campen. Huygens' house, The Hague. Ground plan. Engraving by P. Post.

115. The Plein, with Huygens' house and Mauritshuis. Drawing by Van Call, 1690. Gemeente-Archief, The Hague.

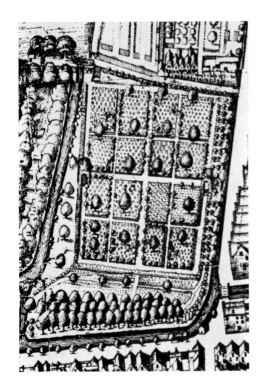

116. Site of Plein. From map by Bos and Van Harn, 1616.

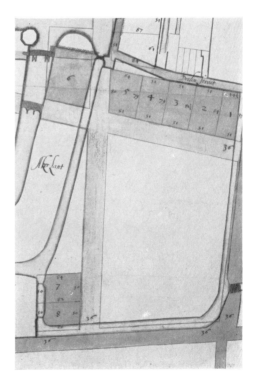

117. Project. Detail. Algemeen Rijksarchief. *6 Mauritshuis. 7-8 Huygens' house.*

118. Van Campen. Mauritshuis. Back pediment.

119. Van Campen. Mauritshuis, The Hague. Begun c. 1633.

120. Honselaarsdijk Palace. 1621 and later. Engraving by C. Elandt.

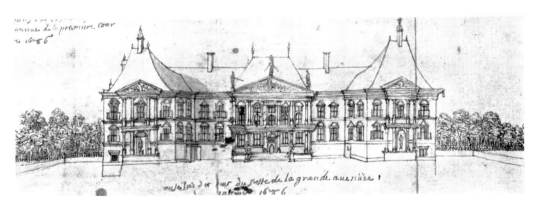

121. Honselaarsdijk Palace. Front façade. Drawing, 1686. Detail. Gemeente-Archief, The Hague.

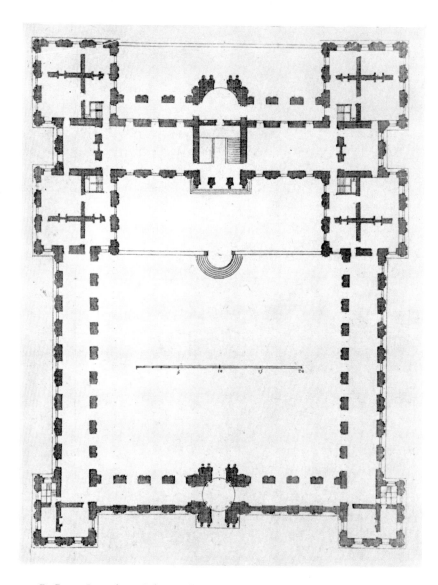

122. De Brosse. Luxembourg Palace, Paris. 1615. Ground plan. From Marot.

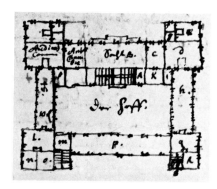

123. Honselaarsdijk. First floor plan. Sketch by
Tessin Riksarkivet, Stockholm.

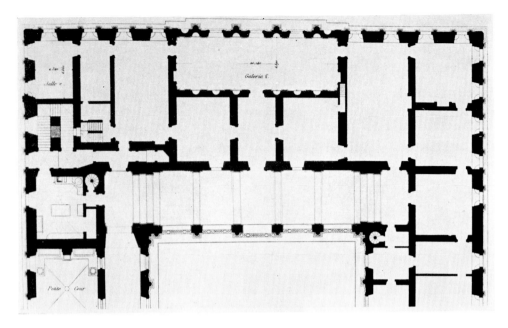

124. Farnese Palace, Rome. First floor plan. Detail. From Letarouilly.

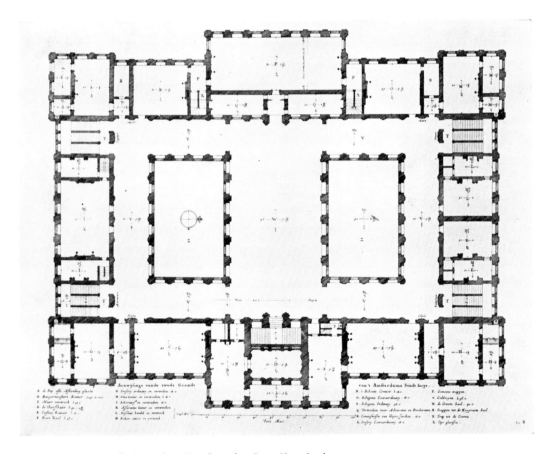

125. Former Town Hall, Amsterdam. First floor plan. From Vennekool.

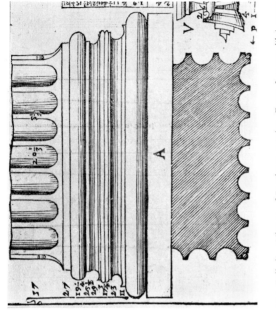

129. Palladio. Pilaster of Pantheon portico. From *I quattro libri*, 1570.

130. Former Town Hall. Burgerzaal. Pilaster. Detail of base.

128. The Pantheon, Rome. Portico. Pilaster. Detail of base.

132. Scamozzi. Ornaments of Corinthian Order. From *L'idea*, 1615.

131. Former Town Hall, Amsterdam. Burgerzaal. Cornice.

134. Former Town Hall. Burgerzaal. Corinthian capital.

133. Former Town Hall. Burgomasters' Chamber. Mantelpiece. Detail.

135. Van Campen. Organ, Alkmaar. Garland.

136. Former Town Hall. Gallery. Garland.

137. The Ara Pacis, Rome. Festoon.

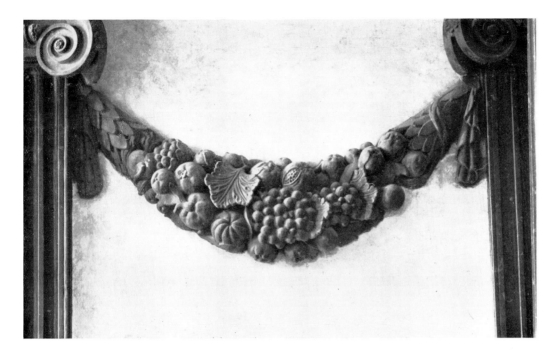

138. Van Campen. Organ, St. Laurenskerk, Alkmaar. 1638-45. Festoon.

139. Former Town Hall, Amsterdam. Gallery. Festoon.

140. J. Duquesnoy the Elder. Tabernacle. 1604. St. Martin, Alost.

141. De Keyser. Tomb of William the Silent . 1614-21. New Church, Delft.

145. De Keyser. Erasmus. 1618-22. Rotterdam.

144. R. or H. Colyns de Nole. St. Bavo. St. Gommarus, Lierre.

146. Rubens. High Altar. c. 1618. Cathedral, Antwerp. Engraving by Lommelin.

147. Rubens. High Altar. c. 1621. St. Charles Borromeo, Antwerp. From painting by Von Ehrenberg. Kunsthistorisch Instituut, Utrecht.

148-9. Rubens. High Altar. Details. St. Charles Borromeo, Antwerp.

151. Rubens. Monogram. c. 1621. St. Charles Borromeo, Antwerp.

150. Rubens. Decoration of Choir. St. Charles Borromeo, Antwerp.

152. Jordaens. Triumph of Prince Frederik Hendrik. Oranjezaal. Huis ten Bosch, The Hague.

153. Rubens. Arch of the Cardinal Infante Ferdinand. 1635. From Gevartius, *Pompa introitus Ferdinandi.*

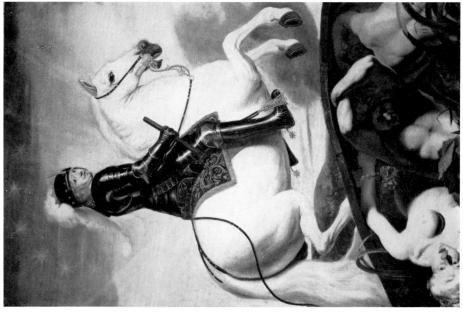

154. Rubens. Prince Ferdinand at Nordlingen. From Gevartius.

155. Van Campen. Prince Frederik Hendrik Crosses the Rivers. Oranjezaal.

157. Van Couwenberch. Doors of Oranjezaal.

156. Rubens. Doors of the Temple of Janus. From Gevartius.

158. L. Duquesnoy the Younger. Tomb of Bishop Triest, 1642-54. Detail. St. Bavo, Ghent.

159. Faydherbe. Tomb of Archbishop Cruesen. 1660. Detail. Cathedral, Malines.

163. J. Duquesnoy the Younger. St. Thomas. Ste Gudule, Brussels.

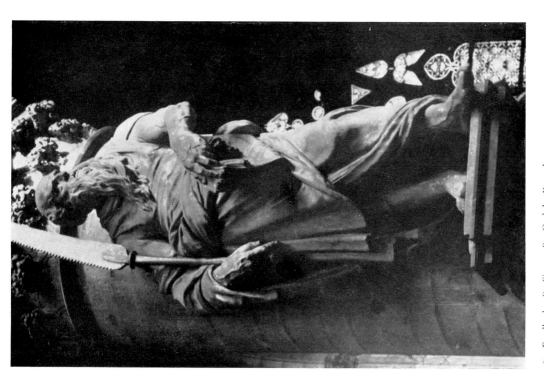

162. Faydherbe. St. Simon. Ste Gudule, Brussels.

164. Quellien. Plantin printer's mark. 1639. Plantin-Moretus Museum, Antwerp.

165. Rubens. Plantin printer's mark. Drawing. c. 1627-8. Plantin-Moretus Museum, Antwerp.

166. Quellien. Model of door-top for Amsterdam Town Hall (see Pl. 43). Rijksmuseum, Amsterdam.

167. F. Duquesnoy. Tomb of Ferdinand van den Eynde. Commissioned 1633. Detail. S. Maria dell' Anima, Rome.

171. F. Duquesnoy. Tomb of Van den Eynde. Detail. S. Maria dell' Anima, Rome.

170. Quellien. Sleeping child. Ivory. 1641. Walters Art Gallery. Baltimore.

172. Quellien. Holy Family. 1644. St. Paul's, Antwerp.

ALLERZOETSTE
JESUS
WEES ONS GENADIG.

H. ANNA
MOEDER DER BEDRUKTEN
BID VOOR ONS.

173. Quellien. Holy Family. Detail.

175. A. Quellien the Younger, High Altar, 1686-9. S. Jacques, Antwerp.

174. Rubens. High Altar. c. 1621. St. Charles Borromeo, Antwerp.

177. Van Logteren. Organ. 1735-8. St. Bavo, Haarlem.

176. Van Campen and Quellien. Organ. c. 1650-5. New Church, Amsterdam.

178-9. Van Campen and Quellien. Organ. Details. New Church, Amsterdam.

180. Former Town Hall, Amsterdam. Front pediment.

181. Former Town Hall, Amsterdam. West pediment.

183. Palladio. Villa Barbaro, Maser. The Chapel.

182. Temple of Castor and Pollux, Naples. Drawing by d'Ollanda. Library, Escorial.

184. Temple of Castor and Pollux, Naples. Pediment. From drawing by d'Ollanda. Escorial Library.

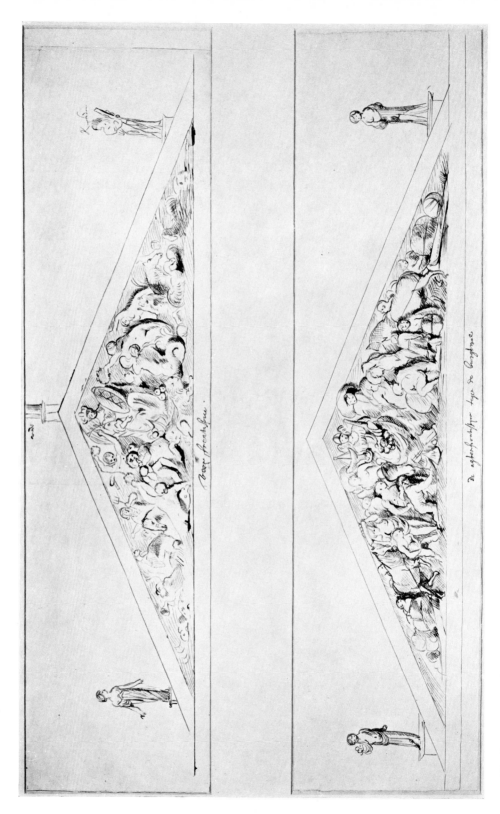

185. Van Campen. Design for pediments of Town Hall. Rijksprentenkabinet, Amsterdam.

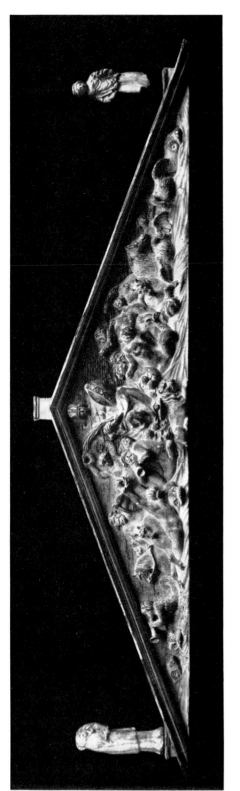

186. Model for Town Hall. c. 1648. Front pediment. Historisch Museum De Waag, Amsterdam.

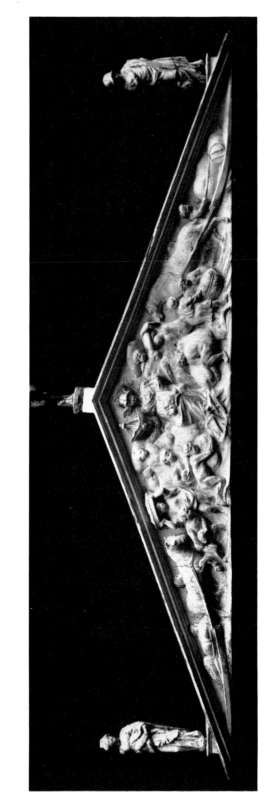

187. Model for Town Hall. West pediment. Historisch Museum De Waag, Amsterdam.

189. Model for fountain for Town Hall. Rijksmuseum, Amsterdam.

188. Amsterdam's first coat of arms. Former Town Hall (see Pl. 87).

190. Front pediment of Town Hall. Project, 1650. From engraving published by Stalpaert.

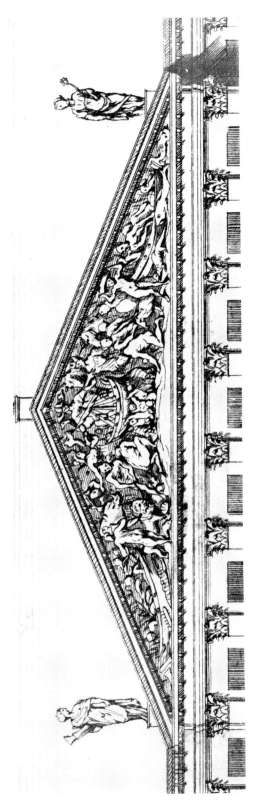

191. West pediment of Town Hall. Project, 1650. From engraving published by Stalpaert.

193. West pediment: The River IJ.

194. West pediment: Attendant of Asia.

192. Model for west pediment. Detail of figure of Africa. Rijksmuseum, Amsterdam.

195-6. Model for west pediment: River IJ and River Amstel. Rijksmuseum, Amsterdam.

197. Model for west pediment: Miners of America.

198. Model for west pediment: American Monkeys. Rijksmuseum, Amsterdam.

199. West pediment: Miners.

200. West pediment: Monkey.

201. Rubens. Adoration of the Magi. Detail. From sketch for painting of 1609. Museum, Groningen.

202. Sacrifice. Detail of relief. Arch of Constantine, Rome.

203. West pediment: Attendant of Asia.

204. West pediment: Attendant of America.

205b. Detail.

205.

TRIO PRINTERS LTD · THE HAGUE